-Ologies
&
-Isms

-Ologies & -Isms

&

-Isms

A Thematic Dictionary

Edited by
Howard G. Zettler, Ph.D.

under the direction of
Laurence Urdang

GALE RESEARCH COMPANY
BOOK TOWER • DETROIT, MICHIGAN 48226

Library of Congress Cataloging in Publication Data

Main entry under title:

-Ologies and -isms.

    Includes index.
    1. English language--Dictionaries. 2. Learning
and scholarship--Terminology. 3. English language--
Suffixes and prefixes. I. Zettler, Howard G.
PE1683.03   423'.1   78-8328
ISBN 0-8103-1014-7

Editor's Foreword

-Ologies and -Isms is a dictionary that, on four counts, deserves the qualifier *unusual.* Its lexicon is drawn mainly from words ending in one of four suffixes, its organizing principle is thematic as well as alphabetic, it concludes with a unique index, and it is intended primarily for those who seek assistance in using the resources of libraries.

Each of these novelties deserves a fuller explanation.

We have all had wide experience in using standard dictionaries, but our familiarity with alphabetization from the left somewhat obscures the fact that much of our knowledge and information has been categorized through terms ending in a few very active suffixes. For example, our scientific and systematic areas of analysis are described in a few hundred words ending in *-ology* or *-ics,* as *psychology* or *physics.* The multitude of English words denoting theories, doctrines, systems, attitudes, or practices end chiefly in (Greek) *-ism* or (Latin-French) *-ity,* as in *pessimism* or *urbanity.* The core of the specialized word list that is *-Ologies and -Isms* consists of nouns ending in *-ologies, -ities, -isms,* and *-ics* and their forms in other parts of speech; for example, among the more than 3,000 words defined, there are 1,261 words ending with *-ism* or *-ist,* 42 ending with *-ity,* 463 with *-ology,* and 150 with *-ic* or *-ics.* A selection of 1,168 terms end in *-graphy, -metry, -philia, -mancy,* and 24 other suffixes. The lexicon contains, in addition, 248 *-phobia* terms, the greatest number currently in print.

The content of *-Ologies and -Isms* renders it a lexicographical pantology (*which see*), and its arrangement of entries and definitions by thematic categories gives it a remarkable utility.

Thematic dictionaries are not, in themselves, novel, for many wordhoards restricted to terms in a science, art, or technology have previously been both successful and useful. But the use of a thematic design in a brief lexicon of learned words covering a multiplicity of areas is a radical innovation. Such an approach makes unnecessary long periods of searching for an appropriate term in a standard dictionary. Inclusion, for instance, of the term **bathygraphy** in the category **SEA** will obviate a fruitless search in a standard dictionary among terms beginning with *ocean-.* Moreover, because terms often fit simultaneously in a variety of categories, *-Ologies and -Isms* includes cross references to other categories and to other terms.

The usefulness of *-Ologies and -Isms* is further enhanced by its unique alphabetical index. Its design enables the book to refer the reader to a category rather than to a page, and therefore permits this reference work to distinguish denotations by category, as for example the philosophical as against the political meaning of **pluralism.** Under this plan, the reader will more readily locate the specific definition he seeks.

As a tool for persons researching or about to initiate research in indexes, bibliographies, and other reference works, *-Ologies and -Isms* will be valuable because of several additional features. It first of all provides definitions which act as foundations for the gathering of broader and deeper information, especially in unfamiliar material. It also contains terms to be found in older scholarly works, terms of the archaic, obsolete, or rare varieties often omitted from current dictionaries. Moreover, it provides both variant spellings and alternate names of terms and, especially where such forms are unusual or various, other parts of speech developed from the entry word. Thus, for instance, for the term describing a tendency to uncontrolled bleeding, **hemophilia,** the reader will note an alternate spelling **(haemophilia)**, an alternate term **(hemorrhaphilia)**, and the noun or adjectival form **hemophiliac.**

We trust that the attempt, in *-Ologies and -Isms,* to design an unusual reference work of the utmost utility will promote the pleasure and satisfaction of its users.

Essex, Connecticut   Howard G. Zettler
December 1977

-OLOGIES AND -ISMS

A

ACTION

automatism an automatic or involuntary action. —**automatist,** *n.*

mannerism a style of action, bearing, thought, or speech peculiar to an individual or a special group. —**mannerist,** *n.* —**manneristic,** *adj.*
See also ATTITUDES and BEHAVIOR.

AGREEMENT

analogy an agreement or correspondence in particular features between things otherwise dissimilar; in literature, the basis for metaphor and simile. —**analogic, analogical,** *adj.*

congruence a correspondence in physical structure or thought; harmony. Also called **congruity.** —**congruent,** *adj.*

similarity a point, feature, or detail in which two items are alike.

AIR

aerobics a system of exercising designed to increase absorption of oxygen by the body. —**aerobic,** *adj.*

aerodynamics the branch of dynamics that studies the motions of air and other gases, esp. with regard to bodies in motion in these substances. —**aerodynamic, aerodynamical,** *adj.* Cf. **aeronautics, aerostatics.**

aeromancy a divination from the state of the air or atmospheric substances, sometimes limited to weather forecasting.

aerometry the science of measuring properties of air; pneumatics. —**aerometric,** *adj.*

aerophobia an abnormal dread of fresh air. —**aerophobe,** *n.*

anemography *Rare.* the recording of the measurement of wind speed by an anemometer. —**anemographic,** *adj.*

anemology   the science of the winds. —**anemological,** *adj.*

anemometry   the recording of the simultaneous measurement of air pressure and of wind speed and direction by an anemometrograph. —**anemometric, anemometrical,** *adj.*

anemophilia   wind-loving, said of plants that are fertilized only through the action of winds. —**anemophile,** *n.* —**anemophilous,** *adj.*

anemophobia   an abnormal fear of drafts or winds. —**anemophobe,** *n.*

koniology, coniology   the study of atmospheric dust and other impurities in the air, as germs, pollen, etc., esp. the effect on plant and animal life.

miasmology   the study of fogs and smogs, esp. those affecting air pollution levels.

pneumatics   a specialty in physics that studies the mechanical properties of air and other gases. Also called **pneumodynamics.**

pneumology   the scientific study of the human respiratory system. —**pneumological,** *adj.*

ALCHEMY

iatrochemistry   1. originally, alchemy devoted to medicinal purposes, especially the alchemy of the period 1525-1660 influenced by the theories of Paracelsus.
2. currently, chemistry for healing purposes. —**iatrochemist,** *n.*

spagyrist   an alchemist.

transmutationist   an alchemist who believed that, in one of several ways, it was possible to change less valuable elements into silver or gold.

ALCOHOL

absinthism   an addiction to absinthe, a liqueur flavored with the narcotic wormwood, *Artemisia absinthium.* —**absinthial, absinthian,** *adj.*

abstinence   a voluntary and habitual self-deprivation, esp. from alcoholic beverages. —**abstinent,** *adj.*

alcoholism   1. an addiction to alcohol, esp. compulsive excessive consumption.
2. the pathological effects of such overindulgence. —**alcoholic,** *n.*

alcoholphilia   an excessive liking for alcoholic beverages. —**alcoholphile,** *n.*

bacchanalianism   1. a devotion to drunken revelry and carousal in honor of Bacchus.
2. a dedication to such behavior on other occasions. —**bacchanalian,** *n., adj.*

dipsomania   an insatiable craving for alcohol; chronic drunkenness. —**dipsomaniac,** *n.* —**dipsomaniacal,** *adj.*

dipsophobia   an abnormal fear of drinking. —**dipsophobe,** *n.*

ebriety   intoxication or inebriation, whether regarded as the condition, the process, or the habit.

fermentology   a science that deals with ferments and fermentation, esp. those concerned with the production of alcoholic beverages. —**ferment-ologist,** *n.*

inebriety   drunkenness.

insobriety   the opposite of sobriety; inebriation.

nephalism   an adherence to the tenets of teetotalism, —**nephalist,** *n.* —**nephalistic,** *adj.*

prohibitionism   **1.** the principles governing the forbidding by law of the manufacture or sale of alcoholic beverages.
2. the interdiction itself. —**prohibitionist,** *n.* —**Prohibition,** *n.*

teetotalism   the principle or conscious practice of complete abstinence from alcoholic beverages. Also called **total abstinence.** —**teetotaler,** *n.*

Volsteadism   the theory or practice of prohibitionism.

ALERTNESS

alacrity   a cheerful readiness, promptitude, or willingness; briskness. —**alacritous,** *adj.*

pantaraxia   any actions aimed at keeping people on their toes. (Nubar Gulbenkian, 1964)

ALMANACS

almanagist   a person who compiles almanacs.

ephemeris   an astronomical almanac giving, as an aid to the astronomer and navigator, the locations of celestial bodies for each day of the year.

ALPHABET

abecedarian, abecedary   a teacher or learner of an alphabet.

analphabetic   **1.** unable to read or write.
2. descriptive of a language written without an alphabet; that is, with a syllabary (Cherokee), in hieroglyphics (ancient Egyptian), in ideograms (Chinese), or in pictograms (American Indian).

literalism   the practice or theory of following the letter or literal sense of something written. —**literalist,** *n.*

metagraphy   the art of transliteration. —**metagraphic,** *adj.*

transliteration   the spelling of a word in one language with the alphabet of another language.

ANATOMY

anthropometry   the study concerned with the measurements of the proportions, size, and weight of the human body. —**anthropometrist,** *n.* —**anthropometric, anthropometrical,** *adj.*

anthropomorphous, anthropomorphic, anthropomorphical human in form; possessing the anatomical features of a human being.

anthropomorphism 1. a representation of God in a human form, or with a human outlook and feelings.
2. the assignment of human qualities to nonhuman creatures. Also called **anthropomorphology.** —**anthropomorphic, anthropometrical,** *adj.*

anthroposcopy *Rare.,Physiology.* the labeling of the type of body structure by nonanthropometric means.

asthenic ectomorphic.

athletic mesomorphic.

eccrinology the branch of anatomy and physiology that studies secretions and the secretory glands.

ectomorphy the condition of having a light, slender body structure. —**ectomorphic,** *adj.*

endomorphy the condition of having a heavy, rounded body structure with a tendency to become fat. —**endomorphic,** *adj.*

eurysomatic endomorphic.

histology a branch of anatomy that deals with the microscopic features of animal and plant tissues. Also called **microscopical anatomy.** —**histologist,** *n.* —**histological,** *adj.*

leptosomic ectomorphic. Also called **leptosomatic.**

mesomorphy the condition of having a muscular, athletic body structure. —**mesomorphic,** *adj.*

myography the measurement of muscular phenomena, such as the velocity and intensity of muscular contractions. —**myographic,** *adj.*

myology 1. the branch of anatomy that studies muscles and musculature.
2. the muscular makeup of an animal or anatomical unit. —**myologic,** *adj.*

pyknic endomorphic.

ANCESTORS

archaism an inclination toward old-fashioned things, speech, or actions, esp. those of one's ancestors. Also called **archaicism.** —**archaist,** *n.* —**archaistic,** *adj.*

atavism the reappearance in the present of a characteristic belonging to a remote ancestor. —**atavist,** *n.* —**atavistic,** *adj.*

ANIMALS

animality 1. the state of being an animal.
2. animal existence or nature in human activity; the animal in man as opposed to the spiritual.

anthropopathism, anthropopathy the assignment of human feelings or passions to something not human, as a deity or an animal. —**anthropopathic,** *adj.*

bestiarian 1. by analogy to **humanitarian,** an advocate of kindness to animals.

2. in Great Britain, an antivivisectionist.

bestiarist a compiler or writer of bestiaries.

bestiary an allegorical or moralizing commentary on real or fabled animals, usually medieval and sometimes illustrated.

bioecology the branch of ecology that studies the interrelationship of plant and animal life in their common environment. —**bioecologist,** *n.* —**bioecologic, bioecological,** *adj.*

doraphobia an intense fear of contact with animal fur or skin. —**doraphobe,** *n.*

epizootiology, epizootology the science concerned with the factors involved in the occurrence and spread of animal diseases. —**epizootiologic, epizootiological,** *adj.*

ethology the study of animal behavior in relation to habitat. —**ethologist,** *n.* —**ethological,** *adj.*

faunology zoogeography.

haruspicy a form of divination from lightning and other natural phenomena, but esp. from inspection of the entrails of animal sacrifices. —**haruspex, aruspex,** *n.* —**haruspical,** *adj.*

morphology the branch of biology that studies the structure and form of animals and plants. —**morphologist,** *n.* —**morphologic, morphological,** *adj.*

organology the study of the organs of plants and animals. —**organologist,** *n.* —**organologic, organological,** *adj.*

sybotism *Rare.* the business and art of raising swine.

taxidermy the art of preparing, stuffing, and mounting the skins of animals so that they appear lifelike. —**taxidermist,** *n.*

theriomancy a form of divination involving observation of the movements of animals. Also called **zoomancy.**

theriomorphism the worship of deities that are partly animal and partly human in form. Also called **therianthropism, theriolatry.** —**theriomorphic, theriomorphous,** *adj.*

thremmatology the branch of biology that studies the breeding of domestic plants and animals.

vulpicide 1. the killing of a fox by methods other than by hunting it with hounds.

2. the killer of a fox.

zoolatry the worship of animal gods. —**zoolater,** *n.* Cf. **theriomorphism.**

zoanthropy a derangement in which a person believes himself to be an animal and acts accordingly. —**zoanthropic,** *adj.*

zoobiology zoology.

zoology the branch of biology that studies and classifies all living creatures. —**zoologist,** *n.* —**zoological,** *adj.*

zoomorphism the attribution of animal form or nature, esp. to a deity. —**zoomorphic,** *adj.*

zoophilia a love of animals. —**zoophile,** *n.*

zoophobia an abnormal dread of animals. —**zoophobe,** *n.*

zoopsychology a branch of psychology that studies animal behavior.

zootechny the principles of animal husbandry. Also called **zootechnics.** —**zootechnician,** *n.* —**zootechnical,** *adj.*

zootheism the worship of animal gods; zoolatry. —**zootheist,** *n.*
See also ZOOLOGY.

ANTHROPOLOGY

cultural anthropology a specialty which studies the creative achievements of societies, esp. those passed on through later generations. Also called **culturology.**

ethnogeny the study of the origin of distinctive groups or tribes. —**ethnogenist,** *n.* —**ethnogenic,** *adj.*

ethnography the branch of anthropology that studies and describes the individual cultures of mankind. —**ethnographer,** *n.* —**ethnographic, ethnographical,** *adj.*

ethnology the study, often comparative, of the origins and development of the races of mankind. —**ethnologist,** *n.* —**ethnologic, ethnological,** *adj.*

ethnocentrism the belief in the superiority of one's own group or culture. —**ethnocentric,** *adj.*

hybridism, hybridity the blending of diverse cultures or traditions.

physical anthropology the branch of anthropology that studies, describes, and interprets the evolutionary changes in man's bodily structure and the classification of modern races. Also called **somatology.** Cf. **cultural anthropology.**

social anthropology the branch of anthropology that studies human societies, emphasizing interpersonal and intergroup relations.

ANTIQUITY

antiquarianism an interest in the customs, art, and social structure of earlier peoples and civilizations. —**antiquarian,** *n., adj.*

archaeology, archeology the scientific study of human remains and artifacts. —**archaeologist,** *n.* —**archaeologic, archaeological,** *adj.*

epigraphy the deciphering and interpreting of ancient inscriptions. —**epigraphist, epigrapher,** *n.* —**epigraphic, epigraphical,** *adj.*

lipsanography *Rare.* the research and composition of treatises about relics. —**lipsanographer,** *n.*

paleography the study of ancient writings, including inscriptions. —**paleographer,** *n.* —**paleographic,** *adj.*

ANTS

formicary, formicarium the dwelling of a colony of ants; anthill or nest.

myrmecology the branch of entomology that studies ants. —**myrmecologist,** *n.*

myrmicophilism, myrmicophily the dependence upon or attraction to ants exhibited by certain myrmicophilous plants and insects. —**myrmicophile,** *n.* —**myrmicophilous,** *adj.*

myrmecophobia **1.** an abnormal fear of ants.
2. the repelling of ants by some plants through hairs or glands. —**myrmecophobic,** *adj.* Cf. **myrmicophilism.**

ARCHERY

toxophilite a student or lover of archery.

toxophily the art or sport of archery.

ARCHITECTURE

Brutalism an aggressive 20th cent. style, usually in rough-textured and unfinished materials, which frankly exhibits both structural and mechanical systems.

Bungaloid a 20th cent. dwelling style, usually of one story, imitative of the true bungalow form characterized by low, sweeping roof gables and a large verandah in the front.

classicism **1.** the employment of compositional formulas and decorative techniques based upon the architecture of ancient Greece or Rome, but often including new ideas.
2. the employment of formulas and decorative techniques, with an emphasis upon the subordination of utility in order to stress perfection of form.

eclecticism an international movement most in vogue from 1820 until about 1930, characterized by almost total freedom of choice among historical styles of both overall composition and decoration in the design of public buildings, the freedom tempered by the intended use or location of the building.

Egyptian Revivalism a style imitative of antique Egyptian temple architecture, most influential after Napoleon's campaign in Egypt and lasting in the U.S. into the early 20th cent.

Federalism an American style based upon the classical theories and decorations of the English Robert Adams and his contemporaries, with lightness and delicacy as its outstanding qualities; practiced from 1775 until overwhelmed by Greek Revivalism, its most typical external features are doorways with fanlights and sidelights (often with attenuated pilasters) and the play of other curved elements against a basically boxlike structure. Also called **Early Federal Style, Early Republican.**

functionalism a philosophy of architectural design rather than a separate style, expressed in Louis Sullivan's "form follows function" and Le Corbusier's concept of a house as a machine for living in, under the premise that buildings ought to express construction, materials, and accommodation of purpose, usually with the assumption that the result would be aesthetically significant. Also called **structuralism.**

Georgianism **1.** in England, the modes of architecture, furniture, decoration, and silver produced from about 1714 to 1830; architecturally, it embraced several styles: Palladian, Early Gothic Revival, Chinese, and various other classical and romantic manners.

2. in America, the architectural style of the English colonies during the 18th cent., based first upon the ideas of Christopher Wren and James Gibbs and later upon the Palladian style. It is typically characterized by construction in red brick with white or colored trim and double-hung windows, central halls, elaborately turned stair balusters, paneled and warmly colored walls, fine woodwork, and white plastered ceilings.

Gothicism, Gothic the general term employed to denote the several phases of European architecture in the period 1100–1530 which employ the pointed arch, or their imitations.

Gothic Revivalism a universal style current since its inception in Britain in the late 18th cent., passing from a period of superficial decoration to one in which true Gothic massing yielded such masterpieces as the British Houses of Parliament and Pittsburgh's Cathedral of Learning.

Greek Revivalism an austere American style of the period 1798–c.1850, embracing in either form or decoration such Greek features as bilateral symmetry, low pitched roofs, frontal porticos with pediments, and horizontal doorheads; often executed in wood and painted white, the structures usually featured modifications of the classical orders and occasional imaginative use of interior vaulting.

Internationalism, International Style a style current since the 1920's which makes use of modern constructional advances to create buildings reflecting characteristic industrial forms and emphasizing both volume and horizontality through ribbon windows, smooth and undecorated wall surfaces, and flat roofs, with contrasts introduced by curved or cylindrical forms and cantilevered projecting features.

Neo-Expressionism a current style emphasizing dynamism achieved by employment of sweeping curves, acute angles, and pointed arches.

New Formalism a current American manner, characterized by buildings that are freestanding blocks with symmetrical elevation, level rooflines (often with heavy, projecting roof slabs), many modeled columnar supports, and frequent use of the arch as a ruling motif to produce a kind of classicism without classical forms.

Palladianism the classical style evolved by the 16th cent. Andrea Palladio featuring harmonic proportion based upon mathematics, extensive use of porticos, a neat contrast between openness and solidity, and features of Roman decoration; partially influential today in the so-called "Palladian motif", a window or other opening consisting of a central high arch flanked by lower rectangular areas, the whole supported by four columns (a feature actually invented before Palladio's time and used only sparingly by him).

Renaissance Revivalism a style originating in England c.1830 and influential in the U.S. from 1850 through 1930, derived from the Renaissance palace architecture of Rome, Florence, and Venice; in the U.S., the structures were executed in masonry, wood, or cast iron.

structuralism See **functionalism**.

ARGUMENT

analogy an agreement or correspondence in particular features between things otherwise dissimilar; the inference that if two things agree with each other in one or more respects, they will probably agree in yet other respects. —**analogous,** *adj.*

apagoge a method of argument in which the proposition to be established is emphasized through the disproving of its contradiction; *reductio ad absurdum.* —**apagogic,** *adj.*

circularism, circularity reasoning or arguing in a circle.

doctrinarianism a stubborn attachment to a theory or doctrine without regard to its practicability. Also called **doctrinairism.** —**doctrinaire,** *n., adj.*

dogmatism **1.** a statement of a point of view as if it were an established fact.
2. the use of a system of ideas based upon insufficiently examined premises. —**dogmatist,** *n.* —**dogmatic,** *adj.*

epagogue a method of induction in which enumeration of particulars leads to the inferred generalization. —**epagogic,** *adj.*

ergotism the practice or habit of quibbling and wrangling; sophistical reasoning. —**ergotize,** *v.*

forensics the art and study of argumentation and formal debate. —**forensic,** *adj.*

heuristic a method of argument in which are made postulates or assumptions that remain to be proven or that lead the arguers to discover the proofs themselves. —**heuristic,** *adj.*

Megarianism Euclid of Megara's Socratic school of philosophy, known for the use of logical paradox and near-specious subtleties.

misology a hatred of argument, debate, or reasoning. —**misologist,** *n.*

noetics the laws of logic; the science of the intellect. —**noetic,** *adj.*

obscurantism the use of argument intended to prevent enlightenment or to hinder the process of knowledge and wisdom. Also called **obscuranticism.** —**obscurantist,** *n.* —**obscurant, obscurantic,** *adj.*

obstructionism deliberate interference with the progress of an argument. —**obstructionist,** *n.* —**obstructionistic,** *adj.*

paralogism, paralogy a method or process of reasoning which contradicts logical rules or formulas, esp. the use of a faulty syllogism (the formal fallacy). Also called **paralogia.** —**paralogist,** *n.* —**paralogistic,** *adj.*

philopolemic *Rare.* related to a love of controversy and argument. —**philopolemist,** *n.*

pilpulist one who uses Talmudic dialectic; a subtle reasoner. —**pilpulistic,** *adj.*

polemicist, polemist a skilled debater in speech or writing. —**polemical,** *adj.*

simplism the tendency to concentrate on a single part of an argument and to ignore or exclude all complicating factors. —**simplistic,** *adj.*

sophism **1.** a specious argument for displaying ingenuity in reasoning or for deceiving someone.
2. any false argument or fallacy. —**sophister,** *n.* —**sophistic,** *adj.*

syllogism a form of reasoning in which two statements are made and a logical conclusion is drawn from them. —**syllogistic,** *adj.*

ARROWS

belomancy a form of divination involving drawing arrows at random from a container.

sagittate shaped like an arrowhead, esp. plant leaves shaped like elongated triangles.

sagittary **1.** pertaining to archery.
2. resembling an arrow; sagittate.

ART

Abstract Expressionism a spontaneous, intuitive painting technique producing nonformal work characterized by sinuous lines. Also called **Action Painting.**

Abstractism a nonrepresentational style in painting or sculpture.

aestheticism **1.** the doctrine that aesthetic standards are autonomous and not subject to political, moral, or religious criteria.
2. used pejoratively to describe those who believe only in "art for art's sake," to the exclusion of all other human activities.

archaism a taste for and imitation of earlier styles, a recurrent phenomenon since ancient times based on the premise that earlier works were somehow purer and simpler. Cf. **primitivism.**

autotelism a nonutilitarian theory of art holding that a work of art is an end in itself. —**autotelic,** *adj.*

classicism **1.** formerly, an imitation of Greek and Roman art.
2. currently, a dedication to the principles of that art: clarity of execution, balance, adherence to recognized standards of form, and conscious craftsmanship. —**classicist,** *n.* —**classicistic,** *adj.*

Cubism a movement in 20th cent. painting in which several planes of an object in the form of cubes or other solids are presented in an arbitrary arrangement using a narrow range of colors or monochrome. —**Cubist,** *n.* —**Cubistic,** *adj.*

Dadaism a revolt by 20th cent. painters and writers in France, Germany, and Switzerland against smugness in traditional art and Western society; their works, illustrating absurdity through paintings of purposeless machines and collages of discarded materials, expressed their cynicism about conventional ideas of form and their rejection of traditional concepts of beauty. —**Dadaist,** *n.*

eclecticism a style that intermixes features borrowed from other artists or differing schools; applied esp. when the result is unsuccessful. —**eclecticist,** *n.*

Expressionism a movement in the 20th cent. that attempted to express feeling and emotion directly by distorting forms, choosing violent subject matter and harsh colors, and keeping the overall design out of balance. —**Expressionist,** *n.* —**Expressionistic,** *adj.*

Fauvism an early movement in 20th cent. painting characterized by an emphasis on the use of unmixed bright colors for emotional and decorative effect. —**Fauvist,** *n.* —**Fauve,** *n., adj.*

Futurism a movement of the 20th cent. attempting to capture in painting the movement, force, and speed of modern industrial life by the simultaneous representation of successive aspects of forms in motion. —**Futurist,** *n.* —**Futuristic,** *adj.*

Gothicism the principles of the paintings, sculptures, stained glass, mosaics, and book illustrations of the period 1200-c.1450, embracing several disparate styles and emphases, —**Gothicist,** *n.*

iconology the description, history, and analysis of symbolic art or artistic symbolism, esp. that of the late medieval and Renaissance periods. Also called **iconography.** —**iconologist,** *n.* —**iconological,** *adj.*

Impressionism a movement in the late 19th cent. in French painting characterized by the goal of reproducing an impression of a subject by use of reflected light and color and the blurring of outlines. —**Impressionist,** *n., adj.* —**Impressionistic,** *adj.*

luminarism a movement in painting concerned with precision in representing light and shade. —**luminarist,** *n.*

luminism a movement in painting concerned with effects of light, esp. the use of broken color in its full intensity with a minimum of shadow effects, applied esp. to many Impressionist and Pointillist artists. —**luminist,** *n.*

mannerism an overemphasis on any distinctive technique of expression, occurring when the manner of expression obscures the feeling or idea expressed in the work of art; considered by many art critics to be a sign of decadence. —**mannerist,** *n.* —**manneristic,** *adj.*

Mannerism a style developed between c.1530 and c.1590 marked by deliberate violations of earlier standards of painting in depicting the artist's idea rather than nature by means of asymmetrical and crowded compositions, elongated and twisted figures, and emphasis upon devices, as foreshortening. The style also affected both architecture and sculpture. —**Mannerist,** *n.*

miniaturist **1.** *Obsolete.* an artist whose task it was to draw in red certain words or letters in manuscripts.
2. a painter of miniature pictures or portraits, as on china or ivory, characterized by fineness of detail.

monochromist one who paints or draws in shades or tints of a single color.

naturalism the goal of artists who attempt to represent a subject without stylization or interpretation, and to create a mirror for natural beauty. —**naturalist,** *n.* —**naturalistic,** *adj.*

Neo-Classicism a European movement of the late 18th cent. differing from earlier classical revivals in that it deliberately and consciously imitated antique models such as those found between 1738-56 in Herculaneum, Paestum, and Pompeii. —**Neo-Classicist,** *n.* —**Neo-Classic, Neo-Classical,** *adj.*

Neo-Impressionism See **Pointillism.**

New Realism the European critical label for **Pop Art.**

origami the Japanese art of paper folding. —**origamist,** *n.*

ornamentalism a use of ornament for decorative purposes, esp. its overuse.

Orphism a shortlived development of Cubism c.1912 which attempted to enliven the original approach by subordinating the geometrical forms and using unmixed bright colors. —**Orphist,** *n.*

Plein-airism the practice of painting in the open air to obtain effects of light and atmosphere not possible in a studio. —**plein-air,** *adj.*

Pointillism   a style of the late 19th cent. based upon some Impressionist techniques and the application of scientific theories of the process of vision; begun by Seurat, who gave it the name Divisionism, it consists of using dots of unmixed color side by side so that the viewer's eye may mix them into the appropriate intermediate color. Also called **Neo-Impressionism.** —**Pointillist,** *n.* —**Pointillistic,** *adj.*

Pop Art   an antitraditional, antiaesthetic glorification of mass culture occurring in Britain and America in the 1960's. It attempts to startle the viewer into extracting significance from such banal everyday objects as greatly enlarged soupcans or huge ice cream cones created in limp plastic.

Post-Impressionism   a late 19th cent. reaction to Impressionism, emphasizing on one hand the emotional aspect of painting and on the other a return to formal structure; the first led to Expressionism; the second, to Cubism. —**Post-Impressionist,** *n.*

pre-Raphaelitism   the principles of the 19th cent. artists and writers who sought to restore the principles and practices thought to be characteristic of Italian art before Raphael. —**pre-Raphaelite,** *n., adj.*

primitivism   **1.** the self-conscious return, for inspiration, to the archaic forms produced by non-Western cultures.
2. the practice of painting in a way alien to academic or traditional techniques, often displaying a highly individual naiveté in interpretation and treatment of subjects. —**primitivist,** *n.* —**primitivistic,** *adj.*

pyrography   the art or process of burning designs on wood or leather, using heated tools. Also called **pyragravure.** —**pyrographer,** *n.* —**pyrographic,** *adj.*

Realism   **1.** naturalism.
2. a movement in the late 19th cent. stressing common rather than individual characteristics as the basis of reality. —**Realist,** *n.* Cf. **naturalism, verism.**

representationalism   the practice of creating recognizable figures, objects, and natural forms in art. Cf. **Abstractism.**

Romanticism   the reflection, in art, of a late 18th cent. literary and philosophical movement in reaction against the intellectuality and rationality of Neo-Classicism. It produced no single artistic style or characteristic but strongly influenced the ideals of imagination, emotion, and the freedom of expression in other media. —**Romanticist,** *n.*

serigraphy   the procedure of making prints through the silk-screen process. —**serigrapher,** *n.*

Surrealism, Superrealism   a controversial movement in art and literature between the two World Wars in which the artist attempted to portray, express, or interpret the workings of the subconscious mind; in painting it found expression in two techniques, the naturalistic (Dali) and the abstract (Miró). —**Surrealist,** *n.* —**Surrealistic,** *adj.*

synchronism an American movement, founded in 1913, based upon Abstractism in unmixed color, usually involving disklike forms. —**synchronist,** *n.* —**synchronistic,** *adj.*

Tachism, Tachisme a movement of the early 1950's which claimed to be in revolt against both Abstractism and naturalism, taking its name from patches of color (Fr. *taches*) placed on canvas spontaneously and by chance, the result being considered an emotional projection rather than an expression or a symbol. —**Tachist, Tachiste,** *n.* Cf. **Abstract Expressionism.**

Verism a naturalistic approach, esp. in portraiture, in which every wrinkle and flaw of the subject is faithfully reproduced; extreme realism. —**Verist,** *n.* —**Veristic,** *adj.* Cf. **naturalism, realism.** *See also DRAWING.*

Vorticism an art movement in England in 1914-15 stimulated by Futurism and by the idea that all artistic creation must begin in a state of strong emotion; its products, intended to establish a form characteristic of the industrial age, tend to use angular, machinelike shapes. —**Vorticist,** *n.*

ARTERIES

aneurism, aneurysm a disease of the artery wall which causes a localized dilatation of the artery and a pulsating tumor.

sphygmology *Med.* the sum of what is known about the pulse.

embolism the sudden obstruction of a blood vessel by a foreign object, as an air bubble or a blood clot.

ASTROLOGY

apotelesm *Archaic.* the casting of horoscopes —**apotelesmatic,** *adj.*

astrology 1. the study that assumes, and professes to interpret, the influence of the stars and planets upon human existence.
2. *Obsolete.* astronomy. —**astrologer, astrologist,** *n.* —**astrological,** *adj.*

genethlialogy the lore which underlies the art of casting genethliacs, or astrological nativities. —**genethlialogic, genethlialogical,** *adj.*

Magianism the teaching and studies of the priestly caste in ancient Media and Persia whose belief in the advent of a savior involved them in intensive astrological research, including the following of a star to Bethlehem (Matthew 2:1-12).

ASTRONOMY

aerolithology the branch of astronomy that studies meteors.

aerolitics the branch of astronomy that studies aerolites, or stony meteors.

areology the astronomical studies of the planet Mars. —**areologist,** *n.* —**areologic, areological,** *adj.*

asterism *Rare.* a constellation or small group of unrelated stars. —**asterismal,** *adj.*

astrogation   the art of navigating in space. Also called **astronavigation.** —**astrogator,** *n.*

astrogeology   a geological specialty that studies celestial bodies.

astrognosy   the branch of astronomy that studies the fixed stars.

astrography   a scientific analysis and mapping of the stars and planets. —**astrographic,** *adj.*

astrolatry   the worship of the heavenly bodies. Also called **Sabaism.** —**astrolater,** *n.*

astromancy   a form of divination involving studying the stars. —**astromancer,** *n.* —**astromantic,** *adj.*

astrometry   the branch of astronomy that studies the dimensions of heavenly bodies, esp. the measurements made to determine the positions and orbits of various stars. —**astrometric, astrometrical,** *adj.*

astronautics   the science of space travel, concerned with both the construction and the operation of vehicles which travel through interplanetary or interstellar space. —**astronautic, astronautical,** *adj.*

astronavigation   a type of navigation involving observations of the apparent positions of heavenly bodies. Also called **celestial navigation, celonavigation.** —**astronavigator,** *n.*

astrophile   a person strongly attracted to knowledge about the stars. —**astrophilic,** *adj.*

astronomy   the science that studies the stars and other features of the material universe beyond the earth's atmosphere. —**astronomer,** *n.* —**astronomical,** *adj.*

astrophysics   the branch of astronomy concerned with the origin, and the chemical and physical nature of heavenly bodies. —**astrophysicist,** *n.*

Copernicanism   the fundamental theoretical basis of modern astronomy, first demonstrated in the early 16th cent. by Copernicus, who showed that the earth and the other planets orbit around the sun. Also called **the Copernican system.** Cf. **Ptolemaism.**

Ptolemaism   the complicated demonstration of Ptolemy, 2nd cent. geographer and astronomer, that the earth is the fixed center of the universe around which the sun and the other planets revolve, now discredited. Also called **the Ptolemaic system.**

Ptolemaist   a supporter of the Ptolemaic explanation of planetary motions.

radioastronomy   the branch of astronomy that studies radio frequencies emitted by the sun, planets, and other celestial bodies.

selenography   the scientific analysis and mapping of the moon's physical features. —**selenographer, selenographist,** *n.* —**selenographic, selenographical,** *adj.*

sideromancy   a form of divination involving observations of the stars.

uranianism *Obsolete.* astronomy.

uranography the branch of astronomy that deals with the description of the heavens by constructing maps and charts, esp. of the fixed stars. Also called **uranology.** —**uranographer, uranographist,** *n.* —**uranographic, uranographical,** *adj.*

uranology **1.** a written description of the heavens and celestial bodies. **2.** another term for astronomy.

ATHLETICS

agonist one who contends for a prize in public games. —**agonistic, agonistical,** *adj.*

agonistics the art of athletic combat or contests in public games.

calisthenics the science, art, or practice of bodily exercises intended to promote strength, health, and grace of movement. —**calisthenic, calisthenical,** *adj.*

contortionist a person who performs gymnastic feats involving distorted postures. —**contortionistic,** *adj.*

trampolinist a person who performs feats of tumbling using a trampoline as a springboard. Also called **trampoliner.** —**trampoline,** *n.*

ATMOSPHERE

aerographics, aerography the branch of meteorology that studies and describes atmospheric conditions. —**aerographer,** *n.* —**aerographic, aerographical,** *adj.*

aerology **1.** *Obsolete.* the branch of meteorology that observed the atmosphere by using balloons, airplanes, etc. **2.** meteorology. —**aerologist,** *n.* —**aerologic, aerological,** *adj.*

aneroid a barometer working in a vacuum.

barograph a barometer which automatically records, on a rotating cylinder, any variation in atmospheric pressure; a self-recording aneroid.

barometry the art or science of barometric observation.

bioclimatology a branch of biology that studies the relationship between living creatures and atmospheric conditions. Also called **biometeorology.** —**bioclimatologist, bioclimatician,** *n.* —**bioclimatological,** *adj.*

ATTITUDES

altruism a concern or regard for the needs of others, entirely without ulterior motive. —**altruist,** *n.* —**altruistic,** *adj.*

amateurism the views and principles of a person who engages in an activity for pleasure rather than profit. Cf. **professionalism.**

animosity an active dislike or energetic hostility that leads to strong opposition.

Arcadianism the dress and conduct suitable to a pastoral existence, usually with reference to the idealized description of pastoral life in literature. —**Arcadian,** *n., adj.*

asceticism a severe self-deprivation for ethical, religious, or intellectual ends. —**ascetic,** *n., adj.*

attitudinarianism the practice of striking poses, either to mask or to express personal feelings. —**attitudinarian,** *n.*

authoritarianism **1.** the habit of conduct, thought, and speech expressing total submission to rigid principles and rules. **2.** the principles and views of the rule maker. —**authoritarian,** *n., adj.*

autotheism the elevation of one's self into being one's god.

bucolicism the conduct and views suitable for a rural, rustic, or pastoral existence. —**bucolic, bucolical,** *adj.*

ceremonialism an addiction to ceremonies or ritualism, esp. in social and other nonreligious contexts. —**ceremonialist,** *n.*

chrematist a person whose chief goal in life is the gaining of wealth. —**chrematistic,** *adj.*

consciencism the personal philosophy of Kwame Nkrumah, a president of Ghana, devised and named by him.

conventionalism a variety of conduct and thought based solely upon the usages, opinions, and practices of one's own society. —**conventionalist,** *n.*

cosmopolitanism the opinions and behavior emerging from the theory that cultural and artistic activities should have neither national nor parochial boundaries. —**cosmopolitan,** *n., adj.*

cynicism the holding or expressing of opinions which reveal disbelief, and sometimes disdain, for commonly held human values and virtues. Also called **cynism.** —**cynic,** *n.* —**cynical,** *adj.* Cf. entry under PHILOSOPHY.

defeatism the views underlying acceptance of the frustration or thwarting of a goal, esp. by the failure to prevent them. —**defeatist,** *n., adj.* Cf. **futilitarianism.**

didacticism the views and conduct of one who intends to teach, often in a pedantic or contemptuous manner, both factual and moral material. —**didact,** *n.* —**didactic,** *adj.*

didascalic *Archaic.* didactic or moralistic in thought, intention, or conduct.

egoism an extreme individualism; thought and behavior based upon the premise that one's individual self is the highest product, if not the totality, of existence. —**egoist,** *n.* —**egoistic,** *adj.*

egotism the practice of thought, speech, and conduct expressing high self-regard or self-exaltation, usu. without skepticism or humility. —**egotist,** *n.* —**egotistical,** *adj.*

emotionalism an undue influence of feelings upon thought and behavior. —**emotionalist,** *n.* —**emotionalistic,** *adj.*

ethicism a conscious tendency to moralize.

fanaticism an extreme and uncritical zeal or enthusiasm, as in religion or politics. —**fanatic,** *n.* —**fanatical,** *adj.*

fatalism the viewpoints of believers in the doctrine that all things are determined by the nature of existence. —**fatalist,** *n.* —**fatalistic,** *adj.* See also **determinism** and **necessarianism.**

feminism the sometimes radical doctrines of contemporary movements to eliminate political, social, and professional discrimination against women. —**feminist,** *n.* —**feministic,** *adj.*

finicalness an undue fastidiousness or overniceness. Also called **finicality.** —**finical,** *adj.*

finicalism *Rare.* a conscious and sometimes affected fastidiousness and undue concern with trifles, esp. those affecting elegance.

finicism *Rare.* finicalness.

fogyism, fogeyism an adherence to old-fashioned or conservative ideas and intolerance of change, often coupled with dullness or slowness of personality. —**fogyish,** *adj.*

formulism the basing of behavior and thinking upon existent categories, formulas, or systems of formulas; traditionalism. —**formulist,** *n.* —**formulistic,** *adj.*

futilitarianism a belief in the uselessness of human endeavor and aspiration; total defeatism. —**futilitarian,** *n., adj.*

gigmanism *Rare.* the habit of narrowmindedness or Philistinism.

gourmetism the theories and standards of connoisseurs in eating and drinking. Cf. **gourmandism.**

Grundyism the censorship of personal conduct based upon narrow and unintelligent conventionalism. —**Grundyist, Grundyite,** *n.*

hermitism the practice of retiring from society and living in solitude, based upon a variety of motives, including religious. Also called **hermitry, hermitship.** —**hermitic, hermitical,** *adj.*

individualism the practice of independence in thought and action on the premise that the development and expression of an individual character and personality are of the utmost importance. —**individualist,** *n.* —**individualistic,** *adj.* Cf. **egoism.**

Klanism the beliefs and practices of Ku Kluxers. Also called **Ku Kluxism, Ku Kluxery.**

malism the conviction that the world is evil.

masculinism masculinity; currently, an attempt to protect masculine traits and qualities against the assaults of the more militant feminist. Cf. **feminism.**

misandry, misandria   an extreme dislike of males, frequently based upon unhappy experience or upbringing. Cf. **misogynism.**

misanthropy   a hatred of mankind; pessimistic distrust of human nature expressed in thought and behavior. —**misanthrope, misanthropist,** *n.* —**misanthropic,** *adj.* Cf. **philanthropy.**

misogynism, misogyny   an extreme dislike of females, based upon training or experience. Cf. **misandry.**

misosophy   *Rare.* a hatred of wisdom. —**misosophist,** *n.*

nihilism   a belief in nothing. —**nihilist,** *n.* —**nihilistic,** *adj.*

nonconformism   a deliberate and conscious refusal to conform to conventional practices or patterns of behavior. —**nonconformist,** *n.* —**nonconformity,** *n.*

objectivity   the views and behavior of one who attempts not to be moved by the emotional content of an event, argument, or problem. Cf. **objectivism.**

opportunism   the conscious policy and practice of taking advantage of circumstances, with little regard for principles. —**opportunist,** *n.* —**opportunistic,** *adj.*

parochialism   a narrowness or pettiness of interests, opinions, or information. —**parochialist,** *n.*

perfectionism   **1.** the religious or philosophical aspiration to be perfect in moral character.
2. a personality trait manifested by the rejection of personal achievements falling short of perfection, often leading to distress and self-condemnation. —**perfectionist,** *n.* —**perfectionistic,** *adj.*

pessimism   a depressed and melancholy viewpoint manifested as a disposition to hold the least hopeful opinion of conditions or behavior. —**pessimist,** *n.* —**pessimistic,** *adj.* Cf. entry under PHILOSOPHY.

philanthropy   a deliberate affection for mankind, shown in contributions of money, property, or work for the benefit of others. —**philanthropist,** *n.* —**philanthropic,** *adj.* Cf. **misanthropy.**

philistinism   the opinions, goals, and conduct of persons deficient in liberal culture. —**philistine,** *n., adj.*

precisionism   an insistence upon perfection in language, morals, or ritual. —**precisionist,** *n.* —**precisionistic,** *adj.*

professionalism   the standards, views, and behavior of one who engages in an activity, esp. sports or the arts, to make his livelihood. —**professional,** *n., adj.* Cf. **amateurism.**

racism   **1.** a belief that human races have distinctive characteristics that

determine their respective cultures, usually involving the idea that one's race is superior and has the right to control others.
2. a belief in a policy of enforcing the asserted right of control. **—racist, n., adj.**

ritualism ceremonialism. **—ritualist,** n. **—ritualistic,** adj.

rubricism a tenacious adherence to rules of behavior or thought; formulism. **—rubrician,** n.

ruralism the motivations for exalting country above city living. **—ruralist, n.**

scientism **1.** *Often Disparaging.* the style, assumptions, techniques, practices, etc., typifying or regarded as typifying scientists.
2. the belief that the assumptions and methods of the natural sciences are appropriate and essential to all other disciplines, including the humanities and the social sciences.
3. scientific or pseudoscientific language. **—scientistic,** adj.

spartanism a devotion to the habits and qualities of the ancient Spartans, esp. to an indomitable spirit and an undaunted hardihood. **—spartan,** n., adj.

skepticism, scepticism a personal disposition toward doubt or incredulity of facts, persons, or institutions. **—skeptic,** n., adj. **—skeptical,** adj. Cf. entry under PHILOSOPHY.

snobbism the double inclination to ape one's superiors, often through vulgar ostentation, and to be proud and insolent with one's inferiors. **—snob,** n. **—snobby,** adj. **—snobbish,** adj.

subjectivity the views and behavior of one who tends to be affected by the emotional qualities of an event, argument, or problem. Cf. **subjectivism.**

suburbanism the doctrines and conduct of those who regard life in suburbia superior to life in cities or country.

traditionalism the tendency to submerge individual opinions or creativity in ideas or methods inherited from the past, distinguished from conventionalism in having reference more to the past than to the present. **—traditionalist,** n. Also called **traditionism.** Cf. entry under CATHOLICISM.

troglodytism **1.** an outlook or activity suitable to a cave dweller, esp. among primitive tribes.
2. the motivation or condition of a modern cave-dwelling recluse, esp. one who has rejected normal society.
3. coarse, brutal behavior, thought to resemble that of a primitive cave dweller. **—troglodyte,** n. **—troglodytic,** adj.

ultraism **1.** an extremist point of view or act.
2. extremism. **—ultraist,** n. **—ultraistic,** adj.

urbanism the views and behavior of those who champion urban living as superior to life elsewhere. **—urbanistic,** adj. Cf. **ruralism, suburbanism.**

AUTOMATION

cybernetics the comparative study of complex electronic devices and the nervous system in an attempt to understand better the nature of the human brain. —**cyberneticist,** *n.* —**cybernetic,** *adj.*

robotism the use of automated machinery or manlike mechanical devices to perform tasks. —**robotistic,** *adj.*

servomechanism a closed-circuit feedback system used in the automatic control of machines, involving an error-sensor using a small amount of energy, an amplifier, and a servomotor dispensing large amounts of power. —**servomechanical,** *adj.*

AVIATION

aerialist one who performs aerial acrobatics, such as a trapeze artist, a tightrope walker, a stunt flier, etc.

aerodonetics *Rare.* the science or art of gliding. —**aerodonetic,** *adj.*

aerodromics the art or science of flying airplanes.

aeronautics **1.** *Archaic.* the science or art of ascending and traveling in the air in lighter-than-air vehicles.
2. the technology or art of flying airplanes. —**aeronaut,** *n.* —**aeronautic, aeronautical,** *adj.*

aerophysics the branch of physics that studies the earth's atmosphere, esp. the effects upon the atmosphere of objects flying at high speeds or at high altitudes.

aerostatics the study of the construction and operation of aerostats, lighter-than-air craft such as balloons or dirigibles, —**aerostatic, aerostatical,** *adj.*

avinosis airsickness.

ornithopter da Vinci's exploratory design for a flying machine moved by flapping wings.

perastadics the science and art of space flying. —**perastadic,** *adj.*

supersonic applied to aircraft moving at speeds beyond 750 mph. (1207.5 Km) at sea level.

radar an acronym for Radio Detecting And Ranging: a method and the equipment used for the detection and direction of a flying object by reflecting radio waves off it.

B

BACTERIA

bacteriology the branch of biology that studies and classifies bacteria. —**bacteriologist,** *n.* —**bacteriologic, bacteriological,** *adj.*

chromatophobia in bacteria, a strong resistance to absorbing stains. —**chromatophobic,** *adj.*

microbiology the branch of biology that studies microorganisms, including bacteria, viruses, fungi, and pathogenic protozoa. —**microbiologist,** *n.*

microphobia, microbiophobia an abnormal fear of microorganisms. —**microphobic,** *adj.*

BALDNESS

acomia baldness. Also called **alopecia, phalacrosis.** —**acomous,** *adj.*

alopecist *Med.* one who treats baldness.

atrichia *Med.* congenital or acquired baldness. Also called **atrichosis.**

calvities, calvity baldness, esp. at the top or back of the head. —**calvous,** *adj.*

peladophobia a dread of baldness.

See also HAIR.

BANISHMENT

ostracism 1. a casting out from social or political society.
2. the ancient Athenian process of temporary banishment by popular vote, using potsherds or tiles for ballots.

petalism a Syracusan method of banishing citizens for five years if they were judged guilty of dangerous influence or ambition; olive leaves were used for ballots.

BAPTISM

Abecedarian a member of a 16th cent. Anabaptist sect who refused to learn to read, arguing that the guidance of the Holy Spirit was sufficient for the understanding of the Bible.

Anabaptism 1. a belief in adult, as opposed to infant, baptism.
2. membership in various Protestant sects advocating adult baptism. —**Anabaptist,** *n., adj.*

antipedobaptism, antipaedobaptism the denial, on scriptural grounds, of the validity of infant baptism. —**antipedobaptist,** *n.*

baptisaphily an interest in collecting Christian baptismal names.

catabaptist an opponent of baptism.

conditional baptism Christian baptism administered when there is doubt whether a person has already been baptized or whether a former baptism is valid.

hemerobaptism the practice of ancient Jewish and early Christian sects involving daily ceremonial baptisms or ablutions. —**hemerobaptist,** *n.*

holobaptism a belief in baptism by immersion. Also called **immersionism.** —**holobaptist,** *n.*

palingenesis   a belief that baptism effects a new birth or regeneration. Also called **palingenesy**. —**palingenesist**, *n*. —**palingenesian**, *adj*.

pedobaptism, paedobaptism   the historic Christian practice of infant baptism. —**pedobaptist**, *n*.

BATHING

balneography   a treatise on baths.

balneology   the study of the therapeutic uses of various types of bathing; hydrotherapy. —**balneologist**, *n*. —**balneologic, balneological**, *adj*.

bathophobia   an intense dislike of bathing.

hydrotherapy   the treatment of diseases through the use of water, whether internal or external, as whirlpool baths, compresses, or drinking mineral waters. Also called **hydrotherapeutics**. —**hydrotherapist**, *n*. —**hydrotherapeutic, hydrotherapeutical**, *adj*.

Kneippism   a 19th cent. treatment of diseases by types of hydrotherapy, as warm or cold baths and walking barefoot in dewy grass.

BEARDS

pogoniasis   *Med*. 1. an excessive growth of beard.
2. the development of a beard by a woman.

pogonology   a treatise on beards. —**pogonologist**, *n*.

pogonophile   an admirer of beards; a student of beards.

pogonotomy   the cutting of beards.

pogonotrophy   the cultivation of beards, beard-growing.

BEAUTY

adonism   the beautification of a person, usu. a male.

aesthetician, esthetician   1. a specialist in aesthetics.
2. a proponent of aestheticism.

aestheticism, estheticism   the doctrine that the principles of beauty are basic and that other principles (the good, the right) are derived from them, applied esp. to a late 19th cent. movement to bring art into daily life.

aesthetics, esthetics   a branch of philosophy dealing with beauty and the beautiful. —**aesthetic**, *n., adj*. —**aesthetical**, *adj*.

cosmetology   the art or practice of the beautification of the skin, hair, or nails. —**cosmetologist**, *n*. —**cosmetological**, *adj*.

philocalist   a lover of beauty.

BEER

labeorphily   the collecting of beer bottle labels. —**labeorphile**, *n*.

meadophily   the study of beer bottle labels.—**meadophile**, *n*.

tegestology   the collecting of beer mats. —**tegestologist,** *n.*

BEES

apiarist   a person who tends bees.

apiary   a beehive or collection of beehives. —**apiarian,** *adj.*

apiology   a specialty within entomology that studies honeybees. —**apiologist,** *n.*

apiphobia, apiophobia   an intense fear of bees. Also called **melissophobia.**

melittology   *Rare.* apiology. —**melittologist,** *n.*

BEHAVIOR

antagonism   a contentiousness toward or opposition to others or their ideas; hostility or antipathy. —**antagonistic,** *adj.*

atrabilarian   **1.** a sad and gloomy individual.
2. an irritable and bad-tempered person. —**atrabilious,** *adj.*

autophoby   *Rare.* an abnormal fear of being egotistical, of referring to oneself.

bestiality   a debased brutality, the opposite of humane activity: "I have lost the immortal part of myself, and what remains is bestial". (*Othello*)

bohemianism   the practice of individualistic, unconventional, and relaxed conduct, often in an artistic context, expressing disregard for or opposition to ordinary conventions. —**bohemian,** *n., adj.*

casuist   **1.** a person who studies and resolves questions of right and wrong in conduct.
2. an oversubtle or specious reasoner. —**casuistic,** *adj.*

casuistry   **1.** the branch of ethics or theology that studies the relation of general ethic principles to particular cases of conduct or conscience.
2. a dishonest or oversubtle application of such principles.

dilettantism   an admiration of or interest in the arts, often used pejoratively to designate a shallow, undisciplined, or frivolous attraction. —**dilettante,** *n., adj.*

dramaticism   the habit of performing actions in a histrionic manner.

ergoism   a pedantic adherence to logically constructed rules.

exhibitionism   **1.** a deliberately conspicuous or exaggerated mode of behavior, intended to gain attention.
2. *Med.* the abnormal practice of indecent exposure. —**exhibitionist,** *n.* —**exhibitionistic,** *adj.*

gelastic   **1.** inclined to laughter.
2. laugh-provoking in conduct or speech.

gnathonism   the extremely obsequious behavior of a sycophant. —**gnathonic,** *adj.*

gourmandism, gormandism 1. a strong penchant for good food; gourmetism; epicurism.
2. gluttony. —**gourmand,** *n., adj.*

histrionicism a tendency to theatrical or exaggerated action. —**histrionics,** *n.* —**histrionic,** *adj.*

histriconism histrionicism.

humoralism, humouralism an obsolete physiological explanation of health, disease, and behavior, asserting that the relative proportions of four elemental bodily fluids or humors (blood-sanguinity, phlegm-sluggishness, black bile-melancholy, and yellow bile-choler) determined a person's physical and mental constitution. —**humoral,** *adj.*

hypercriticism the practice of unreasonable or unjustly severe criticism; faultfinding. —**hypercritic,** *n.,adj.* —**hypercritical,** *adj.*

impubic not yet arrived at puberty; immature. —**impuberty,** *n.*

irascibility a tendency to irritability and sudden fits of anger. Also called **irascibleness.** —**irascible,** *adj.*

juvenilism, juvenility a mode of action or thought characterized by apparent youthfulness (often used pejoratively).

libertinism a tendency to unrestrained conduct, often licentious or dissolute. —**libertine,** *n., adj.*

lionism the pursuit or adulation of celebrities. —**lionize,** *v.*

litigiousness an inclination to dispute or disagree with others; argumentativeness. —**litigious,** *adj.*

macaronism a tendency to foppishness. —**macaroni, maccaroni,** *n.*

martinetism an emphasis on scrupulous attention to the details of methods and procedures in all areas of life. —**martinet,** *n.* —**martinetish,** *adj.*

maudlinism *Rare.* 1. a tendency in temperament to be mawkishly sentimental and tearfully emotional.
2. a degree of drunkenness characterized by mawkish emotionalism. —**maudlin,** *adj.*

mimicism an intense (and sometimes injurious) tendency to mimicry.

narcissism an excessive admiration of oneself. Also called **narcism.** —**narcissist, narcist,** *n.* —**narcissistic, narcistic,** *adj.*

nomadism a rootless, nondomestic, and roving lifestyle. —**nomadic,** *adj.*

nudism the practice of going nude. —**nudist,** *n., adj.*

pococurantism a tendency to conduct expressing indifference, nonchalance, or lack of concern. —**pococurante, pococurantist,** *n.* —**pococurante,** *adj.*

polypragmatism a penchant for meddlesomeness and officiousness. Also occasionally called **polypragmacy, polypragmaty.** —**polypragmatist,** *n.* —**polypragmatic,** *adj.*

pornerastic unchaste, licentious, or lewd in conduct.

praxeology, praxiology the study of human behavior and conduct. —**praxeological,** adj.

protervity a tendency to peevish, petulant, or insolent conduct.

psychagogics, psychagogy a method of affecting behavior by assisting in the choice of desirable life goals. —**psychagogue,** n.

Quixotism a tendency to absurdly chivalric, visionary, or romantically impractical conduct. —**quixotic, quixotical,** adj.

rabulism Rare. a tendency to railing and quibbling. —**rabulistic, rabulous,** adj.

sequacity a tendency to subservience and obsequiousness. Also called **sequaciousness.** —**sequacious,** adj. Cf. **sycophantism.**

seraphism Archaic. an ecstatic devotion, esp. religious.

Shandyism a tendency to whimsical conduct in accord with absurd theories from past ages. [allusion to the actions of Walter, father of the hero in Sterne's Tristram Shandy]

spasmodism a tendency to conduct marked by outbursts of strong emotion. —**spasmodist,** n. —**spasmodic, spasmodical,** adj.

sybaritism a love of luxury. [allusion to Sybaris, a Greek city in Italy noted for its luxury] —**sybarite,** n. —**sybaritic,** adj.

sycophantism the practice of self-serving or servile flattery. —**sycophant,** n. —**sycophantic,** adj.

theatricalism a tendency to actions marked by exaggerations in speech or behavior.

Timonism a personal despair leading to misanthropy. [allusion to Shakespeare's Timon of Athens]

toadyism a fawning flattery, obsequiousness, or sycophancy. —**toady,** n. —**toadyish,** adj.

vagabondism 1. the tendency to wander from place to place without a settled home; nomadism.
2. the life of a tramp; vagrancy. Also called **vagabondage.** —**vagabond,** n., adj.

voyeurism the compulsion to seek sexual gratification by secretively looking at sexual objects or acts; the actions of a Peeping Tom. [allusion to the man who looked at Lady Godiva on her nude ride through Coventry] —**voyeur,** n. —**voyeuristic,** adj.

Yahooism a penchant for rowdyism. [allusion to Swift's characters in Gulliver's Travels]

zealotism, zealotry a tendency to undue or excessive zeal; fanaticism.

BEING

neontology the scientific study of living, usually recent, plants and animals. —**neontologist,** *n.* —**neontologic, neontological,** *adj.* Cf. **paleontology.**

ontology, ontologism the branch of metaphysics that studies the nature of existence. —**ontologist,** *n.* —**ontologic, ontological, ontologistic,** *adj.*

paleontology the scientific study of plants and animals of past geologic ages, usually in fossilized conditions. —**paleontologist,** *n.*

BELLS

campanarian *Rare.* concerned with bells or the manufacture of bells.

campanile a tower for peals of bells or a carillon, usu. freestanding. Also called **campanario.**

campanist a carilloneur.

campanology the science or art of bell ringing. See also **change ringing.** —**campanologist, campanologer,** *n.* —**campanological,** *adj.*

change ringing the art of sounding a ring or set of from 3 to 12 tuned bells according to intricate patterns of sequences.

tintinabulation **1.** the sound made by ringing bells.
2. a tinkling, bell-like sound. —**tintinabular,** *adj.*

BIBLE

biblioclasm the destruction of books, esp. the Bible. —**biblioclast,** *n.*

bibliomancy a technique of divination from books, esp. using passages chosen randomly from the Bible.

colporteur a person who distributes or sells religious tracts or books, esp. Bibles. —**colportage,** *n.*

dittology a double reading or interpretation, esp. of a Bible passage.

Elohist the author of part of the first six books in the Old Testament, so named because of references to God as *Elohim.* Cf. **Yahwist.**

exegetics the branch of theology that specializes in interpretation, or exegesis, of Biblical literature. Historically, exegetes have recognized four levels of meaning in the Bible: the historical or literal, the allegorical, the moral and the anagogical or mystical, putting emphasis on the necessity of a foundation for the latter three in the literal sense. —**exegete,** *n.*

fundamentalism the rationale of conservative American Protestants who regard the Bible as free of errors or contradictions and emphasize its literal interpretation, usu. without reference to modern scholarship. —**fundamentalist,** *n., adj.*

hermeneutics the science of interpretation and explanation, esp. the branch of theology that deals with the general principles of Biblical interpretation. —*Rare.* **hermeneutist,** *n.*

Higher Criticism   the analysis of Biblical materials that aims to ascertain, from internal evidence, authorship, date, and intent. Cf. **Lower Criticism.**

isagogics   a branch of theology that is introductory to actual exegesis, emphasizing the literary and cultural history of Biblical writings. —**isagogic,** *adj.*

literalism   See **fundamentalism** and **Scripturalism.**

Lower Criticism   the study of Biblical materials that intends to reconstruct their original texts in preparation for the tasks of Higher Criticism.

pseudepigrapha   the spurious writings (other than the canonical books and the Apocrypha) professing to be Biblical in character, as the Books of Enoch. —**pseudepigraphic, pseudepigraphical, pseudepigraphous,** *adj.*

Scripturalism   a strict compliance with the literal interpretation of the Bible.

synoptist   a Biblical scholar who arranges side by side excerpts from the first three Gospels to show their resemblances in event, chronology, and language. —**synoptic,** *adj.*

Targumist   1. the writer of a Targum, a translation or paraphrase into Aramaic of a portion of the Old Testament.
2. an authority on Targumic literature. —**Targumic, Targumistic,** *adj.*

tropology   a method of interpreting Biblical literature emphasizing the moral implications of the tropes, or figures of speech, used in its composition. —**tropological,** *adj.*

Yahwist   the author of part of the first six books in the Old Testament, so named because of references to God as *Yahweh* (Jehovah). Cf. **Elohist.**

BIOLOGY

agrobiology   the branch of biology that studies the relation of soil management to the nutrition, growth, and crop yield of plants. —**agrobiologist,** *n.* —**agrobiologic, agrobiological,** *adj.*

autecology   the branch of ecology that studies the relation of an organism to its environment. Cf. **synecology.**

auxanography   the branch of microbiology that studies the rate of growth or inhibition exhibited by individual organisms in various plate-culture media. —**auxanographic,** *adj.*

biogeography   the branch of biology that studies the geographical distribution of animals and plants.

chorology   *Biogeography.* the study of organisms, esp. their migrations and distribution. —**chorologic, chorological,** *adj.*

ctetology   the branch of biology that studies the origin and development of acquired characteristics.

cytology   the branch of biology that studies the structure, growth, and pathology of cells, —**cytologist,** *n.*

ecology, oecology 1. the branch of biology that studies the relations between plants and animals and their environment.
2. the branch of sociology that studies the environmental spacing and interdependence of people and institutions, as in rural or in urban settings. —**ecologist,** *n.* —**ecological,** *adj.*

genetics the branch of biology that studies heredity and variation in plants and animals. —**geneticist,** *n.* —**genetic,** *adj.*

karyology a specialty within cytology that studies the anatomy of cell nuclei with emphasis upon the nature and structure of chromosomes.

Lysenkoism the theories of the Russian geneticist Trofim Lysenko, who argued that somatic and environmental factors have a greater influence on heredity than orthodox genetics has found demonstrable; now generally discredited.

parasitology the branch of biology that studies parasites and parasitism. —**parasitologist,** *n.*

photoperiodism, photoperiodicity the effect on the growth and reproduction of plants or animals of varying exposures to light and darkness. —**photoperiod,** *n.* —**photoperiodic,** *adj.* Cf. **thermoperiodism.**

psychobiology 1. the branch of biology that studies the interactions of body and mind, esp. as exhibited in the nervous system.
2. psychology as studied in terms of biology. —**psychobiologist,** *n.* —**psychobiologic, psychobiological,** *adj.*

symbiosis the living together of two dissimilar organisms; the relationship may be beneficial to both (*mutualism* and *symbiosis*), beneficial to one without effect on the other (*commensalism*), beneficial to one and detrimental to the other (*parasitism*), detrimental to the first without any effect on the other (*amensalism*), or detrimental to both (*synnecrosis*). —**symbiotic,** *adj.*

synecology the branch of ecology that studies the relation of organisms in the mass to their common environment. Cf. **autecology.**

teratology the branch of biology that studies abnormal formations in animals or plants. —**teratologist,** *n.*

thermoperiodism the effect on the growth and reproduction of plants or animals of timed exposures to varied temperatures. —**thermoperiod,** *n.* —**thermoperiodic,** *adj.*

BIRDS

aviary a large cage or enclosure where birds are kept.

avicide the killing of birds.

aviculture the raising or keeping of birds. —**aviculturist,** *n.*

caliology *Rare.* the study of bird's nests.

neossology the study of young birds.

nidology the study of bird's nests. —**nidologist,** *n.*

oology the branch of ornithology that collects and studies birds' eggs. —**oologist,** *n.* —**oologic, oological,** *adj.*

ornithology the branch of zoology that studies birds. —**ornithologist,** *n.* —**ornithologic, ornithological,** *adj.*

ornithomancy, ornithoscopy the observation of birds, esp. in flight, for divination.

penisterophily *Rare.* the raising and training of pigeons.

psittacosis a disease of parrots and other birds communicable to human beings. —**psittacotic,** *adj.*

pterylology the branch of ornithology that studies the areas upon which birds grow feathers. Also called **pterylography.**

BIRTH

obstetrics the branch of medicine that deals with pre- and postnatal care and with the delivery of a child. —**obstetrician,** *n.* —**obstetric, obstetrical,** *adj.*

parturiency the state or condition of bringing forth young or about to begin parturition. —**parturient,** *adj.*

tocology, tokology the science of obstetrics or midwifery.

tocophobia, tokophobia an abnormal fear of childbirth. Also called **maieusiophobia.**

viviparism the bearing of living offspring characteristic of almost all mammals, many reptiles, and some fishes. —**viviparity,** *n.* —**viviparous,** *adj.*

BLACKENING

denigration literally, blackening; commonly, the sullying or defaming of a person, organization, or institution. —**denigrator,** *n.*

melanism a darkening caused by an unusually high amount of pigmentation in the skin, hair, and eyes. Cf. **albinism.**

BLINDNESS

ablepsia, ablepsy a lack or loss of sight. —**ableptical,** *adj.*

cecity blindness.

chionablepsia *Med.* the condition of snow blindness.

nyctalopia the loss of sight in darkness. —**nyctalopic,** *adj.*

typhlology the totality of medical knowledge concerning the causes, treatment, and prevention of blindness.

typhlophile a person who devotes himself to helping the blind.

typhlosis blindness. —**typhlotic,** *adj.*

BLOOD

angiology the branch of anatomy that studies the blood vessels and the lymphatics.

angiopathology the pathology of, or changes seen in, diseased blood vessels.

hemadynamometry the measurement of blood pressure.

hemaphobia, haemaphobia, hemophobia an abnormal fear of the sight of blood. Also called **hematophobia.**

hematidrosis the excretion of bloody sweat.

hematology, haematology the branch of medical science that studies the morphology of the blood and bloodforming tissues. —**hematologist,** *n.* —**hematologic, hematological,** *adj.*

hemautography a method of tracing variations in blood pressure by having an arterial jet mark a special tracing paper. —**hemautograph,** *n.* —**hemautographic,** *adj.*

hemopathology, hematopathology the branch of medical science that studies the diseases of the blood.

hemophilia, haemophilia a tendency to uncontrolled bleeding. Also called **hemorrhaphilia.** —**hemophiliac,** *n., adj.*

phlebotomy a medical treatment involving incision of a vein; bloodletting. Also called **venesection.** —**phlebotomist,** *n.* —**phlebotomize,** *v.* —**phlebotomic, phlebotomical,** *adj.*

toxemia, toxaemia 1. a condition of illness due to the presence in the bloodstream of toxins.
2. popularly, bloodpoisoning. —**toxemic,** *adj.*

BODIES

androgynism the possession of the characteristics of both sexes; hermaphroditism. Also called **androgyneity.** —**androgynous,** *adj.*

ankylophobia a dread of stiff or immobile joints.

biophysiology the branch of biology that studies the growth, morphology, and physiology of organs. —**biophysiologist,** *n.*

chondrology the branch of medical science that studies cartilages.

gynecomastism an excessive development of mammary glands in males. Also called **gynecomastia, gynecomasty.**

hermaphroditism the presence on an individual body of both male and female sex organs. —**hermaphrodite,** *n.* —**hermaphroditic,** *adj.*

kinesiology *Med.* the study of the motions of the human body, esp. as they apply to therapy through corrective exercise. Also called **kinestherapy.** —**kinesiologic, kinesiological,** *adj.*

metaboly *Rare.* the process of metabolism.

nephrology the branch of medical science that studies the kidney. —**nephrologist,** *n.*

physiology 1. the branch of medical science that studies the functions of living organisms or their parts.
2. the organic processes or functions of an organism or any of its parts. —**physiologist,** *n.* —**physiologic, physiological,** *adj.*

somatology the branch of anthropology that studies man's physical characteristics. —**somatologic, somatological,** *adj.* See **physical anthropology.**

spirometry the measurement of the breathing capacity of the lungs. —**spirometer,** *n.*

splanchnology the branch of anatomy that studies the viscera. *See also ANATOMY.*

BONES

agmatology 1. a branch of medical science that studies fractures.
2. a treatise on fractures.

osteology the branch of anatomy that studies the skeleton. —**osteologist, osteologer,** *n.* —**osteologic, osteological,** *adj.*

osteomancy a form of divination involving bones.

osteopathology any disease of the bone.

osteopathy 1. a disease of the bone.
2. a therapeutic system based upon the premise that restoring or maintaining health requires manipulation of the skeleton and muscles to preserve normal structure. —**osteopath, osteopathist,** *n.* —**osteopathic,** *adj.*

BOOKS

bibliognost a person who possesses an encyclopedic knowledge of books and bibliography. —**bibliognostic,** *adj.*

bibliogony the making of books; book production. Also called **bibliogenesis.**

bibliography 1. the science that studies the history of books, noting their physical description, publication, and editions.
2. a list of books on a particular subject.
3. a list of books by a particular author.
4. a list of source materials used or consulted in the preparation of a work or referred to in the text. —**bibliographer,** *n.* —**bibliographic, bibliographical,** *adj.*

bibliokleptomania an abnormal compulsion to steal books. —**biblioklept,** *n.* Cf. **bibliomania.**

bibliology 1. the history of books; bibliography.
2. the study of the doctrines of the Bible. —**bibliologist,** *n.*

bibliomania an excessive fondness for acquiring and possessing books. —**bibliomaniac,** *n.* —**bibliomaniacal,** *adj.*

bibliopegy   the art of binding books. —**bibliopegist,** *n.* —**bibliopegic,** *adj.*

bibliophage   a bookworm (literally, a 'bookeater'). —**bibliophagy,** *n.* —**bibliophagous,** *adj.*

bibliophilism, bibliophily   a love for books, esp. for first or fine editions. —**bibliophile, bibliophilist,** *n.* —**bibliophilic,** *adj.*

bibliophobia   an abnormal dislike for books.

bibliopolism, bibliopoly   the selling of books, esp. rare or secondhand volumes. —**bibliopole, bibliopolist,** *n.* —**bibliopolic,** *adj.*

bibliotaphy   the hoarding or hiding of books, often under lock and key. —**bibliotaph,** *n.* —**bibliotaphic,** *adj.*

bibliotherapy   the therapeutic use of reading material in the treatment of nervous diseases. —**bibliotherapist,** *n.* —**bibliotherapeutic,** *adj.*

grangerism   1. the augmentation of the illustrative material in a book by prints, sketches, and engravings not found in the original edition.
2. the mutilation of books to acquire extra-illustrative materials. —**grangerize,** *v.*

incunabulum   any book printed in the last part of the 15th cent., as Caxton's editions of Chaucer and Malory. —**incunabula,** *n. pl.* —**incunabulist,** *n.* —**incunabular,** *adj.*

philobiblist   a lover of books; bibliophile.

BOTANY

agrostology   the branch of systematic botany that studies grasses. —**agrostologist,** *n.* —**agrostologic, agrostological,** *adj.*

algology   the branch of botany that studies algae. Also called **phycology.** —**algologist,** *n.* —**algological,** *adj.*

ampelography   the branch of botany that studies the cultivation of grapes. —**ampelographer,** *n.*

batology   the branch of botany that studies brambles. —**batologist,** *n.*

botany   a major division of biology that studies all plant life. —**botanist,** *n.* —**botanical,** *adj.* Cf. **zoology.**

bryology   the branch of botany that studies mosses and liverworts. —**bryologist,** *n.*

carpology   the branch of botany that studies the structure of fruits and seeds. —**carpologist,** *n.* —**carpological,** *adj.*

ethnobotany   a specialty in botany that studies the lore and uses of plants as illustrative of the customs of a usu. primitive group. —**ethnobotanist,** *n.* —**ethnobotanic, ethnobotanical,** *adj.*

herbarism   *Archaic.* botany.

Linneanism   a system of botanical nomenclature following the binomial procedures established by the Swede Carl von Linné. —**Linnaean, Linnean,** *adj.*

mycology   **1.** the branch of botany that studies fungi.
2. a catalog of the fungi found in a specific area. —**mycologist,** *n.* —**mycologic, mycological,** *adj.*

phytography   the branch of botany that studies plant measurement and plant taxonomy. —**phytographer, phytographist,** *n.* —**phytographic, phytographical,** *adj.*

phytology   botany.

phytosociology   the branch of ecology that studies the interrelations of plants and plant communities. —**phytosociologist,** *n.* —**phytosociologic, phytosociological,** *adj.*

pomology   **1.** the branch of botany that studies the cultivation of fruit.
2. the science of growing, storing, and processing fruit. —**pomologist,** *n.*

pteridology   the branch of botany that studies ferns. —**pteridologist,** *n.* *See also* PLANTS.

BOXING

pugilism   the art or practice of fighting with fists; boxing. —**pugilistic,** *adj.*

pugilist   a person who fights with his fists; prizefighter.

BRAIN

biofeedback   the process of providing a person with visual or auditory evidence of the quality of an autonomic physiological function so that he may exercise conscious control over it.

cerebrology   **1.** *Obsolete.* the branch of psychology that studies the brain.
2. *Med.* the total knowledge concerning the brain.

cybernetics   *See* AUTOMATION.

menticide   the process of systematically altering beliefs and attitudes, esp. through the use of drugs, torture, or psychological-stress techniques; brainwashing.

psychosurgeon   a specialist who performs brain surgery to treat mental disorders. —**psychosurgery,** *n.*

synectics   a procedure for the stating and solving of problems based upon creative thinking in figurative terms by a small, carefully chosen, and diversely specialized group.

BRASSES

chalcologue   a student of brasses.

chalcomancy   a technique of divination by examining vessels of brass.

chalcotript   one who copies monumental brasses by taking rubbings.

BREVITY

brachylogy   the practice of conciseness in speech or writing.

laconism, laconicism   **1.** the practice of using few words to say much. **2.** a laconic utterance. —**laconic,** *n., adj.* —**laconical,** *adj.*

BUDDHISM

Buddhism   the religion of the followers of Gautama Buddha, whose 6th cent. B.C. doctrines strongly opposed the formalized, mechanical rituals of the Brahman sect in Hinduism; Buddha's teachings offered escape from endless reincarnation, a method of spiritual attainment through correct views and actions (**The Eight-Fold Path**), and a spiritual goal (Nirvana): a soul free from craving, suffering, and sorrow. —**Buddhist,** *n.* —**Buddhistic, Buddhistical,** *adj.*

The Eight-Fold Path   the method of spiritual attainment outlined in Buddha's sermons on the Four Noble Truths: pain, the cause of pain, the cessation of pain, and the path that leads to this cessation, emphasizing in the last right view, thought, speech, action, livelihood, effort, mindfulness, and concentration.

Hinayanism   the earliest development of Buddhism after Buddha's death, emphasizing doctrines and practices originally formulated by Buddha and reflected in the "School of the Elders" (*Theravada*) of the Pali tradition; called "the lesser vehicle," it found followers in southern India and Ceylon.—**Hinayana,** *n., adj.*

Lamaism   a reformation of Buddhism in Tibet intended to bring about stricter discipline in the monasteries; the dominant sect is Ge-lup-Ka (The Virtuous Way), with the patron deity Chen-re-zi (the Bodhisattva of Great Mercy), who is reincarnated as the successive Dalai Lamas. Also called **Ge-lup-Ka.** —**Lamaist,** *n.* —**Lamaistic,** *adj.*

Mahayanism   the "greater vehicle" or second development of Buddhism after the death of its founder as a reaction against the orthodox and conservative ideas of the Hinayana, asserting that Gautama is one of many manifestations of one primordial Buddha and emphasizing good works illustrating the six virtues of generosity, patience, vigor, concentration, and wisdom necessary to ideal Buddhism; its tenets are preserved in Sanskrit texts, later translated into Chinese and Japanese. —**Mahayana,** *n., adj.*

Tantrayana   the mixed form of Buddhism practiced in Tibet, adding to ideas from both major Buddhist developments doctrines and practices from Hindu Tantric sects and the native Tibetan religion of nature worship and magic called Bönism; it combines the Hinayana concept of emancipation through self-discipline and the Mahayana concept of philosophical insight into reality for the sake of others with uniquely Tibetan magical rites and mystical meditation. —**Tantrayanic,** *adj.*

Zenism an outgrowth of Mahayana, the "meditation" sect, developed in Japan from its earlier Chinese counterpart and divided into two branches: *Rinzai,* an austere and aristocratic monasticism emphasizing meditation on paradoxes; and *Sōtō,* a benevolent monasticism with great popular following, emphasizing ethical actions and charity, tenderness, benevolence, and sympathy as well as meditation on whatever occurs as illumination. —**Zen,** *n.* —**Zenic,** *adj.*

BUILDINGS

batophobia 1. an abnormal fear of being too close to buildings.
2. an abnormal fear of heights.

knacker *Brit.* a person who purchases old structures and disassembles them for salvageable materials and scrap.

naology the study of sacred buildings.

BULLS

aficionado an avid and informed devotee of a sport, activity, or art, formerly restricted to bull fighting.

bulldogging *Western U.S.* the seizing of a calf or steer by the horns and throwing it by twisting the head. —**bulldogger,** *n.*

tauricide 1. the killing of a bull.
2. the killer of a bull.

taurobolium a part of an ancient religious rite in which baptism in the blood of a sacrificed bull takes place. Also called **tauroboly.**

taurokathapsia an ancient Cretan sport for both sexes involving grasping the horns of a bull and tumbling over him; bull-leaping.

tauromachy, tauromaquia 1. the art or technique of bullfighting.
2. a bullfight. —**tauromachian, tauromachic,** *adj.*

Taurus 1. the bull, second of the zodiacal constellations.
2. the bull, second of the astrological signs.

BUREAUCRACY

bureaucracy 1. a government typified by a rigid hierarchy of bureaus, administrators, and minor officials.
2. a body of administrators; officialdom.
3. administration characterized by excessive red tape and routine. —**bureaucratic,** *adj.*

officialism 1. any official regulations or procedures.
2. an excessive emphasis on official regulations or procedures.
3. officials in general or collectively.

red-tapeism, red-tapism the practice of requiring excessive paperwork and tedious procedures before official action can be considered or completed.

BURYING

hydriotaphia   a burial in an urn.

taphophilia   a love for funerals.

taphephobia, taphiphobia, taphophobia   an abnormal fear of being buried alive.

BUTTERFLIES

Lepidoptera   an order of insects comprising the butterflies, moths, and skippers, that as adults have four membranous wings more or less covered with scales. —**lepidopterous, lepidopteral,** *adj.*

lepidopterology   a branch of zoology that studies butterflies and moths. —**lepidopterist,** *n.*

C

CALENDAR

embolism   **1.** an intercalation of a day or days in the calendar to correct error.
2. the day or days intercalated. —**embolic, embolismic, embolismical,** *adj.*

heortology   the study of the origin, growth, meaning and history of Christian religious feasts. —**heortological,** *adj.*

menology   **1.** a list or calendar of months.
2. *East.Ch.* a calendar of all festivals for martyrs and saints, with brief accounts of their lives. Also called **Menologion.**
3. a church calendar, listing festivals for saints.

CANCER

carcinogen   a substance capable of producing a cancer. —**carcinogenic,** *adj.*

carcinomophobia, carcinomatophobia, carcinophobia   an abnormal fear of cancer. Also called **cancerophobia.**

CANNIBALISM

anthropophagism, anthropophagy   the consumption of human flesh; cannibalism. —**anthropophagous,** *adj.*

androphagy   cannibalism. —**androphagous,** *adj.*

CATS

ailurophile, aelurophile   a lover of cats. Also called **felinophile.**

ailurophobia, aelurophobia, elurophobia   an abnormal fear of cats. Also called **felinophobia.**

galeophilia   an excessive fondness for cats.

gatophobia an abnormal fear of cats.

CATHOLICISM

anticlericalism an opposition to the influence and activities of the clergy in public affairs. —**anticlericalist,** *n.*

Cahenslyism a 19th cent. plan of the German parliamentarian Cahensly, successfully opposed by American interests, to have the pope divide the foreign-born population of the U.S. into ethnic groups and to appoint bishops and priests of the same ethnic and linguistic background as each group.

catechumenism the condition of a person who is receiving basic instruction in the doctrines of Christianity in preparation for the sacrament of confirmation. Also called **catechumenate.** —**catechumen,** *n.* —**catechumenal, catechumenical,** *adj.*

chrism 1. a sacramental oil.
2. a sacramental anointing, as unction.
3. *East. Ch.* the rite of confirmation.

clericalism 1. an undue influence of the hierarchy and clergy in public affairs and government.
2. the principles and interests of the clergy.
3. the system, spirit, or methods of the priesthood; sacerdotalism. —**clericalist,** *n.* Cf. **laicism.**

Curialism 1. the philosophy and methods of the ultramontane party in the Roman Church.
2. the methods and processes of the Curia Romana, the bureaucracy of congregations and offices which assist the pope in the government of the Roman Church.

decretist 1. a canon lawyer versed in papal decrees on points in ecclesiastical law.
2. a person versed in the decretals. Also called **decretalist.**

ecclesiarchy the control of government by clerics. Also called **hierocracy.** —**ecclesiarch,** *n.*

extrascripturalism the view that the faith and practice of the Church are based in both tradition and the Scriptures. Cf. **fundamentalism** and **Scripturalism.**

Gallicanism the body of doctrines, chiefly associated with French dioceses, advocating the restriction of papal authority, esp. in administrative matters. —**Gallican,** *n., adj.*

Heckerism the teaching of a 19th cent. Paulist priest Isaac T. Hecker, who regarded Catholicism as the religion best suited to promoting human aspirations after liberty and truth and to the character and institutions of the American people. Also called **Americanism.**

Hildebrandism the views of Hildebrand, Pope Gregory VII (1073-85), esp. those underlying his drastic reforms within the Roman Church and his assertion of papal supremacy. Usually called **ultramontanism.** —**Hildebrandic, Hildebrandine,** *adj.*

infallibilism **1.** the belief in or adherence to the dogma of papal infallibility. **2.** the dogma itself.

laicism **1.** the nonclerical, or secular, control of political and social institutions in a society.
2. lay participation in church matters. —**laity,** *n.* Cf. **clericalism.**

Marianism *Rare.* a religious cult based on the veneration of the Virgin Mary.

Maronism an Arabic-speaking Uniat sect in Lebanon, under the authority of the papacy since the 12th cent. but maintaining its Syriac liturgy, married clergy, and practice of communion in both bread and wine. —**Maronite,** *n., adj.*

marranism, marranoism the forced conversion of Jews or Moors in medieval Spain. —**marrano,** *n.*

martyrology **1.** a history or registry of martyrs.
2. the branch of ecclesiastical history that studies the lives and deaths of martyrs.
3. *Rom.Ch.* an official catalog of martyrs and saints, arranged according to the dates of their feast days. —**martyrologist,** *n.* —**martyrologic, martyrological,** *adj.*

Mariolatry, Maryology, Maryolatry the cult of the Blessed Virgin Mary. Earlier, **Marianism.** —**Mariolater,** *n.* —**Mariolatrous,** *adj.*

Molinism the doctrine of the 16th cent. Jesuit Luis Molina, who taught that the work of grace depends on the accord of man's free will. —**Molinist,** *n.*

Novationism a 3rd cent. controversy in the Roman diocese in which Novation, elected bishop of a schismatic group, declared that lapsed Christians could not be received again into the Church. —**Novationist,** *n.*

ostiary **1.** a member of the lowest-ranking of the four minor orders in Roman Catholicism.
2. a doorkeeper of a church.

papism *Usually Disparaging.* authoritarian government under the direction of the pope; Roman Catholicism. Also called **papistry.** —**papist,** *n.* —**papistic, papistical,** *adj.*

papalism **1.** the institution and procedures of papal government.
2. the advocacy of papal supremacy. —**papalist,** *n., adj.*

Petrinism the theological concepts taught by or ascribed to St. Peter. —**Petrinist,** *n.*

popeism, popery   a pejorative term for the papacy.

portiforium   a breviary.

sacerdotalism   the system, practices, or principles underlying the priesthood. —**sacerdotal,** *n., adj.*

simonism   the practice or defense of simony, esp. in ecclesiastical government.

stigmatism   the state of one who has received supernatural stigmata, marks on hands, feet, and side similar to the wounds of Christ. —**stigmata,** *n.* —**stigmatic,** *adj.*

synodist   a member of a council, meeting to consult and decide on church matters. —**synodical, synodal,** *adj.*

traditionalism   adherence to tradition, rather than to revelation, independent Bible study, or individual reasoning, as the authority controlling religious knowledge and practice. —**traditionalist,** *n.* —**traditionalistic,** *adj.*

ultramontanism   the advocacy of the supremacy of the papacy and the papal system, in opposition to those favoring national churches and the authority of church councils. —**ultramontane, ultramontanist,** *n.* —**ultramontanistic,** *adj.*

Uniatism   the union of an Eastern Rite church with the Roman Church in which the authority of the papacy is accepted without loss of separate liturgies or government by local patriarchs. —**Uniat, Uniate,** *n.*

Vaticanism   the doctrine or advocacy of papal supremacy. —**Vaticanist,** *n.*

CAVES

speleology, spelaeology   the branch of geology that explores, studies, and describes caves. —**speleologist,** *n.* —**speleological,** *adj.*

spelunker   a person who explores caves as a hobby. —**spelunk,** *v.*

CELLS

cytology   the branch of biology that studies the structure, function, multiplication, and life history of cells. —**cytologist,** *n.* —**cytologic, cytological,** *adj.*

karyology   a branch of cytology dealing with the structure of cell nuclei, esp. chromosomes. —**karyologic, karyological,** *adj.*

CHANCE

fortuitism   the doctrine that chance is involved in natural events rather than absolute determinism. —**fortuist,** *n.* Cf. **tychism, uniformitarianism.**

fortuity   a chance event, discovery, or occurrence. —**fortuitousness,** *n.* —**fortuitous,** *adj.*

serendipity   a talent for making fortunate discoveries while searching for other things. —**serendipitous,** *adj.*

CHANGE

metabolism the chemical and physical processes in an organism by which protoplasm is produced, sustained, and then decomposed to make energy available. —**metabolize,** *v.*

misoneism an abnormal dislike of novelty or innovation. Also called **neophobia, cainotophobia, cainophobia.**

CHEESE

fromology a knowledge of cheeses.

laclabphily the collecting of cheese labels.

tyromancy *Obsolete.* a divination involving inspection of cheese; esp. as it coagulates.

tyrosemiophily the collecting of Camembert cheese labels.

CHILD

filicide 1. a parent who kills a son or daughter.
2. the killing of a son or daughter by a parent. —**filicidal,** *adj.*

misopedia an abnormal dislike of children. Also called **misopaedia.** —**misopedist,** *n.*

pedagogics the science or art of teaching or education. Also called **pedagogy.** —**pedagogue,** *n.*

pederasty a sexual act between two males, esp. when one is a minor. —**pederast,** *n.*

pediatrics the branch of medicine that studies the diseases of children and their treatment. —**pediatrician,** *n.*

pedodontics, pedodontia a branch of dentistry specializing in children's dental care. —**pedodontist,** *n.*

pedology the branch of medical science that studies the physical and psychological events of childhood. —**pedologist,** *n.* —**pedological,** *adj.*

pedophilia a sexual attraction to children. —**pedophiliac, pedophilic,** *adj.*

pedophobia an abnormal fear of children. —**pedophobiac,** *n.*

prolicide 1. the crime of killing one's own children.
2. a parent who kills his own children. —**prolicidal,** *adj.*

tecnology pedology.

CHINA

Sinicism 1. a trait or custom peculiar to the Chinese.
2. the use in another language of a Chinese word, idiom, or expression.

Sinology the branch of anthropology that studies Chinese culture. —**Sinologist,** *n.* —**Sinological,** *adj.*

CHRIST

adoptionism   the 8th cent. heretical doctrine that Christ in His human nature was the son of God only by adoption; in His spiritual nature, however, He was truly God's son. Also called **adoptianism.** —**adoptionist,** *n., adj.*

Arianism   a 4th cent. doctrine, considered heretical by orthodox Christianity, that Christ was merely the noblest of men and, being of a different substance, was not the son of God. See **heteroousianism.** —**Arian,** *n., adj.* —**Arianistic, Arianistical,** *adj.*

Athanasianism   the teachings of Athanasius, 4th cent. bishop of Alexandria, asserting that Christ is of the same substance as God, adopted by the Council of Nicea as orthodox doctrine. —**Athanasian,** *n., adj.* See **homoousianism, homoiousianism.**

autotheism   the Calvinist doctrine of the separate existence of God the Son, derived from Calvin's assertion that Christ took His person from God, but not His substance. —**autotheist,** *n.* —**autotheistic,** *adj.*

chiliasm   the doctrine that Christ will return to the world in a visible form and set up a kingdom to last 1000 years, after which the world will come to an end. —**chiliast,** *n.* —**chiliastic,** *adj.*

Christology   the branch of theology that studies the personality, attitudes, and life of Christ. —**Christological,** *adj.*

Christophany   one or all of Christ's appearances to men after the resurrection, as recorded in the Gospels.

Docetism   the teaching of an early heretical sect asserting that Christ's body was not human or material, but celestial in substance. —**Docetic,** *adj.*

Dyophysitism   a 5th cent. doctrine that Christ had a dual nature, the divine and the human, united perfectly in Him, but not inextricably blended. —**Dyophysite,** *n.* —**Dyophysitic,** *adj.* Cf. **Monophysitism.**

Dyothelitism, Dyotheletism   the doctrine that Christ had two wills, the human and the divine. Also called **Dyothetism.** —**Dyothelite, Dyothelete,** *n.* Cf. **Monothelitism.**

Eutychianism   a 5th cent. concept, declared heretical, that the human and divine natures were so blended in Christ as to be one nature; Monophysitism. —**Eutychian,** *n.*

heteroousianism   a position in the 4th cent. controversy over Christ's nature, asserting that He and God were of different natures; Arianism. Also called **heterousianism.** —**heteroousian,** *n., adj.*

homoiousianism   a position in the 4th cent. controversy over Christ's nature, asserting that He and God were of similar, but not the same, natures; semi-Arianism. Also called **homoeanism.** —**homoiousian,** *n., adj.*

homoousianism   a position in the 4th cent. controversy over Christ's nature, asserting that He and God are of the same nature; Athanasianism. —**homoousian,** *n., adj.*

Julianism   the heretical theory of Julian, 6th cent. bishop of Halicarnassus, who took the extreme Monophysite position that Christ's human nature had been subsumed in and altered by the divine. —**Julianist,** *n.*

kenoticism   the theological concept that, through His incarnation, Christ humbled or emptied Himself and became a servant for man's sake. —**kenosis, kenoticist,** *n.* —**kenotic,** *adj.*

millenialism   a doctrine that Christ will make a second Advent and that the prophecy in the book of Revelation will be fulfilled with an earthly millenium of peace and righteousness; millenarianism. —**millenialist,** *n.*

millenarianism   **1.** the doctrine of Christ's 1000-year kingdom. **2.** a belief in the millenium; chiliasm. —**millenarian,** *n., adj.* —**millenarist,** *n.*

Monophysitism   a 5th cent. heresy concerning the nature of Christ, asserting that He had only a divine nature or that the human and divine made one composite nature. —**Monophysite,** *n., adj.* —**Monophysitic, Monophysitical,** *adj.*

Monothelitism, Monotheletism   a heretical position of the 7th cent. that Christ's human will had been superseded by the divine. Also called **Monothelism.** —**Monothelite, Monothelete,** *n.* —**Monothelitic, Monotheletic,** *adj.*

Nestorianism   a 5th cent. heresy concerning Christ's nature, asserting that the human and divine were in harmony but separate and that Mary should be considered the Mother of Christ, not of God. —**Nestorian,** *n., adj.*

Patripassianism   a heretical, monophysitic concept of the 2nd and 3rd cent. which held that, in the Crucifixion, the Father suffered equally with the Son. —**Patripassian, Patripassianist,** *n.*

Paulianism   a 3rd cent. heresy concerning the nature of Christ, denying the divine by asserting that Christ was inspired by God and was not a person in the Trinity. —**Paulian, Paulianist,** *n.*

psilanthropism   the doctrine that Christ was merely a human being. —**psilanthropist,** *n.* —**psilanthropic,** *adj.* Cf. **Arianism.**

soteriology   *Theology.* the doctrine of salvation through Jesus Christ. —**soteriologic, soteriological,** *adj.*

theanthropism   the condition of being, simultaneously, both god and man. Also called **theanthropology.** —**theanthropist,** *n.* —**theanthropic,** *adj.*

trinitarianism   the orthodox Christian belief that God exists as the Trinity of the Father, the Son, and the Holy Spirit. —**trinitarian,** *n., adj.*

unitarianism the doctrines of those, including the Unitarian denomination, who hold that God exists only in one person. —**unitarian,** *n., adj.* Cf. **trinitarianism.**
See also HERESY and THEOLOGY.

CHRISTIANITY

anathematism 1. *Obsolete.* the pronouncing of a curse or ban with religious solemnity by ecclesiastical authority; anathematization.
2. a curse or malediction. —**anathema,** *n.*

catechism 1. a manual of instruction in the principles of the Christian religion, usu. in question and answer form.
2. catechetical instruction. —**catechist,** *n.*

Catholicism the doctrines, system, and practice of the Catholic Church, esp. the Roman Catholic Church. —**Catholic,** *n., adj.*

didachist 1. a writer of the anonymous 2nd cent. Christian manual of morals and church practices called the *Didache.*
2. an expert on or student of the *Didache.*

Eastern Orthodoxy the doctrines, systems, and practices of local and national independent churches (including the Greek and Russian Orthodox Churches) in communion with the ecumenical patriarch of Constantinople and adhering to the Nicene Creed and to a common rite celebrated in various languages; **Byzantinism.** —**Eastern Orthodox,** *n., adj.*

election the theological doctrine of God's predestination of individuals as objects of divine mercy and salvation.

Eucratism the practices of a 2nd cent. sect which abstained from marriage, wine, and flesh meat. —**Eucratite,** *n.*

evangelism, evangelicalism the missionary, reforming, or redeeming spirit evident throughout the history of Christianity in various guises or emphases, —**evangelical, evangelistic,** *adj.*

flagellantism 1. the practice of ascetic individuals or groups who practice scourging for the sake of discipline or punishment.
2. (*cap.*) the practice of a 13th and 14th cent. fanatical European sect which practiced scourging to avoid the punishment of God. —**flagellant,** *n., adj.*

infralapsarianism the theological doctrine that man's fall was foreseen and permitted by God, who then decreed election as a method for the salvation of some of mankind. —**infralapsarian,** *n., adj.* Cf. **supralapsarianism.**

kerygma, kerugma 1. the original, oral gospel preached by the apostles.
2. the preaching of the Christian gospel, esp. the activity of the earliest Christian missionaries. —**kerygmatic,** *adj.*

Marcionism the beliefs of an anti-Semitic Gnostic sect in the early Christian church. —**Marcionite,** *n., adj.*

monasticism   1. the rule or system of life in a monastery.
   2. the life or condition of a monk. —**monastic,** *n., adj.* —**monastical,** *adj.*

Paraclete   the Holy Spirit, considered as comforter, intercessor, or advocate.

pneumatology   *Theology.* **1.** the doctrines concerning the Holy Spirit.
   2. the belief in spiritual beings, as angels, between men and God.
   —**pneumatologist,** *n.* —**pneumatologic, pneumatological,** *adj.*

preterism   the belief that the prophecies of the book of Revelation have
   already come to pass. —**preterist,** *n., adj.*

Protestantism   the doctrines and practices of those Western Christian
   churches not in communion with the Roman or Eastern churches.
   —**Protestant,** *n., adj.*

psychopannychism   *Theology.* the doctrine that death causes the soul to
   sleep until the day of resurrection. —**psychopannychist,** *n.* —**psychopannychian, psychopannychistic,** *adj.*

sabbatarianism   1. the practice in Judaism and some Christian groups of
   keeping the seventh day holy.
   2. the practice of keeping Sunday holy and free of work and pleasureful
   activity. —**sabbatarian,** *n., adj.*

sacramentalism   1. the theological doctrines concerning the sacraments.
   2. the doctrines asserting that the sacraments are necessary to salvation as
   a conveyor of grace to a human soul.
   3. an adherent to these doctrines. —**sacramentalist,** *n.*

subordinationism   the theological tenet of progressive declining essence
   within the Trinity. —**subordinationist,** *n.*

supralapsarianism   the theological doctrine asserting that God's plan for the
   salvation of man decreed election before the fall of man and permitted
   the fall as an instrumentality for fulfilling the divine purposes.
   —**supralapsarian,** *n., adj.* Cf. **infralapsarianism.**

tritheism   1. the heretical belief that the Trinity consists of three distinct
   gods.
   2. any polytheistic religion having three gods. —**tritheist,** *n.* —**tritheistic,
   tritheistical,** *adj.*
   See also CATHOLICISM, EASTERN ORTHODOXY, *and* PROTESTANTISM.

CHURCH

ecclesiarch   *East.Ch.* a sacristan.

ecclesioclasticism   *Rare.* an opposition to the church.

ecclesiolatry   an intense devotion to church forms, authority, and traditions.

ecclesiology   1. the science of church building and decoration.
   2. *Theology.* the doctrine of the church.
   3. the policy and operations of the church. —**ecclesiologist,** *n.*
   —**ecclesiologic, ecclesiological,** *adj.*

ecclesiophobia an excessive dislike of the church, its forms, or its doctrines.

Ecumenism, Oecumenism a movement within Christianity toward the recovery of unity among all Christians. —**Ecumenicist,** *n.*

sacrist 1. a sacristan.
2. an official or cleric appointed curator of the vestments, sacred vessels, and relics of a religious body, church, or cathedral.

CITIES

conurbation a composite of urban communities, usu. clustered around the largest.

urbiculture the study of and concern with the special practices and problems of city life.

CLASSIFICATION

systematics the study of classification and methods of classification. —**systematician, systematist,** *n.*

taxonomy, taxology 1. the technique or science of classification.
2. the scientific identification, naming, and classification of living things. —**taxonomist,** *n.* —**taxonomic, taxonomical,** *adj.* Also called **systematy.**

CLEANLINESS

ablutomania an abnormal desire to wash, esp. the hands.

automysophobia an abnormal fear of being dirty.

bromidrosiphobia an abnormal fear of having an unpleasant body odor.

CLIMATE

cryptoclimate the climate of the inside of a building, airliner, or space ship, as differentiated from that on the outside.

meteorology the science that studies climate and weather variations.

phenology the branch of biology that studies the relation between variations in climate and periodic biological phenomena, as the migration of birds or the flowering of plants. —**phenologist,** *n.* —**phenologic, phenological,** *adj.*

CLOUDS

ceilometer an automatic instrument for measuring and recording the distance between the earth and the cloud ceiling by triangulation.

nephology the branch of meteorology that studies clouds. —**nephologist,** *n.*

COCKS

alectoromachy a contest between two cocks; cockfighting. Also called **alectryomachy.**

alectoromancy, alectryomancy a form of divination by recording the corn-covered letters revealed as a cock eats the corn.

CODE

cryptanalysis 1. the procedures and methods used to translate or interpret codes and ciphers.
2. the science or study of such procedures. —**cryptanalyst**, *n.* —**cryptanalytic**, *adj.*

cryptogram a message or writing in code or cipher. Also called **cryptograph**. —**cryptogrammic**, *adj.*

cryptography 1. the science or study of secret writing, esp. codes and ciphers. Also called **cryptology**.
2. the procedures and methods of making and using codes and ciphers. —**cryptographer, cryptographist**, *n.* —**cryptographic**, *adj.*

COLD

cryogenics the branch of physics that studies the production and effects of very low temperatures. —**cryogenic**, *adj.*

cryology 1. the study of snow and ice.
2. the science of refrigeration.

cryophilia *Biology.* a preference for low temperatures. —**cryophile**, *n.* —**cryophilic**, *adj.*

psychrophobia a dread of the cold.

COLLECTIONS AND COLLECTING

addenda the appendixes or supplements gathered to appear at the end of a book.

aerophilately the collecting of airmail stamps.

arctophilist a collector of teddy bears.

argyrothecology the collecting of money boxes, as those found in churches or on dispensing machines.

brandophily the collecting of cigar bands. Also called **cigrinophily.**

cagophily the collecting of keys.

cartophily the collecting of cigarette or chewing gum cards depicting famous people, baseball players, etc.

chrestomathy 1. a collection of literary selections, esp. in a foreign language, as an aid to learning.
2. a collection of literary selections from one author. —**chrestomathic**, *adj.*

compendium a catalog or inventory of brief items on a subject.

compilation a gathering together of written material from a variety of sources.

conchology 1. the collecting of shells.
2. the branch of zoology that studies shells. —**conchologize**, *v.* —**conchologist**, *n.*

copoclephily the collecting of key rings containing advertising. —**copocle-phile,** *n.*

corrigendum a collection, catalog, or list of errors found in a book after its printing and placed, with corrections, on a separate page at the front of the book. Also called **corrigenda.**

credenda *Eccl.,Obsolete.* a collection of writings held by church authorities as to be believed. Cf. **legenda.**

cumyxaphily the collecting of matchboxes.

curiosa a collection of oddities and rarities, especially books.

deltiology the collecting of picture postcards.

discophily the collecting of phonograph records.

doxography the collection and compiling of extracts from ancient Greek philosophers, to which editorial comments are added. —**doxographer,** *n.* —**doxographic,** *adj.*

errinophily the collecting of stamps other than postage stamps, as revenue or tax stamps.

esoterica a collection of items of special, rare or unusual interest, often pornographic.

florilegium **1.** an anthology or collection of brief extracts or writings.
2. an anthology of good writing from the best writers for imitation.

Hebraica a collection of Hebrew materials, usu. literary or historical.

herbalism **1.** the science or art of collecting and dispensing herbs, chiefly medicinal.
2. *Obsolete.* botany.

homologumena, homologoumena the collection of books from the New Testament recognized from the earlier period of the Christian church as authoritative and canonical.

hostelaphily *Brit.* the collecting of outdoor signs from inns.

Judaica a collection of literary or historical materials relating to Judaism or the Jews.

legenda *Eccl., Obsolete.* a collection of materials that may be or are to read, usu. for spiritual or moral edification.

legendary **1.** a compilation of legends.
2. a collection of the lives of the saints.

memorabilia a formal collection of written accounts about matters or events worthy to be remembered.

memoranda an informal collection of data to be remembered or preserved.

militaria a collection of objects or materials illustrating military history.

museology the science of collecting and arranging objects for museums. —**museologist,** *n.*

notaphily   the collecting of bank notes.

numismatics   the collecting of coins or medals. Also called **numismatology.** —**numismatist,** *n.*

philately   the collecting of postage stamps. —**philatelist,** *n.*

phillumeny   the collecting of match box labels and matchbook covers.

philometry   a speciality within philately involving the collecting of first-day covers.

phonophily   the collecting of phonograph records. —**phonophile,** *n.* See also PHONOGRAPH RECORDS.

timbrology   *Archaic.* philately.

vecturist   a collector of tokens used in buses and subways.

COLOR

achromaticity   **1.** the total absence of color.
2. the ability to emit, reflect, or transmit light without breaking down into separate colors. Also called **achromatism.**

acritochromacy   *Med.* an inability to perceive colors effectively; colorblindness.

acyanoblepsia   *Med.* a variety of colorblindness characterized by an inability to distinguish blue.

chromatics   the branch of optics that studies the properties of colors.

chromophobia   an abnormal fear of colors.

Daltonism   *Med.* a red-green colorblindness.

erythrophobia   **1.** an abnormal fear of the color red.
2. an abnormal fear of blushing.
3. *Med.* a neurotic tendency marked by blushing at the slightest stimulus.

pallidity   a faintness or deficiency in color. —**pallid,** *adj.*

COMMUNALISM

Fourierism   a utopian social reform, planned by the French social scientist F. M. Charles Fourier, that organized groups into cooperative phalansters, as Brook Farm. Also called **phalansterianism.** —**Fourierist, Fourierite,** *n.*

Hutterites   in the U.S. and Canada, descendants of Swiss Protestants exiled from their homeland in 1528 for communal living, pacifism, and Anabaptist views, still persecuted for their economic self-sufficiency and their refusal to allow their communities to be assimilated. Also called **Hutterian Brethren.**

kibbutz   a communal farm in Israel, cooperatively owned, with members who receive no pay but who gain housing, clothing, medical care, and education from the cooperative. Also called **kvutzah.** —**kibbutzim,** *n. pl.*

Oneida Perfectionists   a native American communal society active in the middle 19th cent. in Putney, Vt., and Oneida, N.Y., practicing a pooling of all property and communal marriage for eugenic reasons.

Owenism   the social and political theories of Robert Owen, an early 19th cent. British reformer whose emphasis upon cooperative education and living led to the founding of communal experiments, including the illfated community of New Harmony. Ind., purchased from the Rappites. —**Owenite,** *n.*

Rappite   a follower of George Rapp, an early 19th cent. German Pietistic preacher, whose experiments in a religion-based cooperative system involved the founding of Economy, Pa. and Harmonie, Ind. Also called **Harmonite.**

COMMUNISM

Backuninism   a 19th cent. theory of revolution in opposition to Karl Marx's, advocating atheism, destruction of central government, and extreme individualism. Also called **autonomism.**

Bolshevism   a radical wing of the Russian Social Democratic Labor party, favoring revolutionary tactics to achieve full socialization, and under the leadership of Ulyanov (Lenin), setting up from 1917-20 the present Soviet regime. —**Bolshevik, Bolshevist,** *n., adj.*

communism   1. a political and economic theory proposing the replacement of private ownership of goods or capital with common ownership and distribution upon need.
2. (*cap.*) the social and political system based upon revolutionary Marxist socialism and currently practiced in the U.S.S.R. —**communist,** *n., adj.* —**communistic,** *adj.*

cosmopolitanism   the tolerance of or sympathy for noncommunist ideas and institutions, used as a charge against Soviet intellectuals.

deviationism   a position or rationale which departs from the established dogma of a political party, esp. the Communist party. Also called **deviationalism.** —**deviationist,** *n., adj.*

Leninism   the political doctrines of Vladimir Ilich Ulyanov (pen name: Lenin), founder of Bolshevism, architect of the current Soviet government, originator of the Comintern, and author of the imperative that the Soviets lead the proletariat of other nations to revolution and communism. —**Leninist, Leninite,** *n., adj.*

Marxism   1. the doctrines developed from the political, economic, and social theories of Karl Marx, Friedrich Engels, and their followers: dialectical materialism, a labor-based theory of wealth, an economic class struggle leading to revolution, the dictatorship of the proletariat, and the eventual development of a classless society.
2. the contributions to these doctrines in the interpretations of Lenin; Leninism. —**Marxist,** *n., adj.* —**Marxian,** *adj.*

Menshevism the minority wing of the Russian Social Democratic Labor party that in a 1903 convention split from the majority or Bolshevik wing, enabling the latter to direct and win power in the revolution of 1917-20. —**Menshevik,** *n., adj.*

revisionism 1. *Marxism.* any deviation from Marxist theory, doctrines, or practice, esp. to modify revolution to evolution.
2. a movement to reexamine historical information in the light of current knowledge. —**revisionist,** *n., adj.*

Stakhanovism a system of piece-work incentives, speedup, and competition for bonuses and honors introduced into Russia and named after A.G. Stakhanov, whose prodigious mining output is constantly emulated. —**Stakhanovite,** *n., adj.*

Stalinism the communistic theories and practices developed by Joseph Stalin from Marxism and Leninism, esp. his development of the cult of the individual with himself as its center, his advocacy of national revolution, and his extensive use of secret police and slave-labor camps to reduce personal opposition to his power. —**Stalinist,** *n., adj.* —**Stalinistic,** *adj.*

syndicalism a theory of revolutionary politics that, through the actions of labor unions, seeks to establish a society controlled by workers' cooperatives and trade unions. —**syndicalist,** *n., adj.* —**syndicalistic,** *adj.*

Titoism 1. the social, political, and economic theories of Tito (Josip Broz), premier of Yugoslavia.
2. the nationalistic practices of a communist country which deviate from or oppose the directives of the U.S.S.R. —**Titoist,** *n., adj.*

Trotskyism the theories of Leon Trotsky (born Braunstein) on the social, political, and economic implications of communism, esp. his opposition to Stalin in advocating international revolution. —**Trotskyite,** *n., adj.*

CONVERT

neophytism 1. the condition of a new convert to a religious belief.
2. the condition of a newly baptized convert to the early Christian church. —**neophyte,** *n.* —**neophytic,** *adj.*

proselytism 1. the act of becoming or the condition of being a convert to an opinion, political party, or religious group.
2. an active policy of inviting or persuading converts, esp. to a religious position. —**proselyte,** *n.* —**proselyter, proselytist,** *n.* —**proselytistic,** *adj.*

COPYING

hectography, hektography a reproductive process involving a prepared gelatin surface to which the original writing has been transferred. —**hectographic,** *adj.*

pantograph a device for making copies of plans or drawings on a predetermined scale. —**pantographic,** *adj.*

reprography a collective term introduced by UNESCO, for all processes of producing facsimiles of documents.

xerography a process for copying material by charging electrostatic paper in areas corresponding to the printed areas of the original so that powdered resin carrying a negative charge adheres to them. —**xerographic,** *adj.*

CORPSE

autopsy an inspection and dissection of a body after death, usu. to determine the cause of death. Also called **post-mortem examination.**

necrophagy the practice of feeding on carrion. —**necrophagous,** *adj.*

necrophilia, necrophily, necrophilism an abnormal attraction, esp. erotic, for corpses.

necrophobia 1. an abnormal fear of death.
2. an abnormal fear of corpses. Also called **thanatophobia.**

necropsy the examination of a body after death; autopsy.

necrotomy 1. the dissection of corpses.
2. the surgical excision of a piece of dead bone. —**necrotomist,** *n.* —**necrotomic,** *adj.*

resurrectionism the exhuming and stealing of bodies from graves, esp. for dissection; body snatcher. —**resurrection man,** *n.*

COSMOLOGY

cosmism a 19th cent. theory about cosmic evolution developed from contemporary science that regards the cosmos as self-existent and self-acting. —**cosmist,** *n.*

cosmogony 1. a theory about the origin and the evolution of the universe.
2. the branch of astrophysics that studies the origin and evolution of specific astronomical systems and the universe as a whole.
3. cosmology. —**cosmogonist,** *n.* —**cosmogonic,** *adj.*

cosmography 1. the branch of astronomy that maps and describes the main features of the universe.
2. a description or representation of the main features of the universe. —**cosmographer,** *n.* —**cosmographic, cosmographical,** *adj.*

cosmology 1. the branch of astronomy that studies the overall structure of the physical universe.
2. the branch of philosophy that studies the origin, structure, and evolution of the universe, esp. such characteristics as space, time, causality, and freedom. —**cosmologic, cosmological,** *adj.* —**cosmologist,** *n.*

cosmotheism the concept that the universe and God are identical; pantheism. —**cosmotheist,** *n.*

cosmozoism   the concept of the cosmos as alive.

creationism   the belief concerning the creation of the universe, matter, and living organisms out of nothing by a transcendant God. —**creationist,** *n.*

geocentricism   1. the concept that the earth is the center of the universe. 2. *Astronomy.* the measurements or observations that are relative to the center of the earth. Also called **geocentrism.** —**geocentric,** *adj.*

heliocentricism   1. the concept that the sun is the center of the universe. 2. *Astronomy.* the measurements or observations that are relative to the center of the sun. Also called **heliocentrism, heliocentricity.** —**heliocentric,** *adj.*

pancosmism   the theory that the totality of existence comprises only the physical universe in time and space. —**pancosmic,** *adj.*

Pansatanism   a Gnostic theory that considered Satan's to be the controlling will of the universe.

teleologism   the belief that purpose and design control the development of the universe and are apparent through natural phenomena. —**teleologist,** *n.* —**teleology,** *n.*

universology   the science of the universe.

COWARDICE

poltroonery   a spiritless cowardice and faintheartedness. —**poltroon,** *n.*

pusillanimity   a cowardly, irresolute, or fainthearted condition. —**pusillanimous,** *adj.*

CRIME

criminology   the scientific study of crime and criminals. —**criminologist,** *n.* —**criminologic, criminological,** *adj.*

mayhem   *Law.* an intentional crippling, disfigurement, or mutilation of another.

penology   1. the science of the punishment of crime. 2. the science of the management of prisons. —**penologist,** *n.*

recidivism   a repeated relapsing into criminal or delinquent behavior. —**recidivist,** *n.* —**recidivistic, recidivous,** *adj.*

CRITICISM

chorizontist   *Rare.* a critic of Homeric literature who claims the *Iliad* and the *Odyssey* had different authors.

formalism   a critical emphasis upon style, arrangement, and artistic means with limited attention to content. —**formalist,** *n.* —**formalistic,** *adj.*

New Criticism   a critical approach to literature that concentrates upon analysis and explication of individual texts and considers historical and biographical information less important than an awareness of the work's formal architecture. —**New Critic,** *n.*

Zoilism the practice of making bitter, carping, and belittling critical judgements. —**Zoilus, Zoili,** n.

CROWDS

demophil, demophile a person fond of crowds. —**demophilia,** n.

demophobia an intense dislike of crowds.

ochlophobia an abnormal fear of crowds.

D

DAMPNESS

hygrophobia an abnormal fear of water, moisture, or dampness.

psychrometry the measurement of the humidity content of the air by use of a psychrometer. —**psychrometric, psychrometrical,** adj.

DANCING

choreography 1. the art of composing dances for the stage, esp. in conceiving and realizing the movements of the dancers.
2. the technique of representing dance movements through a notational scheme.
3. the art of dancing. Also called **choregraphy, orchesography.** —**choreographer,** n. —**choreographic,** adj.

orchesis the art or skill of dancing, esp. in, or in the style of, the Greek chorus. Also called **orchestics.**

DANTE

Dantesque from or resembling the characters, scenes, or events in Dante's works.

Dantophily the love of Dante or his writings.

DARKNESS

nyctophobia an abnormal fear of darkness or night.

scotophobia an abnormal fear of the dark.

DEAFNESS

Ameslan an acronym for the American Sign Language for the Deaf, a modified manual system.

dactylology the technique of communicating through signs made with the fingers, as in the manual alphabet for the deaf. Also called **dactyliology.**

manualism the teaching of communication through the hands to the deaf. —**manualist,** n.

oralism   1. the principles of the oral method of training the deaf, as lip reading.
2. the support or practice of these principles. —**oralist,** *n.* Cf. **manualism.**

phonautography   a procedure for producing visible records of sound waves or speech sounds, esp. to assist the deaf in using the telephone. Also called **visible speech.** —**phonautographic,** *adj.*

DEATH

ktenology   the science of putting people to death.

necrolatry   the worship of the dead.

necrologist   a writer of obituaries.

necrology   1. an announcement of death; obituary.
2. a list of persons who have died within a certain time. Also called **necrologue.** —**necrologist,** *n.*

necromancy   1. the magic practiced by a witch or sorcerer.
2. a form of divination through communication with the dead; the black art. —**necromancer, necromant,** *n.* —**necromantic,** *adj.*

sindology   the study of shrouds.

taphophilia   an excessive interest in graves and cemeteries.

thanatoid   resembling death; deathly.

thanatology   the study of death or the dead. Also called **thanatism.** —**thanatological,** *adj.*
See also KILLING *and* MURDER.

DECADENCE

cataclasm   a breaking down; disruption. —**cataclasmic,** *n.*

deteriorism   the belief that the universe is gradually breaking down. Cf. **meliorism.**

geratology   the branch of biology that studies aging and its phenomena. Also called **gereology.** —**geratologic, geratologous,** *adj.*

sphacelation   a gangrenous condition.

DEFENSE

apologetics   *Theology.* the study of the methods and content of defenses or proofs of Christianity. —**apologetical,** *adj.*

apologist   a person who defends, in speech or writing, a faith, doctrine, idea, or action.

trierarchy   an ancient Athenian policy allowing private citizens, as part of their civic duty, to fit out triremes for the defense of the city.

DEMONS

ademonist   one who denies the existence of the devil or demons.

cacodemonia a mania that causes a person to believe himself possessed and controlled by an evil spirit. Also called **cacodemonomania.** —**cacodemonic, cacodemoniac,** *adj.*

demonianism 1. a belief in the possibility of possession by a demon. 2. demoniac possession. Also called **demoniacism.** —**demonian,** *adj.* —**demoniac,** *n., adj.*

demonolatry the worship, through propitiation, of ghosts, demons, and spirits.

demonology 1. the study of demons or superstitions about demons. 2. the doctrine of demons. —**demonologist,** *n.* —**demonologic, demonological,** *adj.*

demonomancy a form of divination involving a demon or demons.

demonophobia an abnormal fear of spirits and demons.

exorcism 1. the ceremony which seeks to expel an evil spirit from a person or place. 2. the act or process of exorcising. —**exorcist,** *n.* —**exorcismal, exorcisory, exorcistic, exorcistical,** *adj.*

incubus a demon alleged to lie upon people in their sleep and esp. to tempt women to sexual relations.

nympholepsy 1. an ecstatic variety of demonic possession believed by the ancients to be inspired by nymphs. 2. a frenzy of emotion, as for something unattainable. —**nympholeptic,** *adj.*

pandemonism *Rare.* the worship of spirits dwelling in all forms of nature.

polydemonism, polydaemonism a devotion to a multitude of demonic powers or spirits. —**polydemonistic,** *adj.*

succubus a demon which assumes a female form to tempt men to intercourse. —**succubi, succubae,** *pl.*

DEPTH

bathometer, bathymeter *Oceanography.* a device for ascertaining the depth of water.

bathyalic, bathyal of or concerning the deeper parts of the ocean, esp. those parts between 100 and 1000 fathoms.

bathyclinograph a device for ascertaining vertical currents in the deeper parts of the sea.

bathymetry the measurement of the depths of oceans, seas, or other large bodies of water. —**bathymetric, bathymetrical,** *adj.*

bathyscaphe, bathyscape, bathyscaph *Oceanography.* a small modified submarine for deep-sea exploration, usu. with a spherical observation chamber under the hull.

bathysphere *Oceanography.* a spherical diving apparatus from which to study deep-sea life.

bathythermograph   a device that records the temperature of water as a reflex of depth.

DESERTS

eremite   a religious hermit living alone, often in the desert. —**eremitic**, *adj.*

eremology   the systematic study of desert features and phenomena.

DEVIL

adiabolist   one who denies the existence of the devil.

diabolism   1. belief in or worship of the devil.
2. *Theology.* an action aided or prompted by the devil; sorcery; witchcraft. —**diabolist**, *n.*

diabology   1. the study of the devil.
2. devil lore. Also called **diabolology**.

PanSatanism   a Gnostic doctrine that the material world expresses the personality of Satan.

Satanism   1. the worship of Satan or evil powers.
2. a parody of Christian ceremonies in which the devil is worshipped.
3. diabolical behavior. —**Satanist**, *n.*

DINING

aristology   *Rare.* the art or science of dining. —**aristologist**, *n.*

deipnosophist   a person adept in table conversation.

DIRT

aischrolatreia   a devotion to or worship of filth and obscenity.

automysophobia   *Rare.* an abnormal fear of being dirty.

maculation   1. the act of staining or spotting.
2. the condition of being spotted or stained.
3. a disfiguring spot or stain. —**maculate**, *adj.*

mysophilia   an abnormal attraction to filth.

misophobia, musophobia, mysophobia   an abnormal fear of dirt, esp. of being contaminated by dirt.

DISEASE AND ILLNESS

albinism   the total or partial absence of pigment in skin, hair, and eyes. —**albinic, albinistic, albinal**, *adj.*

argyrism, argyria   a poisoning by silver or salts of silver, causing the skin to become ashy gray.

arthritism   1. a predisposition to gout.
2. a predisposition to joint diseases. —**arthritic, arthritical**, *adj.*

arthropathology   *Med. Sci.* the study of functional and structural changes made by diseases of the joints.

bromism a poisoning produced by excessive use of bromine or bromine compounds. Also called **brominism, bromidism.**

cacesthesia *Med.* a morbid sensation or disordered sensibility.

cacoethes a chronic and overwhelming desire; mania. —**cacoethic,** *adj.*

calciphilia a tendency to calcification.

catalepsy *Pathology, Psychiatry.* a physical condition characterized by a loss of sensation, muscular rigidity, fixity of posture, and often by a loss of contact with surroundings. Also called **catalepsis.** —**cataleptic,** *adj.*

choromania the dancing sickness (epidemic chorea).

cypridophobia an abnormal fear of veneral disease. Also called **venereophobia.**

delitescence *Med.* the sudden disappearance of symptoms or of objective signs of a lesion or disease. —**delitescent,** *adj.*

dyspepsia an impairment of the ability to digest food, usu. a discomfort after meals. —**dyspeptic,** *n., adj.* —**dyspeptical,** *adj.*

eclamptism a toxemia sometimes occurring in late pregnancy marked by visual impairment, headache, and, occasionally, convulsions. Also called **eclampsia.**

emesis an act of vomiting. —**emetic,** *adj.*

erethism 1. an excessive irritability or sensibility to stimulation in any part of the body, esp. the sexual organs.
2. a psychic disturbance characterized by irritability, emotional instability, depression, shyness, and fatigue, often caused by toxicity. —**erethistic, erethitic,** *adj.*

erythrism a redness of beard and hair and a ruddiness of complexion. —**erythristic, erythrismal,** *adj.*

etiology, aetiology 1. the branch of medical science that studies the causes of diseases and the factors underlying their spread.
2. the accumulated knowledge of disease causes. —**etiologist,** *n.* —**etiologic, etiological,** *adj.*

fabism, favism an acute anemia caused by the consumption of fava beans or the ingestion of fava pollen.

glycophilia a condition in which a small amount of glucose produces hyperglycemia.

hemophilia, haemophilia an hereditary tendency, in males, toward a deficiency in coagulation factors in the blood. —**hemophiliac,** *n., adj.*

hyperesthesia, hyperaesthesia 1. an excessive sensitivity of skin in a particular area.
2. an excessive sensitivity of a particular sense, esp. smell.
3. a heightened sensitivity to the environment. —**hyperesthetic,** *adj.*

invalidism a condition of prolonged ill health.

lionism *Rare.* a lion-like appearance of the face caused by leprosy; leontiasis.

lithiasis a condition causing concretions of mineral salts or pebbles (*calculi*) in the pancreas, tear ducts, appendix, or kidneys.

luetism the veneral disease syphilis in any of three stages. —**luetic,** *adj.*

meteorism *Med.* a tendency to uncontrollable flatulence. Also called **typmanites.**

molysomophobia an abnormal fear of infection.

myxomatosis an infectious, highly fatal, virus disease of rabbits, transmitted by mosquitoes.

narcolepsy a condition characterized by an uncontrollable desire for sleep or sudden onsets of sleep. —**narcoleptic,** *adj.*

nosology the branch of medical science that classifies diseases. Also called **nosonomy.** —**nosologist,** *n.* —**nosologic, nosological,** *adj.*

nosophilia an excessive, abnormal desire to be sick. Also called **pathophilia.**

nosophobia an abnormal fear of contracting disease.

pathology **1.** the branch of medical science that studies the origin, nature, and course of diseases. **2.** the conditions and processes of a disease. —**pathologist,** *n.* —**pathologic, pathological,** *adj.*

pathophobia an abnormal fear of disease.

phorology the branch of medical science that studies disease carriers and epidemic or endemic diseases. —**phorologist,** *n.*

phthisiology *Med.* the body of knowledge accumulated about tuberculosis.

poriomania an unconscious tendency to walk away from home; an ambulatory automatism.

psychogenicity a medical theory that the cause of some illnesses is psychological and emotional and not organic. —**psychogenic,** *adj.*

psychopathy a disorder of the mind. —**psychopathic,** *adj.*

pyretology a branch of medical science that studies fevers and their treatment.

rheumatism any disorder of the connective tissue structures of the body, esp. those in the back or the extremities, characterized by pain or stiffness. —**rheumatic,** *adj.*

rheumatology the branch of medical science that studies rheumatism. —**rheumatologist,** *n.*

sialism, sialismus an excessive salivation, often a sign of poisoning.

somatogenic originating in the body or the cells of the body, as a disease. Also called **physiogenic.**

spasmophilia   an extreme tendency to convulsions. —**spasmophile,** *n.*

symptomatology   1. the branch of medical science that studies the symptoms of diseases.
2. the combined symptoms of a particular disease. Also called **semeiology.** —**symptomatologic, symptomatological,** *adj.*

tarantism   a variety of dancing mania, popularly thought to be caused by the bite of a tarantula and to be cured by dancing.

thrombophilia   a tendency to the occurrence of thrombosis.

thyroidism   a condition caused by overactivity of the thyroid gland or excessive doses of thyroid.

tomophobia   an abnormal fear of surgical operations.

traumatophilia   a condition in which a patient takes a subconscious delight in injuries or surgical operations.

valetudinarianism   the condition of being overly concerned with one's health. —**valetudinarian,** *n., adj.*

zoonosis   any disease of lower animals that may be transmitted to man. —**zoonotic,** *adj.*

See also MEDICAL SPECIALITIES *and* REMEDIES.

DISTANCE

odograph   a device that records the distance traveled; a recording odometer or pedograph.

odometer   a device for measuring the distance passed over, as an automobile. Also called **hodometer.**

pedometer   a device that measures the distance walked by counting the number of steps taken.

DOGS

cynanthropy   *Psychiatry.* a delusion in which a person believes himself to be a dog.

cynology   the branch of zoology that studies the dog, esp. its natural history.

cynologist   a specialist in the care and breeding of dogs.

cynophobia   an intense dread of dogs.

DOLLS

pedophobia, paedophobia   an abnormal fear of dolls.

planganologist   a collector of dolls.

DRAWING

chalcography   1. *Archaic.* the art of engraving on copper plates, esp. for printing.
2. the art of drawing with chalks or pastels.

chiaroscuro, chiarooscuro   a technique of painting or drawing using light and shade to achieve a three-dimensional quality. —**chiaroscurist**, *n.*

ichnography   **1.** the rendering of a horizontal section of an object in scale.
2. the rendering of a floor plan of a building in a specific scale; an orthographic projection. —**ichnographic, ichnographical**, *adj.*

isometric projection   the rendering of an object or floor plan in scale as viewed from a stated angle. Cf. **orthographic projection.**

orthographic projection   a rendering of an object or floor plan of a building in scale as viewed perpendicularly from above. Cf. **isometric projection.**

scenography   the rendering of an object on a perspective plane. —**scenographer**, *n.* —**scenographic, scenographical**, *adj.*

skiagraphy   **1.** the technique of filling in the outline of the shadow made by an object to create a pictorial work or shadowgraph.
2. the creation of skiagrams on film with X-rays. —**skiagram**, *n.* —**skiagrapher**, *n.*

stereography   the art of representing the forms of solid bodies on a plane surface. —**stereographer**, *n.* —**stereographic, stereographical**, *adj.*

DREAMS

autism   **1.** a tendency to daydream.
2. *Psychiatry.* an extreme withdrawal into fantasy in thought or behavior, not correctible by external information. —**autistic**, *adj.*

oneirocriticism   the interpretation of dreams. —**oneirocritic**, *n.* —**oneirocritical**, *adj.*

oneirodynia   *Med.* a disturbed sleep, involving nightmare and sometimes sleepwalking.

oneirology   the science and interpretation of dreams. Also called **oneiroscopy.**

oneiromancy   a form of divination involving dreams. —**oneiromancer**, *n.*

DRUGS

cannabism   **1.** addiction to marijuana.
2. a toxic condition caused by excessive use of marijuana.

cinchonology   a branch of pharmacology that studies cinchona and its derivatives, as quinine and quinidine.

cubebism   a toxic condition caused by smoking cubeb or Java pepper, formerly dried and crushed for medicinal purposes.

meconism   an addiction to opium; opium eating. Also called **meconophagism.**

narcomania   an abnormal desire for drugs.

narcosis, narcoma   a condition of stupor or unconsciousness induced by drugs and usu. treatable by medication.

narcoticism 1. the narcosis or narcoma induced by drugs.
2. an addiction to drugs. Also called **narcotism.**

morphiomania an addiction to and intense craving for morphine. Also called **morphinmania.**

opiomania an addiction to opium.

pharmacognosia, pharmacognosis, pharmacognosy the branch of pharmacology that studies the composition, use, and history of drugs. —**pharmacognosist,** *n.* —**pharmacognostic,** *adj.*

pharmacology, pharmacologia the branch of medical science that studies the preparation, uses, and effects of drugs. —**pharmacologist,** *n.* —**pharmacologic, pharmacological,** *adj.*

pharmacopedics, pharmacopedia the branch of medical science that studies drugs and medicinal preparations. —**parmacopedic,** *adj.*

pharmacophobia an abnormal fear of drugs.

pharmacy 1. a drug therapy.
2. the art of preparing drugs and medicines, esp. the discovery of new varieties.
3. the place where drugs are prepared, dispensed, or sold. —**pharmacist,** *n.*

synergism, synergy the joint action of agents, as drugs, that, taken together, produce a greater effect than the sum of their individual effects. —**synergistic,** *adj.*

toxicomania an addiction to drugs, esp. opium or cocaine.

E

EAR

audiology 1. the branch of medical science that studies hearing, esp. impaired hearing.
2. the treatment of persons with impaired hearing. —**audiologist,** *n.*

otalgia an earache.

otiatrics, otiatry *Med.* the therapeutics of ear diseases. —**otiatric,** *adj.*

oticodinia a vertigo resulting from ear disease. Also called **oticodinosis.**

otitis *Med.* any variety of inflammation in the ear. —**otitic,** *adj.*

otology 1. the branch of medicine that studies the ear and its diseases.
2. the treatment of ear disorders. —**otologist,** *n.* —**otologic, otological,** *adj.*

otoscopy a visual inspection of the ear drum and the auditory canal. —**otoscopic,** *adj.*

EARTH

diastrophism   the procession of disturbances in the earth's outer surface that produced continents, oceans, and mountains. —**diastrophe,** *n.* —**diastrophic,** *adj.*

geochronology   the branch of geology that describes the past in terms of geologic rather than human time. —**geochronologist,** *n.* —**geochronologic, geochronological,** *adj.*

geogony   a theory or science about the formation of the earth. —**geogonic,** *adj.*

geology   the science that studies the physical history of the earth, the rocks of which it is composed, and the changes the earth has undergone or is undergoing. —**geologist,** *n.* —**geologic, geological,** *adj.*

geomalism   the tendency of organisms, under the influence of gravity, to be symmetrical. —**geomalic,** *adj.*

geomancy   a form of divination that analyses the pattern of a handful of earth thrown down at random or dots made at random on paper. —**geomancer,** *n.*

geomorphology   the branch of geology that studies the form of the earth's surface. —**geomorphologist,** *n.* —**geomorphologic, geomorphological,** *adj.*

geophagism, geophagy, geophagia   the practice of eating earthy matter, esp. clay or chalk. —**geophagist,** *n.* —**geophagous,** *adj.*

tellurist   a dweller on the earth. Also called **tellurian.**

EARTHQUAKES

bathyseism   an earthquake occurring at very deep levels of the earth.

seismicity   the intensity, frequency, and distribution of earthquakes in a specific area.

seismism   an earthquake. Also called **seism.** —**seismic,** *adj.*

seismogram   the record of an earthquake's vibrations and intensity made by a seismograph.

seismograph   one of various devices for measuring and recording the vibrations and intensities of earthquakes. —**seismographer,** *n.* —**seismographic, seismographical,** *adj.*

seismography   1. the scientific measuring and recording of the shock and vibrations of earthquakes.
2. seismology.

seismology   the branch of geology that studies earthquakes and their effects. —**seismologist,** *n.* —**seismologic, seismological,** *adj.*

seismometer   a special seismograph equipped to measure the actual movement of the ground. —**seismometry,** *n.* —**seismometric,** *adj.*

tromometer   an instrument for detecting or measuring very slight earth tremors.

EASTERN ORTHODOXY

Achephali **1.** any of various Middle Eastern Christian sects in the early church that lacked or rejected theological leaders.
2. a Flagellant. —**Achephalist,** *n.*

charisticary an official in the medieval Greek church who collected the money from a monastery or benefice.

chrismation a sacrament corresponding to confirmation in the Western church in which a baptized person is anointed with chrism.

exarch **1.** in the early church, the head of a major diocese or province.
2. a bishop inferior to a patriarch but superior to a metropolitan.
3. a deputy of a patriarch, either a priest or a bishop.
4. the head of an autonomous church. —**exarchal,** *adj.*

Euchologion the principal service book of Eastern Orthodoxy. Also called **Euchology.**

euchology the study of Eastern Orthodox ritual.

Hesychasm the quietistic practices of a 14th cent. ascetic sect of mystics drawn from the monks of Mt. Athos. Also called **Palamitism.** —**hesychast,** *n.* —**hesychastic,** *adj.* See **quietism.**

iconoclasticism **1.** the practice of opposing the veneration of icons.
2. the practice of destroying icons.
3. (*cap.*) the principles of the religious party in the 8th cent. Eastern church that opposed the use of icons. —**iconoclast,** *n.* —**iconoclastic,** *adj.*

idoloclast an iconoclast.

Sophianism a theological system centering on the Holy Wisdom developed by the 20th cent. Russian priest Sergei Bulgakov. Also called **Sophiology.** —**Sophianist,** *n.*

synaxarist one who reads the synaxarion, or brief narrative of a saint's life, in Eastern Orthodox liturgies.

ECHOES

catacoustics *Rare.* the branch of acoustics that studies echoes. Also called **cataphonics.**

phonocamptics *Obsolete.* the branch of physics that studies reflected sounds.

ECONOMICS

aphnology *Rare.* the science of wealth; plutology.

autarky a national policy of economic self-sufficiency or independence. —**autarkist,** *n.* —**autarkic, autarkical,** *adj.*

bilateralism the practice of promoting trade between two countries through agreements concerning quantity and price of commodities. —**bilateralistic,** *adj.* Cf. **multilateralism.**

capitalism   a system of economics under which ownership of and investment in the means of production and distribution depends chiefly upon corporations and private individuals. —**capitalist,** *n.* —**capitalistic,** *adj.*

cartelism   the practice of controlling production and prices by agreements between or among international companies. —**cartel,** *n.*

Colbertism   the mercantilist theories of Jean Colbert in the 17th cent., esp. his advocacy of high protective tariffs.

commercialism   **1.** the principles, practice, and spirit of commerce.
2. an excessive emphasis on high profit, commercial success, or immediate results.
3. a commercial custom, practice, or expression. —**commercialist,** *n.* —**commercialistic,** *adj.*

Fabianism   a late 19th cent. English movement which favored the gradual development of socialism by peaceful means. —**Fabian,** *n., adj.*

industrialism   a system of social and economic organization based upon highly mechanized industry. —**industrialist,** *n., adj.*

Keynesianism   the economic theories of John Maynard Keynes, English economist, and his advocates, esp. his emphasis upon deficit spending by government to stimulate business investment. —**Keynesian,** *n., adj.*

Malthusianism   the theories of Thomas Malthus, 19th cent. English economist, stating that population growth tends to increase faster than production and that food and necessities will be in short supply unless population growth is restricted or war, disease, and famine intervene. —**Malthusian,** *n., adj.*

mercantilism   a political and economic policy seeking to advance a state above others by accumulating large quantities of precious metals and by exporting in large quantity while importing in small. —**mercantilist,** *n.* —**mercantilistic,** *adj.*

multilateralism   the practice of promoting trade among several countries through agreements concerning quantity and price of commodities, as the Common Market, and, sometimes, restrictive tariffs on goods from outsiders.

Owenism   the principles of social and labor reform along communistic lines developed by Robert Owen in the 19th cent. —**Owenite,** *n.*

peonism   **1.** the practice of persons in servitude, as to work off a debt.
2. convict labor.
3. the state or condition of a peon. Also called **peonage.**

plutology   the branch of economics that studies wealth; theoretical economics.

protectionism   the theory or practice of a method of fostering or developing industry through restrictive tariffs on foreign imports. —**protectionist,** *n., adj.*

ENDS

eschatology *Theology.* any doctrines concerning death, the afterlife, or other final matters. —**eschatological,** *adj.* —**eschatologist,** *n.*

Millerism the preachings of the 19th cent. American William Miller, who believed that the end of the world and the return of Christ would occur in 1843. —**Millerite,** *n.*

teleology, teleologism **1.** *Philosophy.* the doctrine that final causes exist.
2. the study of the evidences of purpose or design in nature.
3. such design or purpose. —**telic, teleological,** *adj.* —**teleologist,** *n.*

ENGLAND

Anglist an authority on England, its language, or its literature.

Anglomania an extreme devotion to English manners, customs, or institutions.

Anglophile one who greatly admires England and things English.

Anglophobia a hatred or fear of England and things English.

ENGLISH

Anglicism **1.** a word, idiom, or feature of the English language occurring in or borrowed by another language.
2. *U.S.* a Briticism.
3. any manner, idea, or custom typical of the English people.

Anglicist an authority on the English language or English literature.

ENGRAVING

burinist an engraver, usu. in metal. Also called **graver.**

glyptology **1.** the art of engraving, especially on gems.
2. the study of this art.

xylography the art of engraving on wood for printing. —**xylographer,** *n.* —**xylographic, xylographical,** *adj.*

ENTOMOLOGY

coleopterology the branch of entomology that studies beetles. —**coleopterist,** *n.*

entomology the branch of zoology that studies insects. —**entomologist,** *n.* —**entomologic, entomological,** *adj.*

polymorphism *Zoology, Botany.* the ability in some plants and animals to occur in several form or color varieties. —**polymorphous,** *n.*

ENVIRONMENT

anthoecology the study of the relationship of flowers and their environment.

anthroposociology　the study of the effects upon each other of environment and race.

autecology　the study of an individual organism, or the species regarded collectively, in relation to environment. —**autecologic, autecological,** *adj.*

bioecology　the study of the interrelation of plants and animals in their common environment. —**bioecologist,** *n.*

ecology　**1.** the branch of biology that studies the relationship of organisms and environments.
2. the branch of sociology that studies the environmental spacing and interdependence of people and their institutions, as in rural or urban settings. —**ecologist,** *n.* —**ecologic, ecological,** *adj.*

ergonomics　the study of the relation of man to the environment in which he works and the application of anatomical, physiological, psychological, and engineering knowledge to the problems involved. Also called **biotechnology.** —**ergonomic,** *adj.*

genecology　a combination of genetics and ecology that studies animal species and their environment. —**genecologist,** *n.* —**genecologic, genecological,** *adj.*

paleoecology　a branch of ecology that studies the relationship of ancient plants and animals and their environments. —**paleoecologic, paleoecological,** *adj.*

synecology　the branch of ecology that studies the relationship between plant and animal communities and their environments. —**synecologic, synecological,** *adj.*

EQUATOR

antipodes　two points on the surface of the earth diametrically opposite each other. —**antipodean,** *n., adj.*

Antiscians, Antiscii　the persons living on opposite sides of the equator but in the same longitude whose shadows at noon fall in opposite directions.

ETHICS

axiology　the branch of philosophy dealing with values, as those of ethics, aesthetics, or religion. —**axiologist,** *n.* —**axiological,** *adj.*

deontology　the branch of philosophy concerned with ethics, esp. that branch dealing with duty, moral obligation, and right action. —**deontologist,** *n.* —**deontological,** *adj.*

eudaemonism, eudaemonics, eudemonism　the ethical doctrine that the basis of morality lies in the tendency of right actions to produce happiness, esp. in a life governed by reason rather than pleasure. —**eudaemonist,** *n.*

moralism　the practice of morality, as distinct from religion. —**moralist,** *n.* —**moralistic,** *adj.*

utilitarianism   the ethical doctrine that virtue is based upon utility, and that behavior should have as its goal the procurement of the greatest happiness for the greatest number of persons. —**utilitarian,** *n., adj.*

EVIL

invultuation   a form of witchcraft involving melting a wax image of the intended victim or, in voodoo, sticking it with pins.

malism   the belief that the world is essentially bad or evil.

ponerology   the branch of theology that studies sin and evil.

EVOLUTION

Darwinism   the theory of evolution by natural selection of those species best adapted to survive the struggle for existence. —**Darwinian,** *n., adj.*

Lamarckism   the theory of organic evolution advanced by the French naturalist Lamarck that characteristics acquired by habit, diseases, or adaptations to change in environment may be inherited. —**Lamarckian,** *adj.*

phylogeny   the history of the development of a plant, animal, or racial type. —**phylogenist,** *n.* —**phylogenetic,** *adj.*

primordialism   a devotion to the conditions which existed at the beginning of creation.

tychism   1. the theory that chance is involved in evolution and that variation within a species is accidental.
2. the belief that chance rather than mere determinism operates in the cosmos. Cf. **uniformitarianism.**

uniformitarianism   1. *Philosophy.* a doctrine that the universe is governed only by rigid, unexceptionable law.
2. *Geology.* the concept that current geological processes explain all past geological occurrences. —**uniformitarian,** *n., adj.*

EYES

astigmatism   a defect in a lens, eye, or mirror which causes rays from one direction not to focus at one point. —**astigmatic,** *adj.*

hypermetropia   the condition of farsightedness. —**hypermetropic,** *adj.*

myopia   the condition of nearsightedness. —**myopic,** *adj.*

oculist   a physician who specializes in ophthalmology.

ommatophobia   an abnormal fear of eyes.

ophthalmology   the branch of medical science that studies the eyes, their diseases, and defects. —**ophthalmologist,** *n.* —**ophthalmologic, ophthalmological,** *adj.*

optician   a person who makes and sells glasses after prescriptions prepared by an oculist or optometrist.

optology *Archaic.* the testing of the eyes for lenses.

optometry the practice or profession of testing eyes for defects in vision and the prescribing of corrective glasses. —**optometrist,** *n.* —**optometrical,** *adj.*

orthoptics the art of treating visual defects by exercise and retraining in visual habits. —**orthoptist,** *n.* —**orthoptic,** *adj.*

retinoscopy a method of determining the refractive error of an eye using an ophthalmoscope to illuminate the retina through the lens of the eye. Also called **skiascopy.** —**retinoscopist,** *n.*

F

FACE

physiognomy, physiognomics 1. the art of determining character or personal qualities from the features or form of the body, esp. the face. 2. divination by examining the features of a face. —**physiognomist,** *n.* —**physiognomic, physiognomical,** *adj.*

prosopography 1. *Obsolete.* a description of the face. 2. a biographical sketch containing a description of a person's appearance, qualities, and history. 3. a collection of biographical articles. 4. the preparation of such a collection. —**prosopographer,** *n.*

FADS

faddism an inclination for adopting fads. —**faddist,** *n.* —**faddish,** *adj.* —**faddishness,** *n.*

mania a manifestation of intense enthusiasm for something; craze or fad, as *musicomania.*

FAITH

fideism a reliance, in a search for religious truth, on faith alone. —**fideist,** *n.* —**fideistic,** *adj.*

pistic referring to or having a pure and genuine faith.

pistology the branch of theology that studies the characteristics of faith.

FASCISM

Bundist a member of the German—American Volksbund, a U.S. pro-Nazi organization of the 1930's and 1940's. —**Bund,** *n.*

Falangism the doctrines of the Falange, the fascist party of Spain. —**Falangist,** *n.*

fascism 1. the tenets of a centralized totalitarian and nationalistic government which strictly controls finance, industry, and commerce,

practices rigid censorship and racism, and eliminates opposition through secret police.
2. such a government, as that of Italy under Mussolini. —**fascist,** *n.* —**fascistic,** *adj.*

Hitlerism the tenets of German fascism as developed by Adolf Hitler; Nazism. —**Hitlerite,** *n., adj.*

Nazism the German form of fascism, esp. that of the National Socialist (Naz*ionalsozialist*) Workers' Party under Adolf Hitler. —**Nazi,** *n., adj.*

putschism a method of revolution or overthrow involving secret planning, suddenness, and speed, as Hitler's 1938 invasion of Austria. —**putschist,** *n.*

Rexist a member of the Belgian pro-fascist party of the 1930's.

FATHER

misopaterism the hatred of one's father. —**misopaterist,** *n.*

patriarchy **1.** a form of community in which the father or oldest male is the supreme authority in the family, clan, or tribe, and descent is traced through the male line.
2. government by males, with one as supreme. —**patriarchist,** *n.* —**patriarchic, patriarchical,** *adj.*

patricentric tending to move toward or centering upon the father. Cf. **matricentric.**

FATIGUE

kopophobia an abnormal fear of mental or physical exhaustion.

ponophobia an abnormal fear of fatigue, esp. through overworking.

FAVORITISM

nepotism a favoritism shown to nephews or other relatives, as in politics or business. —**nepotist,** *n.* —**nepotic,** *adj.*

partisanism **1.** a favoritism shown to members of one's own party, faction, sect, or cause.
2. a strong adherence to the tenets of one's party, faction, sect, or cause. —**partisan,** *n., adj.*

FEAR

panophobia **1.** a nonspecific fear, a state of general anxiety.
2. an abnormal fear of everything. Also called **panphobia, pantaphobia, pantophobia.** —**panophobe,** *n.* —**panophobic,** *adj.*

phobophobia **1.** an abnormal fear of being afraid, a fear of fear itself.
2. a fear of phobias.

polyphobia an abnormal fear of many things.

FEET

chiropody   an earlier and still frequent term for podiatry. —chiropodist, *n.* —chiropodial, *adj.*

podiatry   a medical specialty concerned with the care and treatment of the foot. —podiatrist, *n.* —podiatric, *adj.*

podology   podiatry.

FERMENTATION

enzymology   the branch of biochemistry that studies enzymes. —enzymologist, *n.*

zymology   the branch of biochemistry that studies fermentation. Also called zymetology.

zymometer   a device for determining degrees of fermentation.

zymotic   1. caused by or causing fermentation.
2. causing or referring to infectious diseases.

zymurgy   a branch of applied chemistry that studies fermentation processes, as in brewing.

FIGURES OF SPEECH

apophasis   *Rhetoric.* a spoken or written figure in which an assertion is made in the midst of a denial, as in Mark Antony's funeral speech for Caesar. Also called paralipsis. —apophasic, *adj.*

apostrophe   a variety of personification in which the dead, absent, or inanimate are addressed as if present. —apostrophic, *adj.*

hypallage   the deliberate movement for effect and emphasis of one of a group of nouns from a more natural position to one less natural, as Virgil's "the trumpet's Tuscan blare" for "the Tuscan trumpet's blare." —hypallactic, *adj.*

hyperbole   *Rhetoric.* 1. an obvious and intentional exaggeration.
2. an extravagant statement or figure of speech not intended to be taken literally, as "She's as big as a house." —hyperbolic, *adj.* Cf. litotes.

hysteron proteron   a figure of speech in which what logically should come last comes first, as *bred and born* and *thunder and lightning.*

litotes   an understatement, esp. one in which an affirmative is expressed by the negative of the contrary, as in "it's not unpleasant."

meiosis   an expressive understatement, esp. litotes. —meiotic, *adj.*

metonymy   the use of the name of a part of an object or a related object to denote, as in "A sail, a sail" for a ship. —metonymic, *adj.*

paronomasia   a play on words; pun.

personification   the attribution of personality to an inanimate object or abstraction, as "*the table tripped me.*" Also called *prosopopoeia.* —personificative, *adj.*

syllepsis   the use of a word with the same syntactic relation to two adjacent words, in a literal sense with one and a metaphorical sense with the other, as in "the ships collided, and the sailors and many dreams were drowned." —**sylleptic,** *adj.*

synecdoche   the use of a part for a whole or a whole for a part, the special for the general or the general for the special, as in "a Rockefeller" for a rich man or "wheels" for transportation. —**synecdochic, synecdochical,** *adj.*

tropology   1. the use of figurative language in writing.
2. a treatise on figures of speech or tropes. —**tropologic, tropological,** *adj.*

zeugma   the use of a word grammatically related to two adjacent words, but inappropriate for one of them, as in "he loved both his wife and his wallet." —**zeugmatic,** *adj.*
See also RHETORIC.

FILMS

bioscope   1. a film projector of the early 20th cent.
2. *Brit.* a motion-picture theater.

cinematics   the art or principles of making motion pictures.

cinematography   the art or technique of motion-picture photography. —**cinematographer, cinematographist,** *n.* —**cinematographic,** *adj.*

continuity   a motion-picture scenario arranging action, dialogue, and scenes in the order to be shown on the screen.

scenarist   the writer of scenarios for motion pictures.

FINANCE

cambism   the theory and practice of commercial exchange. Also called **cambistry.** —**cambist,** *n.*

cambist   1. a dealer in bills of exchange.
2. a handbook listing the exchange values of moneys and the weights and measures of many countries.

cambistry   the branch of economics that studies commercial exchange, esp. international money values.

FINGERS

dactyliomancy   a form of divination involving finger rings.

dactylitis   an inflammation of a finger or toe.

dactylography   the study of fingerprints. —**dactylographer,** *n.* —**dactylogram,** *n.* —**dactylographic,** *adj.*

dactylonomy   *Rare.* the practice of counting on the fingers.

dactyloscopy   the comparison of fingerprints for identification. —**dactyloscopist,** *n.* —**dactyloscopic,** *adj.*

FIRE

arsonist a person who destroys property by fire, for revenge, insurance, etc.

incendiarism the deliberate destruction of property by fire; arson. —**incendiary,** *n., adj.*

pyrogenous *Geology.* produced by the action of heat, hot solutions, etc. —**pyrogenic,** *adj.*

pyrography the process of burning designs on wood or leather with a heated tool. —**pyrograph,** *n.* —**pyrographer,** *n.* —**pyrographic,** *adj.*

pyrolatry the worship of fire.

pyromancy a form of divination involving fire or flames.

pyromania the persistent compulsion to start fires.

pyrophobia an abnormal fear of fire.

FIREWORKS

pyrotechnics 1. the art of making and using fireworks.
2. a brilliant and dazzling display, as of eloquence, wit, virtuosity, etc. Also called **pyrotechny.** —**pyrotechnist,** *n.* —**pyrotechnic, pyrotechnical,** *adj.*

pyrotechnist, pyrotechnician a person skilled in the use and handling of fireworks.

FISH

ichthyism, ichthyismus a toxic condition caused by toxic fish roe.

ichthyolatry the worship of fish or of fish-shaped idols.

ichthyology 1. the branch of zoology that studies fishes.
2. a zoological treatise on fish. —**ichthyologist,** *n.* —**ichthyological,** *adj.*

ichthyomancy a form of divination involving the heads or entrails of fish.

ichthyophagy the practice of eating or subsisting on fish. —**ichthyophagist,** *n.* —**ichthyophagous,** *adj.*

ichthyophobia 1. a ritual avoidance of fish, esp. under the pressure of taboo.
2. an abnormal fear of fish.

piscatology *Rare.* the art or science of fishing. —**piscator,** *n.*

planktology, planktonology the branch of biology that studies plankton, esp. as the sustenance of planktivorous fish.

potanadromous *Ichthyology.* concerned with movements of fish up and down stream in a single watershed.

FLAGS

vexillary a standard bearer.

vexillium 1. a military standard or banner carried by ancient Roman troops.
2. the men serving under such a banner.

vexillology the study of flags and flag design. —**vexillologist,** *n.* —**vexillological,** *adj.*

FLESH

creophagism, creophagy the use of flesh meat for sustenance. —**creophagous,** *adj.*

omophagia *Rare.* the eating of raw meat, esp. as part of an initiation ritual. —**omophagic,** *adj.*

FLOWERS

anthoecology the branch of ecology that studies the relationship of flowers and their environment.

anthography *Botany.* the description of flowers.

anthomania *Rare.* an extreme love for flowers.

anthophagy the habit, as of larvae, of feeding on flowers. —**anthophagous,** *adj.*

anthophobia an abnormal fear of flowers.

floriculture the cultivation of flowers, esp. of decorative flowering plants, usu. on a commercial scale. —**floriculturist,** *n.* —**floricultural,** *adj.*

floriferous flower-bearing.

ikebana the Japanese art of flower arrangement, esp. for the home.

FOOD AND NUTRITION

accubation *Rare.* the act or habit of reclining at meals.

alimentology *Med.* the science of nutrition.

anorexia a lack of appetite, usu. for psychological reasons.

autophagy, autophagia *Med.* 1. the eating of one's own body. 2. the nutrition of the body by its own tissues, as in dieting. —**autophagous,** *adj.*

botulism a toxic condition caused by a neurotoxin in improperly canned or preserved food.

bromatology *Rare.* the science of food.

cibophobia an abnormal fear of food. Also called **sitophobia, sitiophobia.**

commensalism the practice of eating together at the same table. Also called **commensality.** —**commensal,** *n., adj.*

epicureanism the habit of refined, often luxurious, enjoyment of sensuous pleasures, esp. of food. —**epicurean,** *n., adj.*

Fletcherism the practice of eating only when hungry and in small amounts, and esp. chewing one's food thoroughly. —**Fletcherite,** *n.* —**Fletcherize,** *v.*

fruitarianism the practice of subsisting chiefly on fruit. —**fruitarian,** *n., adj.* Cf. **vegetarianism.**

gastronomy   the art or science of good eating. —gastronome, gastronomist, *n.* —gastronomic, *adj.*

magirics   *Rare.* the science or art of cooking. —magirist, *n.*

phagophobia   an abnormal fear of eating.

polyphagia, polyphagy   1. a desire for all kinds of food. 2. *Med.* excessive or gluttonous consumption of food. —polyphagian, *n.* —polyphagic, polyphagous, *adj.*

trophology   *Med.* the science of nutrition; alimentology.

tsiology   a treatise on tea.

vegetarianism   the practice of subsisting chiefly on vegetables. —vegetarian, *n., adj.*

FOREIGNERS

androlepsy   *Law.* the seizure of foreign subjects to enforce a claim for justice or other right against their nation.

xenophobia   an abnormal fear or hatred of foreigners and strange things.

FORM

geomorphology   *Physical Geog.* the study of the characteristics, origins, and development of land forms. —geomorphologist, *n.* —geomorphologic, geomorphological, *adj.*

morphology   1. the study of the form or structure of anything. 2. the branch of biology that studies the form and structure of plants and animals. See also geomorphology. —morphologist, *n.* —morphologic, morphological, *adj.*

FOSSILS

ichnology   the branch of paleontology that studies fossil footprints. —ichnological, *adj.*

paleobiology, palaeobiology   the branch of paleontology that studies fossil plants and animals. —paleobiologist, *n.* —paleobiologic, paleobiological, *adj.*

paleobotany, palaeobotany   the branch of paleology that studies fossil plants, esp. their origin, structure, and growth. —paleobotanist, *n.* —paleobotanic, paleobotanical, *adj.*

paleontology, palaeontology   1. the science of the forms of life existing in prior geologic periods from their fossilized remains. 2. an article on paleontology. —paleontologist, *n.* —paleontologic, paleontological, *adj.*

pyrochromatography   a process for detecting traces of organic elements in fossils by using heat or fire.

scatology   the branch of paleontology that studies fossil excrement.

FRANCE

Francophobia, Gallophobia a hatred of France or things French.

Gallomania a fondness or prejudice for French life, manners, etc.

Gallophil, Gallophile a person, not French, who loves France. Also called **Francophile.**

FREEDOM

eleutheromania *Rare.* a strong desire for freedom.

heteronymy **1.** the condition of being under the rule or domination of another.
2. the condition of being under the moral control of something or someone external; an inability to be self-willing. —**heteronymous,** *adj.*

libertarianism **1.** the advocacy of freedom, esp. in thought or conduct.
2. *Theology.* the advocacy of the doctrine of free will. —**libertarian,** *n.,* *adj.* Cf. **necessitarianism.**

liberticide **1.** the destruction of freedom.
2. the destroyer of freedom. —**liberticidal,** *adj.*

FUTURE

catopromancy, catoptromancy a form of divination involving a crystal ball or mirrors.

chiromancy, cheiromancy a form of divination involving analysis of the appearance of a hand; palmistry.

chronomancy a divination to determine the precise time for action.

oracularity the skill, condition, or an instance of being oracular.

prognostication **1.** the act of forecasting or prophesying.
2. a forecast or prediction. —**prognosticator,** *n.* —**prognosticative,** *adj.*

pythoness **1.** a woman held to be possessed by an oracle; prophetess.
2. a woman with powers of divination.

vaticide **1.** the killing of a prophet.
2. the killer of a prophet. —**vaticidal,** *adj.*

vaticination **1.** the act of prophesying.
2. the thing foretold. —**vaticinator,** *n.*

See also DIVINATION.

G

GAMBLING

hazard **1.** a dice game played with two dice; craps.

2. a dice game played with three dice; chuck-a-luck or birdcage.

3. something risked, as money in a gambling game.

philocubist   a devotee of games involving dice.

sortition   the casting of lots, as in a gambling game.

totalizator   a machine used in pari-mutuel betting.

GEMS

gemmology   the science of gemstones. Also called **gemology.** —**gemmologist,** *n.* —**gemmological,** *adj.*

glyptography   the art of carving or engraving upon gemstones. —**glyptographer,** *n.* —**glyptographic,** *adj.*

glyptology   the science or study of carved or engraved gemstones. Also called **glyptic.**

lapidary   **1.** one who cuts, polishes, or engraves precious stones.

2. a cutter of gemstones, esp. diamonds.

3. the art of cutting gemstones.

4. a connoisseur of cut gemstones and the art of their cutting. —**lapidarist,** *n.* —**lapidarian,** *adj.*

lapidist   a lapidary.

GEOGRAPHY

geography   **1.** the science that studies and describes the surface of the earth and its physical, biological, political, economic, and demographic characteristics and the complex interrelations among them.

2. the topographical features of a specific area.

3. a book on this subject. —**geographer,** *n.* —**geographic, geographical,** *adj.*

hypsography   the branch of geography that studies land areas above sea level to measure and map them. —**hypsographic, hypsographical,** *adj.*

orography   the branch of physical geography that studies mountains and mountain systems. —**orographic, orographical,** *adj.*

paleogeography   the branch of geography that studies the features of the earth of past geologic times. —**paleogeographer,** *n.* —**paleogeographic, paleogeographical,** *adj.*

telmatology   a branch of physical geography that studies wet lands, as marshes or swamps.

topology   the study of the physical features of a specific place or area, usu. accompanied by maps or charts showing relationships and elevations. —**topologist,** *n.* —**topologic, topological,** *adj.*

GEOLOGY

aerogeology   the use of aerial observation and photography in the study of geological features. —**aerogeologist,** *n.*

aphanitism a minuteness of rock texture so fine that individual grains are invisible to the naked eye. —**aphanite,** *n.*

archeogeology, archaeogeology the branch of geology that studies the formations of the remote past.

catastrophism the theory that geological changes have been caused by sudden upheaval rather than by gradual and continuing processes. —**catastrophist,** *n.* Cf. **uniformitarianism.**

crustalogy the study of the surface of the earth or the moon.

geognosy a branch of geology that studies the constituent parts of the earth, its atmosphere and water, its crust, and its interior condition. —**geognosist, geognost,** *n.* —**geognostic,** *adj.*

geotectology the branch of geology that studies the structure of the earth's crust; structural geology. Also called —**geotectonics.** —**geotectonic,** *adj.*

glaciology the branch of geology that studies the nature, distribution, and movement of glaciers and their effects upon the earth's topography. —**glaciologist,** *n.* —**glaciological,** *adj.*

limnology the branch of geology that studies ponds and lakes. —**limnologist,** *n.*

lithology the branch of geology that studies the mineral composition and structure of rocks, usu. macroscopically. —**lithologic, lithological,** *adj.* Cf. **petrography.**

mineralogy the branch of geology that studies the physical and chemical structures of minerals. —**mineralogist,** *n.*

neptunism the now obsolete theory that all rock surfaces were formed by the agency of water. —**neptunist,** *n.* Cf. **plutonism.**

oryctology mineralogy. Also called **oryctognosy.**

paleopedology a branch of pedology that studies the soils of past geologic times.

petrography the branch of geology that describes and classifies rocks, usu. after microscopic study. —**petrographer,** *n.* —**petrographic, petrographical,** *adj.* Cf. **lithology.**

petrology the branch of geology that studies the origin, structure, composition, changing, and classification of rocks. —**petrologist,** *n.* —**petrologic, petrological,** *adj.*

plutonism the theory that all rock surfaces have solidified from magmas, some at great depths below the surface of the earth. —**plutonist,** *n.* Cf. **neptunism.**

stratigraphy a branch of geology that studies the classification, correlation, and interpretation of stratified rocks. —**stratigrapher,** *n.* —**stratigraphic, stratigraphical,** *adj.*

uniformitarianism   the thesis that early geological processes were not unlike those observed today. —**uniformitarian,** *n.* Cf. **catastrophism.**

GESTURE

chironomy, cheironomy   1. the science of gesture.
2. the art of conducting singers of Gregorian chant through hand gestures to mark the rise or fall of the melody. —**chironomic,** *adj.*

kinemics   *Linguistics.* the study of units of gestural expression.

kinesics   *Linguistics.* a systematic study of nonverbal body gestures, as smiles, hand motions, or jerks, in their relation to human communication; body language. Also called **pasimology.** —**kinesic,** *adj.*

GHOSTS

Doppelgänger, doubleganger   a supposedly ghostly counterpart or double of a living person.

eidolism   a belief in ghosts.

eidolon   a phantom or apparition.

spectrology   the study of ghosts, phantoms, or apparitions. Also called **spookology.** —**spectrological,** *adj.*

GOD AND GODS

acosmism, akosmism   a denial of, or disbelief in, the existence of an external world or of a world distinct from God. —**acosmist,** *n.* —**acosmic,** *adj.*

adevism   the denial of legendary gods. —**adevist,** *n.*

agnosticism   the tenet that neither the existence nor the nature of God is known or knowable. —**agnostic,** *n., adj.*

allotheism   the worship of strange or foreign gods.

aniconism   1. the worship of an object symbolizing, but not representing, God.
2. an opposition to icons or idols. —**aniconic,** *adj.*

animism   1. the belief that natural objects and phenomena, and the universe itself, possess souls and consciousness.
2. the belief in spiritual beings or agencies. —**animist,** *n.* —**animistic,** *adj.*

anthropolatry   the deification and worship of a human being.

anthropomorphism   the assignment of human shape and attributes to gods, animals, etc. —**anthropomorphist,** *n.* —**anthropomorphic, anthropomorphical, anthropomorphistic,** *adj.*

anthropopathism, anthropopathy   the assignment of human feelings to a god or inanimate object. —**anthropopathite,** *n.* —**anthropopathic,** *adj.*

anthropophuism   the assignment of human nature and emotions to God. —**anthropophuistic,** *adj.*

anthropotheism the belief that the gods have human nature, or are only deified men.

Atenism the monotheistic religious system of the Egyptian pharaoh Ikhnaton, emphasizing the worship of the sun god Aten (Aton).

atheism the absolute denial of the existence of God or any other gods. —**atheist,** *n.* —**atheistic,** *adj.*

Baalism the worship, in ancient Canaan or Phoenicia, of any of a variety of chief deities referred to as *Baal,* 'lord'. —**Baalite,** *n.* —**Baalistic,** *adj.*

bitheism a belief in two gods. —**bitheist,** *n.* —**bitheistic,** *adj.*

chrematheism *Obsolete.* the worship of inanimate objects as usefully divine.

deicide 1. the killing of a god.
2. the killer of a god. —**deicidal,** *adj.*

deism the acknowledgement of the existence of a god upon the testimony of reason and of nature and its laws, and the rejection of the possibility of supernatural intervention in human affairs and of special revelation. —**deist,** *n.* —**deistic,** *adj.*

demiurgism the belief, in Platonism and some Gnostic sects, that the material and sensible world was created by a subordinate god under the direction of the Supreme Being. —**demiurge,** *n.* —**demiurgic,** *adj.*

euhemerism the belief that the mythological gods were merely early kings and heroes deified. —**euhemerist,** *n.* —**euhemeristic,** *adj.*

henotheism a belief in one supreme or specially venerated god who is not the only god. —**henotheist,** *n.*

hylotheism the identification of God with matter or the universe. —**hylotheist,** *n.*

isiac relating to the religious practices and objects involving the goddess Isis.

Mammonism the pursuit of material wealth and possessions, esp. a dedication to riches that is tantamount to devotion. —**Mammonist, Mammonite,** *n.*

Mazdaism the worship of Ahura Mazda in Zoroastrianism as the source of all light and good.

mechanomorphism the concept that God is a mechanical force and that the universe is governed by natural laws. —**mechanomorphic,** *adj.* Cf. **deism.**

misotheism *Rare.* a hatred of gods or God.

Mithraism an eclectic oriental mystery cult whose deity was Mithras, the savior hero of Persian myth, admitting only men. —**Mithraist,** *n.* —**Mithraic,** *adj.*

monolatry the worship of one god without excluding belief in others.

monotheism   the doctrine of or belief in only one God. —**monotheist,** *n.*

noumenalism   the doctrine of the existence of noumena, whose existence is understood only by intellectual intuition, without the aid of the senses. —**noumenalist,** *n.*

panentheism   the belief that the world is part, though not all, of God. —**panentheist,** *n.*

pantheism   the identification of God with the universe as His manifestation. —**pantheist,** *n.*

Parsiism, Parseeism   the Zoroastrianism of southwest India, with religious literature in the Parsi dialect. —**Parsi,** *n.*

phallicism   the worship of the phallus as symbolic of the generative power of nature. —**phallicist, phallist,** *n.*

physitheism   **1.** the assignment to God of a physical shape.
2. deification of the powers or phenomena of nature.

polytheism   a belief in, or worship of, many gods. —**polytheist,** *n.*

psychotheism   the doctrine that God is pure spirit.

Sethite, Sethian   a member of a Gnostic sect that regarded Seth, son of Adam, as the father of a pure race and considered the serpent as its deity.

theanthropism   **1.** the attributing of human characteristics to God; anthropomorphism.
2. a belief in the divinity of a human being.
3. a belief in God's becoming man. Also called **theanthroposophy.** —**theanthropist,** *n.*

theism   **1.** a belief in the existence of God or gods.
2. a belief in one god as creator and ruler of the universe, without rejection of special revelation. —**theism,** *n.* Cf. **deism.**

theocentrism, theocentricity   the belief that God is the center of all truth in the universe. —**theocentric,** *adj.*

theocrasy, theocrasia   **1.** a mingling of the attributes of several deities into one.
2. a union of an individual soul with God, esp. through contemplation.

theogony   **1.** the origin of the gods.
2. a genealogical account of the origin of the gods. —**theogonist,** *n.*

theolepsy   *Archaic.* a seizure or possession by a deity. —**theoleptic,** *n.*

theology   the study of God and His relationship to the universe. —**theologist,** *n.* —**theological,** *adj.*

theomachist   a person or a god who resists the divine will of God or the gods. —**theomachy,** *n.*

theomancy   a form of divination involving divinely inspired oracles or others inspired by God.

theomania   a religious madness in which a person believes he is God or inspired by God.

theophobia   an abnormal fear of God.

theurgy   1. the working of some divine or supernatural agency in human affairs.
2. the art of invoking deities or spirits for aid or information or knowledge unachievable through human reason.
3. a divine act; miracle.
4. a system of supernatural knowledge or powers believed bequeathed to the Egyptian Platonists by beneficent deities. —**theurgist,** n. —**theurgic, theurgical,** adj.

tritheism   1. a belief in three gods.
2. a Christian heresy holding that the Trinity consists of three distinct gods. —**tritheist,** n.

Zemiism   the religion of the Taino tribes of the West Indies, involving the invocation of Zemis, spirits or supernatural beings often dwelling in objects.

zoomorphism   the attribution of animal form or nature to a deity.

GOOD

agathism   the belief that all things incline toward the good. —**agathist,** n.

agathology   the doctrine or science of the good.

GOVERNMENT

absolutism   the theory and exercise of complete and unrestricted power in government. —**absolutist,** n., adj. —**absolutistic,** adj. See **autarchy, autocracy, despotism, dictatorship, monarchy, obligarchy.**

anarchism   1. a political theory advocating the elimination of governments and governmental restraint and the substitution of voluntary cooperation among individuals.
2. the methods and practices of anarchists. —**anarchist,** n. —**anarchic,** adj. Cf. **nihilism.**

apartheid   the policy of strict racial segregation and political and economic discrimination against coloreds and blacks practiced in the union of South Africa.

archology   1. the science of government.
2. the science of origins.

autarchy   1. an absolute sovereignty.
2. an autocratic government.
3. autarky. —**autarch,** n. —**autarchic, autarchical,** adj.

autocracy   1. a government in which one person has unrestricted control over others.
2. a country with an autocratic system. —**autocrat,** n. —**autocratic,** adj.

autonomy 1. the power or right of self-government. 2. a self-governing community. —**autonomous,** *adj.*

biarchy the rule of a nation, state, or community by two persons.

bicameralism 1. a legislative body having two branches, houses, or chambers. 2. advocacy of bicameral structure. —**bicameralist,** *n.* —**bicameral,** *adj.* Cf. **unicameralism.**

caciquism the domination in Spanish and Latin American areas of local political bosses. Also called **caciquismo.**

centralism a system, esp. in government, in which power and administration are concentrated in a central group or institution. —**centralist,** *n., adj.* —**centralistic,** *adj.*

colonialism the implementation of various political, economic, and social policies to enable a state to maintain or extend its authority and control over other territories. —**colonialist,** *n., adj.* —**colonialistic,** *adj.*

condominium *Internat. Law.* a joint sovereignty over a colony or dependent territory by several states. —**condominate,** *v.*

constitutional monarchy a system in which the powers of a monarch are defined and limited by law.

cosmocracy a control of the whole world.

decarchy, dekarchy the control of a governmental system by ten persons. Also called **decadarchy.**

democracy a form of government in which sovereign power resides in the people and is exercised by them or by officers they elect to represent them. —**democrat,** *n.* —**democratic,** *adj.* Cf. **republicanism.**

despotism 1. a form of government with a ruler having absolute authority; autocracy. 2. a system ruled by a tyrant or dictator having absolute, usu. oppressive power. —**despot,** *n.* —**despotic,** *adj.*

dictatorship 1. a despotic system ruled by a dictator possessing absolute power and absolute authority. 2. the office of a dictator. —**dictatorial,** *adj.*

doulocracy, dulocracy *Rare.* a government controlled by slaves.

diarchy, dyarchy a government controlled by two rulers; biarchy. —**diarch,** *n.*

dynasticism 1. a system of government in which a sequence of rulers is derived from the same family, group, or stock. 2. the reign of such a sequence. —**dynast, dynasty,** *n.*

endarchy a centralized government.

ergatocracy a government controlled by workers.

fascism 1. the tenets of a centralized, totalitarian and nationalistic government which strictly controls finance, industry, and commerce, practices rigid censorship and racism, and eliminates opposition through secret police.
2. such a government, as that of Italy under Mussolini. —**fascist**, *n.* —**fascistic**, *adj.*

federalism 1. a union of states under a central government distinct from that of the separate states, who retain certain individual powers under the central government.
2. (*cap.*) the principles of the American Federalist party, esp. its emphasis during the early years of the U.S. on a strong central government. —**federalist**, *n., adj.* —**federalistic**, *adj.*

feudalism a European system flourishing between 800-1400 based upon fixed relations of lord to vassal and all lands held in fee (as from the King), and requiring of vassal-tenants homage and service. —**feudal, feudalistic**, *adj.*

hagiarchy 1. a system of government by priests.
2. a state so governed.

hagiocracy 1. a system of rule by persons considered holy.
2. a state so governed.

hecatonarchy a system of rule by 100 persons.

justicialism a fascistic theory of government in Argentina under the Peron administration involving government intervention and economic control to ensure social justice and public welfare; Peronism.

kakistocracy a system of rule by the worst men.

kritarchy *Rare.* the rule, over ancient Israel, of the judges.

legitimist a supporter of legitimate authority, esp. of claims to a throne based on the rights of heredity. —**legitimism**, *n.*

matriarchy a society organized with the mother as head of the tribe or clan, with descent being traced through the female line. —**matriarch**, *n.* —**matriarchal**, *adj.*

monarchy 1. a governmental system in which supreme power is actually or nominally held by a monarch.
2. supreme power and authority held by one person; autocracy. —**monarchical**, *adj.*

monocracy a system ruled by one person; autocracy.

neocracy a government by amateurs.

Nihilism the principles of a Russian revolutionary movement in the late 19th cent. advocating the destruction of government as a means to anarchy and often employing terrorism and assassination to assist its program. —**nihilist**, *n., adj.* —**nihilistic**, *adj.*

oligarchy   1. a system of rule by a few persons.
2. the people who form such a government. —**oligarch,** *n.* —**oligarchic,** *adj.*

panarchy   *Rare.* a realm or dominion that includes the universe.

pantisocracy   a utopian community where all are equal and all rule. —**pantisocratist,** *n.* —**pantisocratic, pantisocratical,** *adj.*

patriarchism   a patriarchal government in a society or a church. —**patriarchist,** *n.*

patriarchy   a society organized to give supremacy to the father or the oldest male in governing a family, tribe, or clan. —**patriarch,** *n.*

plutocracy   1. the rule of the rich or wealthy.
2. the rich or wealthy who govern under such a system. —**plutocrat,** *n.*

ptochocracy   a system of rule by the poor.

regalism   the tenets of royal supremacy, esp. in church affairs.

republicanism   the principles of a theory of government in which the supreme power rests in the body of citizens entitled to vote and exercised by representatives they elect directly or indirectly and by an elected or nominated president.

stratocracy   a system of rule by the military.

serfism   a feudal social and economic system in which persons of the lower class are bound to the soil, subject to the will of and service for their lord, and transferable to the new owner if the land is sold or otherwise deeded.

tanistry   an early Irish rule of succession in which the successor to a Celtic chief was chosen from among eligible males during the chief's lifetime. —**tanist,** *n.*

statism, stateism   1. the principle of concentrating major political and economic controls in the state.
2. the support of the sovereignty of the state. —**statist,** *n., adj.*

Technocracy   1. a theory and movement of the 1930's advocating the control of production and distribution by technicians and engineers.
2. a system of government based on this theory. —**Technocrat,** *n.* —**Technocratic,** *adj.*

tetrarchy   1. the Roman practice of dividing authority over provinces among four governors.
2. a system of rule by four authorities. —**tetrarch, tetrarchate,** *n.* —**tetrarchic, tetrarchical,** *adj.*

thearchy   1. a system of government by God or a god.
2. an order or system of deities. —**thearchic,** *adj.*

theocracy   1. a system of government in which God or a deity is the civil ruler; thearchy.
2. a system of government by priests; hagiarchy.
3. a state under such a form of rule. —**theocrat,** *n.* —**theocratic,** *adj.*

timocracy 1. *Platonism.* a state in which a love of honor and glory is the guiding principle of the rulers.

2. *Aristotelianism.* a state in which the ownership of property is a qualification for office. —**timocratic, timocratical,** *adj.*

totalitarianism 1. a system of highly centralized government in which one political party or group takes control and grants neither recognition nor tolerance to other political groups.

2. autocracy in one of its several varieties.

3. the character or traits of an autocratic or authoritarian individual, party, government or state. —**totalitarian,** *n., adj.*

triarchy 1. the rule of a nation, state, or community by three persons.

2. a set of three joint rulers. Usu. called *triumvirate.*

3. a country divided into three governments.

4. a group of three districts or three countries, each under its own ruler.

tribalism 1. the customs, life, and organization of a tribal society.

2. a strong loyalty to one's tribe, party, or group.

tuchungism the former Chinese practice of governing provinces through warlords or *tuchuns.*

unicameralism 1. a system of government having a single legislative chamber.

2. an advocacy of unicameral structure. —**unicameralist,** *n.* —**unicameral,** *adj.*

vassalism 1. the feudal system of lands held in fee and of mandatory vassal-tenant homage, fealty, and service.

2. the condition of a person owing homage and fealty to a superior; vassalage.

GRAMMAR

agrammatism *Med.* a neurological defect resulting in an inability to use words in grammatical sequence.

amphibology 1. an ambiguity of language.

2. a word, phrase, or sentence that can be interpreted variously because of uncertainty of grammatical construction rather than ambiguity of the words used, as "John met his father when he was sick." Also called —**amphiboly.** —**amphibological, amphibolous,** *adj.*

anacoluthon a lack of grammatical sequence or coherence, as "He ate cereal, fruit, and went to the store". Also called **anacoluthia.** —**anacoluthic,** *adj.*

grammarianism 1. *Rare.* the principles of the study of grammar followed by a grammarian.

2. excessive emphasis upon the fine points of grammar and usage, esp. as a shibboleth; dedication to the doctrine of correctness; grammatism.

grammaticism   a principle or a point of grammar.

grammatism   excessively pedantic behavior about grammatical standards and principles. —**grammatist,** *n.*

parataxis   the placing together of phrases, clauses, or sentences without conjunctive words, as *I came, I saw, I conquered.* —**paratactic,** *adj.*

periphrastic   referring to the ability in some languages to use function words instead of inflections, as *the hair of the dog* for *dog's hair.* —**periphrasis,** n.

solecism   a violation of conventional usage and grammar, as "I are sixty year old". —**solecist,** *n.* —**solecistic, solecistical,** *adj.*

syllepsis   the use of a word or expression to perform two syntactic functions, esp. to apply to two or more words of which at least one does not agree in logic, number, case, or gender, as in Pope's line "See Pan with flocks, with fruits Pomona crowned". —**sylleptic, sylleptical,** *adj.*

GRANDEUR

megalomania   1. *Psychiatry.* a form of mental illness marked by delusions of greatness, wealth, or power.
2. an obsession with doing extravagant or grand things. —**megalomaniac,** *n.*

paranoia   *Psychiatry.* a slowly progressive personality disorder marked by delusions, esp. of persecution and grandeur. —**paranoid, paranoiac,** *adj.*

GRASSES

agrostography   a description of grasses. —**agrostographer,** *n.*

agrostology   the branch of systematic botany that studies grasses. —**agrostologist,** *n.*

GRAVITY

baragnosis   *Med.* the absence of the power to recognize weight through the senses; the absence of barognosis.

barognosis   *Med.* the conscious perception of weight, esp. through cutaneous and muscular nerves.

barology   *Archaic.* a branch of physics that studied weight and its relationship to gravity.

geotropism   *Botany.* the response of a plant to the force of gravity. —**geotropic,** *adj.*

telekinesis   the production of motion in a body, apparently without the use of material force, a power long claimed by mediums and magicians. Also called **teleportation.** —**telekinetic,** *adj.*

tidology   the science or theory of tides.

GREECE AND GREEKS

Hellenism 1. the culture and ideals of the ancient Greeks.
2. the use of a Greek idiom in writing in another language.
3. the adoption or imitation of ancient Greek language, thought, art, or customs. —**Hellenist,** *n.*

Ionicism 1. *Architecture.* use or imitation of the Ionic order in construction or decoration.
2. the culture and ideals of ancient Ionia and the Ionians.
3. an Ionian idiom appearing in the midst of material in another language or in the dialect of Athens (Attic). Also called **Ionism.**

Panhellenism 1. the idea of a union of all Greeks in a single political body.
2. advocacy of the idea of such a union. —**Panhellenist,** *n.* —**Panhellenic,** *adj.*

Philhellenism a habit of friendship or support for the Greeks. —**Phillenist,** *n.* —**Philhellenic,** *adj.*

GROWTH

auxology *Obsolete. Med.* the science of growth, esp. applied to microorganisms. Also called **auxanology.**

bathmism a hypothetical vital force, thought to control growth and the function of nutrition.

teratology *Biology.* the study of malformations or abnormal growth in animals or vegetables. —**teratologist,** *n.* —**teratological,** *adj.*

GUIDE

valet-de-place a man who acts as guide to strangers and travelers.

courier *Brit.* a person hired by travelers to make arrangements for a tour and to act as guide.

H

HAIR

alopecia 1. a loss of hair, feathers, or wool.
2. baldness. —**alopecic,** *adj.*

electrology the use of electrolysis for removing moles, warts, or excess hair. —**electrologist,** *n.*

hirsutism 1. a condition of shaggy hairiness.
2. *Biology, Zoology.* the state of being covered with long, stiff hairs. —**hirsute,** *adj.*

pilosism, pilosity an excessive hairiness; furriness. —**pilose,** *adj.*

trichoanesthesia *Med.* a loss of hair sensibility.

trichobezoar   a hairball.

trichology   *Med.* the scientific study of hair and its diseases. —**trichologist,** *n.*

tricopathy   *Med.* any disease of the hair. —**tricopathic,** *adj.*

tricophagy   the practice of eating hair.

trichosis   **1.** *Med.* any disease or abnormal growth of the hair. **2.** a heavy growth of hair.

trichotillomania   *Med.* an abnormal desire to pull out one's own hair, esp. by delirious patients. Also called **trichologia.**

HANDS

ambidextrianism   **1.** the ability to use both hands equally well. **2.** an unusual cleverness. **3.** deceitfulness. Also called **ambidexterity.** —**ambidextrous,** *adj.*

chiragra   a pain in the hand.

chirapsia   a friction caused by rubbing skin with the hand; massage.

chirocosmetics   a beautifying of the hands. —**chirocosmetic,** *adj.*

chirognomy, cheirognomy   the theories and activity of palmistry. —**chirognomist,** *n.*

chirology, cheirology   *Rare.* the study of the hands.

chiromancy, cheiromancy   a form of divination by the examination of the hand; palmistry.

chiroplasty   the plastic surgery of the hand.

chirothesia   the imposition of hands, usu. on the head, in certain rituals, as confirmation and ordination.

chirotony   **1.** *Eccl.* the extending of the hands in blessing during certain rituals. **2.** an election by show of hands.

mancinism   the state of left handedness.

palmistry   the art of telling a person's character, past, or future by the lines, marks, and mounts on his palms. —**palmist,** *n.*

prestidigitation   the performance of tricks and illusions by the quick and skillful use of the hands; conjuring; sleight of hand. Also called **prestigiation.** —**prestidigitator,** *n.* —**prestidigitatorial, prestidigitatory,** *adj.*

sexdigitism   the condition of six-fingeredness.

HAPPINESS

ataraxia   a state of tranquility free from anxiety and emotional disturbance. —**ataraxic,** *adj.*

athedonia   an inability to be happy. —**athedonic,** *adj.*

cherophobia an abnormal fear of gaiety.

eudemonics, eudaemonics 1. an art or means of acquiring happiness; eudaemonism.

2. the theory of happiness. —**eudemonia,** n. —**eudemonic, eudemonical,** adj.

euphoria, euphory 1. a state of happiness and well-being.

2. Psychiatry. an exaggerated state of happiness, with no foundation in truth or reality. —**euphoric,** adj.

macarism the practice of making others happy through praise and felicitation. —**macarize,** v.

HEAD

bumpology a sarcastic term for phrenology. —**bumpologist,** n.

cephalomancy a form of divination involving the head.

cephalometry the science of measuring the dimensions of the human head. —**cephalometer,** n. —**cephalometric,** adj.

craniology the science that studies the size, shape, and other features of human skulls. —**craniologist,** n. —**craniological,** adj.

craniometry the science of measuring skulls. —**craniometrist,** n. —**craniometric, craniometrical,** adj.

cranioscopy the observation, examination, and description of the human skull. —**cranioscopist,** n. —**cranioscopical,** adj.

macrocephaly a condition in which the head or cranial capacity is unusually large. —**macrocephalic,** adj.

phrenology a system by which an analysis of character and of the development of faculties is attempted by studying the shape and protuberances of the skull. —**phrenologist,** n. —**phrenologic, phrenological,** adj.

HEALTH

anorexia Psychiatry. a lack of appetite and inability to eat, often traceable to abnormal psychological attitudes.

dyscrasia Med. an unhealthy condition, esp. an imbalance of physiologic or constitutional elements, often of the blood. —**dyscrasic, dyscratic,** adj. Cf. **eucrasia.**

dyspepsia, dyspepsy 1. a condition of impaired digestion.

2. indigestion. —**dyspeptic,** adj.

eucrasia 1. Med. a normal state of health; good health.

2. physical well-being. —**eucrasic, eucratic,** adj. Cf. **dyscrasia.**

eupepsia, eupepsy a condition of good digestion. —**eupeptic,** adj.

hygiastics Rare. hygienics.

hygieology, hygiology Rare. the science of hygiene; hygienics.

hygienics 1. the branch of medical science that studies health and its preservation; hygiene.
2. a system of principles for promoting health. —**hygienist,** *n.* —**hygienic,** *adj.*

hypochondriacism, hypochondriasis 1. *Psychiatry.* an abnormal state characterized by emotional depression and imagined ill health, often accompanied by symptoms untraceable to any organic disease.
2. an excessive concern and conversation about one's health. —**hypochondriac,** *n.* —**hypochondriacal,** *adj.*

valetudinarianism 1. a condition of poor health.
2. a state of being concerned with health, often excessively.
3. invalidism. —**valetudinarian,** *n., adj.*

HEARING

audiclave an instrument that aids hearing.

audioanalgesia *Med.* a pain in the ear; earache.

auditognosis *Med.* the sense by which sounds are understood and interpreted.

audiometry a testing of hearing ability by frequencies and various levels of loudness. —**audiometrist, audiometrician,** *n.* —**audiometric,** *adj.*

otocleisis a closure of the hearing passages.

otomyasthenia *Med.* a weakness of the ear muscles causing poor selection and amplification of sounds. —**otomyasthenic,** *adj.*

otophone 1. an external appliance used to aid hearing; a hearing aid.
2. *Med.* a tube used in the auscultation of the ear.

otosis a defect in hearing causing a false impression of sounds made by others.
See also EARS.

HEART

anginophobia an abnormal fear of angina pectoris.

cardioangiology *Med.* the specialty that treats the heart and the blood vessels.

cardiocentesis *Med.* the surgical puncture or incision of the heart. Also called **cardiopuncture.**

cardiodynamics the branch of medical science that studies the forces and motions involved in the heart's actions.

cardiodynia *Med.* a pain in the heart.

cardiogenesis *Med. Science.* the study of the development of the heart in the embryo.

cardiograph an instrument to record the action of the heart. —**cardiographer,** *n.* —**cardiographic,** *adj.*

cardiography *Med.* the technique of graphically recording some physical or functional features of heart action.

cardiokinetic 1. an agent that stimulates action of the heart.
2. stimulating the action of the heart.

cardiology *Med. Science.* the study of the heart and its functions. —**cardiologist,** *n.* —**cardiologic, cardiological,** *adj.*

cardiomalacia *Med.* a disease causing a softening of the muscle of the heart.

cardiomegaly *Med.* an abnormal enlargement of the heart.

cardiomyopathy *Med.* a general term designating the early stages of diseases of heart muscles.

cardiopaludism *Med.* a heart disease caused by malaria and marked by increases in heart rhythm and doubled beating.

cardiopathy any disease or disorder of the heart. —**cardiopath,** *n.*

cardiophobia an abnormal fear of heart diseases.

cardioversion *Med.* the restoration of proper heart rhythm by electrical shock.

crotism the condition of having a single (*mono-*), double (*di-*), etc. heartbeat.

HEAT

actinism the ability of light and heat and other forms of radiant energy to cause chemical changes, as hormonal changes in birds so that they migrate or brood. —**actinic,** *adj.*

geothermometry the branch of geology that measures temperatures deep below the surface of the earth; geologic thermometry.

tepidity a moderate warmth; lukewarmness. —**tepid,** *adj.*

thermatology *Med. Science.* the study of heat as a medical remedy or therapy. Also called **thermotherapy.**

thermochemistry the branch of chemistry that studies the relationship of heat to chemical changes, including the production of energy. —**thermochemist,** *n.* —**thermochemical,** *adj.*

thermodynamics the branch of physics that studies the relationship of heat and mechanical energy and the conversion, in various materials, of one into the other. —**thermodynamicist,** *n.* —**thermodynamic, thermodynamical,** *adj.*

thermogenesis the production of heat, esp. in an animal body by physiological processes. —**thermogenic, thermogenous,** *adj.*

thermography 1. *Engineering.* a method of measuring surface temperatures by using luminescent materials.
2. a printing or photocopying process using infrared rays and heat.

3. a process of photography using far-infrared radiation; thermal photography. —**thermographer,** *n.* —**thermographic,** *adj.*

thermology *Archaic.* the science and study of heat. Also called **thermotics.**

thermoluminescence *Atomic Physics.* any luminescence appearing in materials upon application of heat, caused by electron movement which increases as the temperature rises. —**thermoluminescent,** *adj.*

thermolysis *Physiology.* the dispersion of heat from the body. —**thermolytic,** *adj.*

thermometry the branch of physics that deals with the measurement of temperature. —**thermometric,** *adj.*

thermophobia an abnormal fear of heat.

thermoscope a device for giving an approximation of the temperature change of a substance by noting the accompanying change in its volume. —**thermoscopic,** *adj.*

thermotaxis **1.** *Biology.* the movement of an organism toward or away from a source of heat.
2. *Physiology.* the regulation of body temperature by various physiological processes. —**thermotactic, thermotaxic,** *adj.*

HEIGHTS

acrophobia an abnormal fear of being at great heights.

altimetry the science of measuring heights, as with an altimeter. —**altimetrical,** *adj.*

cremnophobia an abnormal fear of precipices.

hypsiphobia, hypsophobia an abnormal fear of high places.

hypsography a branch of geography that deals with the measurement and mapping of the varying elevations of the earth's surface above sea level. —**hypsographic, hypsographical,** *adj.*

HEREDITY

genetics **1.** *Biology.* the science of heredity, studying resemblances and differences in related organisms and the mechanisms which explain these phenomena.
2. the genetic properties and phenomena of an organism. —**geneticist,** *n.* —**genetic,** *adj.*

heredofamilial *Med.* referring to a disorder or disease having a history of occurrence within a family and thought to be hereditary.

Mendelism the laws of inheritance through genes, discovered by Gregor J. Mendel. —**Mendelian,** *n., adj.*

radiogenetics a division of radiobiology that studies the effects of radioactivity upon factors of inheritance in genetics. —**radiogenic,** *adj.*

telegony   the supposed transmission of hereditary characteristics from one sire to offspring subsequently born to other sires by the same female.

HERESY

Agnoetism   **1.** the tenet of a 4th cent. Arian sect that God's omniscience was restricted to contemporary time.
2. the tenet of a 6th cent. Monophysite sect that Christ possessed no omniscience. —**Agnoete, Agnoite,** *n.*

Albigensianism   the beliefs and principles of an 11th cent. Catharist sect of southern France, exterminated in the 13th cent. by order of Pope Innocent III. See **Catharism.** —**Albigenses,** *n. pl.* —**Albigensian,** *n., adj.*

Apollinarianism   a late 4th cent. Christological doctrine asserting that Christ had a perfect divine nature, an imperfect human nature, and a mind replaced by the Logos. —**Apollinarian,** *n., adj.*

Berengarianism   the beliefs of Berengar de Tours, 11th cent. French churchman, esp. his denial of transubstantiation. —**Berengarian,** *n., adj.*

Cainism, Cainitism   the beliefs of a 4th cent. Gnostic sect, esp. that the Old Testament concerns a demiurge and not God and that Cain, whom they revered, had been maligned. —**Cainite,** *n.*

Catharism   the beliefs of several sects in medieval Europe, esp. the denial of infant baptism, purgatory, the communion of saints, images, and the doctrine of the Trinity; the abrogation of the institution of marriage; and the practice of rigorous asceticism. —**Cathar, Cathari, Catharist,** *n.* —**Catharistic,** *adj.*

Cyrillianism   the monophysitic tenet of Cyril, 5th cent. archbishop of Alexandria, that Christ had only one nature, a composite of the human and the divine. —**Cyrillian,** *n., adj.*

Donatism   a heretical cult in N. Africa during the 4th through 7th cents. that emphasized high morality and rebaptism as necessary for church membership and considered invalid a sacrament celebrated by an immoral priest. —**Donatist,** *n.* —**Donatistic,** *adj.*

Ebionism, Ebionitism   the beliefs of a Judaistic Christian Gnostic sect of the 2nd cent., esp. partial observation of Jewish law, rejection of St. Paul and gentile christianity, acceptance of only one Gospel (Matthew), and an early adoptionist Christology. —**Ebionite,** *n.* —**Ebionitic,** *adj.*

Gnosticism   the beliefs and practices of pre-Christian and early Christian sects, condemned by the church, esp. the conviction that matter is evil and that knowledge is more important than faith, and the practice of esoteric mysticism. —**Gnostic,** *n., adj.*

heresiarch   **1.** the originator of a heresy.
2. the leader of a group of heretics.

heresimach   a fighter of heresy and heretics.

heresiography   a systematic exposition on heresy.

heresiology   1. *Theology.* the study of heresies.
2. a reference work on heresies. —**heresiologist,** *n.*

heresy   1. a religious opinion or doctrine at variance with accepted doctrine.
2. a wilful and persistent rejection of any article of the faith by a baptized member of the Roman Catholic Church.
3. any belief or theory strongly at variance with established opinion. —**heretic,** *n.* —**heretical,** *adj.*

heretication   1. the judgement or denunciation of a belief as heretical.
2. the denunciation of a person as a heretic. —**hereticator,** *n.*

heretocide   *Rare.* 1. the killing of a heretic.
2. the killer of a heretic. —**heretocidal,** *adj.*

Jansenism   a heretical doctrine of the 17th and 18th cents. denying freedom of the will, accepting absolute predestination for part of mankind and condemnation to hell for the others, and emphasizing puritanical moral attitudes. —**Jansenist,** *n., adj.*

Manichaeism, Manicheism, Manicheanism   1. the doctrines and practices of the dualistic religious system of Manes, a blending of Gnostic Christianity, Buddhism, Zoroastrianism, and other elements, esp. doctrines of a cosmic conflict between forces of light and darkness, the darkness and evilness of matter, and the necessity for a sexual, vegetarian asceticism.
2. any similar dualistic system, considered heretical by orthodox Christian standards, —**Manichean,** *n., adj.* —**Manicheistic,** *adj.*

modalism   the theological doctrine that the members of the Trinity are not three separate persons but modes or forms of God's self-expression. —**modalist,** *n.* —**modalistic,** *adj.*

monergism   the doctrine advanced by some Lutheran theologians that spiritual renewal is exclusively the activity of the Holy Spirit. —**monergist,** *n.* —**monergistic,** *adj.* Cf. **Synergism.**

Patarinism   1. the beliefs and practices of 11th cent. Bulgarian Manicheans who migrated to the Pataria section of Milan. Also called **Pataria.**
2. the beliefs and practices of various Cathari sects in France and Bulgaria. —**Patarine, Patarene,** *n.*

Pelagianism   the heretical doctrines of Pelagius, 4th cent. British monk, esp. a denial of original sin and man's fallen spiritual nature, and an assertion that man's goodness was sufficient for him to work out his salvation without the assistance of the Holy Spirit. —**Pelagian,** *n., adj.*

Photinianism   the heresy of Photinus, 4th cent. bishop of Sirmium, deposed because he denied the divinity of Christ.

Priscillianism   the concepts of Priscillian, 4th cent. bishop of Avila, executed for heresies influenced by Manichaeism, Docetism, and modalism. —**Priscillianist,** *n., adj.*

quietism a 17th cent. Christian mystical theory, originated in Spain by Molinos and promulgated in France by Fenelon, involving passive contemplation and surrender of the will to God, and indifference to the demands of the self or the outside world, declared heretical through efforts of the Inquisition. —**quietist,** *n., adj.*

Sabellianism the modalistic doctrines of Sabellius, 3rd cent. prelate, esp. that the Trinity has but one divine essence and that the persons are only varying manifestations of God. Also called **Modalistic Monarchianism.** —**Sabellian,** *n., adj.*

Semi-Pelagianism a theological doctrine, hereticated in the 5th cent., that accepted the doctrine of original sin but asserted that man's turning to God of his own free will and not after the provocation of the Holy Ghost begins the process of spiritual rebirth. Cf. **Pelagianism.**

Socinianism the heretical tenets of Faustus Socinius, a 16th cent. Italian theologian, denying the divinity of Christ, the existence of Satan, original sin, the atonement, and eternal punishment, explaining sin and salvation in rationalistic terms. —**Socinian,** *n., adj.*

synergism an ancient heretical doctrine, extant since the 3rd cent., which holds that spiritual renewal is a cooperative endeavor between a person and the Holy Ghost. —**synergist,** *n.* —**synergistic,** *adj.* Cf. **Pelagianism, semi-Pelagianism.**

Theopaschitism Patripassianism. —**Theopaschite,** *n.*

Valentinianism a 2nd cent. blending of Egyptian Gnosticism and Christianity into a system of heretical doctrines, esp. the denial that Christ took his human nature from the Virgin Mary. —**Valentinian,** *n., adj.*

See also CHRIST.

HINDUISM

Ayurvedism, Ayurveda the conventional Hindu system of medicine, founded chiefly on naturopathy and homeopathy. —**Ayurvedic,** *adj.*

Brahmanism, Brahminism the doctrines and practices of Brahmans and orthodox Hindus, characterized by the caste system, a diverse pantheism, and primary devotion to Brahma, the creator-god of the Hindu trinity.

Krishnaism the worship of Krishna as the eighth incarnation of the god Vishnu, the preserver-god of the Hindu trinity.

Ramaism the worship of Rama, a hero of Hindu epic, as an incarnation of the god Vishnu. —**Ramaite,** *n.*

Shaktism, Saktism 1. a Hindu sect worshipping Shakti as a mother goddess under such names as Kali and Durga through contemplation and humility; right-hand Shaktism.

2. a Hindu Tantric sect worshipping Shakti as the feminine principle of generation through rites involving ritual eating and orgy; left-hand Shaktism. —**Shakta, Shakti,** *n., adj.* See also **tantrism.**

Sivaism, Shivaism, Saivism a cult made up of the worshippers of Siva, the destroyer-god of the Hindu trinity. —**Sivaite,** *n.*

sutteeism the Hindu practice or custom of a widow's willing cremation upon her husband's funeral pyre, now forbidden. —**suttee, sati,** *n.*

Tantrism 1. the teachings of the Tantras, Sanskrit religious writings concerned with mysticism and magic rituals.
2. the beliefs and practices of Hindu adherents to the Tantras in place of the Vedas, esp. magic rituals for healing, averting evil, and union with the female creative principle.
3. *Buddhism.* Tantrayana. —**Tantrist,** *n.* —**Tantric,** *adj.*

thuggeeism, thuggee a semi-religious Hindu cult with a highly organized system of murder and robbery, suppressed in India in the 19th cent. Also called **thuggery.** —**thug,** *n.*

Vaishnavism the worship of Vishnu in any of his forms or incarnations. —**Vaishnava, Vaishnavite,** *n.*

Vedaism, Vedism 1. the teachings of the Vedas, the four most sacred writings of Hinduism.
2. an adherence to these teachings; orthodox Hinduism. —**Vedaic, Vedic,** *adj.*

Vedantism the beliefs and practices of Vedanta, an orthodox Hindu philosophy emphasizing the teachings on contemplation found in the Vedas. —**Vedantic,** *adj.*

Yogism, Yoga 1. an orthodox Hindu philosophical system concerned with the liberation of the self from its noneternal elements or states.
2. any system of exercises and disciplines for achieving such liberation of self. —**Yogi, Yogin,** *n.*

HISTORY

cyclicism the belief that history repeats itself, as in the writings of Arnold Toynbee. Also called **cyclicity.** —**cyclic,** *n.*

Etruscology the study of the Etruscan civilization, esp. its language and artifacts. —**Etruscologist,** *n.*

genealogy 1. a record or account of the ancestry and descent of a person, family, or group.
2. the study of family ancestries or histories.
3. descent from an original form or progenitor; lineage. —**genealogist,** *n.* —**genealogic, geneological,** *adj.*

historicism 1. a theory that history is determined by immutable laws.
2. a theory that all cultural phenomena are historically determined and that all historians should study a period on its own merits.

3. A search for the laws of historical evolution.
4. A profound or an excessive respect for historical institutions, as traditions or laws. Also called **historism.** —**historicist,** *n., adj.*

historiography **1.** the body of literature concerned with historical matters. **2.** the methods of historical research and presentation. **3.** an official history —**historiographer,** *n.* —**historiographic, historiographical,** *adj.*

historiology the study or knowledge of history.

medievalist **1.** an expert in medieval history, literature, art, architecture, etc. **2.** a person devoted to the art, culture, or spirit of the Middle Ages.

monism the theory that there is only one causal factor in history, as intellect or nature. —**monist,** *n.* —**monistic,** *adj.*

Orientalist a specialist in Oriental history, art, literature, etc.

HOMOSEXUALITY

homoeroticism, homoerotism **1.** the tendency to obtain sexual gratification from a member of the same sex. **2.** homosexual activity. —**homoerotic,** *adj.*

lesbianism the practice of homosexual relations between women. —**lesbian,** *n., adj.*

tribadism, tribady a sexual activity between women which imitates heterosexual intercourse. —**tribade,** *n.* —**tribadic,** *adj.*

uranianism *Obsolete.* homosexuality.

uranism *Med.* the practice of homosexuality between males. —**uranist,** *n.*

urningism male homosexuality. Also called **urnism.** —**urning,** *n.*

HOMESICKNESS

nostalgia **1.** a longing to go back to one's home; homesickness. **2.** a longing for experiences, things, and relationships belonging to the past. —**nostalgic,** *adj.*

nostalgy *Archaic.* nostalgia.

nostomania *Med.* an abnormal nostalgia.

HORSES

farrier **1.** one who shoes horses; a shoeing smith. **2.** *Brit.* one who treats the ailments of horses, esp. a person not fully qualified as a veterinarian.

hippology the study of horses.

hippomobile a vehicle drawn by a horse.

hippopathology *Vet. Med.* the study and treatment of the diseases of the horse.

hippophile   a lover of horses.

hippophobia   an abnormal fear of horses.

knacker   **1.** *Brit.* a person who buys and slaughters worn-out domestic animals, as horses, for animal food or fertilizer.
2. *Dial. Eng.* a worn-out domestic animal, as a horse.

leucippotomy   the cutting of white horses on hillsides, thought to be a symbol of Odin, as near Uffington, England.

HOUSES

domatophobia   the abnormal fear of being in a house.

ecophobia, oecophobia, oikophobia   **1.** an abnormal fear of home surroundings.
2. an aversion to home life.

gazumping   *Brit.* swindling or cheating by raising the agreed-upon price of a house before closing agreements have been signed.

HUMOR

Atticism   a concise witticism or well-turned phrase. —**Atticist,** *n.*

buffoonism   **1.** a tendency to amuse others by tricks, jokes, unusual gestures, and strange gestures.
2. a tendency toward coarse joking. Also called **buffoonery.** —**buffoon,** *n.* —**buffoonish,** *adj.*

facetiae   **1.** amusing or witty writings and remarks.
2. coarsely witty stories or books. —**facetious,** *adj.*

jocosity   **1.** the habit of joking or jesting.
2. a joke or a jest.   .
3. the state or quality of humorousness or playfulness. —**jocose,** *adj.*

Pantagruelism   the habit of dealing with serious matters in a spirit of good and sometimes cynical good humor. [allusion to Rabelais' satirical novels *Gargantua* (1534) and *Pantagruel* (1532), esp. to the behavior of Gargantua's huge son] —**Pantagruelian,** *adj.*

HUNTING

cynegetics   the sport of hunting. —**cynegetic,** *adj.*

venation   *Archaic.* the sport or occupation of hunting. —**venatic, venatical, venational,** *adj.*

venerer   a hunter.

venery   **1.** *Archaic.* the sport, practice, or art of hunting or the chase.
2. the animals that are hunted.

HYPNOSIS

Mesmerism   **1.** hypnosis as induced by Dr. F. A. Mesmer through animal magnetism, a 19th cent. therapy.

2. hypnotism.

3. a compelling attraction; fascination. —**mesmerization,** *n.* —**mesmerist, mesmerizer,** *n.*

odylism   the theory of od, a hypothetical force formerly held to pervade all nature and to reveal itself in magnetism, mesmerism, chemical action, etc. —**odylic,** *adj.*

I

IDEAS

conceptualism   the philosophical doctrine that universals exist only in the mind, a compromise between nominalism and realism. —**conceptualist,** *n.* —**conceptualistic,** *adj.* Cf. **nominalism, realism.**

counteridea   *Rare.* in logic, a contrary.

misocainea   an abnormal dislike for new ideas.

neoteric   a modern person; one accepting new ideas and practices.

sophiology   **1.** the science of ideas.
2. Sophianism.

IDIOCY

cretinism   *Med.* a congenital deficiency of the thyroid secretion causing deformity and idiocy. —**cretinoid,** *adj.* —**cretinous,** *adj.*

idiotism   **1.** the condition of an idiot, esp. an extreme degree of mental deficiency, usu. a mental age of less than three or four years; idiocy.
2. idiotic conduct or action, esp. in a normal person. —**idiotic,** *adj.*

mongolism   *Med.* the abnormal condition of a child born mentally deficient, with a flattened skull, narrow slanting eyes, and a short, flat-bridged nose. Also called **Down's syndrome.** —**mongolic,** *adj.*

IMAGES

effigiation   *Archaic.* the creation of an image or effigy of something. —**effigiate,** *v.*

iconoclasm   **1.** the practice of destroying images, esp. those created for religious veneration.
2. the practice of opposing cherished beliefs or traditional institutions as being founded on error or superstition.
3. the doctrines underlying these practices. —**iconoclast,** *n.* —**iconoclastic,** *adj.*

iconolatry   the worship or adoration of images. Also called **idolatry.** —**iconolater,** *n.*

iconology 1. the study of images.
  2. iconography. —**iconologist,** *n.* —**iconological,** *adj.*

IMPROVEMENT

eugenics 1. the science of improving a breed or species through the careful selection of parents.
  2. the science applied to the improvement of the human race. —**eugenicist,** *n.* —**eugenic,** *adj.*

deoppilation *Rare.* the removal of obstacles and obstructions.

meliorism the doctrine that the world tends to get better or may be made better by human effort. —**meliorist,** *n., adj.* —**melioristic,** *adj.* Cf. **deteriorism.**

INANIMATE OBJECTS

abiology the study of inanimate things.

animatism the assignment to inanimate objects, forces, and plants of personalities and wills, but not souls. —**animatistic,** *adj.* Cf. **animism.**

resistentialism the apparently perverse or spiteful behavior of inanimate objects.

INSANITY

demonianism 1. *Obsolete.* the doctrine of demoniac possession.
  2. *Archaic.* demonomania. —**demonian,** *n., adj.*

demonomania *Med.* a monomania in which a person believes he is possessed of devils. Also called **demonopathy.**

diabolepsy *Med., Obsolete.* a state in which a person believes he is possessed by a devil or has been endowed with supernatural powers.

lyssophobia an abnormal fear of becoming insane.

maniaphobia an abnormal fear of madness.

megalomania 1. *Med.* a form of mental illness characterized by the unreasonable conviction in the patient of his own greatness, goodness, power or wealth.
  2. an obsession with extravagant or grand actions. —**megalomaniac,** *n., adj.*

paranoidism *Med.* a state resembling paranoia. —**paranoid,** *n., adj.*

INSECTS

acarophobia a fear of itching or of those insects which cause it.

coleopterology the branch of entomology that studies beetles and weevils. —**coleopterological,** *adj.*

dipterology the branch of entomology that studies the order of insects **Diptera,** including houseflies, mosquitoes, and gnats.

entomology   the branch of zoology that studies insects. —**entomologist,** *n.* —**entomological,** *adj.*

hemipterology   the branch of entomology that studies the order *Hemiptera,* including bedbugs, squashbugs, and aphids.

hymenopterology   the branch of entomology that studies the order *Hymenoptera,* including bees, wasps, and ants.

neuropterology   the branch of entomology that studies the order *Neuroptera,* including lacewings and ant lions.

orthopterology   the branch of entomology that studies the order *Orthoptera,* including cockroaches, grasshoppers, and mantises.

pediculophobia   an abnormal fear of lice. Also called **phthiriophobia.**

pediculosis   an infestation with lice; lousiness. —**pediculous,** *adj.*

ISLAM

Alcoranist   a strict follower of the Koran.

Babism, Babiism   the doctrines and practices of a 19th cent. Persian sect that formed the basis for the current Baha'i organization, regarded as heretical by orthodox Muslims because its leader proclaimed himself to be the Imam Mahdi, the expected twelfth Imam of the Shiite sect, who would establish justice on earth. —**Babist,** *n.*

Islamism   the religion of Islam; Mohammedanism. —**Islamist,** *n.* —**Islamitic,** *adj.*

Kaabism   the tradition in Islam of venerating a shrine in Mecca through pilgrimage and prayers made after turning in its direction. —**Kaaba,** *n., adj.*

Senusism, Sanusism   a 19th cent. Islamic brotherhood observing a strict and ascetic religious orthodoxy and practicing militant political activity. Also called **Senusiya, Sanusiya.** —**Senusi, Sanusi,** *n.*

Shiism   the doctrines and practices of Shi'a one of the two major branches of Islam, regarding Ali, the son-in-law of Muhammed, as the Prophet's legitimate successor. —**Shiite,** *n., adj.*

Sufiism, Sufism   the beliefs and practices of an ascetic, retiring, and mystical sect in Islam. —**Sufi,** *n., adj.*

Sunnism   the doctrines and practices of the largest of the two major branches of Islam, regarding as legitimate the first four caliphs after Muhammed's death and stressing the importance of the traditional portion of Muslim law (the Sunna). —**Sunnite,** *n., adj.*

talismanist   *Obsolete.* a Muslim holy man.

J

JOBS

arbalist, arbalest   a crossbowman. Also called **arcubalist.**

cameist   **1.** a maker of cameos.
2. a collector of or authority on cameos.

chekist   a member of the Russian secret police called *Cheka.*

dragoman   an interpreter, esp. in the Middle East.

modiste, modist   a maker and seller of fashionable gowns and millinery for women.

oecist, oekist   a colonizer.

paysagist   a painter of landscapes.

vitrailist   a maker or designer of stained glass.

JUDAISM

cabalism   **1.** the principles or doctrines of the cabala, a system of theosophy, theurgy, and mystical Scriptural interpretive methods originated by rabbis about the 8th cent. and affecting later Christian thinkers.
2. an interpretation made according to these doctrines.
3. an extreme traditionalism in theological concepts or Biblical interpretation.
4. obscurantism, esp. that resulting from the use of obscure vocabulary. —**cabalist,** *n.* —**cabalistic,** *adj.*

Haggada, Haggadah, Aggada, Aggadah   **1.** the explanatory matter in rabbinic and Talmudic literature, interpreting or illustrating the Scriptures.
2. a book in which is printed the liturgy for the Seder service. —**haggadic, haggadical,** *adj.*

Haggadist   **1.** a student of the Haggada.
2. a writer of the Haggada.

Halaka, Halakah, Halachah   the entire body of Jewish law, comprising Biblical laws, oral laws transcribed in the Talmud, and subsequent codes altering traditional teachings. —**Halakist, Halachist,** *n.* —**Halakic,** *adj.*

Hasidism, Chasidism   **1.** the beliefs and practices of a mystical sect, founded in Poland about 1750, characterized by an emphasis on prayer, religious zeal, and joy. —**Hasidic,** *adj.* —**Hasidim,** *n. pl.*
2. the beliefs and practices of a pious sect founded in the 3rd cent. B.C. to resist Hellenizing tendencies and to promote strict observance of Jewish laws and rituals. Also called **Assideanism.**

Hebraism the thought, spirit, and practice characteristic of the Hebrews. —**Hebraist,** *n.* —**Hebraistic, Hebraistical,** *adj.*

Messianism **1.** a belief in a Messiah coming to deliver the Jews, restore Israel, and rule righteously, first mentioned by the Prophet Isaiah.
2. the Christian belief that Jesus Christ was the Messiah prophesied.
3. the vocation of a Messiah. —**Messianic,** *adj.*

Phariseeism, Pharisaism **1.** the beliefs and practices of an ancient Jewish sect, esp. strictness of religious observance, close adherence to oral laws and traditions, and belief in an afterlife and a coming Messiah. Cf. **Sadduceeism.**
2. (l.c.) the behavior of a sanctimonious and self-righteous person. —**Pharisee, pharisee** *n.* —**Pharisaic, pharisaic,** *adj.*

Philonism the philosophy of Philo Judaeus, 1st cent. B.C. Alexandrian, combining Judaism and Platonism and acting as a precursor of Neoplatonism. —**Philonian,** *adj.* —**Philonic,** *adj.*

rabbinism the beliefs, practices, and precepts of the rabbis of the Talmudic period. —**rabbinic, rabbinical,** *adj.*

Sabbatarianism the beliefs and principles underlying a strict observance of the Sabbath. —**Sabbatarian,** *n., adj.*

Sadduceeism, Sadducism the beliefs and practices of an ancient Jewish sect made up largely of the priestly aristocracy and opposing the Pharisees in both political and doctrinal matters, esp. literal and less legalistic interpretation of the Jewish law, rejection of the rabbinical and prophetic traditions, and denying immortality, retribution in a future life, and the existence of angels. —**Sadducee,** *n.* —**Sadducean,** *adj.*

Talmudism **1.** the teachings of the collection of Jewish law and tradition called the Talmud.
2. the observance of and adherence to these teachings. —**Talmudist,** *n.* —**Talmudic,** *adj.*

Torah **1.** the first five books of the Old Testament; the Pentateuch.
2. a scroll of these scriptures in Hebrew used for liturgical purposes. Also called **Sepher Torah.**
3. the entire body of Jewish law and tradition as found in the Old Testament and the Talmud.

tosaphist a writer of tosaphoth.

tosaphoth the explanatory and critical glosses made usu. in the margins of Talmudic literature.

Zealotism the beliefs, activities, and spirit of an ancient radical group in Judea that advocated overthrowing Roman rule.

Zionism a worldwide Jewish movement for the establishment in Palestine of a national homeland for Jews. —**Zionist, Zionite,** *n.* —**Zionist, Zionistic,** *adj.*

K

KILLING

amicicide　*Rare.* **1.** the murder of one friend by another.
2. the killer of a friend.

euthanasia　**1.** the act of putting to death without pain a person incurably ill or suffering great pain; mercy killing.
2. an easy, painless death. —**euthanasic,** *adj.*

parricidism　the murder of a parent or close relative. —**parricide,** *n.* —**parricidal,** *adj.*

regicidism　the murder of a king. —**regicide,** *n.* —**regicidal,** *adj.*

tyrannicide　**1.** the killing of a tyrant.
2. the killer of a tyrant. —**tyrannicidal,** *adj.*

KNOWLEDGE

acatalepsy　the Skeptic doctrine that knowledge cannot be certain. —**acataleptic,** *n.* See **Skepticism.**

agnoiology, agnoeology　*Archaic.* the study of human ignorance.

chrestomathics　the teaching of useful knowledge. —**chrestomathic,** *adj.* See also **chrestomathy.**

empiricism　a system of acquiring knowledge that rejects all *a priori* knowledge and relies solely upon observation, experimentation, and induction. Also called **empirism.** —**empiricist,** *n., adj.*

encyclopedism　**1.** the command of a wide range of knowledge.
2. the writings and thoughts of the 18th cent. French Encyclopedists, esp. an emphasis on scientific rationalism. —**encyclopedist,** *n.*

epistemology　the branch of philosophy that studies the origin, nature, methods, validity, and limits of human knowledge. —**epistemologist,** *n.* —**epistemological,** *adj.* —**epistemic,** *adj.*

epistemophilia　an excessive love or reverence for knowledge. —**epistemophiliac,** *n., adj.*

gnosiology, gnoseology　the philosophy of knowledge and the human faculties for learning. —**gnosiological, gnoseological,** *adj.*

Illuminism　**1.** the beliefs or claims of certain religious groups or sects that they possess special religious enlightenment. —**Illuminati,** *n.*
2. (*l.c.*) the claim to possess superior knowledge. —**Illuminist, illuminist,** *n.*

intellectualism　**1.** the exercise of the intellect.
2. a devotion to intellectual activities.
3. an excessive emphasis on intellect and a resulting neglect of emotion. —**intellectualistic,** *adj.*

intuitionalism 1. *Metaphysics.* the doctrine that the reality of perceived external objects is known intuitively, without the intervention of a representative idea.
2. *Metaphysics.* the doctrine that knowledge rests upon axiomatic truths discerned intuitively.
3. *Ethics.* the doctrine that moral values and duties can be perceived directly. Also called **intuitionism. —intuitionalist,** *n.* **—intuitionist,** *n.*

maieutics the method used by Socrates in bringing forth knowledge through questions and insistence upon close and logical reasoning. **—maieutic,** *adj.*

mentalism the doctrine that objects of knowledge have no existence except in the mind of the perceiver. **—mentalist,** *n.* **—mentalistic,** *adj.* See **Berkeleyism.**

misology a hatred of reason, reasoning, and knowledge. **—misologist,** *n.*

pansophism 1. the possession of universal knowledge. See **pansophy.**
2. the claim to such enlightenment. **—pansophist,** *n.* **—pansophistical,** *adj.*

pansophy 1. a universal wisdom or encyclopedic learning.
2. a system of universal knowledge; pantology. **—pansophic,** *adj.*

pantology a systematic survey of all branches of knowledge. **—pantologist,** *n.* **—pantologic, pantological,** *adj.*

philonoist 1. *Rare.* a lover of learning.
2. (*cap.*) an advocate of Philonism. Also called **Philonist.**

polyhistor a person of exceptionally wide knowledge; polymath. **—polyhistoric,** *adj.*

polymathy the possession of learning in many fields. **—polymath,** *n., adj.*

sciolism a superficial knowledge, esp. when pretentiously revealed. **—sciolist,** *n.* **—sciolistic, sciolous,** *adj.*

sciosophy a supposed knowledge of natural and supernatural forces, usu. based upon tradition rather than ascertained fact, as astrology and phrenology. **—sciosophist,** *n.*

specialism 1. a devotion or restriction to a particular pursuit, branch of study, etc.
2. a field of specialization within a science or area of knowledge, as otology within medicine. **—specialist,** *n.* **—specialistic,** *adj.*

L

LABOR

Luddism the beliefs of bands of early 19th cent. English workmen that attempted to prevent the use of laborsaving machinery by destroying it. Also called **Ludditism. —Luddite,** *n.*

Whitleyism a system of permanent voluntary boards in English industries in which both management and workers settle matters of wages, hours, etc. —**Whitley Council,** *n.*

LAND

absenteeism the practice of extensive or permanent absence from their property by owners. —**absentee,** *n.*

fiefdom *Medieval Hist.* the land over which a person exercises control after vows of vassalage and service to an overlord. See **feudalism.**

LANGUAGE

Americanism a word, phrase, or idiom peculiar to American English. Cf. **Anglicism.**

aptotic of or relating to languages that have no grammatical inflections.

Aramaism a word, phrase, idiom, or other characteristic of Aramaic occurring in a corpus written in another language.

aulicism *Obsolete.* a courtly phrase or expression. —**aulic,** *adj.*

Bascology the study of the Basque language and culture.

bilingualism 1. the ability to speak two languages.
2. the use of two languages, as in a community. Also called **bilinguality.** —**bilingual, bilinguist,** *n.* —**bilingual,** *adj.*

Briticism a word, idiom, or phrase characteristic of or restricted to British English.

Celticism 1. a word, phrase, or idiom characteristic of Celtic languages in material written in another language.
2. a Celtic custom or usage.

Chaldaism an idiom or other linguistic feature peculiar to Chaldean, esp. in material written in another language. —**Chaldaic,** *n., adj.*

colloquialism a word, phrase, or expression characteristic of ordinary or familiar conversation rather than formal speech or writing, as "She's out" for "She is not at home." —**colloquial,** *adj.*

cryptography 1. the science or study of secret writing, esp. code and cipher systems.
2. the procedures and methods of making and using secret languages, as codes or ciphers. —**cryptographer,** *n.* —**cryptographist,** *n.* —**cryptographic, cryptographical, cryptographal,** *adj.*

cryptology 1. the study of, or the use of, methods and procedures for translating and interpreting codes and ciphers; cryptanalysis.
2. cryptography. —**cryptologist,** *n.*

demotist a student of demotic language and writings.

demotic 1. of or relating to the common people; popular.

2. of, pertaining to, or noting the simplified form of hieratic writing used in ancient Egypt.

3. (*cap.*) of, belonging to, or connected with modern colloquial Greek. Also called **Romaic.**

dialecticism **1.** a dialect word or expression.
2. dialectal speech or influence.

Gallicism **1.** a French linguistic peculiarity.
2. a French idiom or expression used in another language.

glottogonist *Linguistics.* an expert on the origin of language. —**glottogonic,** *adj.*

Hebraism **1.** an expression or construction peculiar to Hebrew. —**Hebraist,** *n.*
2. the character, spirit, principles, or customs of the Hebrew people. —**Hebraistic,** *adj.* —**Hebraic,** *adj.*

Hibernianism **1.** an Irish characteristic.
2. an idiom peculiar of Irish English. Also called **Hibernicism.** —**Hibernian,** *adj.*

holophrasis, holophrase the ability, in certain languages, to express a complex idea or entire sentence in a single word, as the imperative *Stop!* —**holophrasm,** *n.* —**holophrastic,** *adj.*

idiolect *Linguistics.* a person's individual speech pattern.

Idoism the advocacy of an artificial language based on Esperanto. —**Ido,** *n.* —**Idoist,** *n.* —**Idoistic,** *adj.*

Latinism **1.** a mode of expression imitative of Latin.
2. a Latin word, phrase, or expression in the midst of material in another language. —**Latinize,** *v.*

lexicography the writing or compiling of dictionaries. —**lexicographer,** *n.* —**lexicographic, lexicographical,** *adj.*

linguistician a person skilled in the science of language. Also called **linguist.**

localism a custom or manner of speaking peculiar to one locality. Also called **provincialism.** —**localist,** *n.* —**localistic,** *adj.*

monoglot a person capable in only one language.

morphology **1.** a branch of linguistics that studies and describes patterns of word formation, including inflection, derivation, and compounding, usu. in a single language.
2. the patterns of a particular language. —**morphologist,** *n.* —**morphological,** *adj.*

pasigraphy **1.** an artificial international language using signs and figures instead of words.
2. any artificial language, as Esperanto. —**pasigraphic,** *adj.*

philology **1.** the study of written records to determine their authenticity, original form, and meaning.

2. linguistics, esp. historical. —**philologist, philologer,** *n.* —**philologic, philological,** *adj.*

phonetics   1. the science or study of speech sounds and their production, transmission, and perception, and their analysis, classification, and transcription.
2. *Linguistics.* the science or study of speech sounds with respect to their role in distinguishing meanings among words.
3. the phonetic system of a particular language. —**phonetician,** *n.* —**phonetic, phonetical,** *adj.* Cf. **phonology.**

phonology *Linguistics.* **1.** the branch of linguistics that studies the history and theory of sound changes in a language or in two or more languages comparatively.
2. the phonetics and phonemics of a language at a stated time; synchronic phonology. —**phonologist,** *n.* —**phonological,** *adj.* See also LINGUISTICS.

Polonist   a specialist in Polish language, literature, and culture.

polyglottism   the ability to use or to speak several languages. —**polyglot,** *n., adj.*

provincialism   a word, phrase, or idiom that is characteristically provincial; localism.

Scotticism, Scoticism, Scottishism   1. a feature characteristic of Scottish English.
2. a predilection for things Scottish.

semantics   *Linguistics.* **1.** the study of the meaning of words.
2. the study of linguistic development by examining and classifying changes in meaning. —**semanticist,** *n.* —**semantic,** *adj.*

sematology   semantics.

semeiology, semiology   the study or science of signs; semantics. —**semeiologist,** *n.* —**semeiologic, semeiological,** *adj.*

Semiticism   a word, phrase, or idiom from a Semitic language, esp. in the context of another language.

semology   semantics.

slangism   a slangy expression or word.

Slavicism   a word, phrase, expression, form, or usage characteristic of a Slavic language, esp. in the context of another language.

Sumerology   the study of the language, history, and archeology of the Sumerians. —**Sumerologist,** *n.*

transatlanticism   a word, phrase, or idiom in English which is common to both Great Britain and the United States.

vernacularism   1. a word, phrase, or idiom from the native and popular language (as opposed to *literary* and *learned*).
2. the use of the vernacular. —**vernacular,** *n., adj.*

Yankeeism 1. a Yankee characteristic or character.
2. *Brit.* a linguistic or cultural trait peculiar to the United States.
3. *U.S. South.* a linguistic or cultural trait peculiar to the states siding with the Union during the Civil War.
4. *U.S. North.* a linguistic or cultural trait peculiar to the New England states.

Yiddishism a word, phrase, or idiom from Yiddish, esp. in the context of another language.

LANGUAGE STYLES

aeolism a tendency to longwindedness. —**aeolistic,** *adj.*

anadiplosis *Rhetoric.* the repetition in the first part of a clause of a word or phrase from the end of the preceding clause or sentence, esp. as a persuasive device.

aposiopesis *Rhetoric.* the deliberate failure to complete a sentence in order to convey exasperation or imply a threat. —**aposiopetic,** *adj.*

battology a futile repetition in speech or writing.

Billingsgate a coarse, vulgar, violent, or abusive language. [allusion to the scurrilous language used by fishwives in Billingsgate market, London]

chiasmus *Rhetoric.* a reversal in the order of words in two otherwise parallel phrases, as "flowers are lovely, love is flowerlike" (Coleridge). —**chiastic,** *adj.*

causticism, causticity a sharp, tart wittiness. Also called **causticness.**

concettism any writing characterized by conceits (*concetti*), as elaborate and fanciful figures of speech, as in the opening lines of T.S. Eliot's "Prufrock."

epigrammatism 1. the composition of brief witty, ingenious, or pointed statements.
2. the composition of short, concise poems, often satirical, displaying a witty or ingenious thought. —**epigrammatist,** *n.* —**epigrammatic,** *adj.*

epiphora *Rhetoric.* the repetition of a word or words at the end of two or more successive clauses, phrases, or verses, as "I should do Brutus wrong and Cassius wrong." Also called **epistrophe.** Cf. **anaphora.**

Euphuism 1. an elaborate prose style invented by John Lyly c. 1580, characterized by bountiful figures of speech, Latinisms, extended similes, frequent antitheses, and highly involved syntax.
2. any similar ornate style of writing or speaking. —**euphuistic,** *adj.* Cf. **Gongorism.**

Gongorism a Spanish verse style invented by the 17th cent. poet Luis de Gongora y Argote, characterized by a studied obscurity, an emphasis on Latin terms and syntax, allusions to classical myths, and lavish use of metaphors, hyperbole, paradoxes, neologisms, and antitheses. Also called **cultismo** or **culteranismo.** —**Gongoristic, Gongoresque,** *adj.*

heterophemism, heterophemy an unconscious tendency to use words other than those intended. Cf. **Spoonerism.**

illeism the tendency in some individuals to refer to themselves in the third person. —**illeist,** *n.*

laconicism, laconism a tendency to use few words to express a great deal; conciseness. —**laconic,** *adj.*

lexiphanicism 1. *Archaic.* the use of excessively learned and bombastic terminology.
2. an instance of this language style. —**lexiphanic,** *adj.*

logorrhea 1. an excessive or abnormal volubility, sometimes incoherent.
2. talkativeness. —**logorrheic,** *adj.*

lucidity the quality, state, or art of clarity in thought and style. —**lucidness,** *n.* —**lucid,** *adj.*

macaronic a piece of prose or verse characterized by a mixture of two languages, as a medieval Christmas carol.

macrology an excessive wordiness.

metaphrasis, metaphrase the practice of making a literal translation from one language into another (as opposed to paraphrase). —**metaphrast,** *n.* —**metaphrastic, metaphrastical,** *adj.*

parrhesia a tendency to boldness and frankness of speech; freedom of expression, as in much modern literature.

pedestrianism a style lacking in vitality, imagination, or distinction; prosiness. —**pedestrian,** *adj.*

pellucidity the quality, state, or art of writing or speaking in a fashion that is easy to understand. —**pellucidness,** *n.* —**pellucid,** *adj.*

periphrasis 1. a roundabout way of speaking or writing; circumlocution.
2. an expression in such fashion. —**periphrastic,** *adj.*

perissology *Archaic.* a pleonasm.

platitudinarianism 1. an addiction to spoken or written expression in platitudes.
2. a staleness or dullness of both language and ideas. —**platitudinarian,** *n.*

pleonasm 1. the use of unnecessary words to express an idea; redundancy.
2. an instance of this, as *true fact.*
3. a redundant word or expression. —**pleonastic,** *adj.*

proverbialism the composing, collecting, or customary use of proverbs. —**proverbialist,** *n.*

psilology a love of vacuous or trivial talk.

Ronsardism the composition of verse after the manner of Ronsard, characterized by neologisms and dialectal forms.

sardonicism a style of speaking or writing characterized by bitter, contemptuous, or scornful derision.

Spoonerism the transposition of initial or other sounds of words, usually by accident, as *check my cash* for *cash my check*. [after the Rev. W. A. Spooner, 1844-1930, noted for such slips] —**spoonerize,** *v.*

stichometry the practice of expressing the successive ideas in a prose composition in single lines corresponding to natural cadences or sense divisions. —**stichometric, stichometrical,** *adj.*

tuism 1. the use of the second person, as in apostrophe.
2. in certain languages, the use of the familiar second person in cases where the formal third person is usually found and expected.
3. an instance of such use.

verbalism 1. a verbal expression, as a word or phrase.
2. the way in which something is worded.
3. a phrase or sentence devoid or almost devoid of meaning.
4. a use of words regarded as obscuring ideas or reality; verbiage.

witticism a remark or expression possessing cleverness in perception and choice of words.
See also RHETORIC.

LAUGHTER

Abderian relating to foolish or excessive laughter. [allusion to Democritus, the laughing philosopher, born in Abdero]

geloscopy, gelotoscopy a form of divination that determines a person's character or future from the way he laughs.

risibility 1. the ability or disposition to laugh.
2. a humorous awareness of the ridiculous and absurd.
3. laughter.

LAW

anomie, anomy, anomia a state or condition of individuals or society characterized by an absence or breakdown of social and legal norms and values, as in the case of an uprooted people. —**anomic,** *adj.*

antinomia, antinomy a real or apparent contradiction in a statute. —**antinomic, antinomian,** *adj.*

antinomianism the theological doctrine maintaining that Christians are freed from both moral and civil law by God's gift of grace. —**antinomian, antinomist,** *n.*

asportator the person who carries away stolen goods. —**asportation,** *n.*

asseveration the solemn affirmation of the truth of a statement. —**asseverative,** *adj.*

avowtry the crime of adultery.

barrator a person guilty of barratry. —**barratrous,** *adj.*

barratry the offense of frequently exciting or stirring up suits and quarrels between others.

battery an intentional act that, directly or indirectly, is the legal cause of a harmful contact with another's person, whether as an unlawful touching or striking or by any substance put into motion by an agressor.

cavear a legal notice to beware; a notice placed on file until the caveator can be heard. —**caveator,** *n.* —**caveatee,** *n.*

compurgation in medieval law, a form of trial wherein a defendant could assert his innocence and then call eleven neighbors to swear to their belief in his innocence, thereby allowing him to go free. Also called *trial by wager of law.* —**compurgator,** *n.* —**compurgatory,** *adj.*

contumacy the contemptuous disobedience of a court order; refusal to submit to authority. —**contumacious,** *adj.*

criminalism an act or action having the character of a crime. Also called **criminality.** —**criminal,** *n., adj.*

culpability 1. the condition of blameworthiness, criminality, censurability.
2. *Obsolete.* guilt. —**culpable,** *adj.*

Draconianism any unreasonable harshness or severity in laws. —**Draconian,** *adj.*

fiduciary a person to whom property or power is entrusted for the benefit of another. —**fiducial,** *adj.*

Justinianist an expert on the codification and revision of Roman laws ordered by the 6th cent. Byzantine emperor Justinian. —**Justinian code,** *n.*

latrocination a robbery committed by force or violence; pillage. Also called **latrocinium.**

legalism a strict and usu. literal adherence to the law. —**legalistic,** *adj.*

litigiomania a compulsion for involving oneself in legal disputes.

litigious excessively inclined to litigation. —**litigiousness,** *n.*

mayhem, maihem 1. in early common law, the crime of wilfully inflicting an injury which deprived the victim of the ability to defend himself.
2. a malicious injury which disables or disfigures the person of another.

nomism the practice of religious legalism, esp. the basing of standards of good actions upon the moral law.

nomography 1. the art of drafting laws.
2. a treatise on the drawing up of laws. —**nomographer,** *n.* —**nomographic,** *adj.*

nomology the science of law. —**nomologist,** *n.* —**nomological,** *adj.*

pandectist 1. the writer of a complete code of the laws of a country.
2. the writer of a complete digest of materials on a subject. —**pandect,** *n.*

pettifogger 1. a lawyer whose practice is of a small or petty character; a lawyer of little importance.
2. a shyster lawyer. —**pettifoggery,** *n.*

publicist   an expert in public or international law.

symbolaeography   the drawing up of legal documents. —**symbolaeographer,** *n.*

LEARNING

academicism   **1.** the mode of teaching or of procedure in a private school, college, or university.
2. a tendency toward traditionalism or conventionalism in art, literature, music, etc.
3. any attitudes or ideas that are learned or scholarly but lacking in worldliness, common sense, or practicality. Also called **academism.** —**academic,** *n., adj.* —**academist,** *n.*

academism   **1.** the philosophy of the school founded by Plato.
2. academicism. —**academist,** *n.* —**academic, academical,** *adj.*

didacticism   **1.** the practice of valuing literature, etc., primarily for its instructional content.
2. an inclination to teach or lecture others too much, esp. preaching and moralizing.
3. a pedantic, dull method of teaching. —**didact,** *n.* —**didactic,** *adj.*

monism   *Epistemology.* a theory that the object and datum of cognition are identical.

didactics   the art or science of teaching.

Froebelist   a person who supports or uses the system of kindergarten education developed by Friedrich Froebel, 1782-1852, German educational reformer. Also called **Froebelian.**

pedagogics, paedogogics   the science or art of teaching or education. —**pedagogue, pedagog,** *n.* —**pedagogic, pedagogical,** *adj.*

pedagogism   **1.** the art of a teacher.
2. teaching that is pedantic, dogmatic, and formal.

pedagogy   **1.** the function or work of a teacher; teaching. —**pedagogue,** *n.*
2. the art or method of teaching; pedagogics. —**pedagogist,** *n.*

pedanticism   **1.** the character or practices of a pedant, as excessive display of learning.
2. a slavish attention to rules, details, etc. —**pedantry,** *n.* —**pedant,** *n.* —**pedantic,** *adj.*

propaedeutics   the basic principles and rules preliminary to the study of an art or science. —**propaedeutic, propaedeutical,** *adj.*

educationist   **1.** *Brit.* an educator.
2. a specialist in the theory and methods of education. Also called **educationalist.**

tyrology   *Rare.* a set of instructions for beginners.

LEAVES

defoliant   a preparation for defoliating plants and trees, esp. for agricultural or military purposes.

defoliation   the loss or shedding of leaves, esp. prematurely. —**defoliate,** *v., adj.*

effoliation   the removal of leaves from a tree or shrub.

LIES AND LYING

accismus   *Rhetoric.* an affected or false refusal.

autothaumaturgist   one who pretends to be notable or mysterious.

mythomania   *Psychiatry.* an abnormal propensity to lie, exaggerate, or twist the truth.

mythophobia   an abnormal fear of making false statements.

pseudomania   *Psychiatry.* **1.** pathological lying.
2. a false or pretended mental disorder.

Sinonism   an act of perfidy. [allusion to Sinon, whose false tale persuaded the Trojans to allow the wooden horse within the walls of Troy]

LIFE

abiogenesis   *Biology.* the production of living organisms from inanimate matter. Also called **spontaneous generation.** —**abiogenetic,** *adj.*

biochemistry   the study of the chemical processes that take place in living organisms. —**biochemist,** *n.* —**biochemical,** *adj.*

cytogenetics   the branch of biology that studies the structural basis of heredity and variation in living organisms from the points of view of cytology and genetics. —**cytogeneticist,** *n.* —**cytogenetic, cytogenetical,** *adj.*

cytopathology   *Med.* the branch of pathology that studies the effects of disease on the cellular level. —**cytopathologic, cytopathological,** *adj.*

macrobiotics   the branch of biology that studies longevity. —**macrobiosis,** *n.* —**macrobiotist,** *n.*

mechanism   *Philosophy.* the theory or doctrine that all the phenomena of the universe, esp. life, can ultimately be explained in terms of physics and chemistry, and that the difference between organic and inorganic lies only in degree. —**mechanist,** *n.* —**mechanistic,** *adj.*

parthenogenesis   *Biology.* the development of an egg or seed without fertilization. —**parthenogenetic,** *adj.*

physiology   the branch of biology that studies the functions and vital processes of living organisms. —**physiologist,** *n.* —**physiological,** *adj.*

vitalism   **1.** *Philosophy.* the doctrine that phenomena are only partly controlled by mechanistic forces and are in some measure self-determining.
2. *Biology.* the doctrine that the life in living organisms is caused and

sustained by a vital principle that is distinct from all physical and chemical forces. —**vitalist,** *n.* —**vitalistic,** *adj.* Cf. **mechanism.**

zoism 1. *Philosophy.* a doctrine that the phenomena of life are controlled by a vital principle, as Bergson's *elan vital.*
2. a high regard for animal life.
3. a belief in animal magnetism. —**zoist,** *n.* —**zoistic,** *adj.*

LIGHT

lithophany the process of impressing porcelain objects, as lamp bases, with figures that become translucent when light is placed within or behind them. —**lithophany,** *n.* —**lithophanic,** *adj.*

lucubration 1. the practice of reading, writing or studying at night, esp. by artificial light; to "burn the midnight oil."
2. the art or practice of writing learnedly. —**lucubrator,** *n.* —**lucubrate,** *v.*

phengophobia an abnormal fear of daylight.

photometry the measurement of the intensity of light. —**photometrician, photometrist,** *n.* —**photometric,** *adj.*

photophily the tendency to thrive in strong light, as plants.

photopathy a pathologic effect produced by light, as swelling (*photoncia*).

photophobia 1. an abnormal fear of light.
2. a painful sensitivity to light, esp. visually. Also called **photodysphoria.**
3. a tendency to thrive in reduced light, as plants.

LIGHTNING

astraphobia an abnormal fear of lightning. Also called **astrapophobia.**

keraunography, ceraunography the recording of occurrences of lightning and thunder on a time scale attached to a revolving drum. —**keraunograph,** *n.* —**keraunographic,** *adj.*

keraunophobia, ceraunophobia an abnormal fear of thunder and lightning.

keraunoscopia, ceraunoscopia, keraunoscopy a form of divination involving thunder and lightning.
See also THUNDER.

LINGUISTICS

allomorphic referring to any of the alternate contextually determined phonetic shapes of a morpheme, as *es* in *dresses,* which is an allomorph of the English plural morpheme. See **morphemics, morpheme.** —**allomorph,** *n.*

allophonic referring to any of the alternate contextually determined phonetic shapes of a phoneme, as the *p* in *spit* and *tip,* which are allophones of the English phoneme */P/.* See **phonemics, phoneme.** —**allophone,** *n.*

diachronism, diachrony the study and description of the change or development in the structural systems of a language over a stated period of time. Also called **historical linguistics.** —**diachronic,** *adj.* Cf. **synchronic linguistics.**

dialectology   **1.** the study of dialects and dialect features.
2. the linguistic features of a dialect. —**dialectologist,** *n.* —**dialectician,** *n.*

echoism   **1.** the formation of sounds like those in nature; onomatopoesis.
2. the tendency of paired sounds to become more similar phonetically, as the *d* sound in iced tea has become a *t;* assimilation. —**echoic,** *adj.*

glossology   an archaic term for linguistics.

glottochronology   a statistical and lexical study of two languages deriving from a common source to determine the time of their divergence, as English and German. —**glottochronologist,** *n.* —**glottochronological,** *adj.*

glottology   the science of linguistics.

morphemics   the study and description of the morphemes of a language. —**morphemicist,** *n.*

morpheme   any of the minimal grammatical units of a language that cannot be divided into smaller independent grammatical parts, as *wait* and -*ed* in *waited,* but that can have alternate phonetic shapes. See **allomorphic.** —**morphemic,** *adj.*

morphophoneme   **1.** a class of phonemes that are allomorphs of the same morpheme, as the *f* and *v* in *knife* and *knives.*
2. the designation of the class by the arbitrary selection of one of its members, as F in *knife* and *knives.* —**morphophonemic,** *adj.*

morphophonemics   **1.** the study of the relations between morphemes and their phonetic realizations, components, or distribution contexts.
2. the body of data concerning these relations in a specific language. —**morphophonemicist, .n.** —**morphophonemic,** *adj.*

phoneme   any of a small set of basic units of sound, different for every language, by which utterances are represented. In English, the difference in sound and meaning between *tip* and *dip* indicates the existence of the alveolar phonemes / t / and / d /. —**phonemic,** *adj.*

phonemics   **1.** the study and description of phonemes and phonemic systems.
2. the phonemic system of a given language. —**phonemicist,** *n.*

psycholinguistics   the study of the relationships between language and the behavioral mechanisms of its users, esp. in language learning by children. —**psycholinguist,** *n.* —**psycholinguistic,** *adj.*

structuralism   an emphasis in research and description upon the systematic relations of formal distinctions in a given language. Also called **structural linguistics.** —**structuralist,** *n.*

synchronic linguistics   the study of the phonological, morphological, and syntactic features of a language at a stated time. Also called **descriptive linguistics.** Cf. **diachronism.**

transformationalist 1. an advocate or student of the theory of transformational grammar.
2. referring to a system of grammatical analysis that uses transformations of base sentences to explain the relations between thought and its syntactic manifestation and to express the relations between elements in a sentence, clause, or phrase, or between different forms of a word or phrase, as active or passive forms of a verb.

vocalism *Phonetics.* the system of vowels in a given language.

LITERARY STUDY

criticism 1. the act or art of analyzing the quality of something, esp. a literary or artistic work, a musical or dramatic performance, etc.
2. a critical comment, article, or essay; critique. —**critic,** *n.*

epistolography the art or practice of writing letters. —**epistolographic,** *adj.*

paleography 1. ancient forms of writing, as in inscriptions, documents, and manuscripts.
2. the study of ancient writings, including decipherment, translation, and determination of age and date. —**paleographer,** *n.* —**paleographic,** *adj.*

scholiast an ancient commentator on the classics, esp. the writing of marginalia (*Scholia*) on grammatical and interpretive cruxes. —**scholiastic,** *adj.*

storiology the systematic study of folk lore and folk literature, esp. concerning origin and transmission. —**storiologist,** *n.*

LITERATURE

anecdotalism 1. the writing or telling of short narratives concerning an interesting, amusing, or curious incident or event.
2. an excessive use of anecdotes, as sometimes in the conversation of the aged. —**anecdotalist,** *n.*

antiphrasis the satirical or humorous use of a word or phrase to convey an idea exactly opposite to its real significance, as Shakespeare's "honorable men" for Caesar's murderers. —**antiphrastic,** *adj.*

belletrism, belles-lettrism the view that literature is a fine art, esp. as having a purely aesthetic function. —**belletrist,** *n.* —**belles lettre,** *n.* —**belletristic,** *adj.*

bowdlerism the expurgation of a literary work in a highly prudish manner. —**bowdlerize,** *v.*

centonism the practice, esp. in verse, of writing by arranging quotations from other authors. Also called **centonization.** —**cento,** *n.* —**centonical,** *adj.*

classicalism 1. an imitation of Greek or Roman literature.
2. classicism. —**classicalize,** *v.*

cloacal referring to literature intentionally filled with obscenity and indecency.

genteelism   **1.** a polished style and graceful form in literary works.
  2. false standards of refinement.
  3. a word thought by its user to be socially superior to a common term, as *serviette* for *napkin.*

gothicism   a style in fictional literature characterized by gloomy settings, violent or grotesque action, and a mood of decay, degeneration, and decadence. —**gothicist,** *n.* —**gothic,** *adj.*

juvenilia   **1.** the literary compositions produced in an author's youth.
  2. literary productions intended for the young.

Kiplingism   **1.** a style resembling or having the features of the literary style of Rudyard Kipling.
  2. an attitude of superiority over and sympathy for nonwhite peoples, as found in "Gunga Din." —**Kiplingesque,** *adj.*

melodramaticism   an emphasis in narrative or dramatic literary works on the sensational in situation or action. —**melodramatist,** *n.* —**melodramatic,** *adj.*

mimesis   an imitation, used in literary criticism to indicate Aristotle's theory of imitation. —**mimetic,** *adj.*

parody   **1.** a humorous or satirical imitation of a serious piece of literature, musical composition, person, etc.
  2. the genre of literary composition represented by such imitations.
  3. a poor or feeble imitation. —**parodist,** *n.* —**parodistic,** *adj.*

regionalism   a quality in literature that is the product of its fidelity to a particular geographical section, accurately representing its habits, speech, manners, history, folklore, and beliefs, as Thomas Hardy and Wessex. —**regionalist,** *n.* —**regionalistic,** *adj.*

teratology   **1.** a type of mythmaking or story telling in which monsters and marvels are featured.
  2. a collection of such stories. —**teratologist,** *n.* —**teratological,** *adj.*

sillography   the writing of satires. —**sillographer,** *n.*

sentimentalism   an excessive indulgence in sentiment or emotionalism, predominance of feeling over reason and intellect, as the death scene of Little Nell in Dickens' *Old Curiosity Shop.* —**sentimentalist,** *n.*

sensationalism   **1.** the use of subject matter, language, or style designed to amaze or thrill.
  2. such subject matter, language, or style itself. —**sensationalist,** *n.* —**sensationalistic,** *adj.*

Zolaism   **1.** an overemphasis on the coarser sides of life.
  2. the objective types of naturalism and determinism underlying Zola's novelistic methods.

M

MAGIC

abracadabrism a reliance upon incantations or charms, often inscribed upon amulets, to ward off calamity. —**abracadabra,** *n.*

apotropaism the acting out of magic rites or the recital of incantatory formulas to ward off evil. —**apotropaic,** *adj.*

gramarye, gramary **1.** any book of occult learning.
   2. occult learning, magic.

illusionist a conjurer or magician who creates illusions, as by sleight of hand.

jujuism an African variety of magical fetishism characterized by the wearing of an exotic amulet called a *juju.* —**jujuist,** *n.*

obeahism **1.** a kind of sorcery practiced by the Negroes of Africa, the West Indies, and elsewhere. Also called **obi** and **obism.**
   2. the wearing of an obeah, a fetish or charm. Also called **obi.**

powwowism the belief among American Indians that a ceremony characterized by magic, feasting, and dancing can cure disease, ensure the success of a hunt or battle, etc. —**powwow,** *n.*

prestidigitation the art of legerdemain; sleight of hand. —**prestidigitator,** *n.* —**prestidigitatorial, prestidigitatory,** *adj.*

sorcery the art, practices, or spells of a person who is supposed to exercise supernatural powers through the aid of evil spirits; black magic; witchery. —**sorcerer,** *n.* —**sorcerous,** *adj.*

talisman **1.** an object believed to possess occult powers, worn as an amulet or charm.
   2. any amulet or charm. —**talismanic,** *adj.*

theurgist a magician who practices the art or science of persuading or compelling a supernatural being to do or refrain from doing something. —**theurgy,** *n.* —**theurgic, theurgical,** *adj.*

voodooism, voudouism **1.** the religious rites or practices, including magic or sorcery, of West Indian Negroes.
   2. the practice of sorcery. —**voodooist,** *n.*

wizardry the art or practice of a wizard; sorcery; magic. —**wizard,** *n., adj.*

Zendicism **1.** *Middle East.* the practice of atheism.
   2. *Middle East.* the practice of heretical magic, esp. with fire. —**Zendic, Zendik,** *n.* —**Zendaic,** *adj.*

MALE

andric of or belonging to a male.

androcentric   emphasizing or highly influenced by masculine points of view or interests.

androcracy   the domination of society and politics by males. —**androcratic,** *adj.* Cf. **gyneocracy.**

androgenesis   *Biology.* the condition of an embryo which contains only paternal chromosomes; male parthenogenesis. —**androgenetic,** *adj.*

androphilia   a preference for males. —**androphilic,** *adj.*

androphobia   **1.** an abnormal fear of men.
2. a hatred of males.

misandry, misandria   in women, an abnormal aversion to males.

MAN

agriology   the study of the customs of uncivilized people, usu. on the comparative level. —**agriologist,** *n.* —**agriological,** *adj.*

animalism   the theory that human beings lack a spiritual nature; animality. —**animalist,** *n.* —**animalistic,** *adj.*

anthropography   the branch of anthropology that describes the varieties of mankind and their geographical distribution. —**anthropographer,** *n.* —**anthropographic,** *adj.*

anthropophobia   an abnormal fear of people.

anthroponomy   *Rare.* the branch of anthropology that studies the interrelation of the laws regulating human behavior and environment. Also called **anthroponomics.** —**anthroponomist,** *n.* —**anthroponomical,** *adj.*

anthropophilic   of insects, attracted to human beings.

anthroposophy   a movement developed from theosophy by Rudolf Steiner, Austrian social philosopher, to develop the faculty of cognition and the awareness of spiritual reality. —**anthroposophist,** *n.* —**anthroposophical,** *adj.*

antilapsarian   a person who denies the doctrine of the fall of man.

demography   the science of vital and social statistics, as of the deaths, births, marriages, etc., of populations. —**demographer,** *n.* —**demographic,** *adj.*

demology   the study of human activities and social conditions. —**demological,** *adj.*

demophobia   a hatred of people.

ergonomics   the study of the various factors affecting man in his working environment. Also called **biotechnology.** —**ergonomic,** *adj.*

ethnography   a branch of anthropology that studies and describes individual human cultures. —**ethnographer,** *n.* —**ethnographic, ethnographical,** *adj.* Cf. **cultural anthropology.**

ethology   *Philosophy.* the science proposed by John Stuart Mill for the study of the character formation in humans. —**ethologic, ethological,** *adj.*

humanism 1. any system or mode of thought or action in which human interests, values, and dignity are taken to be of primary importance, as in moral judgments.
2. a devotion to or study of the humanities.
3. a theory of the life of man as a responsible being behaving independently of a revelation or deity. Also called **naturalistic, scientific,** or **philosophical humanism.** —**humanist,** *n.* —**humanistic,** *adj.*

hylicism, hylism 1. the materialist theories of the early Ionic philosophers. —**hylicist,** *n.*
2. the doctrines concerning the lowest of three Gnostic orders of mankind, the material or fleshly, unsaveable as sons of the devil. Cf. **pneumatism, psychism.**
3. the theory that regards matter as the principle of evil, as in dualistic theology or philosophy. —**hylic,** *adj.*

misanthropism, misanthropy a hatred or distrust of all people. —**misanthrope,** *n.* —**misanthropic,** *adj.*

paleoethnography the ethnography of the prehistoric races of man.

philanthropism 1. an affection for mankind, esp. as manifested in the devotion of work or wealth to persons or socially useful purposes.
2. activity revealing this affection. —**philanthropist,** *n.* —**philanthropical,** *adj.*

pneumatism the doctrines concerning the highest of three Gnostic orders of mankind, those who have received spiritual gifts and are therefore by nature capable of salvation. Cf. **hylicism, psychism.**

psychism the doctrines concerning the second of three Gnostic orders of mankind, those endowed with souls and free wills, saveable through the right use of the latter. Cf. **hylicism, pneumatism.**

sociogram a diagram of the pattern of preferred relationships in a social group. —**sociography,** *n.* —**sociographic,** *adj.*

sociology 1. the science or study of the origin, development, organization, and functioning of human society.
2. the science of fundamental laws of social behavior, relations, institutions, etc. —**sociologist,** *n.* —**sociological,** *adj.*

sociometry the measurement of attitudes of social acceptance or rejection among members of a social grouping. —**sociometrist,** *n.* —**sociometric,** *adj.*

trichotomy *Theology.* the division of human nature into body, soul, and spirit. —**trichotomic, trichotomous,** *adj.*

MANUSCRIPTS

codicology the study of early manuscripts.

diplomatics the critical study of original historical documents, as registers, treaties, and charters, esp. from medieval periods.

diplomatic text   an edition of a manuscript that faithfully reproduces each leaf of the original separately.

palimpsest   a parchment from which earlier writing has been partially or completely removed by scraping so that it may be used again. —**palimpsestic,** *adj.*

scriptorium   a room in a monastery for the writing or copying of manuscripts.

MAPS

atlas   a bound collection of maps.

cartography   the production of maps, including construction of projections, design, compilation, drafting, and reproduction. Also called **chartography, chartology.** —**cartographer,** *n.* — **cartographic,** *adj.*

chorography   1. a description, map, or chart of a particular region or area. **2.** the art of preparing such descriptions or maps. —**chorographer,** *n.* —**chorographic,** *adj.*

topography   1. the detailed mapping or description of the features of a relatively small area, district, or locality. **2.** the relief features or surface configuration of an area. —**topographer,** *n.* —**topographic,** *adj.*

MARRIAGE

adelphogamy   the form of marriage in which brothers have a common wife or wives. —**adelphogamic,** *adj.*

bigamy   the possession of more than one wife or one husband at a time. —**bigamist,** *n.* ⊷**bigamous,** *adj.*

digamism, digamy   a second legal marriage after the termination of a first marriage by death or divorce. Also called **deuterogamy.** — **digamist,** *n.* —**digamous,** *adj.*

endogamy   the custom of marrying only within one's tribe or similar social unit. —**endogamic, endogamous,** *adj.*

exogamy   the practice of marrying only outside one's tribe or similar social unit. —**exogamic, exogamous,** *adj.*

gamomania   1. *Obsolete.* a form of mania characterized by strange and extravagant proposals of marriage. **2.** an excessive longing for the married state.

gamophobia   an abnormal fear of marriage.

misogamy   a hatred of marriage. —**misogamist,** *n.* —**misogamic,** *adj.*

monandry   the custom of marriage to only one man at a time. —**monandrous,** *adj.*

monogamy   the custom of marriage to one wife or one husband at a time. —**monogamous,** *adj.*

morganatic designating or pertaining to a marriage between a man of high rank and a woman of lower station with the stipulation that their offspring will have no claim to his rank or property.

polyandry the practice of having two or more husbands at a time. —**polyandrous,** *adj.*

polygamy the practice of being married to more than one person at a time. —**polygamous,** *adj.*

polygyny the practice of having two or more wives at a time. —**polygynous, polygynious,** *adj.*

MARS

areography *Astronomy.* a topographical description of the planet Mars.

areology *Astronomy.* the observation and study of the planet Mars. —**areologist,** *n.* —**areologic, areological,** *adj.*

MARY

hyperdulia the veneration offered by Roman Catholics to the Virgin Mary as the most exalted of human beings.

Mariolatry an excessive and proscribed veneration of the Virgin Mary. —**Mariolater,** *n.* —**Mariolatrous,** *adj.*

Mariology **1.** the body of belief and doctrine concerning the Virgin Mary. **2.** the study of the Virgin Mary. —**Mariologist,** *n.*

MATHEMATICS

algorism **1.** the Arabic system of numbering.
2. the method of computation with the Arabic figures 1 through 9, plus the zero; arithmetic.
3. the rule for solving a specific kind of arithmetic problem, as finding an average; algorithm. —**algorist,** *n.* —**algorismic,** *adj.*

Euclidean, Euclidian **1.** of or pertaining to Euclid and his postulates.
2. adopting the geometrical postulates of Euclid.

philomathy **1.** *Rare.* a love of learning.
2. a love of mathematics. —**philomath,** *n.* —**philomathic, philomathical, philomathean,** *adj.*

geodesy the branch of applied mathematics that studies the measurement and shape and area of large tracts, the exact position of geographical points, and the curvature, shape, and dimensions of the earth. Also called **geodetics.** —**geodesist,** *n.* —**geodetic, geodetical,** *adj.*

Pythagoreanism, Pythagorism the doctrines and theories of Pythagoras, ancient Greek philosopher and mathematician, and the Pythagoreans, esp. number relationships in music theory, acoustics, astronomy, and geometry (the Pythagorean theorem for right triangles), a belief in metempsychosis, and mysticism based on numbers. —**Pythagorean,** *n.,* *adj.* —**Pythagorist,** *n.*

porism *Rare.* a kind of geometrical proposition of ancient Greek mathematics arising during the investigation of some other proposition either as a corollary or as a condition that will render a certain problem indeterminate. —**porismatic,** *adj.*

topology a branch of mathematics that studies the properties of geometrical forms that remain invariant under certain transformations, as bending or stretching. —**topologist,** *n.* —**topologic, topological,** *adj.*

theorematist a person who discovers or formulates a mathematical theorem. —**theorematic,** *adj.*

MATTER

hylozoism *Philosophy.* the doctrine that all matter has life. —**hylozoist,** *n.* —**hylozoistic,** *adj.*

materialism **1.** the philosophical theory that regards matter and its phenomena as the only reality and explains all occurrences, including the mental, as due to material agencies.
2. attention to or emphasis on material objects, needs, and considerations, with a disinterest in or rejection of intellectual and spiritual values. —**materialist,** *n.* —**materialistic,** *adj.*

monism *Metaphysics.* any of various theories holding that there is only one basic substance or principle that is the ground of reality, as materialism or mechanism. —**monist,** *n.* —**monistic, monistical,** *adj.*

rheology *Chemistry and Geology.* the study of the flow and deformation of colloids, esp. pastes. —**rheologist,** *n.* —**rheologic, rheological,** *adj.*

somatology *Obsolete.* the branch of physics that studies the properties of matter. Cf. **physical anthropology, physical geology.**

MEASUREMENT

baculometry the measurement of distance or lines by means of a stave or staff.

metrology the study and science of measures and weights. — **metrologist,** *n.* —**metrological,** *adj.*

kymography, cymography **1.** the measuring and recording of variations in fluid pressure, as blood pressure.
2. the measuring and recording of the angular oscillations of an aircraft in flight, with respect to an axis or axes fixed in space. —**kymograph,** *n.* —**kymographic,** *adj.*

MEDIA

feuilletonism **1.** the practice of European newspapers of allowing space, usu. at the bottom of a page or pages, for fiction, criticism, columnists, etc.

2. the practice of writing critical or familiar essays for the feuilleton pages. —**feuilletonist,** *n.*

journalism   1. the occupation of reporting, writing, editing, photographing, or broadcasting news.

2. the occupation of running a news organization as a business.

3. the press, printed publications and their employees.

4. an academic program preparing students in reporting, writing, and editing for periodicals and newspapers. —**journalist,** *n.* —**journalistic,** *adj.*

propagandism   1. the action, practice, or art of propagating doctrines, as in the Society for the Propagation of Christian Knowledge.

2. the deliberate spreading of information or ideas to promote or injure a cause, nation, etc. —**propagandist,** *n.* —**propagandistic,** *adj.*

publicist   1. a press agent or expert in public relations.

2. a person who is expert in or writes on current public or political affairs.

videologist   a television enthusiast.

MEDICAL SPECIALTIES

anaplasty   *Obsolete.* any restorative or plastic surgery.

anesthesiology   the branch of medical science that studies anesthesia and anesthetics. —**anesthesiologist,** *n.*

epidemiology   1. the study of the relationships of the various factors determining the frequency and distribution of diseases in a human community.

2. the field of medicine that attempts to determine the exact causes of localized outbreaks of disease. —**epidemiologist,** *n.* —**epidemiologic, epidemiological,** *adj.*

Galenism   the medical system of Galen, a blend of humoralism and Pythagorean number lore. —**galenic,** *adj.* Cf. **humoralism.**

helcology   that branch of medical science that studies ulcers.

heterology   1. an abnormality in tissue structure, arrangement, or manner of formation.

2. the study of abnormalities in tissue structure or organization. —**heterologous,** adj.

iatrology   1. the science of medicine or healing.

2. *Rare.* a treatise on medicine and physicians.

immunology   the branch of biomedical science that studies immunity from disease and the production of such immunity. —**immunologist,** *n.* —**immunologic, immunological,** *adj.*

neonatology   the art and science of diagnosis and treatment of the newborn. —**neonatologist,** *n.*

neuromechanism   the structure and arrangement of the nervous system in relation to function.

neuropathology   the branch of medicine that studies and treats the morphological and other features of nervous system disease. —**neuropathologist,** *n.* —**neuropathologic, neuropathological,** *adj.*

oncology   1. the study of tumors.
2. the totality of medical knowledge concerning tumours. —**oncologist,** *n.* —**oncologic,** *adj.*

organicism   1. the theory that all symptoms are due to organic disease.
2. the theory that each of the organs of the body has its own special constitution. —**organicist,** *n.* —**organicistic,** *adj.* Cf. **psychogenicity, psychosomatics.**

orthopedics   the branch of surgery that is specially concerned with the preservation and restoration of function of the skeletal system, its articulations and associated structures. —**orthopedist,** *n.* —**orthopedic,** *adj.*

osteology   1. the scientific study of bones and their diseases.
2. the totality of medical knowledge concerning the bones of the skeletal system. —**osteologist,** *n.* —**osteologic, osteological,** *adj.*

posology   1. the science of medicinal dosage.
2. a system of dosage. —**posologic, posological,** *adj.*

proctology   the branch of medicine concerned with the disorders of the rectum and anus. —**proctologist,** *n.* —**proctologic, proctological,** *adj.*

psychiatry   the branch of medicine that is concerned with the study, treatment, and prevention of mental illness, using both medical and psychological therapies. —**psychiatrist,** *n.* --**psychiatric,** *adj.*

psychopathology   1. the branch of medicine that studies the causes and nature of mental disease.
2. the pathology of mental disease. —**psychopathologist,** *n.* —**psychopathologic, psychopathological,** *adj.*

psychosomatics   the branch of medical science that studies the relation between psychical and emotional states and physical symptoms. —**psychosomaticist,** *n.* —**psychosomatic,** *adj.*

sarcology   *Archaic.* the anatomy of the soft parts of the body. Cf. **osteology.**

somatism   the belief that emotional and mental disorders are of physical origin and caused by bodily lesions. —**somatist,** *n.*

stethography   1. the use of a recording instrument to register movements of the chest.
2. the use of an instrument to record sounds made by the action of the heart. Also called **phonocardiography.** —**stethographic,** *adj.*

stomatology   the branch of medicine concerned with the diagnosis and treatment of diseases of the mouth. —**stomatologist,** *n.* —**stomatologic, stomatological,** *adj.*

toxicology the scientific study of poisons, their detection and actions, and the treatment of the conditions they cause. —**toxicologist,** *n.* —**toxicologic, toxicological,** *adj.*

traumatology the science of wounds and their treatment. —**traumatologist,** *n.*

virology the branch of medical science that studies viruses and the diseases they cause. —**virologist,** *n.* —**virological,** *adj.*

MEDITATION

contemplation **1.** a full or deep consideration; reflection.
2. the practices of certain monastic groups that withdraw from active life for prayer and meditation. —**contemplative,** *n., adj.*

rumination the act of musing or meditation. —**ruminator,** *n.* —**ruminative,** *adj.*

omphaloskepsis a form of religious meditation practiced by Eastern mystics who stare fixedly at their own navels to induce a mystical trance. Also called **omphalism.**

TM the abbreviation for *transcendental meditation,* a form of contemplation in which the mind, released by the repetition of a mantra, becomes calm and creative. Cf. **Yogism.**

MEMORY

amnesia a loss or lack of memory. —**amnesiac,** *n.* —**amnesic,** *adj.*

anamnesis **1.** a reminiscence.
2. (*cap.*) the section of Christian liturgies rehearsing the sacrifice of Christ and ending "Do this in remembrance of me." —**anamnestic,** *adj.*

cryptomnesia the occurrence in consciousness of images not recognized as produced by the memory and its storage of events and scenes. —**cryptomnesic,** *adj.*

deja vu *Psychology.* the illusion of having previously experienced something actually being encountered for the first time.

mnemonics the process or technique of improving, assisting, or developing the memory. Also called **mnemotechnics.** —**mnemonic,** *adj.*

mnestic related to or concerning memory.

panmnesia the belief that every mental impression remains in the memory.

paramnesia *Psychiatry.* a distortion of memory in which fact and fancy are confused.

MENTAL STATES

corybantism *Med.* a frenzied, sleepless delirium accompanied by wild and frightening hallucinations. Also called **corybantiasm.**

dereism a mode of thinking directed away from reality and toward fantasy without cognizance of ordinary rules of logic. —**dereistic,** *adj.*

hypomania a mild mania.

mania **1.** a type of manic-depressive psychosis, exemplified by rapidly changing ideas, extremes of emotion, and physical overactivity.
2. any violent or abnormal behaviour. —**maniac,** *n.* —**maniacal,** *adj.*

monomania **1.** a partial insanity in which psychotic thinking is confined to one subject or group of subjects.
2. an excessive interest in or enthusiasm for a single thing, idea, or the like; obsession. —**monomaniac,** *n.* —**monomanical,** *adj.*

neolalia **1.** any speech that contains new words unintelligible to a hearer.
2. *Med.* the speech of a psychotic containing new combinations of words unknown to a hearer.

oniomania an excessive desire to buy articles of all kinds. —**oniomaniac,** *n.*

orthopsychiatry the branch of psychiatry that deals with incipient disorders of mind and conduct, esp. in childhood and youth. —**orthopsychiatrist,** *n.* —**orthopsychiatric, orthopsychiatrical,** *adj.*

paralogia, paralogy a reasoning disorder characterized by inappropriate responses to questions and illusional or delusional speech. —**paralogical,** *adj.*

psychoanalysis the method developed by Freud and others for treating neuroses and some other disorders of the mind. —**psychoanalyst,** *n.* —**psychoanalytic,** *adj.*

psychodiagnostics *Clinical Psychology.* **1.** the science or art of making a personality evaluation.
2. the diagnosis of a mental disorder. —**psychodiagnostic,** *adj.*

psychodynamics the systematic study of personality in terms of past and present experiences in relation to motivation. —**psychodynamic,** *adj.*

psycholepsy an attack of mental inertia and hopelessness following a period of elation, esp. in sufferers from neurosis. —**psycholeptic,** *adj.*

psychometrics, psychometry the measurement of mental traits, abilities, and processes. —**psychometrist,** *n.* —**psychometric,** *adj.*

psychopathology *Med.* the science of the diseases of the mind. —**psychopathologist, psychopathist,** *n.* —**psychopathologic, psychopathological,** *adj.*

psychopharmacology the study of drugs that effect emotional and mental states. —**psychopharmacologic, psychopharmacological,** *adj.*

psychostatics **1.** the study of the circumstances under which mental processes occur.
2. the theory that conscious states are made up of elements capable of separating and joining without loss of essential identity. —**psychostatic, psychostatical,** *adj.*

psychotherapy the science or method of treating psychological abnormalities and disorders by psychological techniques, esp. by psychoanaly-

sis, group therapy, or consultation. —**psychotherapist,** *n.* —**psychotherapeu-tic,** *adj.*
See also INSANITY and PSYCHOLOGY.

METEORITES

aerolithology   the science of aerolites, whether meteoric stones or meteorites. Also called **aerolitics.**

astrolithology   the study of meteorites. Also called **meteoritics.**

meteorist   a specialist in the study of meteorites.

MIND

behaviorism   the doctrine that observed behavior provides the only valid data of psychology. —**behaviorist,** *n., adj.* —**behavioristic,** *adj.*

dianoia   the capacity for, process of, or result of discursive thinking. —**dianoetic,** *adj.*

dianoetic   relating to the operation of the mind through logical rather than intuitive thought processes; intellectual activity.

noetic   **1.** of or pertaining to the mind.
2. originating in or apprehended by the intellect. See also **noetics.**

nomology   the science of the laws of the mind. —**nomologist,** *n.* —**nomological,** *adj.*

Pelmanism   a system of mental development exercises.

psychobiology   the study of the relations or interrelations between body and mind, esp. as exhibited in the nervous system. —**psychobiologist,** *n.* —**psychobiologic, psychobiological,** *adj.*

psychology   the science that studies the mind and mental processes, feelings, and desires. —**psychologist,** *n.* —**psychologic, psychological,** *adj.*

psychopathy   a mental disorder. —**psychopath,** *n.* —**psychopathic,** *adj.*

psychophobia   an abnormal fear of the mind.

psychophysics   the branch of psychology that studies the relationships between physical stimuli and resulting sensations and mental states. —**psychophysicist,** *n.* —**psychophysic, psychophysical,** *adj.*

MIRACLES

thaumatology   the study or lore of miracles.

thaumaturgy   the working of wonders or miracles; magic. —**thaumaturgist,** *n.* —**thaumaturge, thaumaturgus,** *n.* —**thaumaturgic, thaumaturgical,** *adj.*

MISSILES

ballistics   **1.** the science or study of the motion of projectiles.
2. the art or science of designing projectiles for maximum flight performance. —**ballistician,** *n.* —**ballistic,** *adj.*

ballistophobia   an abnormal fear of missiles.

MOB

ochlocracy   a rule or government by a mob. —**ochlocrat,** *n.* —**ochlocratic, ochlocratical,** *adj.*

ochlophobia   an abnormal fear of crowds or mobs. —**ochlophobist,** *n.* —**ochlophobic,** *adj.*

MONEY

aphnology   *Rare.* the science of wealth.

bimetallism   the use of two metals jointly as a monetary standard with fixed values in relation to one another. —**bimetallist,** *n.* —**bimetallistic,** *adj.*

cambism, cambistry   the theory and practice of exchange in commerce, esp. in its international features. —**cambist,** *n.*

chrematistics   **1.** the study of wealth.
2. any theory of wealth as measured in money. —**chrematistic,** *adj.*

gombeenism   *Irish.* the lending of money at usurious interest. —**gombeen,** *n.* —**gombeen-man,** *n.*

mammonism   the greedy pursuit of riches.

monometallism   **1.** the use of only one metal, usu. gold or silver, as a monetary standard.
2. the use of only one metal for coinage. —**monometallist,** *n.*

plutolatry   an excessive devotion to wealth.

plutology   *Economics.* the scientific study or theory of wealth.

plutomania   **1.** an abnormal craving for wealth.
2. a mania characterized by delusions of wealth.

symmetalism   a system of coinage based on a unit of two or more metals in combination, each of a specified weight. —**symetallic,** *adj.*

MONKS

anchoritism   the practice of retiring to a solitary place for a life of religious seclusion. —**anchorite, anchoret,** *n.* —**anchoritic, anchoretic,** *adj.*

Benedictinism   **1.** the rule for monastic life composed by St. Benedict, used by several religious orders.
2. membership in an order of monks founded in Monte Cassino by St. Benedict about 530 A.D. —**Benedictine,** *n., adj.*

cenobitism, coenobitism   the action of or motivation for becoming a member of a religious order living in a monastery or convent. —**cenobite,** *n.* —**cenobitic,** *adj.*

Cistercianism   the rule of an order of monks and nuns founded in 1098 in Citeaux, France. —**Cistercian,** *n., adj.*

hebdomadary   a member of a monastic chapter or convent assigned for the period of a week to celebrate the community mass and to lead the recitation of the diurnal.

monachism the religious and work activities of a monk; monasticism. —**monachist**, *adj.* —**monachal**, *adj.*

monasticism a regularized program of religious observance, asceticism, and work followed in a monastery; monachism. —**monastic**, *n., adj.*

religious a member of a monastic order.

MONSTERS

teratism, teratosis, a love of monsters or marvels.

teratoid *Biology.* resembling a monster.

teratology 1. the writing or collecting of fantasies containing monsters and prodigies.
2. *Biology.* the scientific study of monstrosities or abnormal formations in plants or animals. —**teratologist**, *n.* —**teratological**, *adj.*

teratophobia an abnormal fear of monsters or of bearing a monster.

MOODS

cyclothymia a temperament characterized by cyclic alterations of mood between elation and depression. —**cyclothyme**, *n.* — **cyclothymic**, *adj.*

dysthymia extreme anxiety and depression accompanied by obsession. —**dysthymic**, *adj.*

MOON

selenography the branch of astronomy that deals with the charting of the moon's surface. —**selenographer, selenographist**, *n.* —**selenographic, selenographical**, *adj.*

selenolatry the worship of the moon.

selenology the branch of astronomy that studies the physical characteristics of the moon. —**selenologist**, *n.* —**selenological**, *adj.*

selenomancy a form of divination involving observation of the moon.

MOTHER

matricentric tending to move toward or centering upon the mother. Cf. **patricentric**.

matricide 1. the killing of one's mother.
2. the killer of his or her mother. —**matricidal**, *adj.*

momism an excessive attachment and devotion of children to their mothers, resulting in a child's dependence and failure to achieve emotional emancipation.

MOUNTAINS

acrophile   a lover of high mountains; a mountaineer.

orogenesis   the process of the formation of mountains. Also called **orogeny.** —**orogenic,** adj.

orography, oreography   Physical Geog. the study of mountains and mountain systems. —**orographic, orographical,** adj.

orology, oreology   the scientific study of mountains. —**orologist,** n. —**orological,** adj.

orometry   the measurement of mountains. —**orometric,** adj.

orophilous   Botany. referring to orophytes, a class of plants growing on mountains below the timberline.

MOVEMENT

kinetics   the branch of physics that studies the motion of masses in relation to the forces acting on them.

tropism   the tendency of a plant, animal, or part to move or turn in response to an external stimulus, as sunlight or temperature. —**tropistic,** adj.

MURDER

androphonomania   a homicidal mania.

fratricide   **1.** the killing of a brother.
2. the killer of a brother. —**fratricidal,** adj.

homicide   **1.** a general term for murder; the killing of another human being.
2. the murderer of another. —**homicidal,** adj.

sororicide   **1.** the action of killing one's sister.
2. the person who kills a sister. —**sororicidal,** adj.
See also DEATH and KILLING.

MUSIC

agogics   the theory that accent within a musical phrase can also be expressed by modifying the duration of certain notes rather than only by modifying dynamic stress. —**agogic,** adj.

atonalism   **1.** the composition of music without a definite key; dodecaphony.
2. the music so written. Also called **atonality.** —**atonalist,** n. —**atonal, atonalistic,** adj.

choralism   **1.** the techniques of choral singing.
2. the composition of music for chorus illustrative of a cognizance of choral techniques and the possibilities and limitations of choral singing. —**choralistic,** adj.

chromaticism   the use of the chromatic scale or chromatic halftones in musical compositions. Cf. **diatonicism.**

citharist, kitharist a performer on an ancient Greek form of lyre called a cithara.

contrapuntist 1. a composer of music employing counterpoint figures, as fugues.
2. a performer of music employing counterpoint figures. Also called **contrapuntalist.**

diatonicism the use of the diatonic scale of five whole tones and two halftones in the composition of music. Also called **diatonism.** Cf. **chromaticism.**

dodecaphony, dodecaphonism the composition of music employing the twelve-tone scale. Also called **dodecatonality** and **atonality.** —**dodecaphonist,** n. —**dodecaphonic,** adj.

doxology a short hymn expressing praise to God. —**doxological,** adj.

fuguism 1. the composition of fugues.
2. the performance of fugues. —**fuguist,** n.

gambist a performer on the viola da gamba.

Gregorianist Obsolete. a person versed in Gregorian chant. Also called **Gregorian.**

hymnody 1. the singing of hymns; hymnology.
2. the composition of hymns.
3. a study of hymns and their composers.
4. the preparation of expository material and bibliographies concerning hymns; hymnography. —**hymnodist,** n.

melodramaticism the writing of romantic, sensational stage plays interspersed with songs and orchestral music. —**melodramatist,** n. —**melodramatic,** adj.

melograph a mechanical device for recording on paper the notes of keyboard music while it is being played.

melomania an abnormal liking for music and melody. —**melomaniac,** n., adj. —**melomane,** n.

musicology the scholarly and scientific study of music, as in historical research, theory of composition, etc. —**musicologist,** n. —**musicological,** adj.

ophicleidist a performer on the ophicleide, an instrument in the brass section of the orchestra developed from the wooden serpent.

pandiatonicism 1. the composition of music using all seven notes of the diatonic scale in a manner free from classical harmonic restrictions.
2. the music written in this style. —**pandiatonic,** adj.

polytonalism the practice of using combinations of notes from two or more keys in writing musical compositions. Also called **polytonality.** —**polytonalist,** n. —**polytonal,** adj.

psalmody **1.** the art, practice, or act of singing psalms in worship services.
2. a collection of psalms. —**psalmodist,** *n.* —**psalmodial, psalmodic, psalmodical,** *adj.*

threnody a song, musical composition, or literary work created to honor or commemorate the dead; a funeral song. —**threnodist,** *n.* —**threnodic,** *adj.*

verismo, verism the artistic use of commonplace, everyday, and contemporary material in opera, esp. some 20th cent. Italian and French works, as *Louise.* —**verist,** *n., adj.* —**veristic,** *adj.*

MYSTICISM

Boehmenism, Behmenism the mystical teachings of Jakob Boehme, an influence on George Fox and Quakerism. —**Boehmenist, Boehmist, Boehmenite,** *n.*

Bourigianism the mystical theories of Antoinette Bourignon (1616-80), popular in the Netherlands and in Scotland.

epoptic referring to an initiate in the highest grade in the Eleusinian mysteries. —**epopt,** *n.* —**epoptae,** *n. pl.*

mystagogics, mystagogy **1.** the principles, doctrines, and practices of mysticism.
2. the interpretation of mysteries, as the Eleusinian. —**mystagogue,** *n.* —**mystagogic, mystagogical,** *adj.*

mystagogue a teacher of mystical doctrines.

omphalopsychism the practice of staring at one's navel to induce a mystical trance. Also called **omphaloskepsis.** —**omphalopsychite,** *n.*

theosophy, theosophism **1.** any of various forms of philosophical or religious thought claiming a mystical insight into the divine nature and natural phenomena. ˙
2. (*cap.*) the system of belief and practice of the Theosophical Society. —**theosophist,** *n.* —**theosophical,** *adj.*
See also BUDDHISM and HINDUISM.

MYTHS

mythicist **1.** a student of myths.
2. an interpreter of myths.

mythoclast an opponent of myths. —**mythoclastic,** *adj.*

mythologem a recurrent pattern, event, or theme in myths, as an explanation of the change of seasons; folklore motifs.

mythogenesis **1.** the establishment and development of myths.
2. the tendency to create myths or to give mythical status to a person or event. Also called **mythogeny.** —**mythogenetic,** *adj.*

mythologer a narrator of myths and legends.

mythography **1.** the collecting of myths.

2. the recording of myths in writing.

3. a critical collection of myths. —**mythographer, mythographist,** *n.*

mythology **1.** a body of myths, as that of a particular people or relating to a particular person.

2. a collection of myths.

3. the science of myths. —**mythologist,** *n.* —**mythological,** *adj.*

mythopoesis the creation of myths. —**mythopoeist,** *n.* —**mythopoeic,** *adj.*

mythos, mythus **1.** myth.

2. mythology.

3. the interrelationship of value structures and historical experiences of a people, usu. given expression through the arts.

N

NAKEDNESS

gymnopedia, gymnopaedia a religious choral dance performed at ancient Greek festivals by naked youths. —**gymnopedic,** *adj.*

gymnophobia an abnormal fear of nakedness.

gymnosophy the tenets of an ancient Hindu ascetic cult in which the members wore little or no clothing. —**gymnosophist,** *n.* —**gymnosophical,** *adj.*

naturism a cult of nudity for reasons of health. —**naturist,** *n.* —**naturistic,** *adj.*

nudism the practice of going nude. —**nudist,** *n., adj.*

NAMES

anthroponymy a branch of onomastics that studies personal names. —**anthroponymist,** *n.*

antonomasia **1.** the use of an epithet or appellative for an individual's name, as *his excellency.*

2. the use of a proper name to express a general idea or to designate others sharing a particular characteristic, as *a Rockefeller.* —**antonomastic,** *adj.*

caconymic pertaining to a bad or objectionable name.

eponymism the derivation of names for tribes, nations, or places, from that of a person, whether real or imaginary. Also called **eponymy.** —**eponymous, eponymic,** *adj.*

filionymic *Rare.* a name derived from that of a son.

hypocorism **1.** the creation or use of pet names, as Dick for Richard.

2. a pet name.

3. baby talk. —**hypocoristic,** *adj.*

metronymic, matronymic a name derived from a mother or a female ancestor.

onomancy, nomancy a form of divination involving observation of the letters of a name.

onomasticon a dictionary of proper names. —**onomastic,** *adj.*

onomastics the science or study of the origin and forms of proper names. Also called **onomatology.** —**onomastic,** *adj.*

onomatomania a preoccupation with words or names.

onomatophobia an abnormal fear of a certain name or word.

paedonymic a name derived from one's child.

patronymic a name derived from a father or paternal ancestor.

poecilonymy the simultaneous use of several names or synonyms for one thing.

polyonymy the use of various names for one thing. —**polyonymous,** *adj.*

toponym 1. a place name.
2. a personal name derived from a place name.

toponymy 1. the study of the place names of a district.
2. *Anatomy.* the nomenclature of the regions of the body. —**toponymic, toponymical,** *adj.*

NATIONALISM

chauvinism a zealous and belligerent patriotism. —**chauvinist,** *n.* —**chauvinistic,** *adj.*

civism 1. the attitudes and behavior of a good citizen.
2. *Obsolete.* a devotion to the cause of the French revolution of 1789.

ethnomania a fanaticism favoring ethnic or racial autonomy. —**ethnomaniac,** *n., adj.*

jingoism extreme or eccentric national loyalty that is hostile to the interests of any other nation. —**jingo, jingoist,** *n.* —**jingoistic,** *adj.*

Junkerism the militaristic, authoritarian spirit or character of the East Prussian aristocracy. —**Junker,** *n., adj.*

nationalism 1. the spirit or aspirations of a country.
2. a devotion to the interests of one's own country.
3. a desire for national advancement.
4. the policy of asserting the interest of one's own nation, as separate from the interest of another nation and the common interest of all nations. —**nationalist,** *n., adj.* —**nationalistic,** *adj.*

patriotism a devoted love, support, and defense of one's country; national loyalty. —**patriot,** *n.* —**patriotic,** *adj.*

NATURE

anthropopsychism   the assignment of a humanlike soul to nature. —**anthropopsychic,** *adj.*

azoology   the study of inanimate nature.

conservationist   a person who advocates the conservation of the natural resources of a country or region. —**conservational,** *adj.*

etiology, aetiology   **1.** the science of causation.
2. the science of the causes of natural phenomena.
3. *Med.* all of the factors involved in the occurrence of a disease. —**etiologic, etiological,** *adj.*

physiolatry   the worship of nature. —**physiolater,** *n.* —**physiolatrous,** *adj.*

physiosophy   the body of wisdom about nature.

physitheism   **1.** the assignment of a physical form to a god.
2. the deification and worship of natural phenomena; physiolatry.

physiurgic   produced by natural rather than divine or human forces.

NERVES

neuralgia   a sharp and paroxysmal pain along the course of a nerve. —**neuralgic,** *adj.*

neuroanatomy   *Med.* the branch of anatomy that studies the anatomy of the nervous system. —**neuroanatomical,** *adj.*

neurasthenia   **1.** *Med.* a nervous debility and exhaustion, as from overwork or prolonged nervous strain.
2. popularly, a nervous breakdown. —**neurasthenic,** *adj.*

neuritis   **1.** an inflammation in a nerve.
2. a continuous pain in a nerve, associated with paralysis, loss of reflexes, and sensory disturbances. —**neuritic,** *adj.*

neurology   the branch of medical science that studies the nerves and the nervous system, esp. the diseases that affect them. —**neurologist,** *n.* —**neurological,** *adj.*

neuromimesis   *Med.* a psychosomatic disease. —**neuromimetic,** *adj.*

neuropathology   the pathology of the nervous system. —**neuropathologist,** *n.* —**neuropathologic, neuropathological,** *adj.*

neuropsychiatry   the branch of medicine dealing with diseases affecting the mind and the nervous system. —**neuropsychiatrist,** *n.* —**neuropsychiatric,** *adj.*

neurotomy   the cutting of a nerve, as to relieve neuralgia. —**neurotomist,** *n.*

NOSE

mycteric   pertaining to the nasal cavities.

nasillate   to speak or sing through the nose.

nasology a scientific study of the nose. —**nasologist,** *n.* —**nasological,** *adj.*

nasoscope an electrically lighted instrument for examining the nasal cavities. —**nasoscopic,** *adj.*

rhinology the branch of medical science that studies the nose and its diseases. —**rhinologist,** *n.* —**rhinologic, rhinological,** *adj.*

NOVELTY

cainophobia an abnormal fear of novelty. Also called **cainotophobia.**

esotericism 1. the holding of secret doctrines; the practice of limiting knowledge to a small group.
2. an interest in items of a special, rare, novel, or unusual quality. Also called **esoterism.** —**esoterist,** *n.*

esoterica a collection of items of a special, rare, novel, or unusual quality.

neolatry *Rare.* the worship of novelty. —**neolater,** *n.*

misoneism a hatred of novelty. Also called **neophobia.**

philoneism an excessive love of novelty. Also called **neophilism.**

NUMBERS

abacist a skilled user of the abacus.

acalculia *Psychiatry.* an inability to work with figures; a mental block concerning calculation.

arithmancy a form of divination involving numbers. Also called **arithmomancy.**

arithmomania 1. an obsession with numbers.
2. a compulsion to count things.

numerology a system of occultism based upon numbers. —**numerologist,** *n.* —**numerological,** *adj.*

O

OBSCENITY

aischrolatreia 1. the cult of the obscene.
2. the worship of filth.

aischrology the vocabulary of obscenity; linguistic filthiness.

coprology 1. the introduction of obscenity into art and literature.
2. obscene literature.
3. the study of obscene literature.
4. the study of or preoccupation with excrement. Also called **scatology.**

coprophilia a love of obscenity.

rhyparography the painting of sordid and obscene subjects. —**rhyparographer,** *n.* —**rhyparographic,** *adj.*

scatology the study of or preoccupation with excrement or obscenity. Also called **coprology.** —**scatologic, scatological,** *adj.*

ODORS

anosmia *Med.* the absence of the sense of smell; olfactory anesthesia. Also called **anosphrasia.** —**anosmic,** *adj.*

olfactology the branch of medical science that studies the sense of smell. —**olfactologist,** *n.*

osmatic dependent chiefly on the sense of smell for the ability to relate to surroundings. Also called **osmic.**

osmatism the ability to perceive odors. —**osmatic,** *adj.*

osmonosology *Med.* the study of the sense of smell, esp. its disorders. —**osmonologist,** *n.*

osmophobia an abnormal fear of odors.

osphresiology *Med.* the sum of information concerning odors and olfaction. Also called **osmology.**

osphresiophilia an inordinate love of smells.

osphresiophobia an abnormal dislike of odors.

parosmia *Med.* a disorder of the sense of smell. Also called **parosphresia, parosphresis.**

OLD AGE

gerascophobia the fear of growing old.

geratology the study of the decline of life, as in old age. —**geratologic, geratological, geratologous,** *adj.*

geriatrics **1.** *Med.* the science dealing with the diseases, debilities, and care of aged persons.
2. the study of the physical process and problems of aging; gerontology. —**geriatric,** *adj.* —**geriatrist, geriatrician,** *n.*

geriatry the care of the aged.

gerodontics a dental specialty concerned with the care and treatment of the dental problems of the aged. —**gerodontist,** *n.*

geromorphism the condition of appearing older than one is.

gerontology the branch of science that studies aging and the special problems of the aged. Also called **gerocomy.** —**gerontologist,** *n.* —**gerontological,** *adj.*

nostology *Med., Obsolete.* the study of senility.

senectitude the condition of old age.

senicide the killing off of the old men in a tribe. —**senicidal,** *adj.*

ORGANISMS

anabolism *Biology, Physiology.* the synthesis in living organisms of more complex substances from simpler ones. —**anabolic,** *adj.* Cf. **catabolism.**

catabolism, katabolism *Biology, Physiology.* the destructive processes of chemical change in living organisms, characterized by the breaking down of complex substances into simpler ones, with a release of energy. —**catabolic,** *adj.*

histology **1.** the branch of biology that studies tissues of organisms. **2.** the structure, esp. the microscopic structure, of organic tissues. Also called **histiology.** —**histologist,** *n.* —**histologic, histological,** *adj.*

phenology, phaenology the study of the effects of climate on animal and plant life. —**phenologist,** *n.* —**phenological, phenologic,** *adj.*

ORIGINS

archology the science of origins.

derivation the source from which something is derived; origin. —**derivative,** *n., adj.*

glottogony the study of the origin of language. —**glottogonic,** *adj.*

inchoation a beginning; origin. —**inchoate, inchoative,** *adj.*

incipiency the state or fact of beginning or commencing. —**incipient,** *adj.*

provenance the place of origin; source. Also called *provenience.*

P

PAIN

algolagnia a tendency toward strong sexual pleasure in inflicting or enduring pain. —**algolagnist,** *n.* —**algolagnic,** *adj.* Cf. **masochism, sadism.**

algogenic producing pain.

algophilia a love of pain.

algophobia an extreme fear of pain. See also **odynophobia.**

cephalalgia *Med.***1.** a pain in the head. **2.** a headache. Also called **cephalgia** and **cephalodynia.**

dolor, dolour **1.** *Obsolete.* a physical pain. **2.** mental anguish. **3.** grief; sorrow.—**dolorous,** *adj.*

hemicrania **1.** *Med.* a pain or aching on one side of the head. **2.** migraine.

longuanimity a silent suffering while planning revenge. —**longuanimous,** *adj.*

masochism 1. *Psychiatry.* a condition in which sexual gratification is achieved through suffering physical pain and humiliation, esp. inflicted on oneself.
2. any gratification gained from pain or deprivation inflicted or imposed on oneself. —**masochist,** *n.* —**masochistic,** *adj.*

odontalgia *Med.* a pain in a tooth. —**odontalgic,** *adj.*

odynophobia an abnormal fear of pain.

otalgia *Med.* an earache. —**otalgic,** *adj.*

sadism 1. *Psychiatry.* a sexual gratification gained through causing physical pain or humiliation.
2. any enjoyment in being cruel. —**sadist,** *n.* —**sadistic,** *adj.* Cf. **masochism.**

sadomasochism a condition of disturbed and destructive personality marked by the presence of both sadistic and masochistic traits. —**sadomasochist,** *n.* —**sadomasochistic,** *adj.*

stoicism 1. an indifference to pleasure or pain.
2. (*cap.*) the philosophy of the Stoics. —**stoic,** *n., adj.* —**stoical,** *adj.*

torminal 1. *Med.* pertaining to or characterized by a griping pain.
2. *Med.* pertaining to tormina, or colic.

zoosadism *Med.* a sadism directed toward animals. —**zoosadist,** *n.* —**zoosadistic,** *adj.*

PARENTS

compaternity the spiritual relationship between godparents, or between them and the actual parents of a child.

matricide 1. the killing of one's mother.
2. the killer of a maternal parent. —**matricidal,** *adj.*

parenticide the crime of parricide.

parentalism 1. the behavior of a parent.
2. the assumption by a non-parent of superior authority over a child; paternalism.

parentation *Archaic.* the performance of funeral rituals for one's parents.

parricide 1. the act of killing one's parent or other close relative.
2. the person who commits such an act. —**parricidal,** *adj.*

patricide 1. the killing of one's father.
2. the killer of a paternal parent. —**patricidal,** *adj.*

PAST

aboriginality the condition of being first in a place and of having a relatively simple nature. —**aboriginal,** *n., adj.*

antediluvianism an adherence to or fondness for ancient things or customs. —**antediluvian,** *n., adj.*

antiquarianism   an interest in the culture of antiquity, esp. that of classical Greece and Rome. —**antiquary, antiquarian,** *n.* —**antiquarian,** *adj.*

archaeolatry   a devotion to archaism. —**archaeolater,** *n.* —**archaeolatrous,** *adj.*

archaism   an inclination toward old-fashioned things, speech, etc. Also called **archaicism.** —**archaist,** *n.* —**archaic,** *adj.*

futurism   the seeking of life's meaning and fulfillment in the future. —**futurist,** *n.* —**futuristic,** *adj.* Cf. **archaism.**

medievalism   a strong fondness or admiration for the culture, mores, etc., of the Middle Ages. —**medievalist,** *n.* —**medievalistic,** *adj.*

paletiology, palaetiology   an explanation of events of the past through the laws of causation. —**palaetiological,** *adj.*

paleology   the study of antiquities. —**paleologist,** *n.* —**paleological,** *adj.*

paleopathology   *Med.* the study of diseases from former times as found in fossils and mummified remains.

palynology   the branch of paleontology that studies spores, pollen, and microorganisms, both living and fossil. —**palynological,** *adj.*

papyrology   the study of papyrus manuscripts. —**papyrologist,** *n.* —**papyrological,** *adj.*

philarchaist   *Obsolete.* one devoted to the archaic. —**philarchaic,** *adj.*

PERCEPTION

Berkeleianism, Berkeleyanism   the system of philosophical idealism developed by George Berkeley, esp. his tenet that the physical world does not have an independent reality but exists as a perception of the divine mind and the finite mind of man. Also called **Berkeleyism.** —**Berkeleian, Berkeleyan,** *n., adj.*

chromesthesia   *Med.* the association of imaginary sensations of color with actual perceptions of hearing, taste, or smell. Also called **photism** and **color hearing.**

kinesthesia   *Med.* the sense by which movement, weight, position, etc., are perceived. —**kinesthetic,** *adj.*

synesthesia, synaesthesia   *Med.* a secondary sensation accompanying an actual perception, as the perceiving of sound as a color or the sensation of being touched in a place at some distance from the actual place of touching. —**synesthetic, synaesthetic,** *adj.* See **chromesthesia.**

PERSONALITY

characterology   the study of character, esp. its development and its variations. —**characterologist,** *n.* —**characterologic, characterological,** *adj.*

saponacity   an ingratiating but evasive conduct, a slippery personality. —**saponaceous,** *adj.*

unicism   the quality of uniqueness. Also called **unicity.** —**unicist,** *n.*

-PHILIA

claustrophilia   an abnormal desire to be closed in, to shut all windows and doors. —**claustrophile,** *n.* —**claustrophilic,** *adj.*

laparotomaphilia   the abnormal desire to undergo abdominal surgery for simulated reasons.

mysophilia   an abnormal attraction to filth.

nyctophilia   an abnormal preference for the night over the day.

PHILOSOPHY

actualism   the doctrine that all reality is animate, in motion, or in process. —**actualist,** *n.* —**actualistic,** *adj.*

Aristotelianism   the philosophy of Aristotle, esp. an emphasis upon formal deductive logic, upon the concept that reality is a combination of form and matter, and upon investigation of the concrete and particular. —**Aristotelian,** *n., adj.*

atomism   the theory that minute, discrete, finite, and indivisible elements are the ultimate constituents of all matter. Also called **atomic theory.** —**atomist,** *n.* —**atomistic, atomistical,** *adj.*

Averroism   the philosphy of Averroës, chiefly Aristotelianism tinged with Neoplatonism, asserting the unity of an active and divine intellect common to all while denying personal immortality. Also called **Averrhoism.** —**Averroist,** *n.* —**Averroistic,** *adj.*

Bergsonism   the philosophy of Henri Bergson, emphasizing time or duration as the central fact of experience, and asserting the existence of the élan vital as an original life force governing all organic processes in a way that can be explained only by intuition, not by scientific analysis. —**Bergsonian,** *n., adj.*

Cartesianism   the philosphy of Rene Descartes and his followers, esp. its emphasis on logical analysis, its mechanistic interpretation of physical nature, and its dualistic distinction between thought (mind) and extension (matter). —**Cartesian,** *n., adj.*

Cynicism   a Greek philosophy of the 4th cent. B.C. advocating the doctrines that virtue is the only good, that the essence of virtue is self-control and individual freedom, and that surrender to any external influence is beneath the dignity of man. —**Cynic,** *n.* —**Cynical,** *adj.*

descendentalism   the doctrines of a school of philosophy emphasizing empiricism and positivism. —**descendentalist,** *n.* —**descendental, descendentalistic,** *adj.* Cf. **transcendentalism.**

determinism   1. the doctrine that all facts and events result from the operation of natural laws.
2. the doctrine that all events, including human choices and decisions, are

necessarily determined by motives, which are regarded as external forces acting on the will. —**determinist,** *n.* —**deterministic,** *adj.*

doxography   the compiling of extracts from ancient Greek philosophers, with editorial commentary. —**doxographer,** *n.* —**doxographical,** *adj.*

dualism   **1.** any theory in any field of philosophical investigation that reduces the variety of its subject matter to two irreducible principles, as good/evil or natural/supernatural.
2. *Metaphysics.* any system that reduces the whole universe to two principles, as the Platonic Ideas and Matter. —**dualist,** *n.* —**dualistic,** *adj.*

dynamism   any of various theories or philosophical systems that seek to explain natural phenomena by the action and interaction of forces, as mechanism or Leibnizianism. —**dynamist,** *n.* —**dynamistic,** *adj.* See also **vitalism.**

dysteleology   a doctrine denying the existence of a final cause or purpose in life or nature. —**dysteleologist,** *n.* —**dysteleological,** *adj.* Cf. **teleology.**

eclecticism   **1.** the use or advocacy of a method involving the selection of doctrines from various systems and their combination into a unified system of ideas.
2. such a system. —**eclectic,** *n., adj.*

Eleaticism   a school of philosophy founded by Parmenides and its doctrines, esp. those contributed by Zeno asserting the unreality of motion or change. —**Eleatic,** *adj.*

emanationism   a theory of the origin of the world by a series of emanations from the Godhead. Also called **emanatism.** —**emanationist,** *n.* —**emanational,** *adj.*

empiricism   **1.** the doctrine that all ideas and categories are derived from sense experience and that knowledge cannot extend beyond experience, including observation, experiment, and induction.
2. an empirical method or practice. —**empiricist,** *n.* —**empirical,** *adj.*

entelechy   *Vitalism.* a vital agent or force directing growth and life. —**entelechial,** *adj.* Cf. **teleology.**

Epicureanism   the philosophical system of Epicurus, holding that the natural world is a series of fortuitous combinations of atoms, and that the highest good is freedom from disturbance and pain. Also called **Epicurism.** —**Epicurean,** *n., adj.*

epiphenomenalism   the doctrine that consciousness is a mere accessory and accompaniment of physiological processes and is powerless to affect these processes. —**epiphenomenalist,** *n.* —**epiphenomenal,** *adj.*

essentialism   **1.** a philosophical theory asserting that metaphysical essences are real and intuitively accessible.
2. a philosophical theory giving priority to the inward nature, true

substance, or constitution of something over its existence. —**essentialist,** *n.* —**essentialistic,** *adj.* Cf. **existentialism.**

existentialism   1. the doctrine that man forms his essence in the course of the life resulting from his personal choices.
2. an emphasis upon man's creating his own nature as well as the importance of personal freedom, decision, and commitment. Also called **philosophical existentialism.** —**existentialist,** *n., adj.*

fatalism   the doctrine that all things are subject to fate or inevitable predestination and that man is ultimately unable to prevent inevitabilities. —**fatalist,** *n.* —**fatalistic,** *adj.* Cf. **determinism.**

Gnosticism   the doctrines of any of various dualistic sects among the Jews and the early Christians who claimed possession of superior spiritual knowledge, explained the creation of the world in an emanational manner, and condemned matter as evil. See also **Cainism, Ebionism, Manicheanism, Valentinianism.** —**Gnostic,** *n., adj.*

gradualism   a theory maintaining that two seemingly conflicting notions are not radically opposed, but are part of a gradually altering continuity. —**gradualist,** *n., adj.* —**gradualistic,** *adj.*

Hegelian dialectic   an interpretive method, orig. used to relate specific entities or events to the absolute idea, in which an assertable proposition (*thesis*) is necessarily opposed by its apparent contradiction (*antithesis*), and both reconciled on a higher level of truth by a third proposition (*synthesis*). Also called **Hegelian triad.**

Hegelianism   the philosophy of Hegel and his followers, characterized by the use of a special dialectic as an analytical and interpretive method. —**Hegelian,** *n., adj.*

holism   the theory that whole entities, as fundamental components of reality, have an existence other than as the mere sum of their parts. —**holist,** *n.* —**holistic,** *adj.*

humanitarianism   1. *Ethics.* the doctrine that man's obligations are concerned wholly with the welfare of the human race.
2. *Theology.* the doctrine that man may achieve perfection without divine assistance. —**humanitarian,** *n., adj.*

hylomorphism   the theory derived from Aristotle that every physical object is composed of two principles, an unchanging prime matter and a form deprived of actuality with every substantial change of the object. —**hylomorphist,** *n.* —**hylomorphic,** *adj.*

idealism   any system or theory that maintains that the real is of the nature of thought or that the object of external perception consists of ideas. —**idealist,** *n.* —**idealistic,** *adj.*

illusionism   a theory or doctrine that the material world is wholly or nearly wholly an illusion. —**illusionist,** *n.* —**illusionistic,** *adj.*

instrumentalism   a pragmatic philosophy holding that it is the function of thought to be a means to the control of environment, and that the value and truthfulness of ideas is determined by their usefulness in human experience or progress. —**instrumentalist,** *n., adj.*

irrationalism   **1.** a theory that nonrational forces govern the universe.
   2. any attitude or set of beliefs having a nonrational basis, as nihilism. —**irrationalist,** *n., adj.* —**irrationalistic,** *adj.*

Kantianism   the philosophy of Kant, asserting that the nature of the mind renders it unable to know reality immediately, that the mind interprets data presented to it as phenomena in space and time, and that the reason, in order to find a meaningful basis for experience or in order for ethical conduct to exist, may postulate things unknowable to it, as the existence of a soul. —**Kantist,** *n.* —**Kantian,** *adj.*

Leibnizianism, Leibnitzianism   the philosophy of Leibniz and his followers, esp. monadism and the theory of preestablished harmony, the theory that this is the best of all possible worlds because God has chosen it (satirized by Voltaire in *Candide*), and proposals for a scientific language and a method of symbolic computation. —**Leibnizian, Leibnitzian,** *n., adj.*

libertarianism   **1.** one who advocates liberty, esp. with regard to thought or conduct.
   2. the philosophical doctrine of free will. Cf. **necessitarianism, determinism, fatalism.** —**libertarian,** *n., adj.*

materialism   the theory that regards matter and its various guises as constituting the universe, and all phenomena, including those of the mind, as caused by material agencies. —**materialist,** *n.* —**materialistic,** *adj.*

mechanism   **1.** the theory that everything in the universe is produced by matter in process, and capable of explanation by the laws of chemistry and physics.
   2. the theory that a natural process is machinelike or as explainable in terms of Newtonian mechanics. —**mechanist,** *n.* —**mechanistic,** *adj.*

meliorism   the doctrine that the world tends to become better of itself, or that it may improve more rapidly by proper human assistance. —**meliorist,** *n.* —**melioristic,** *adj.* Cf. **optimism, pessimism.**

mentalism   the doctrine that objects of knowledge have no existence except in the mind of the perceiver, as in Berkeleianism. —**mentalist,** *n.* —**mentalistic,** *adj.*

monadism   **1.** the Leibnizian doctrine of monads as unextended, indivisible, and indestructible entities that are the ultimate constituent of the universe and a microcosm of it. Also called **monadology.**
   2. the doctrine of Giordano Bruno concerning monads as basic and irreducible metaphysical units that are psychically and spatially individuated. —**monadistic,** *adj.*

monism 1. *Metaphysics.* a theory that only one basic substance or principle exists as the ground of reality. Cf. **dualism.**
2. *Metaphysics.* a theory that reality consists of a single element. Cf. **pluralism.**
3. *Epistemology.* a theory that the object and the sense datum of cognition are identical. —**monist,** *n.* —**monistic, monistical,** *adj.*

naive realism the theory that the world is perceived exactly as it is. Also called **natural realism** or **commonsense realism.** Cf. **idealism, realism.**

necessitarianism the doctrine of the determinism of the will by antecedent causes, as opposed to that of the freedom of the will. Also called **necessarianism.** Cf. **determinism, fatalism, libertarianism.** —**necessitarian,** *n., adj.*

Neoplatonism, NeoPlatonism a philosophical system originated in Alexandria in the 3rd cent. A.D., founded on Platonic doctrine, Aristotelianism, and Oriental mysticism, with later influences from Christianity. —**Neoplatonist,** *n.* —**Neoplatonic,** *adj.*

Nietzscheism the philosphy of Nietzsche, esp. its emphasis on the will to power as the chief motivating force of both the individual and society. Also called **Nietzscheanism.** —**Nietzschean,** *n., adj.*

noumenalism any of several philosophical concepts regarding the noumenon. —**noumenalist,** *n.*

noumenon 1. *Kantianism.* that which can be the object only of a purely intellectual, nonsensuous intuition, the thing-in-itself.
2. *Kantianism.* an unknowable object (as God), the existence of which is not capable of proof.
3. an object of purely mental apprehension as distinguished from an object of sense perception; abstraction. —**noumenal,** *adj.*

objectivism 1. any of various philosophical theories stressing the external or objective elements of cognition.
2. *Ethics.* any theory asserting that the moral good is objective and not influenced by human feelings. —**objectivist,** *n., adj.*

optimism 1. the belief that good is ultimately triumphant over the evil in the world.
2. the Leibnizian doctrine that this is the best of all possible worlds.
3. the belief that goodness pervades reality. —**optimist,** *n.* —**optimistic,** *adj.*

organicism the theory that vital activities stem not from any single part of an organism but from its autonomous composition. —**organicist,** *n.* —**organicistic,** *adj.* Cf. **holism, mechanism, vitalism.**

Origenism the doctrines developed or ascribed to the 3rd cent. Christian theologian Origen, esp. an attempt to develop a Christian philosophy combining Platonism and the Scriptures. —**Origenist,** *n.* —**Origenistic,** *adj.*

panlogism 1. the doctrine that the universe is a realization or act of the Logos.

2. the Hegelian doctrine that logos or reason informs the asbolute or absolute reality. —**panlogist,** *n.* —**panlogical, panlogistic, panlogistical,** *adj.*

panpsychism the doctrine that each object in the universe has a mind or an unconscious psyche, and that all physical occurrences involve the mental. —**panpsychist,** *n.* —**panpsychistic,** *adj.*

Peripateticism 1. the philosophy of Aristotle, who taught while walking.
2. the followers of Aristotle and his school of philosophy. —**Peripatetic,** *n.,* *adj.*

pessimism 1. the doctrine that all things naturally tend to evil.
2. the doctrine that this is the worst of all possible worlds. Cf. **Leibnizianism.**
3. the doctrine that the evil and pain in the world outweigh goodness and happiness, and that the world is basically evil. —**pessimist,** *n.* —**pessimistic,** *adj.* Cf. **meliorism, optimism.**

phenomenalism the doctrine that phenomena are the only objects of knowledge or the only form of reality. —**phenomenalist,** *n.* —**phenomenalistic,** *adj.*

phenomenology 1. the study of phenomena.
2. the philosophical system of Husserl and his followers, esp. the careful description of phenomena in all areas of experience. —**phenomenologist,** *n.* —**phenomenologic, phenomenological,** *adj.*

Platonism the philosophy of Plato and his followers, esp. the doctrine that physical objects are imperfect and impermanent representations of unchanging ideas, and that knowledge is the mental apprehension of these ideas or universals. —**Platonist,** *n.* —**Platonistic,** *adj.*

pluralism 1. a theory positing more than one principle or basic substance as the ground of reality. Cf. **dualism, monism.**
2. a theory that reality consists, not of an organic whole, but of two or more independent material or spiritual entities. —**pluralist,** *n.* —**pluralistic,** *adj.*

positivism 1. a philosophical system developed by Auguste Comte, concerned with positive facts and phenomena, the first verified by the methods of the empirical sciences, the second explainable by scientific laws. Also called *Comtism.*
2. a contemporary philosphical movement stressing the task of philosophy as criticizing and analyzing science, and rejecting all transcendental metaphysics. Also called **logical positivism.** —**positivist,** *n.* —**positivistic,** *adj.*

pragmatistism the pragmatist philosophy of C.S. Peirce, esp. his work in logic and problems in language. —**pragmaticist,** *n.*

pragmatism a philosophical system stressing practical consequences and values as standards by which the validity of concepts are to be determined. —**pragmatist,** *n.* —**pragmatistic,** *adj.*

probabilism the doctrine, introduced by the Skeptics and influential in the sciences and social sciences in modified form, that certainty is impossible and that probability suffices to govern belief and action. —**probabilist,** *n.* —**probabilistic,** *adj.*

purposivism any of various theories of nature or of animal and human behavior based upon teleological doctrines. —**purposivist,** *n.*

Pyrrhonism 1. the Skeptic doctrines of Pyrrho and his followers, esp. the assertion that, since all perceptions tend to be faulty, the wise man will consider the external circumstances of life to be unimportant and thus preserve tranquility.
2. an extreme or absolute skepticism. —**Pyrrhonist,** *n.* —**Pyrrhonian, Pyrrhonic,** *n., adj.*

rationalism 1. the doctrine that knowledge is gained only through the reason, a faculty independent of experience.
2. the doctrine that all knowledge is expressible in self-evident propositions or their consequences. —**rationalist,** *n.* —**rationalistic,** *adj.*

realism 1. the doctrine that universals have a real objective existence. Cf. **idealism.**
2. the doctrine that objects of sense perception have an existence independent of the act of perception. —**realist,** *n.*

relationism 1. a doctrine asserting the existence of relations as entities.
2. a theory maintaining the conditioning of any ideological perspective or system by its sociocultural context. —**relationist,** *n.*

relativism any theory maintaining that criteria of judgment vary with individuals and their environments; relationism. —**relativist,** *n.* —**relativistic,** *adj.*

Rosminianism the philosophy of Antonio Rosmini-Serbati, 19th cent. Italian philospher and ecclesiastic, who taught that the idea of true being is inborn and that through it true knowledge is made potential. —**Rosminian,** *n., adj.*

Scotism the philosophy of John Duns Scotus, medieval Scholastic, esp. his proposal that philosphy and theology be made separate disciplines. —**scotist,** *n.* —**Scotistic, scotistical,** *adj.*

sensationalism 1. the doctrine that all ideas are derived from and essentially reducible to sense perceptions. Also called **sensualism.**
2. *Ethics.* the doctrine that the good is to be judged only by or through the gratification of the senses. Also called **sensualism.** —**sensationalist,** *n.* —**sensationalistic,** *adj.*

Skepticism, Scepticism the doctrines or opinions of philosophical Skeptics, esp. the doctrine that a true knowledge of things is impossible or that all knowledge is uncertain. —**Skeptic,** *n.* Cf. **Pyrrhonism.**

solipsism the theory that only the self exists or can be proved to exist. —**solipsist,** *n.* —**solipsistic,** *adj.*

Stoicism the school of philosophy founded by Zeno, who asserted that men should be free from passion, unmoved by joy or grief, and submit without complaint to unavoidable necessity. —**Stoic,** *n., adj.*

subjectivism **1.** *Epistemology.* the doctrine that all knowledge is limited to experiences by the self, and that all transcendant knowledge is impossible.

2. *Ethics.* the theory that certain states of feeling or thought are the highest good.

3. *Ethics.* the doctrine that the good and the right can be distinguished only by individual feeling. —**subjectivist,** *n.* —**subjectivistic,** *adj.*

syncretism the attempted reconciliation of different or opposing principles, practices, or parties, as in philosophy or religion. —**syncretic, syncretical, syncretistic, syncretistical,** *adj.*

teleology **1.** the doctrine that final causes (purposes) exist.

2. the study of the evidences of design or purpose in nature.

3. such a design or purpose.

4. the belief that purpose and design are a part of or apparent in nature.

5. *Vitalism.* the doctrine that phenomena are guided by both mechanical forces and goals of self-realization. —**teleologist,** *n.* —**teleologic, teleological,** *adj.*

Thomism the theological and philosophical doctrines of St. Thomas Aquinas and his followers. —**Thomist,** *n.* —**Thomistic,** *adj.*

transcendentalism **1.** any philosophy based upon the doctrine that the principles of reality are to be discovered only through the analysis of the processes of thought, as Kantianism.

2. a philosophy emphasizing the intuitive and spiritual above the empirical, as the philosphy of Emerson. —**transcendentalist,** *n.* —**transcendentalistic,** *adj.*

tutiorism *Casuistry.* a position in the probabilistic controversy of the 16th and 17th cents. maintaining that, in the absence of moral certitude, only the most rigorous of any probable courses of ethical action should be taken. Also called **rigorism.** —**tutiorist,** *n.*

vitalism **1.** the doctrine that phenomena are only partly controlled by mechanical forces and are in some measure self-determining. Cf. **mechanism, organicism.**

2. the doctrine that ascribes the functions of a living organism to a vital principle (as élan vital) distinct from physical or chemical forces. —**vitalist,** *n., adj.* —**vitalistic,** *adj.*

voluntarism any theory that regards the will rather than the intellect as the fundamental agency or principle in human activities and experience, as Nietzscheism. —**voluntarist,** *n.* —**voluntaristic,** *adj.*

PHOBIAS *

Noun forms end in -*phobe* and adjective forms end in -*phobic,* unless otherwise noted.

acarophobia   a fear of skin infestation by mites or ticks.

acousticophobia   an abnormal fear of noise.

albuminurophobia   a fear of albumin in one's urine as a sign of kidney disease.

amathophobia   an abnormal fear of dust.

anginophobia   an abnormal fear of quinsy or other forms of sore throat.

aphephobia   an abnormal fear of touching or being touched. Also called **haphephobia, haptephobia.**

arachnephobia   an abnormal fear of spiders.

asthenophobia   an abnormal fear of weakness.

astrophobia   an abnormal fear of the stars.

ataxiophobia   an abnormal fear of disorder. Also called **ataxophobia.**

aurophobia   a dislike of gold.

bacillophobia   an abnormal fear of germs. Also called **bacteriophobia.**

bathmophobia   an abnormal fear of walking.

batrachophobia   an abnormal fear of frogs and toads.

cathisophobia   an abnormal fear of sitting down.

catoptrophobia   an abnormal fear of mirrors.

Celtophobia   an intense dislike of Celts.

cholerophobia   an intense fear of cholera.

chrematophobia   an intense fear or dislike of wealth.

chronophobia   an abnormal discomfort concerning time.

cometophobia   an abnormal fear of comets.

coprophobia   an abnormal fear of excrement.

crystallophobia   an abnormal fear of glass. Also called **hyalophobia.**

deipnophobia   an abnormal fear of dining and dinner conversation.

demonophobia   an abnormal fear of spirits.

diabetophobia   an intense fear of diabetes.

dinophobia   an abnormal fear of whirlpools.

diplopiaphobia   an abnormal fear of double vision.

dromophobia   an abnormal fear of crossing streets.

dysmorphophobia   an abnormal dread of deformity, usu. in others.

eisoptrophobia   an abnormal fear of termites. Also called **isopterophobia.**

emetophobia   an abnormal fear of vomiting.

entomophobia   an abnormal fear of insects.

eosophobia   an abnormal fear of the dawn.

eurotophobia   an abnormal fear of female genitals.

febriphobia   an abnormal fear of fever.

galeophobia   an abnormal fear of sharks.

gamophobia   an abnormal fear of marriage.

gephyrophobia   an abnormal fear of crossing a bridge.

Germanophobia   a dislike of Germany, its people, or its culture. Also called **Teutophobia, Teutonophobia.**

geumophobia   an abnormal fear of tastes or flavors.

graphophobia   a dislike for writing.

gringophobia   in Spain or Latin America, an intense dislike of white strangers.

hagiophobia   an intense dislike for saints and the holy.

hamartophobia   an abnormal fear of error or sin.

hedonophobia   an abnormal fear of pleasure.

heliophobia   an abnormal sensitivity to the effects of sunlight.

homilophobia   a hatred for sermons.

hydrophobia   **1.** an abnormal fear of water.
2. the occurrence in humans of rabies.

hydrophobophobia   an abnormal fear of rabies.

hygrophobia   an abnormal fear of liquids in any form, esp. wine and water.

hylephobia   an intense dislike for wood.

hypengyophobia   an abnormal fear of responsibility.

iatrophobia   an abnormal fear of going to the doctor.

ichthyophobia   an abnormal fear of fish.

Judophobism, Judophobia   a hatred of the Jews and Jewish culture. Also called **Judaeophobia.**

kakorrhaphiophobia   an abnormal fear of failure or defeat.

kynophobia, cynophobia   an abnormal fear of pseudorabies.

laliophobia   an abnormal fear of talking. Also called **lalophobia.**

lepraphobia   an abnormal fear of leprosy.

levophobia   an abnormal fear of objects on the left side of the body.

meningitophobia   an abnormal fear of meningitis.

merinthophobia   an abnormal fear of being bound.

metallophobia   an abnormal fear of metals.

meteorophobia   an abnormal fear of meteors.

monopathophobia   an abnormal fear of sickness in a specified part of the body.

motorphobia an abnormal fear or dislike of motor vehicles.
musicophobia an intense dislike of music.
negrophobia a strong dislike or fear of Negroes.
noctiphobia an abnormal fear of the night.
nudophobia, nudiphobia an abnormal fear of nakedness.
odontophobia an abnormal fear of teeth, especially those of animals.
olfactophobia an abnormal fear of smells. Also called **osmophobia.**
ombrophobia an abnormal fear of rain.
onomatophobia an abnormal fear of a certain name.
papaphobia an intense fear or dread of the pope or the papacy.
paralipophobia an abnormal fear of neglect of some duty.
paraphobia an abnormal fear of sexual perversion.
parasitophobia an abnormal fear of parasites.
parthenophobia an extreme aversion to young girls.
pellagraphobia an abnormal fear of catching pellagra.
peniaphobia an abnormal fear of poverty.
phagophobia an abnormal fear of eating.
philosophobia an abnormal fear of philosophy or philosophers.
phonophobia an abnormal fear of noise.
photangiophobia an abnormal fear of photalgia, pain in the eyes caused by light.
phthiriophobia an abnormal fear of lice.
phthisiophobia an abnormal fear of tuberculosis.
pnigophobia an abnormal fear of choking.
politicophobia a dislike or fear of politicians.
proctophobia *Med.* a mental apprehension in patients with a rectal disease.
proteinphobia a strong aversion to protein foods.
psychrophobia an abnormal fear of cold temperatures.
pyrexiophobia an abnormal fear of fever.
pyrophobia an abnormal fear of fire.
rhabdophobia an abnormal fear of being beaten.
rhypophobia an abnormal fear of filth.
Russophobia an excessive fear or dislike of Russians.
Satanophobia an excessive fear of Satan.
scabiophobia an abnormal fear of scabies.
scopophobia an abnormal fear of being looked at. Also called **scoptophobia.**
siderophobia an abnormal fear of the stars.

spectrophobia an abnormal fear of specters or phantoms.

syphiliphobia, syphilophobia an abnormal fear of becoming infected with syphilis.

tabophobia an abnormal fear of a wasting sickness.

tapinophobia an abnormal fear of small things.

teleophobia a dislike and rejection of teleology.

telephonophobia an abnormal fear of using the telephone.

theatrophobia an abnormal fear of theaters.

tomophobia an abnormal fear of surgical operations.

tonitrophobia, tonitruphobia an abnormal fear of thunder.

traumatophobia an excessive or disabling fear of war or physical injury.

tridecaphobia an abnormal fear of the number 13. Also called **triskaidekaphobia.**

tremophobia an abnormal fear of trembling.

trichinophobia an abnormal fear of trichinosis. Also called **trichophobia, trichopathophobia.**

tuberculophobia an abnormal fear of tuberculosis.

tyrannophobia an intense fear or hatred of tyrants.

Uranophobia an abnormal fear of homosexuals and homosexuality.

urophobia an abnormal fear of passing urine.

vaccinophobia an abnormal fear of vaccines and vaccination.

vermiphobia an abnormal fear of worms.

xerophobia an abnormal fear of dryness and dry places like deserts.

PHONOGRAPH RECORDS

audiophile a person especially interested in high-fidelity sound equipment and recordings on tape or discs.

audiophilia 1. the state or condition of an audiophile.
2. the state of one who listens to high-fidelity equipment solely for the quality of reproduction. —**audiophilic,** *adj.*

discophily, diskophily the zealous study and collection of phonograph records. Also called **phonophily.** —**discophile, diskophile,** *n.*

disc jockey, disk jockey 1. the announcer who conducts a radio broadcast consisting of recorded music, informal talk, commercials, etc.
2. the announcer and player of recorded music in a discotheque.

discography, diskography 1. a list of musical recordings, usu. with commentary, often concerning one composer, performer, or performing group.
2. the analysis, history, or classification of musical recordings.
3. the methods of such analysis or classification. —**discographer, diskographer,** *n.* —**discographical,** *adj.*

gramophile   *Brit.* a lover and collector of phonograph records.

PHOTOGRAPHY

actinography   1. the measurement of the intensity of radiation with a recording actinometer, usually by the photochemical effect.
2. the calculation of suitable exposure times in photography through the use of a recording actinometer. —**actinographic,** *adj.*

cinematics   the process or art of making motion pictures; cinematography. —**cinematic,** *adj.*

electrography   an apparatus for electrically transmitting pictures. —**electrograph,** *n.* —**electrographic,** *adj.*

reprography   a collective term for all kinds of processes used for the facsimile reproduction of documents or books.

telephotography   1. the art or process of photographing distant objects by using a telephoto lens or a telescope with a camera.
2. electrography. —**telephotographic,** *adj.*

time lapse photography   the motion-picture photography of a slow and continuous process, as the sprouting of a seed, at regular intervals, esp. by exposing one frame at a time.

vectography   a stereoscopic process involving two superimposed images polarized at 90˚ to each other and viewed through polarizing glasses for a three-dimensional effect. —**vectograph,** *n.* —**vectographic,** *adj.*

PHYSICAL CHARACTERISTICS

elasticity   *Physics.* the property of a substance that makes it possible to change its length, volume, or shape in direct response to a force and to recover its original form upon the removal of a force. —**elastic,** *adj.*

malleability   the property of a substance that makes it capable of being extended or shaped by hammering or by pressure from rollers. —**malleable,** *adj.*

plasticity   the property of a substance that makes it capable of being molded, given shape, or being made to assume a desired form. —**plastic,** *adj.*

rigidity   the property of a substance that renders it inflexible, stiff, or nonpliable. —**rigid,** *adj.*

vitreosity   a state or quality resembling that of glass, as in hardness, brittleness, transparency, glossiness, etc. —**vitreous,** *adj.*

PHYSICS

astaticism   the condition of constant, uninterrupted variability of direction or position. —**astatic,** *adj.*

crystallography   the science that studies crystallization and the forms and structures of crystals. —**crystallographer,** *n.* —**crystallographic, crystallographical,** *adj.*

energetics the branch of physics that studies energy and its transformation. —**energeticist,** *n.* —**energeticistic,** *adj.*

geophysics the physics of the earth, including oceanography, volcanology, seismology, etc. —**geophysicist,** *n.* —**geophysical,** *adj.*

oscillography the study of the wave-forms of changing currents, voltages, or any other quantity that can be translated into electricity, as light or sound waves. —**oscillographic,** *adj.*

physics the science that studies matter and energy in terms of motion and force. —**physicist,** *n.*

plenism the theory that nature contains no vacuums. —**plenist,** *n.* Cf. **vacuism.**

tribology the science and technology of friction, lubrication, and wear.

vacuism the theory that nature permits vacuums. —**vacuist,** *n.*

PLACES

nostopathy *Rare.* an abnormal fear of returning to familiar places.

topophobia *Rare.* an abnormal fear of certain places. —**topophobe,** *n.*

PLANETS

celidography a description of the surface markings of the sun or a planet. —**celidographer,** *n.*

exobiology the branch of biology that studies life beyond the earth's atmosphere, as on other planets.

planetoid *Astronomy.* any of thousands of small celestial bodies that revolve about the sun in orbits chiefly between those of Mars and Jupiter ranging in diameter from one mile to 480 miles. Also called **asteroids, minor planets.** —**planetoidal,** *adj.*

PLANTS

acidophobia in plants, an inability to accommodate to acid soils. —**acidophobic,** *adj.* Cf. **basophobia.**

aquapontics *Botany.* the cultivation of plants in nutrient solutions, usu. for commercial purposes. —**aquapontic,** *adj.*

auxography *Botany.* the measurement of the swelling and shrinking of parts of plants. —**auxographic,** *adj.*

basophobia, basiphobia in plants, an inability to accommodate to alkaline soils. —**basophobic,** *adj.* Cf. **acidophobia.**

cecidiology, cecidology *Biology.* the study of galls produced on trees and plants by fungi, insects, or mites.

crescograph a device for making apparent to the eye the successive stages of plant growth. —**crescographic,** *adj.* Cf. **time lapse photography.**

cumaphytism the procedures involved in adapting plants for growth under surf conditions. —**cumaphytic,** *adj.*

dendrophilia *Botany.* the apparent preference of some plants, as orchids, to grow in or near trees. —**dendrophilous,** *adj.*

epiphyte *Botany.* a plant that grows in a commensal relationship upon another, gaining its nutrients and water from rain, dust, etc. Also called **air plant** or **aerophyte.** —**epiphytic, epiphytical,** *adj.*

epiphytology *Botany.* the study of the character, ecology, and causes of plant diseases, as blight, which destroy a large number of susceptible plants in a large area simultaneously.

floristry the art or skill of a florist.

halophytism the ability of certain plants to grow normally in soils having a high mineral salt content. —**halophyte,** *n.* —**halophytic,** *adj.*

heliophilia an attraction or adaptation to sunlight, as the sunflower. —**heliophile,** *n.* —**heliophilic, heliophilous,** *adj.*

heliotropism the tendency in some plant species to turn toward or follow the sun. —**heliotrope,** *n.* —**heliotropic,** *adj.*

hydrophytism the ability of certain plants to grow naturally in water or in highly moist soils. —**hydrophyte,** *n.* —**hydrophytic,** *adj.*

lichenology *Botany.* the study of lichens. —**lichenologist,** *n.* —**lichenologic, lichenological,** *adj.*

mangonism *Obsolete.* any procedure for raising plants under other than natural conditions of growth.

mesophytism the ability of certain plants to grow naturally in moderate but constant moisture. —**mesophyte,** *n.* —**mesophytic,** *adj.*

morphology *Biology.* the study of the form and structure of plants and animals. —**morphologist,** *n.* —**morphologic, morphological,** *adj.*

muscology *Botany.* the study of mosses.

mycology *Botany.* the study of fungi.

ombrophily the capacity of some plants to thrive in the midst of copious rain. Also called **hydrophily.** —**ombrophilic, ombrophilous,** *adj.*

orchidology the branch of botany or horticulture that studies orchids. —**orchidologist,** *n.*

organology *Biology.* the study of the structure and organs of plants and animals. —**organologist,** *n.* —**organologic, organological,** *adj.*

pedology the science that studies the composition and qualities of soils. —**pedologist,** *n.* —**pedological,** *adj.*

philobotanist *Rare.* a lover of plants.

photonasty *Botany.* the tendency in certain plant species to respond to light by developing sufficient cellular force or growth on one side of an axis to change the form or position of the axis, as in the opening and closing of the flowers of four-o'clocks. —**photonastic,** *adj.*

photoperiodism *Botany.* the study of the relative amounts of light and darkness in a 24-hour period required to best effect the growth, reproduction, and flowering of plant species or the growth and reproduction of animals. Also called **photoperiodicity.** —**photoperiodic, photoperiodical,** *adj.*

photophilia, photophily *Botany.* the necessity, in some plants species, for exposure to strong light. —**photophile, photophilic, photophilous,** *adj.*

phytoillumination **1.** *Botany.* the study of the effects of varying periods of artificial light upon plant growth.
2. the growing of plants under agricultural lamps, usu. fluorescent, for domestic or commercial purposes.

phytoserology *Serology.* the identification, classification, and study of plant viruses.

pleomorphism, pleomorphy the existence of a plant or animal in two or more distinct forms during a life cycle; polymorphism. —**pleomorphic, pleomorphous,** *adj.*

saprophytism the ability of certain plants to live in dead or decaying organic matter. —**saprophyte,** *n.* —**saprophytic,** *n., adj.*

thermonasty *Botany.* the tendency in certain plant species to respond to temperature changes by developing a sufficient cellular force or growth on one side of an axis to change the form or position of the axis, as in the closing or folding of rhododendron leaves in cold air. —**thermonastic,** *adj.* Cf. **photonasty.**

thermoperiodism *Botany.* the study of the relative day and night temperatures required, in a 24-hour period, to achieve the best growth, reproduction, or flowering of plant species or the growth and reproduction of animals. Also called **thermoperiodicity.** —**thermoperiodic, thermoperiodical,** *adj.* Cf. **photoperiodism.**

thermotropism the tendency in some plant species to turn toward or away from a source of heat. —**thermotropic, thermotropical,** *adj.*

tulipomania a mania for planting and growing tulips, esp. such a mania in Holland in the 1630's, when a sum equivalent to $5200 was paid for a single bulb. —**tulipomaniac,** *n.*

uredinology a branch of mycology that studies rusts.

vernalization the shortening of the growth period before the blossoming and fruiting of a plant by exposing the seed, bulb, or seedling to high or low temperatures. Also called **jarovization.** —**vernalize,** *v.*

xerophilia, xerophily the ability of some plants in desert or salt marsh areas to store water internally. —**xerophilous**, *adj.*

xerophytism the natural adaptation of plants living under desert or marsh conditions in order to store water internally. —**xerophyte**, *n.* —**xerophytic**, *adj.*

PLEASURE

epicurism, epicureanism **1.** the cultivation of a refined taste, as in food, art, music, etc.; connoisseurship.
2. a devotion or adaptation to luxurious tastes, esp. in drinking and eating, or to indulgence in sensual pleasures. —**epicure**, *n.* —**epicurean**, *n., adj.* Cf. **Epicureanism.**

hedonism **1.** *Ethics.* the doctrine that pleasure or happiness is the highest good. Cf. **Epicureanism, endaemonism.**
2. a devotion to pleasure as a way of life. —**hedonist**, *n.* —**hedonistic**, *adj.*

stoicism **1.** a form of conduct conforming to the precepts of the Stoics.
2. a form of conduct characterized by patience, impassivity, repression of emotion, or indifference to pain and pleasure. —**stoic**, *n., adj.* —**stoical**, *adj.*

POISON

alexipharmac, alexipharmic *Med.* a remedy for or antidote against poison or infection. —**alexipharmic**, *adj.*

botulism *Pathology.* a disease of the nervous system caused by botulin developments in spoiled foods eaten by animals and man; a variety of bacterial food poisoning.

cantharidism *Med.* a toxic condition caused by the misuse of the counter-irritant and diuretic cantharides.

ergotism *Pathology.* a condition caused by eating rye or some other grain infected with ergot fungus or by an overdose of an ergot medicinal agent.

iophobia an abnormal fear of poisons.

mithridatism *Med.* the production of immunity against the action of a poison by consuming it in gradually larger doses. —**mithridatize**, *v.*

mycetism *Med.* any of a variety of toxic conditions produced by poisonous mushrooms. Also called **mycetismus.**

plutonism a poisoning caused by exposure to radioactive plutonium.

plumbism *Pathology.* an acute toxic condition caused by the absorption of lead into the body by skin contact, ingestion, or inhalation; lead poisoning. Also called **saturnism.**

ptyalism *Med.* an excessive salivation, usu. associated with chronic mercury poisoning. Also called **salivation.**

salmonellosis *Med.* an illness caused by food tainted with certain species of salmonella bacteria; a variety of bacterial food poisoning.

thebaism *Archaic.* a toxic condition produced by thebaine, a derivative of opium.

toxicology the branch of medical science that studies the effects, antidotes, detection, etc., of poisons. —**toxicologist,** *n.* —**toxicologic, toxicological,** *adj.*

toxiphobia an abnormal fear of poisoning. Also called **toxicophobia.** —**toxiphobe, toxiphobiac,** *n.* Cf. **iophobia.**

venenation the process of being poisoned, esp. with the venom of animals, as snakes or scorpions.

POLITICS

agrarianism the doctrine of an equal division of landed property and the advancement of agricultural groups. Also called **agrarian reform.** —**agrarian,** *adj.*

analytical stasiology an attempt, through the construction of conceptual frameworks, to develop a science of political parties.

Arabism a devotion to Arab interests, custom, culture, ideals, and political goals.

anythingarianism the holding of no particular belief, creed, or political position. —**anythingarian,** *n.*

Arnoldist a follower of Arnold of Brescia, 12th cent. Italian political reformer, esp. his attacks upon clerical riches and corruption, and upon the temporal power of the pope.

Babouvism a social and political doctrine advocating egalitarianism and communism. —**Babouvist,** *n.*

Chartism the principles of a movement or party of English political reformers, chiefly working men, from 1838 to 1848, advocating better working and social conditions for laborers in its People's Charter (1838). —**Chartist,** *n.*

Boloism the practice, during war, of promoting propaganda and defeatist activities favoring an enemy country.

brinkmanship the technique or practice in foreign policy of manipulating a dangerous situation to the limits of tolerance or safety in order to secure advantage, esp. by creating diplomatic crises. Also called **brinksmanship.**

boodleism *U.S. slang.* the practice of bribery or illicit payments, esp. to or from a politician. Also called **boodling.** —**boodler,** *n.*

Bourbonism 1. an adherence to the ideas and system of government developed by the Bourbons.
2. an extreme conservatism, esp. in politics. —**Bourbonist,** *n.* —**Bourbonian, Bourbonic,** *adj.*

bossism *U.S.* a control by bosses, esp. political bosses.

communalism 1. a theory or system of organization in which the major

political and social units are self-governing communes, and the nation is merely a federation of such groups.
2. the principles or practices of communal ownership. —**communalist,** *n.* —**communalistic,** *adj.* Cf. **communism, socialism.**
See also COMMUNALISM.

conservatism 1. the disposition to retain what is established and to practice a policy of gradualism rather than abrupt change.
2. the principles and practices of political conservatives, esp. of the British Conservative Party. —**conservative,** *n., adj.*

collectivism the socialist principle of control by the state of all means of productive or economic activity. —**collectivist,** *n., adj.* —**collectivistic,** *adj.*

constitutionalism 1. the principles of the form of government defined by a constitution.
2. an adherence to these principles.
3. constitutional rule or authority. —**constitutionalist,** *n.*

continentalism 1. an attitude or policy of favoritism or partiality to a continent.
2. a policy advocating a restriction of political or economic relations to the countries of one continent. —**continentalist,** *n.*

czarism 1. an autocratic government.
2. dictatorship. Also called **tzarism, tsarism.** —**czarist,** *n., adj.*

egalitarianism a social and political philosophy asserting the equality of all men, esp. in their access to the rights and privileges of their society. —**egalitarian,** *n., adj.*

demagogism, demagoguism, demagogy the art and practice of gaining power and popularity by arousing the emotions, passions, and prejudices of the people. Also called **demagoguery.**

expansionism a policy of expansion, as of territory or currency. —**expansionistic,** *adj.*

Falangism the doctrines and practices of the Spanish fascist party. —**Falangist,** *n., adj.*

Fenianism the principles and practices of an Irish revolutionary organization founded in New York in 1858, esp. its emphasis on the establishment of an independent Irish republic. —**Fenian,** *n., adj.*

Gandhism, Gandhiism the principles of Mohandas Gandhi, Indian political and spiritual leader, esp. his principles of passive resistance and noncooperation in gaining social and political reforms. —**Gandhist, Gandhiist,** *n.* —**Gandhian,** *adj.*

Ghibellinism the principles of the imperial and aristocratic party of medieval Italy, esp. their support of the German emperors.—**Ghibelline,** *n., adj.* Cf. **Guelphism.**

gradualism the principle or policy of achieving a goal, as political or economic, by gradual steps rather than by sudden and drastic innovation. —**gradualist,** *n., adj.* —**gradualistic,** *adj.*

Guelphism, Guelfism the principles and practices of the papal and popular party in medieval Italy. —**Guelphic, Guelfic,** *adj.* Cf. **Ghibellinism.**

Guesdism the principles of Marxian socialism as interpreted by the French socialist, editor, and writer Jules Guesde. —**Guesdist,** *n., adj.*

institutionalism 1. the system of institutions or organized societies devoted to public, political, or charitable, or similar purposes. **2.** a strong attachment to established institutions, as political systems or religions. —**institutionalist,** *n.*

ideology the body of doctrine, myth, symbol, etc., with reference to some political or cultural plan, as that of communism, along with the procedures for putting it into operation. —**ideologist,** *n.* —**ideologic, ideological,** *adj.*

irredentism 1. a national policy advocating the acquisition of some region in another country by reason of common linguistic, cultural, historical, ethnic, or racial ties. **2.** (*cap.*) the policies of a 19th cent. Italian party which sought to annex parts of certain neighboring regions with chiefly Italian populations. —**irredentist,** *n., adj.*

isolationism the policy or doctrine directed toward the isolation of a country from the affairs of other nations by a deliberate abstention from political, military, and economic agreements. —**isolationist,** *n.*

jusquaboutism, jusquaboutisme a policy of self-sacrificing and determined radicalism. —**jusquaboutist,** *n., adj.*

liberalism 1. a political or social philosophy advocating the freedom of the individual, parliamentary legislatures, governmental assurances of civil liberties and individual rights, and nonviolent modification of institutions to permit continued individual and social progress. **2.** the principles and practice of a liberal political party. —**liberalist,** *n., adj.* —**liberalistic,** *adj.*

Locofocoism the doctrines of the Locofocos, a radical faction of the New York City Democrats, organized in 1835 to oppose the conservatives in the party. —**Locofoco,** *n.*

Loyalism 1. a dedication to the British cause during the American revolution; Toryism. **2.** an adherence to the cause of the republic during the Spanish Civil War. —**Loyalist,** *n.*

Machiavellianism 1. the principles of government set forth in *The Prince* of Machiavelli, in which political expediency is exalted above morality and the use of craft and deceit to maintain authority or to effectuate policy is recommended. Also called **Machiavellism.**

2. activity characterized by subtle cunning, duplicity, or bad faith. —**Machiavellian,** *n., adj.*

Malanism the principles and attitudes of Daniel F. Malan, prime minister of the Union of South Africa 1948-1954, whose policies of apartheid and Afrikaner supremacy were first made law during his term of office.

McCarthyism 1. *U.S.* the practice of making accusations of disloyalty, esp. of pro-Communist activity, often unsupported or based on doubtful evidence.
2. any attempt to restrict political criticism or individual dissent by claiming it to be unpatriotic or pro-Communist.

militarism 1. the principle of maintaining a large military establishment.
2. the policy of regarding military efficiency as the supreme ideal of the state, and the subordinating of all other ideals to those of the military. —**militarist,** *n.* —**militaristic,** *adj.*

moderantism the principle or policy of moderation, esp. in politics and international relations. —**moderantist,** *n.*

mugwumpism 1. the practice of independence, esp. in politics.
2. an inability to make up one's mind, esp. in politics; neutrality on controversial issues. Also called **mugwumpery.** —**mugwump,** *n.* —**mugwumpian, mugwumpish,** *adj.*

Nazism, Naziism the principles and practices of the National Socialist Workers' Party under Adolf Hitler from 1933 to 1945. —**Nazi,** *n., adj.*

neutralism the practice or policy of remaining neutral in foreign affairs. —**neutralist,** *n.*

nonpartisanism the practice or policy of nonsupport for established or regular political parties. Also called **nonpartisanship.** —**nonpartisan,** *n., adj.*

nothingarianism the holding of no belief, creed, or political position. —**nothingarian,** *n.*

partisanism an action or spirit of partiality for a specific political party. Also called **partisanship.** —**partisan,** *n., adj.*

physiocratism the principles and doctrines of political economists following the ideas of Francois Quesnay in holding that an inherent natural order adequately controlled society and advocating a laissez-faire economy based on land as the best system to prevent interference with natural laws. —**physiocrat,** *n.* —**physiocratic,** *adj.*

pluralism 1. *Eccl.* the holding of two or more church offices by a single person.
2. the state or condition of a common civilization in which various ethnic, racial or religious groups are free to participate in and develop their common cultures.
3. a policy or principle supporting such cultural plurality. —**pluralist,** *n.* —**pluralistic,** *adj.*

popular sovereignty 1. the doctrine that sovereign power is vested in the people and that those chosen by election to govern or to represent must conform to the will of the people.
2. *U.S. Hist.* a doctrine, held chiefly before 1865 by anti-abolitionists, that new territories should be free of federal interference in domestic matters, esp. concerning slavery.

populism 1. the principles and doctrines of any political party asserting that it represents the rank and file of the people.
2. (*cap.*) the principles and doctrines of a late 19th cent. American party, esp. its support of agrarian interests and a silver coinage. —**populist,** *n.* —**populistic,** *adj.*

progressivism 1. the principles and practices of those advocating progress, change, or reform, esp. in political matters. Also called **progressism.**
2. (*cap.*) the doctrines and beliefs of the Progressive party in America. —**progressivist,** *n.*

proletarianism the practices, attitudes, social status, or political condition of an unpropertied class dependent for support on daily or casual labor. —**proletarian,** *n., adj.*

psephology the study of elections. —**psephologist,** *n.* —**psephological,** *adj.*

radicalism 1. the holding or following of principles advocating drastic political, economic, or social reforms. Cf. **conservatism, gradualism.**
2. the principles or practices of radicals.

royalism the support or advocacy of a royal government. —**royalist,** *n., adj.* —**royalistic,** *adj.*

sanscullotism any extreme republican or revolutionary principles. —**sanscullotist,** *n.* —**sanscullotic, sanscullotish,** *adj.*

separatism an advocacy of separation, esp. ecclesiastical or political separation, as the secession of U.S. states before the Civil War. —**separatist,** *n.*

Sinarquism a secret Mexican counter-revolutionary movement, advocating the return to christian social standards and opposing communism, labor unions, conscription, and pan Americanism. —**Sinarquist,** *n.*

socialism 1. a theory or system of social organization advocating placing the ownership and control of capital, land, and means of production in the community as a whole.
2. the procedures and practices based upon this theory.
3. *Marxist theory.* the first stage in the transition from capitalism to communism, marked by imperfect realizations of collectivist principles. —**socialist,** *n., adj.* —**socialistic,** *adj.*

Spartacist 1. a member of a German socialist party founded in 1918.
2. an extreme socialist. [allusion to Spartacus, leader of a slave revolt against Rome, 73-71 B.C.]

suffragism any advocacy of the granting or extension of the suffrage to those now denied it, esp. to women. —**suffragist,** *n.*

syndicalism **1.** an economic system in which workers own and manage an industry.
2. a revolutionary form or development of trade unionism, originating in France, aiming at possession and control of the means of production and distribution, and the establishment of a corporate society governed by trade unions and workers' cooperatives. —**syndicalist,** *n.* —**syndicalistic,** *adj.*

territorialism **1.** the principle of the political predominance of the landed classes; landlordism.
2. the theory of church policy vesting supreme ecclesiastical authority in a civil government, as in 16th cent. Germany. Also called **territorial system.** —**territorialist,** *n.*

terrorism **1.** a method of government or of resisting government involving domination or coercion by various forms of intimidation, as bombing or kidnapping.
2. the state of fear and terror so produced. —**terrorist,** *n.* —**terroristic,** *adj.*

Toryism **1.** a support of the British cause during the American Revolution.
2. an advocacy of conservative principles opposed to reform and radicalism.
3. the actions of dispossessed Irishmen in the 17th cent. who were declared outlaws and noted for their outrages and cruelty.
4. the principles of a conservative British party in power until 1832. —**Tory,** *n., adj.,* —**Toryish,** *adj.*

ultraism **1.** the principles of those who advocate extreme points of view or actions, as radicalism.
2. extremist activities. —**ultraist,** *n., adj.* —**ultraistic,** *adj.*

utopian socialism an economic theory based on the premise that voluntary surrender by capital of the means of production would bring about the end of poverty and unemployment. Cf. **socialism.**

POPE

antipope a pope set up in opposition to another who has been canonically chosen.

chirograph, cheirograph an apostolic letter written by and signed by the pope.
See also CATHOLICISM.

POTTERY

ceramics, keramics **1.** the art and technology of making objects of clay and other materials treated by firing.
2. articles of earthenware, porcelain, etc. —**ceramist, ceramicist,** *n.*

ceramography an historical or descriptive work on pottery.

POVERTY

depauperation actions which impoverish or reduce in quality. Also called **depauperization.** —**depauperate,** *n., v.*

dispauperization *Law.* actions which withdraw legal status as a pauper. —**dispauperize,** *v.*

pauperism the state or condition of utter poverty. Also called **pauperage.**

Poplarism **1.** *Brit.* a policy in local governments of providing relief for the poor, often excessive in amount. **2.** *Brit.* any similar policy of government spending that leads to higher taxes. —**Poplarist,** *n.*

ptochocracy a form of rule by beggars or the poor.

ptochology the scientific study of pauperism, unemployment, etc.

PRAISE

dyslogistic conveying disapproval or censure; uncomplimentary. Cf. **eulogistic.**

encomiast a person who writes or utters formal praise or eulogy. —**encomiastic,** *adj.*

eulogistic conveying approval, praise, and laudation. Also **eulogistical.** —**eulogist,** *n.*

panegyrist a person who writes or speaks a formal and elaborate commendation or eulogy.

PREGNANCY

cyesis *Med.* the condition of pregnancy.

cyesiology *Obsolete.* that part of medical science that studies pregnancy.

gravidity the state or condition of pregnancy. —**gravidness,** *n.* —**gravid,** *adj.*

pregnancy the state, condition, or quality of being with child.

PRINTING

algraphy an offset process which uses an aluminum plate instead of a lithographic stone. Also called **aluminography.** —**algraphic,** *adj.*

electrotypy the process of preparing a facsimile printing surface, involving the depositing of a thin copper or nickel shell by electrolytic action in a mold of the original and backing it with a lead alloy. —**electrotyper, electrotypist,** *n.* —**electrotypic,** *adj.*

glyphography a process for making letterpress plates by engraving a waxed copper plate, dusting with zinc, and preparing an electrotype. —**glyphographer,** *n.* —**glyphographic,** *adj.*

lithography **1.** the art or process of producing a picture or writing on a flat,

specially prepared stone, with some oily or greasy substance marking the items to be printed, and of taking ink impressions from this on paper.
2. a similar process in which the stone is replaced by a zinc or aluminum plate. —**lithographer,** *n.* —**lithographic,** *adj.*

oleography the production of chromolithographs printed in oil colors on canvas or cloth as well as on paper. —**oleographic,** *adj.*

thermography a technique for imitating an engraved appearance, as on business cards, by dusting areas already printed with a powder attracted only to the inks, and using heat to fuse the ink and powder. —**thermographer,** *n.* —**thermographic,** *adj.*

xylography the art of engraving on wood or of printing from such engravings. —**xylographer,** *n.* —**xylographic, xylographical,** *adj.*
See also COPYING.

PRONUNCIATION

cacoepy the habit of unacceptable or bad pronunciation.

cacology **1.** a defectively produced speech.
2. socially unacceptable enunciation.
3. nonconformist pronunciation.

lallation *Phonetics.* **1.** the replacement of *l* for *r* in speech.
2. the mispronunciation of *l.* Cf. **lambdacism.**

lambdacism *Phonetics.* the mispronunciation of double *l,* giving it the sound of *y* or *ly.* Also called **labdacism.**

nasalism a tendency toward nasality in pronouncing words. Also called **nasality.**

orthoepy the study of correct pronunciation. —**orthoepist,** *n.* —**orthoepic, orthoepical, orthoepistic,** *adj.*

paragoge the addition of a sound or group of sounds at the end of a word, as in the nonstandard *idear* for *idea.* —**paragogic, paragogical,** *adj.*

rhotacism *Phonetics.* **1.** a misarticulation of the sound *r* or the substitution of another sound for it.
2. the excessive use of the sound *r.*
3. *Phonology.* replacement of the sound *z* by *r* in Indo-European languages, as Ger. *wesen,* Eng. *were.* —**rhotaticize,** *v.* —**rhotacistic,** *adj.*

traulism a stammering and stuttering speech.

PROTESTANTISM

adiaphorism a tolerance of conduct or beliefs not specifically forbidden in the Scriptures. —**adiaphorist,** *n.* —**adiaphoristic,** *adj.* See **Flacianism, Philippism.**

Adventism the principles and practices of certain Christian denominations which maintain that the Second Advent of Christ is imminent. Also called **Second Adventist.** —**Adventist,** *n., adj.*

Amyraldism   the doctrines and practices of a liberal form of Calvinism established in France in the 17th cent., esp. its doctrines of universal atonement and salvation for all.

Arminianism   the doctrines and teaching of Jacobus Arminius, 17th cent. Dutch theologian, who opposed the Calvinist doctrine of absolute predestination and maintained the possibility of universal salvation. —**Arminian,** *n., adj.*

Brownism   the views and doctrines of Robert Browne, the first formulator of the principles of Congregationalism. —**Brownist,** *n.* —**Brownistic,** *adj.*

Buchmanism   1. the principles of the international movement called Moral Re-Armament or of the Oxford Group.
2. the belief in or adherence to these principles. —**Buchmanite,** *n., adj.*

Calvinism   1. the doctrines of John Calvin or his followers, esp. emphasis upon predestination and limited atonement, the sovereignty of God, the authority of the Scriptures, total depravity, and the irresistibility of grace. Cf. **Arminianism.**
2. adherence to these doctrines. —**Calvinist,** *n., adj.* —**Calvinistic, Calvinistical,** *adj.*

Christadelphianism   the doctrines of a premillenial sect founded in the U.S. in the mid-19th cent., esp. its denial of Trinitarianism and its acceptance of Unitarian and Adventist doctrines. —**Christadelphian,** *n., adj.*

Congregationalism   1. the doctrine and governmental practices of Congregational churches.
2. a form of church government in which each congregation is autonomous. —**Congregationalist,** *n., adj.*

cirplanology   the history and study of Methodist circuit plans.

consociationism   the theory or practice of associations or confederations of religious societies, usu. for purposes of fellowship. —**consociational,** *adj.*

Darbyism   the doctrines and practices of the Plymouth Brethren. —**Darbyite,** *n.*

denominationalism   1. the policy or spirit of denominations or sects.
2. the tendency to divide into denominations or sects. —**denominationalist,** *n.*

ecumenism   the doctrines and practices of the ecumenical movement, esp. among Protestant groups since the 1800's, aimed at developing worldwide Christian unity and church union. Also called **ecumenicalism, ecumenicism.**

Episcopalianism   1. the Protestant Episcopal Church of the Anglican communion.
2. adherence to the policy and practice of the Episcopal Church. —**Episcopalian,** *n., adj.* —**Episcopal,** *adj.*

episcopalism   a theory of church polity asserting that supreme ecclesiastical authority belongs to all bishops collectively and not to an individual except by delegation. Cf. **Gallicanism, ultramontanism.**

Flacianism   the Lutheran doctrines and treatises of Matthias Flacius Illyricus, esp. his attacks úpon Melanchthon and others for distorting Luther's teachings and emphasizing adiaphorism. —**Flacian,** *n. See* **Philippism.**

fundamentalism   1. a conservative movement in 20th cent. American Protestantism in reaction to modernism, asserting esp. the inerrancy of the Scriptures as an historical record and as a guide to faith and morals, and emphasizing, as matters of true faith, belief in the virgin birth, the sacrifice and death of Christ upon the cross, physical resurrection, and the Second Coming.
2. an adherence to the doctrines and practices of this movement. —**fundamentalist,** *n., adj.*

Huguenotism   the doctrines and practices of the Calvinistic communion in France in the 16th and 17th cents. —**Huguenot,** *n.* —**Huguenotic,** *adj.*

Hussitism   the doctrines of a reformist and nationalistic movement initiated by John Huss ın Bohemia about 1402, esp. its reflection of Wycliffite emphases upon clerical purity, communion in both bread and wine for the laity, and the supreme authority of the Scriptures. Also called **Hussism.** —**Hussite,** *n., adj.*

Koreshanity   the doctrines and beliefs of an American communal religious society founded in 1886, esp. its goal of reforming both church and state and their mutual relationship to God. —**Koreshan,** *adj.*

Laudianism   the policies and practices of William Laud, Archbishop of Canterbury and opponent of Puritanism, esp. his assertion that the Church of England preserves more fully than the Roman communion the orthodoxy of the early Christian church, his support of the divine right of Kings and bishops, and his influence upon an architecture blending Gothic and Renaissance motifs. —**Laudian,** *n., adj.*

liberalism   a movement in modern Protestantism that emphasizes freedom from tradition and authority, the adjustment of religious beliefs to scientific conceptions, and the spiritual and ethical content of Christianity. —**liberalist,** *n., adj.* —**liberalistic,** *adj.*

Lollardism   1. the religious teachings of John Wycliffe, 14th cent. English theologian, religious reformer, and Bible translator.
2. adherence to these teachings, esp. in England and Scotland in the 14th and 15th cents. Also called **Lollardry, Lollardy, Wycliffism.** —**Lollard,** *n., adj.*

Lutheranism   1. the religious doctrines and church polity of Martin Luther, 16th cent. German theologian, author, and leader of the Protestant Reformation.

2. adherence to these doctrines or membership in the Lutheran Church. —**Lutheran,** *n., adj.*

Methodism **1.** the religious teachings and church polity of John Wesley, 18th cent. English theologian and evangelist, or those of his followers. **2.** the doctrines, polity, beliefs, and rituals of the Methodist Church, founded by Wesley, esp. its emphasis on personal and social morality. —**Methodist,** *n., adj.*

Mormonism **1.** the doctrines and polity of the Church of Jesus Christ of Latter-day Saints, founded in the U.S. in 1830 by Joseph Smith, esp. its adoption of the *Book of Mormon* as an adjunct to the Bible. **2.** adherence to these doctrines or membership in the Mormon Church. Also called **Mormondom.** —**Mormon,** *n., adj.*

nonconformism **1.** the state or practice of nonadherence to an established church or its doctrine, discipline, or polity. **2.** (*cap.*) the condition of a Protestant in England who is not a member of the Church of England; dissenterism. —**nonconformist,** *n., adj.*

nonjurorism **1.** the practice of refusing to take a required oath, as of allegiance. **2.** (*cap.*) the action of Church of England clergymen who refused, in 1689, to swear allegiance to William and Mary. —**nonjuror,** *n.*

Pajonism a theological doctrine proposed by the 17th cent. French theologian Claude Pajon, esp. its emphasis upon the indirect rather than direct influence of the Holy Spirit upon an individual.

Pentecostalism the beliefs and practices of certain Christian groups, often fundamentalist, that emphasize the activity of the Holy Spirit, stress a strict morality, and seek emotional spiritual experiences in worship rituals. —**Pentecostal,** *n., adj.*

Philippism *Rare.* the doctrines of Philip Melanchthon, 16th cent. German Protestant reformer, esp. his rebuttals to the allegations of the Flacians that his attitude toward certain teachings of Martin Luther was adiaphoristic. —**Philippist,** *n.* —**Philippistic,** *adj.*

Pietism **1.** a movement, begun in the 17th cent. German Lutheran Church, exalting the practice of personal piety over religious orthodoxy and ritual. **2.** the principles and practices of the Pietists. —**Pietist,** *n.* —**Pietistic, Pietistical,** *adj.*

Presbyterianism **1.** the doctrines, polity, and practices of Presbyterian churches, esp. a Calvinist theology and a representative system of church government. **2.** a system of church government in which ministers and congregationally elected elders participate in a graded series of legislative bodies and administrative courts. —**Presbyterian,** *n., adj.*

Puritanism **1.** the principles and practices of a movement within 16th cent. Anglicanism, demanding reforms in doctrine, polity, and worship, and greater strictness in religious discipline, chiefly in terms of Calvinist principles.

2. a political party developed from the religious movement in the 17th cent. that successfully gained control of England through revolution and briefly attempted to put Puritan principles to work on all levels of English life and government.

3. *U.S.* the principles and practices of the Congregationalist members of the religious movement who, migrating to America in 1620, attempted to set up a theocratic state in which clergy had authority over both religious and civil life. —**Puritan,** *n., adj.*

Quakerism   the principles and beliefs of the Society of Friends, a creedless sect founded in England about 1650 by George Fox, esp. its emphasis upon the Inward Light of each believer, its rejection of oaths, and its opposition to all wars. Also called **Quakerdom.** (Terms made from *quake* are never used to or between members of the Society, who prefer *Friend* or *thee.*) —**Quaker,** *n., adj.*

restorationism   the belief in a temporary future punishment and a final restoration of all sinners to the favor of God. Also called **restitutionism.** —**restorationist,** *n.*

revivalism   that form of religious activity which manifests itself in evangelistic services for the purpose of effecting a religious awakening. —**revivalist,** *n.* —**revivalistic,** *adj.*

Russellites   the former name of the sect called Jehovah's Witnesses.

salvationism   **1.** any religious teachings in which are emphasized doctrines concerning the saving of the soul.
2. the doctrines of the saving of the soul.
3. evangelism, esp. that calling for individuals to make open and public conversions. —**salvationist,** *n.* —**salvational,** *adj.*

sectarianism   the spirit or tendencies of sectarians, esp. adherence or excessive devotion to a particular sect, esp. in religion. —**sectarian,** *n., adj.*

Shakerism   the principles, beliefs, and practices of a millenial sect called the United Society of Believers in Christ's Second Coming, originating in England in the Shaking Quakers sect and brought to the U.S. in 1774 by Mother Ann Lee, esp. an emphasis on communal and celibate living, on the dual nature of Christ as male and female, on their dances and songs as part of worship, and their honest, functional craftsmanship. —**Shaker,** *n., adj.*

Stundism   the doctrines and practices of a Russian Protestant denomination founded about 1860, esp. their emphasis upon evangelism, piety, and communal Bible study and prayer. —**Stundist,** *n.*

Swedenborgianism, Swedenborgism   the doctrines, beliefs, and practices of the Church of the New Jerusalem, founded by the followers of Emmanuel Swedenborg in the late 18th cent., esp. its assertion that Christ is God

Himself and not the Son of God, and its reliance upon accounts of mystical appearances of Christ to Swedenborg. —**Swedenborgian,** *n., adj.*

syncretism   the attempted reconciliation or union of different or opposing principles, practices, parties, or denominations, as in the late 19th and 20th cent. discussions between Anglo-Catholics and Roman authorities. —**syncretic, syncretical, syncretistic, syncretistical,** *adj.*

Tractarianism   the religious opinions and principles of the Oxford movement within Anglicanism, esp. in its *Tracts for the Times,* a series of ninety treatises published between 1833 and 1841. —**Tractarian,** *n., adj.*

Ubiquitism   the doctrine that the body of Christ is present everywhere, held by some Lutherans and others. —**Ubiquitarian,** *n., adj.*

Utraquism   the doctrines and practices of the Calixtins, a Hussite group demanding communion in both wafer and wine. —**Utraquist,** *n.*

Unitarianism   the beliefs, principles, and practices of the Unitarian denomination, esp. its doctrine that God is one being, and its emphasis upon autonomous congregational government. —**Unitarian,** *n., adj.*

Universalism   **1.** the theological doctrine that all men will finally be saved or brought back to holiness and God.
   2. the doctrines and practices of the Universalist denomination. —**Universalist,** *n., adj.* —**Universalistic,** *adj.*

Wesleyanism   the evangelical teachings of John Wesley; Methodism. Also called **Wesleyism.** —**Wesleyan,** *n., adj.*

Whitefieldism   the principles, teachings, practices, and techniques of George Whitefield, English Methodist revivalist, who, after a request from Wesley that he visit America, made seven visits after 1738 and gained a reputation as an eloquent and fiery preacher, becoming a model for future American revivalists.

Wycliffism   See **Lollardism.**

PROVERBS

aphorism   a terse saying embodying general truths, as "Clothes make the man." —**aphorist,** *n.* —**aphorismic, aphorismical, aphoristic,** *adj.*

apothegmatist   a creator of short, pithy instructive sayings; aphorist. —**apothegmatic, apothegmatical,** *adj.*

gnomonology   **1.** a collection or anthology of gnomes or aphorisms.
   2. aphoristic writing.

maximist   a person who composes or repeats maxims.

paroemia   a rhetorical proverb. —**paroemiac,** *adj.*

paroemiography, paremiography   **1.** the writing of proverbs.
   2. the collecting of proverbs. —**paroemiographer,** *n.*

paroemiology   the study of proverbs. —**paroemiologist,** *n.*

PSYCHOLOGY

alienism the study or treatment of mental diseases, esp. in their relation to legal problems. —**alienist,** *n.*

anima *Jungianism.* **1.** the inner personality that is turned toward the unconscious of the individual. Cf. **persona.**
2. the feminine principle, esp. as present in men. Cf. **animus.**

animus *Jungianism.* the masculine principle, esp. as present in women.

behaviorism the theory or doctrine that observed behavior provides the only valid data of psychology. —**behaviorist,** *n., adj.* —**behavioristic,** *adj.*

Couéism a method of self-help stressing autosuggestion, introduced into America by the French psychotherapist Emile Coué c. 1920 and featuring the slogan "every day in every way I am getting better and better."

cryptesthesia, cryptaesthesia the innate ability to be clairvoyant, as in parapsychological experiments. —**cryptesthetic,** *adj.*

eidology the study of mental imagery.

hypnotism **1.** the science dealing with the induction of hypnosis, esp. for therapeutic purposes.
2. the act of inducing hypnosis; hypnotizing.
3. hypnosis. —**hypnotist,** *n.* —**hypnotistic,** *adj.*

metapsychology **1.** a speculation dealing systematically with concepts extending beyond the present limits of psychology as an empirical science.
2. a conception in psychoanalytic theory of mental processes involving causal relations, structural placement, and functional value. —**metapsychological,** *adj.*

neuroticism a neurotic condition; psychoneurosis.

pansexualism **1.** the pervasion of all conduct and experience with sexual emotions.
2. the theory which regards all desire and interest as derived from sex instinct. Also called **pansexuality.** —**pansexualist,** *n.*

parapsychology the branch of psychology that studies psychic phenomena, as telepathy, clairvoyance, extrasensory perception, and the like. —**parapsychological,** *adj.*

persona *Jungianism.* the public personality; the façade, front, or mask presented to cope with the demands of a situation or environment and not representative of the inner personality of an individual. Cf. **anima.**

reactology the scientific study of psychological reactions. —**reactologist,** *n.* —**reactological,** *adj.*

reflexology the study of behavior and its interpretation according to a concept that regards behavior as a combination of simple and complex reflexes. —**reflexologist,** *n.* —**reflexological,** *adj.*

telepathy a communication between minds by some nontechnological means other than sensory perception. —**telepathist,** *n.* —**telepathic,** *adj.* See also MIND and MENTAL STATES.

PUN

adnomination *Obsolete.* the act of wordplay; punning. Also called **agnomination, annomination.**

equivoque, equivoke 1. an equivocal term or ambiguous expression. 2. a play upon words; pun.

paronomasia 1. *Rhetoric.* the use of a word in different senses or the use of words similar in sound for effect, as humor or ambiguity; punning. 2. a pun. —**paronomastic,** *adj.*

PUZZLES

enigmatography the art or skill of composing enigmas. —**enigmatographer,** *n.*

enigmatology the analysis of enigmas.

logogriph 1. an anagram, or a puzzle involving anagrams. 2. a puzzle in which a certain word and all other words formed from its letters must be guessed from indications given in verses. —**logogriphic,** *adj.*

logology the pursuit of word puzzles or puzzling words. —**logologist,** *n.*

Q

QUESTIONING

catechesis a method of oral instruction involving question and answer techniques. —**catechist,** *n.*

catechetics that part of theological training that deals with the imparting of religious knowledge through catechesis and printed catechisms. —**catechetic, catechetical,** *adj.*

R

RABIES

hydrophobia in human beings, the disease called rabies.

lyssophobia an abnormal fear of rabies. See also **hydrophobophobia.**

RACE

anthroposociology the sociological study of race using anthropological methods. —**anthroposociological,** adj.

Aryanism 1. a doctrine propagandized by Nazism asserting that the so-called Aryan peoples were superior to all others in the practice of government and the development of civilization.
2. a belief in this doctrine and acceptance of its social and ethical implications, esp. with regard to the treatment of so-called inferior races, as Jews. —**Aryanist,** n.

biracialism the principle or practice of combining or representing two separate races, as white and Negro, on governing boards, committees, etc. —**biracialist, biracial,** adj.

cacogenics Biology. the study of the operation of factors that cause degeneration in offspring, esp. as applied to factors unique to separate races. Also called **dysgenics.** —**cacogenic,** adj.

ethnocracy a government controlled by a particular race or national group. —**ethnocratic,** adj.

ethnogeography the study of the geographical distribution of racial groups and the relationship between them and their environments. —**ethnogeographer,** n. —**ethnogeographic,** adj.

ethnopsychology the psychology of races and peoples. —**ethnopsychological,** adj.

eugenism the blend of factors and influences most suitable for the improvement of the inherited characteristics of a breed or race, esp. the human race. —**eugenic,** adj. Cf. **eugenics.**

genocide 1. the deliberate and systematic extermination of a racial or national group.
2. an actor in this process. —**genocidal,** adj.

Gobinism the theory or doctrine that the white race in general and the Germanic race in particular are superior to all other peoples.

interracialism the principles, beliefs, and attitudes influencing actions aimed at improving relations among differing races. —**interracial,** adj.

miscegenation 1. the interbreeding of members of different races.
2. cohabitation or marriage between a man and woman of different races, esp., in the U.S., between a Negro and a white person.
3. the mixing or mixture of races by interbreeding.

racialism the belief in or practice of the doctrine of racism. —**racialist,** n. —**racialistic,** adj.

segregationist a person who favors, encourages, or practices segregation, esp. racial isolation. Cf. **apartheid.**

RADIATION

bolometry   the measurement of minute amounts of radiant energy, esp. infrared spectra. —**bolometrist,** *n.* —**bolometric,** *adj.*

radiesthesia   the sensitivity of some humans to radiation of various kinds, as in water divining or non-medical diagnosis. —**radiesthetic,** *adj.*

RAILROADS

ferroequinology   a mock classical term for enthusiasm about railroads. —**ferroequinologist,** *n.*

siderodromophobia   an abnormal fear of railroads or traveling on trains.

RAIN

hyetography   the study of the geographical distribution of rainfall by annual totals. —**hyetographic, hyetographical,** *adj.*

hyetology   *Rare.* the branch of meteorology that studies rainfall. —**hyetologist,** *n.* —**hyetological,** *adj.*

nucleation   the process of seeding a cloud, as with silver iodide, to produce rainfall. —**nucleator,** *n.*

ombrology   the branch of meteorology that studies rain. —**ombrological,** *n.*

ombrophobia   an abnormal fear of rain.

pluviography   the branch of meteorology that measures rainfall and snowfall automatically. —**pluviographic, pluviographical,** *adj.*

pluviometry   the branch of meteorology concerned with the measurement of rainfall. —**pluviometric, pluviometrical,** *adj.*

udometry   the measurement of rainfall with any of various types of rain gauges. —**udometric,** *adj.*

READING

dyslexia   an impairment of the ability to read because of a brain defect. Also called *alexia.* —**dyslexic,** *adj.*

strephosymbolia   *Med.* **1.** a disorder of perception causing objects to seem as if reversed in a mirror.
2. a reading difficulty characterized by confusion between similar but oppositely oriented letters (*b-d,* etc.) and a tendency to reverse direction in reading. —**strephosymbolic,** *adj.*

RELIGION

Adamitism   the practice of going naked for God; the beliefs of some ascetic sects in ritual nakedness. —**Adamite,** *n.* —**Adamitic,** *adj.*
See also **gymnosophy.**

angelology   **1.** *Theology.* the doctrine or theory concerning angels.
2. the beliefs concerning angels.

apocalypticism *Theology.* **1.** any doctrine concerning the end of the temporal world, esp. one based on the Revelations of St. John the Divine. **2.** the millenial doctrine of the Second Advent and the reign of Jesus Christ on earth. —**apocalyptic, apocalyptical,** *adj.*

Bahaism the doctrines and practices of a sect growing out of Babism and reflecting some attitudes of the Islamic Shi'a sect, but with an emphasis on tolerance and the essential worth of all religions. —**Bahaist,** *n., adj.* —**Bahai,** *n.*

Caodaism, Caodism the doctrines of an Indochinese religion, esp. an amalgamation of features from Buddhism, Taoism, Confucianism, Christianity, and spiritualism. —**Caodaist,** *n.*

devotionalism the quality or state of a person markedly characterized by religious devotion. —**devotionalist,** *n.*

Druidism the doctrines and practices of an order of Celtic priests in ancient Britain, Gaul, and Ireland. —**Druid,** *n., adj.* —**Druidic, Druidical,** *adj.*

dualism *Theology.* **1.** the doctrine of two independent divine beings or eternal principles, one good and the other evil. **2.** the belief that man embodies two parts, as body or soul. —**dualist,** *n.* —**dualistic,** *adj.*

fanaticism the character, spirit, or conduct of a person with an extreme and uncritical enthusiasm or zeal, as in religion or politics. —**fanatic,** *n.*

heathenism **1.** a belief or practice of heathens.
2. pagan worship; idolatry.
3. irreligion.
4. barbaric morals or behavior. —**heathenistic,** *adj.*

hieraticism the principles, attitudes, and practices of priests as a group, both Christian and non-Christian. —**hieratic,** *adj.*

inspirationist a person who adheres to a theory or doctrine of divine influence, inspiration, or revelation, esp. concerning the Scriptures.

Jainism a dualistic, ascetic religion founded in the 6th cent. B.C. by a Hindu reformer as a revolt against the caste system and the vague world spirit of Hinduism. —**Jain,** *n., adj.* —**Jainist,** *n.*

legalism *Theology.* **1.** the doctrine that salvation is gained through good works.
2. the judging of conduct in terms of strict adherence to precise laws. —**legalist,** *n.* —**legalistic,** *adj.*

manaism **1.** the doctrine of a generalized, supernatural force or power, which may be concentrated in objects or persons.
2. belief in mana. —**manaistic,** *adj.*

mysticism **1.** the doctrine that an immediate spiritual intuition of truth or an intimate spiritual union of the soul with God can be achieved through contemplation and spiritual exercises.

2. the beliefs, ideas, or practices of mystics.

nullifidian   a person who has no religion; a religious skeptic.

occultism   a belief that certain secret, mysterious, or supernatural agencies exist and that human beings may communicate with them or have their assistance. —**occultist,** *n., adj.*

ontologism   *Philosophy.* the doctrine that the human intellect has as its proper object the knowledge of God, that this knowledge is immediate and intuitive, and that all other knowledge must be built on this base. —**ontologist,** *n.* —**ontologistic,** *adj.*

Ophism   the doctrines and beliefs of certain Gnostic sects that worshipped serpents as the symbol of the hidden divine wisdom and as having benefitted Adam and Eve by encouraging them to eat the fruit of the tree of knowledge. Also called **Ophitism.** —**Ophite,** *n.* —**Ophitic,** *adj.*

Orphism   the religion of the Orphic mysteries, a cult of Dionysus (Bacchus) ascribed to Orpheus as its founder, esp. its rites of initiation and doctrines of original sin, salvation, and purification through reincarnations. Also called **Orphicism.** —**Orphic,** *n., adj.*

paganism   **1.** a hedonistic spirit or attitude in moral or religious matters.

2. the beliefs and practices of pagans, esp. polytheists.

3. the state of being a pagan. —**paganist,** *n., adj.* —**paganistic,** *adj.*

pneumatology   the doctrine or theory of spiritual beings. —**pneumatologist,** *n.* —**pneumatologic, pneumatological,** *adj.*

Rosicrucianism   the principles, institutions, or practices of the Rosicrucian Order, esp. claims to various forms of occult knowledge and power, and esoteric religious practices. —**Rosicrucian,** *n., adj.*

Scientology   the doctrines and beliefs of a religious movement founded in the mid-20th cent. by L. Ron Hubbard, esp. an emphasis upon man's immortal spirit, reincarnation, and an extrascientific method of psychotherapy (dianetics). —**Scientologist,** *n., adj.*

secularism   **1.** a view that religion and religious considerations should be ignored or excluded from social and political matters.

2. an ethical system asserting that moral judgments should be made without reference to religious doctrine, as reward or punishment in an afterlife. —**secularist,** *n., adj.* —**secularistic,** *adj.*

shamanism   **1.** the tenets of the primitive religion of northern Asia, esp. a belief in powerful spirits who can only be influenced by shamans in their double capacity of priest and doctor.

2. any similar religion, as among American Indians. —**shamanist,** *n.* —**shamanistic,** *adj.*

Shintoism   the doctrines and practices of Shinto, the native religion of

Japan, esp. its system of nature and ancestor worship. —**Shinto,** *n., adj.* —**Shintoistic,** *adj.*

simonism the practices of simony, esp. the making of a profit out of sacred things. —**simonist,** *n.* —**simoniac,** *n., adj.* —**simoniacal,** *adj.*

Taoism **1.** a philosophical system evolved by Lao-tzu and Chuang-tzu, esp. its advocacy of a simple and natural life and of noninterference with the course of natural events in order to have a happy existence in harmony with the Tao. **2.** a popular Chinese religion, purporting to be based on the principles of Lao-tzu, but actually an eclectic polytheism characterized by superstition, alchemy, divination, and magic. Also called **Hsüan Chiao.**

theomania a religious ecstasy in which the devotee believes that he is the deity.

theomorphism the state or condition of being formed in the image or likeness of God. —**theomorphic,** *adj.*

theophany a manifestation or appearance of God or a god to man. —**theophanic, theophanous,** *adj.*

theophilanthropism the doctrines or tenets of a deistic society in post-Revolutionary Paris that hoped to replace the outlawed Christian religion with a new religion based on belief in God, the immortality of the soul, and personal virtue. —**theophilanthropist,** *n.* —**theophilanthropic,** *adj.*

Zoroastrianism the doctrines and practices of a dualistic Iranian religion, esp. the existence of a supreme deity, Ahura Mazda, and belief in a cosmic struggle between a spirit of good and light and a spirit of evil and darkness. Also called **Zoroastrism, Zarathustrism, Mazdaism.** —**Zoroastrian,** *n., adj.*
See also GOD AND GODS.

REMEDIES

acology *Archaic.* the science of therapeutic remedies.

aliptic *Obsolete.* an ointment.

allopathy the method of treating diseases by using agents that produce effects different from those of the disease. —**allopath, allopathist,** *n.* —**allopathic,** *adj.* Cf. **homeopathy.**

bibliotherapy *Psychiatry.* the therapeutic use of books and magazines in the treatment of mental illness or shock. —**bibliotherapist,** *n.* —**bibliotherapeutic,** *adj.*

chemotherapy *Med.* the treatment of disease by the use of chemicals which have a toxic effect on the microorganisms causing the disease or which selectively destroy tumor tissues. —**chemotherapist,** *n.* —**chemotherapeutic,** *adj.*

chiropractic **1.** a therapeutic system based on the doctrine that disease is

the result of interference with nerve function and that adjusting the segments of the spinal column will restore a normal condition.
2. a chiropractor. —**chiropractor,** *n.*

cryotherapy *Med.* a method of treatment involving applications of cold. Also called **crymotherapy.**

diathermy *Med.* a method of treatment involving the production of heat in the body by electric currents. Also called **diathermia.** —**diathermic,** *adj.*

homeopathy, homoeopathy the method of treating diseases by drugs which produce symptoms similar to those of the disease. —**homeopathist,** *n.* —**homeopath,** *n.* —**homeopathic,** *adj.*

homeotherapy *Med.* a method of therapy using an agent that is similar to but not identical with the causative agent of the disease. —**homeotherapeutic,** *adj.*

iatralipsis a method of treatment involving anointing and rubbing. Also called **iatraliptics.**

naturopathism, naturopathy a method of treating disease, using food, exercise, heat, etc. to assist the natural healing process. —**naturopath,** *n.* —**naturopathic,** *adj.*

osteopathy a method of treating ailments on the premise that they result from the pressure of misplaced bones on nerves, and are curable by manipulation. —**osteopath,** *n.* —**osteopathic,** *adj.*

physiotherapy the treatment of disease, bodily defects, or bodily weaknesses by physical remedies, as massage, special exercises, etc., rather than by drugs. —**physiotherapist,** *n.*

polychrest a drug that serves as a remedy for several diseases. —**polychrestic,** *adj.*

psychotherapy the science or method of treating psychological abnormalities or disorders by psychological techniques. —**psychotherapist,** *n.* Cf. **psychiatry.**

REPTILES

herpetology *Zoology.* the study of reptiles and amphibians. —**herpetologist,** *n.* —**herpetologic, herpetological,** *adj.*

herpetophobia an abnormal fear of reptiles. Also called **ophidiophobia.**

RHETORIC

anaphora *Rhetoric.* the repetition of a word or words at the beginning of two or more successive verses or sentences, as the repetition of *Blessed* in the Beatitudes. —**anaphoral,** *adj.*

antiphrasis the use of a word in a sense opposite to its proper meaning. —**antiphrastic, antiphrastical,** *adj.*

aposiopesis a sudden breaking off in the middle of a sentence as if unable or unwilling to proceed. —**aposiopetic,** *adj.*

palilogy, palillogy   the immediate repetition of a word for emphasis, as "the living, the living, he shall praise thee" (Isaiah 38:19).

paromologia   an apparent concession made to an opponent in an argument that really serves to strengthen one's own argument.
See also FIGURES OF SPEECH.

RIVERS

potamology   the study of rivers. —**potamologist,** *n.* —**potamological,** *adj.*

potamophobia   a morbid fear of rivers.

ROCKS

lithoidolatry   the worship of rocks and stones. —**lithoidolater,** *n.* —**lithoidolatrous,** *adj.*

lithoidology   *Rare.* the study of rocks.

lithomancy   a form of divination involving rocks or stones.

pessomancy   a form of divination involving pebbles. Also called **psephology.**

petroglyphy   the study of drawings or carvings made on rocks by a member of a prehistoric or primitive people. —**petroglyph,** *n.* —**petroglyphic,** *adj.*

S

THE SACRED

hierology   1. the learning or literature concerning sacred things.
2. hagiological materials. —**hierologist,** *n.* —**hierologic, hierological,** *adj.*

hieromancy   a form of divination involving sacrificial remains or sacred objects.

hierophobia   an abnormal fear of sacred objects.

SAINTS

Bollandist   any of the editors of the *Acta Sanctorum,* a critical and official hagiology begun by the Jesuits in the 17th cent.

hagiography   the writing and critical study of the lives of the saints; hagiology. —**hagiographer,** *n.* —**hagiographic, hagiographical,** *adj.*

hagiolatry   the veneration, or the worship, of saints. —**hagiolater,** *n.* —**hagiolatrous,** *adj.*

hagiology   1. the branch of literature comprised of the lives and legends of the saints.
2. a biography or narrative of the life of a saint or saints.
3. a collection of such biographies. —**hagiologist,** *n.* —**hagiologic, hagiological,** *adj.*

SEA

bathyclinograph a device used for measuring vertical currents in deep ocean areas.

bathygraphy the scientific exploration of the sea with sonic instruments. —**bathygraph, bathygram,** *n.*

marigraphy *Rare.* the measurement of the rise and fall of tides. Also called **mareography.** —**marigraphic,** *adj.*

oceanography the branch of physical geography that studies oceans and seas. —**oceanographer,** *n.* —**oceanographic, oceanographical,** *adj.*

oceanology oceanography.

Thalassa *Classical Mythology.* the personification of the sea.

thalassocracy the sovereignty of the seas. —**thalassocrat,** *n.*

thalassography **1.** the branch of oceanography that studies smaller bodies of water, as bays, sounds, gulfs, etc. **2.** oceanography in general. —**thalassographer,** *n.* —**thalassographic, thalassographical,** *adj.*

thalassophobia an abnormal fear of the sea.

SEALS

sigillography the study of seals. —**sigillographer,** *n.* —**sigillographic,** *adj.*

sphragistics the scientific study of seals and signet rings. —**sphragistic,** *adj.*

SELF

autophilia a kind of self-love; narcissism. —**autophile,** *n.* —**autophilic,** *adj.*

autophobia, autophoby an abnormal fear of being by oneself. Also called **eremiophobia, eremophobia, monophobia.**

biosophy a mode of life based on intuition and self-education in order to improve one's character. —**biosophist,** *n.*

egomania a psychologically abnormal egotism. —**egomaniac,** *n.*

egotheism a deification of self.

extraversion, extroversion *Psychology.* **1.** the act of directing one's interest outward or to things outside the self. **2.** the state of having thoughts and activities satisfied by things outside the self. —**extravert,** *n.* —**extraversive, extravertive,** *adj.* Cf. **introversion.**

introversion *Psychology.* **1.** the act of directing one's interest inward or toward the self. **2.** the state of being interested chiefly in one's own inner thoughts, feelings, and processes. —**introvert,** *n.* —**introvertive, introversive,** *adj.*

ipsism an individual identity; selfhood. Also called **ipseity.**

monology **1.** the habit of talking to oneself; soliloquizing. **2.** *Obsolete.* a monologue. —**monologist,** *n.* —**monologic, monological,** *adj.*

SEX

184

nosism *Archaic.* the use of *we* in speaking of oneself.
See also ATTITUDES.

SEX

algolagnia the finding of sexual pleasure in suffering or inflicting physical pain; sadomasochism. —**algolagnist,** *n.* —**algolagnic,** *adj.*

amphierotism *Rare.* bisexuality. —**amphierotic,** *adj.*

anaphrodisia *Med.* the absence or loss of sexual desire. Also called **sexual anesthesia.**

autoeroticism *Psychoanalysis.* the arousal and satisfaction of sexual desires within or by oneself, usu. by masturbation. Also called **autoerotism.** —**autoerotic,** *adj.*

carnalism, carnality the practice of finding satisfaction in activities related to fleshly desires and appetites, esp. the sexual. —**carnal,** *adj.*

coitophobia an abnormal fear of sexual intercourse. Also called **cyprido-phobia, genophobia.**

coprophilia 1. the use of obscene or seatological language for sexual gratification.
2. a love of obscenity.
3. *Psychiatry.* an abnormal interest in feces, esp. as a source of sexual excitement.

eonism *Psychiatry.* the adoption, by a male, of feminine mannerisms, clothing, etc. Also called **transvestism, transvestitism.**

eroticism 1. the erotic or sexual quality of something.
2. the use of sexually arousing or stimulating materials in literature, drama, art, etc.
3. the condition of being sexually stimulated.
4. a sexual drive or tendency.
5. an abnormally persistent sexual drive. Also called **erotism.**

erotophobia an abnormal fear of sexual feelings and their physical expression. Also called **miserotia.**

fetishism *Psychiatry.* the compulsive use of some object or part of the body as a sexual stimulus, as a shoe, underclothes, a lock of hair, etc. Also called **fetichism.** —**fetishistic,** *adj.*

gerontophilia a sexual attraction to the elderly. —**gerontophile,** *n.* —**geron-tophilic,** *adj.*

hetaerism, hetairism 1. the practice of concubinage.
2. a social system characterized by its regarding women as common property. —**hetaerist,** *n.* —**hetaeristic,** *adj.*

leccator *Law.* a lecherous person.

necrophilia a sexual attraction to the dead. —**necrophile,** *n.* —**necrophilic,** *adj.*

necrosadism   the mutilation of a corpse in order to excite or satisfy sexual urges. —**necrosadist,** *n.*

nymphomania   *Pathology.* an excessive sexual desire in a female. Also called **uteromania.** Cf. **satyriasis.**

onanism   **1.** the practice of pre-ejaculatory withdrawal during intercourse. **2.** masturbation. —**onanist,** *n.* —**onanistic,** *adj.*

panderism   **1.** the practice of acting as a go-between in amorous intrigues; pander.
2. the action of soliciting customers for a prostitute or of procuring women for sexual purposes; procurer; pimp.
3. the practice of catering to or profiting from the vices and weaknesses of others. Also called **panderage.**

paraphilia   the practice of, indulgence in, or addiction to unusual sexual activities. —**paraphilic,** *adj.*

partialism   **1.** an emphasis of sexual interest upon one part of the body.
2. a form of fetishism in which the sexual stimulus is a part of the body, as pictures of feet.

priapism   **1.** *Pathology.* a continuous erection of the penis, esp. as the result of a disease.
2. a prurient action or display. —**priapismic,** *adj.*

proxenetism   the practice of pimping by females.

satyriasis   *Pathology.* an abnormal, uncontrollable sexual desire in men. Also called **satyrism, satyromania.** —**satyr,** *n.* —**satyric,** *adj.*

scopophilia   *Psychiatry.* **1.** the deriving of sexual pleasure from viewing nude bodies, sexual acts, or erotic photographs; voyeurism. Also called **passive scopophilia.**
2. an abnormal desire to be seen, esp. genitally; exhibitionism. Also called **active scopophilia.** Also called **scoptophilia.** —**scopophiliac,** *n.* —**scopophilic,** *adj.*

sexology   the study of normal and abnormal sexual behavior. —**sexologist,** *n.* —**sexological,** *adj.*

voyeurism   the practice of gaining sexual gratification by looking at sexual acts, erotic pictures, etc. —**voyeur,** *n.* —**voyeuristic,** *adj.*

zoophilia   a desire for sexual activity with animals. —**zoophilist,** *n.* —**zoophilic, zoophilous,** *adj.*
See also HOMOSEXUALITY.

SHARPNESS

aichmophobia   an abnormal fear of pointed objects.

belonephobia   an abnormal fear of pins and needles.

SHIPS

barratry *Law.* an act of fraud by a master or crew at the expense of the owners of a ship or the owners of its cargo. Also called **barretry.** —**barratrous,** *adj.*

pallograph an instrument for recording the vibrations of a steamship. —**pallographic,** *adj.*

SIN

hamartiology *Theology.* the study or science of the doctrine of sin. Cf. **ponerology.**

peccatiphobia, peccatophobia an abnormal fear of sinning.

SIZE

dwarfism *Med.* the condition of being dwarfed or a dwarf. Also called **nanism.**

gigantism *Pathology.* the condition of abnormally great development in size or stature of the whole body or any of its parts, most often caused by a pituitary disorder.

nanism *Med.* the condition of dwarfishness, as opposed to **gigantism.**

scintilla a spark; a trace; a minute particle.

SKIN

albinism *Med.* a congenital absence of pigment in the skin, hair, and eyes, ranging in scope from partial to total. Also called **albinoism.** —**albino,** *n.* —**albinotic,** *adj.*

dermatoglyphics 1. the patterns of ridges of skin on the fingers and palm and the bottom of the feet.
2. the science dealing with the study of these patterns. —**dermatoglyphic,** *adj.*

dermatography *Anatomy.* a description of the skin. —**dermatographic,** *adj.*

dermatographia *Med.* a condition in which lightly touching or scratching the skin causes raised, reddish marks. Also called **dermatographism, dermographia, dermographism.** —**dermatographic,** *adj.*

dermatology the science that studies the skin and its diseases. —**dermatologist,** *n.* —**dermatological,** *adj.*

dermatophobia an abnormal fear of skin disease. Also called **dermatosiophobia, dermatopathophobia.**

leprology the brand of medical science that studies leprosy and its treatment. —**leprologist,** *n.*

SLAVES

abolitionism the movement for the abolition of slavery, esp. Negro slavery in the U.S. —**abolitionist,** *n.*

helotism   the condition or quality of being a helot; serfdom or slavery. Also called **helotage, helotry.**

odalisque, odalisk   a female slave or concubine in a harem, esp. in that of the Sultan of Turkey.

SLEEP

Braidism   the practice of hypnotism by Dr. James Braid, British physician, in the mid-19th cent.

hypnology   the science dealing with the phenomena of sleep and hypnotism. —**hypnologist,** *n.* —**hypnologic, hypnological,** *adj.* Cf. **Mesmerism.**

hypnopedia, hypnopaedia   the art or process of learning while asleep by means of lessons recorded on disk or tapes.

hypnophobia   an abnormal fear of sleep.

lunambulism   the condition of sleep walking only in the moonlight. —**lunambulist,** *n.* —**lunambulistic,** *adj.* Cf. **somnambulism, noctambulism.**

narcohypnia   *Med.* a numbness often felt upon waking from sleep.

narcolepsy   *Pathology.* a condition characterized by frequent and uncontrollable lapses into deep sleep. —**narcoleptic,** *adj.*

narcotherapy   *Psychiatry.* 1. a method of treating certain mental disorders by inducing sleep through barbiturates.
2. a type of psychotherapy involving the use of hypnotic drugs. Also called **narcoanalysis.** —**narcotherapist,** *n.*

noctambulism   the condition of sleepwalking; somnambulism. Also called **noctambulation.** —**noctambulist, noctambule,** *n.* —**noctambulous, noctambulant, noctambulistic,** *adj.*

somnambulism   the condition of sleepwalking. —**somnambulant,** *n., adj.* —**somnambulist,** *n.* —**somnambulistic,** *adj.*

somniloquism   the tendency to talk in one's sleep. —**somniloquist,** *n.* —**somniloquous,** *adj.*

somnolence   the condition of drowsiness or sleepiness. Also called **somnolency.** —**somnolent,** *adj.*

SMOKE

acapnotic   a nonsmoker.

capnomancy   a form of divination involving smoke.

empyromancy   a form of divination involving fire and smoke.

misocapnist   a hater of tobacco smoke. —**misocapnic,** *adj.*

SNAKES

ophidiophobia   an abnormal fear of snakes. Also called **ophiophobia.**

ophiolatry   the worship of snakes. —**ophiolator,** *n.*

ophiology   the branch of herpetology that studies snakes. —**ophiologist,** *n.* —**ophiologic, ophiological,** *adj.*

ophiomancy   a form of divination involving snakes.

SOCIETY

anthropophobia   an abnormal fear of people, esp. in groups.

chemocracy   a Utopian society in which all foods and other material needs will be prepared by chemical processes. —**chemocrat,** *n.*

sociogram   *Sociology.* a diagram representing the pattern of preferred relationships between individuals in a group.

sociology   **1.** the science or study of the origin, development, organization and functioning of human society.
2. the science of the fundamental laws of social relations, institutions, etc. —**sociologist,** *n.* —**sociologic, sociological,** *adj.*

sociometry   the measurement of social attitudes within a group by sampling expressions of social acceptance or rejection. —**sociometrist,** *n.* —**sociometric,** *adj.*

solidarism   *Sociology.* a theory that the possibility of founding a social organization upon a solidarity of interests is to be found in the natural interdependence of members of a society. —**solidarist,** *n.* —**solidaristic,** *adj.*

totemism   **1.** the practice of having a natural object or animate being, as a bird or animal, as the emblem of a family, clan, or group.
2. the practice of regarding such a totem as mystically related to the family, clan, or group and therefore not to be hunted.
3. a system of tribal organization according to totems. —**totemic,** *adj.*

SOILS

agrology   the branch of soil science dealing esp. with crop production. —**agrologist,** *n.* —**agrological,** *adj.*

edaphic   pertaining to or caused by particular soil conditions, as texture or drainage, rather than by climatic conditions.

edaphology   pedology.

paleopedology, palaeopedology   the branch of pedology that studies the soil conditions of past geologic ages.

pedology   the branch of agriculture that studies soils; soil science. —**pedologist,** *n.* —**pedologic, pedological,** *adj.*

SONGS AND SINGING

balladism   the writing or singing of ballads. —**balladist,** *n.*

melismatics   the practice of composing phrases of several notes to be sung on one syllable of text, as in plainsong.
See also MUSIC.

SOUL

creationism *Theology.* a doctrine that God creates a new soul for every human being born. —**creationist,** *n.* —**creationistic,** *adj.*

metempsychosis **1.** the passage of a soul from one body to another.
2. the rebirth of the soul at death in another body, either human or animal. —**metempsychic, metempsychosic, metempsychosical,** *adj.*

nullibism the denial that the soul exists. —**nullibist,** *n.*

panpsychism *Philosophy.* the doctrine that each object in the universe has either a mind or an unconscious soul. —**panpsychist,** *n.* —**panpsychistic,** *adj.*

polypsychism the belief that one person may have many souls or modes of intelligence. —**polypsychic, polypsychical,** *adj.*

psychagogy the leading of the soul, esp. that of a person recently dead. —**psychagogue,** *n.* —**psychagogic,** *adj.*

psychorrhagy the manifestation of a person's soul to another, usu. at some distance from the body. —**psychorrhagic,** *adj.*

traducianism *Theology.* the doctrine that a new human soul is generated from the souls of the parents at the moment of conception. —**traducianist,** *n.* —**traducianistic,** *adj.*

transmigrationism any of various theories of metempsychosis or re- incarnation, as the Hindu doctrines of Karma.

SOUNDS

acoustics **1.** *Physics.* the study of sound and sound waves.
2. the qualities or characteristics of a space, as an auditorium, that determine the audibility and fidelity of sounds in it. —**acoustician,** *n.* —**acoustic,** *adj.*

cacophony **1.** a harshness of sound.
2. discordant noise. —**cacophonic, cacophonous,** *adj.*

diacoustics *Rare.* the science of sounds refracted through various media.

euphony **1.** an agreeableness in sounds; a pleasantness to the ear; harmoniousness.
2. *Phonetics.* a harmoniousness in speech sounds, esp. in word choices emphasizing various patterns of consonants or vowels. —**euphonic, euphonical, euphonious,** *adj.*

homonym a word having the same pronunciation and spelling as another, but having a different meaning or origin, as *tear* 'rip'/ *tear* 'race'. Also called **homograph.** —**homonymic, homonymous,** *adj.*

homophone a letter, word, or symbol having the same sound as another but having a different meaning, regardless of sameness or difference in spelling, as *choir*/ *quire*. —**homophonic, homophonous,** *adj.*

onomatopoeia a word formed to imitate the sound of the intended meaning. —**onomatopoeic, onomatopoetic, onomatopoietic, onomatopoeial,** *adj.*

SPACES

agoraphobia an abnormal fear of being in or crossing open spaces.

cenophobia, kenophobia an abnormal fear of open spaces.

claustrophobia an abnormal fear of enclosed spaces. Also called **cleisiophobia.**

SPEECH

acyrology 1. an incorrectness in diction.
2. cacology. —**acyrological,** *adj.*

alogy, alogia *Med.* an inability to speak, esp. as the result of a brain lesion.

aphasia *Pathology.* an impairment or loss of the faculty of understanding or using spoken or written language. —**aphasiac,** *n.* —**aphasic,** *n., adj.*

biloquism the ability to speak in two distinct voices. —**biloquist,** *n.*

biolinguistics the study of the relations between physiology and speech. —**biolinguist,** *n.*

dyslalia *Med.* a defect in the ability to make sounds, caused by neurological disorders involving the organs of articulation.

dyslogy, dyslogia *Pathology.* an inability to express ideas or reasoning in speech because of a mental disorder.

dysphemia *Psychology.* any neurotic disorder of speech; stammering.

echolalia 1. *Psychiatry.* the uncontrollable and immediate repetition of sounds and words from others.
2. the imitation by an infant of the vocal sounds produced by others, occurring as a natural stage of speech development. —**echolalic,** *adj.*

glossolalia an ecstatic, usu. unintelligible speech uttered in the worship services of any of several sects stressing emotionality and religious fervor. Also called **speaking in tongues.** —**glossolalist,** *n.*

glossophobia an abnormal fear of speaking in public or of trying to speak.

haplology *Grammar.* the syncope or loss of a syllable within a word, as *syllabication* for *syllabification.* —**haplologic,** *adj.*

lalopathology the branch of medical science that studies disorders of speech. —**lalopathy,** *n.* —**lalopathic,** *adj.*

lalophobia an abnormal fear of speaking.

logopedia, logopaedia *Pathology.* the science that studies speech defects and their treatment. Also called **logopedics, logopaedics.** —**logopedic,** *adj.*

mutism *Psychiatry.* a conscious or unconscious refusal to make verbal responses to questions, present in some mental disorders.

paralogia a disorder of the faculty of reasoning, characterized by disconnected and meaningless speech.

parrhesia a tendency to free or bold speech.

phonology **1.** the study of speech sounds, from either or both the phonetic and phonemic viewpoints.
2. the phonetic and phonemic systems of a language. —**phonologist,** *n.* —**phonological,** *adj.*

psittacism a mechanical, repetitive, and usu. meaningless speech.

sigmatism a faulty pronunciation of sibilant sounds.

solecism **1.** an ungrammatical or substandard usage, as *he are.*
2. any breach of good manners or etiquette. —**solecist,** *n.* —**solecistic, solecistical,** *adj.*

syneresis *Phonetics.* the contraction of the sound of two consonants or two vowels into one, esp. the contraction of two vowels to form a diphthong. Also called **synaeresis.**

ventriloquism the art or practice of speaking so that the voice seems not to come from the speaker but from another source, as from a mechanical doll. Also called **ventriloquy, gastriloquism.** —**ventriloquist,** *n.* —**ventriloquistic,** *adj.*
See also PRONUNCIATION.

SPELLING

cacography the practice or defect of incorrect spelling. —**cacographer,** *n.* —**cacographic, cacographical,** *adj.*

hetericism *Rare.* the study of nonphonetic spelling. —**hetericist,** *n.*

heterography **1.** the practice of spelling in a way contrary to standard usage.
2. the use of the same letters or combinations of letters to represent different sounds, as in English *tough* and *dough.* —**heterographic, heterographical,** *adj.*

orthography **1.** the art of writing words according to accepted usage; correct spelling.
2. that part of grammar that treats of letters and spelling.
3. a method of spelling. —**orthographer,** *n.* —**orthographic,** *adj.*

phonography any phonetic spelling, writing, or shorthand system. —**phonographer, phonographist,** *n.* —**phonographic, phonographical,** *adj.*

SPIRITS AND SPIRITUALISM

aedist a pretender to inspiration.

mediumism **1.** a belief that another person can serve as an instrument through which another personality or supernatural agency can communicate.
2. the art or practice of such a spiritualistic medium. —**mediumistic,** *adj.*

pneumatology 1. *Theology.* the belief in intermediary spirits between men and God.
2. the doctrine or theory of spiritual beings. —**pneumatologist,** *n.*

poltergeist a spirit which makes its presence known by noises, knockings, and throwing things.

psychography 1. the reception of written spirit messages through a medium; spirit writing.
2. the production of images of spirits on film without the use of a camera, believed to be caused by spiritualistic forces. —**psychographic,** *adj.*

spiritualism 1. the belief that the dead survive as spirits that can communicate with the living, esp. through a medium, a person particularly susceptible to their influence.
2. the practices or phenomena associated with this belief. —**spiritualist,** *n.* —**spiritualistic,** *adj.*
See also DEMONS.

STEALING

biblioklept a book stealer.

bibliokleptomania 1. a kleptomania specializing in books.
2. the motivations of a biblioklept. —**bibliokleptomaniac,** *n.*

brigandism the practice of pillage, often destructive, usually practiced by a band of robbers. Also called **brigandage.** —**brigand,** *n.* —**brigandish,** *adj.*

kleptomania, cleptomania *Psychology.* an irresistible impulse to steal, esp. when the thief can afford to pay. —**kleptomaniac,** *n.*

kleptophobia, cleptophobia an abnormal fear of thieves or of loss through thievery.

ladronism 1. *SW. U.S.* an act of thievery.
2. *Scot. Dial.* blackguardism and roguery. —**ladrone, ladron,** *n.*

plagiarism 1. the verbatim copying or imitation of the language, ideas, or thoughts of another author and representing them as original work.
2. the material so appropriated. —**plagiarist,** *n.* —**plagiaristic,** *adj.*

STRENGTH AND WEAKNESS

asthenia *Med.* any of several conditions characterized by lack or loss of strength and energy, as neurasthenia, myasthenia, or somasthenia. —**asthenic,** *adj.*

hamartia 1. an error in judgment, a missing of the mark.
2. *Greek Tragedy.* an error in judgment or action, usu. caused by a weakness or flaw in the tragic protagonist's character. Also called **tragic flaw.**

hypopotencia, hypopotency *Med.* a condition of diminished power, esp. of diminished electrical activity of the cerebral cortex.

impotency   1. a condition of reduced or absent power; weakness.
2. a complete failure of sexual power, esp. in the male. Also called **impotence, impotentness.** —**impotent,** *adj.*

omnipotence   the state or quality of being infinite in power, authority, or might. —**omnipotent,** *adj.*

SUN

celidography   *Archaic.* a description of the surface markings on a planet or the spots on the sun.

coronagraphy   the observation of the corona of the sun by use of a telescope modified to simulate an eclipse. —**coronagraphic,** *adj.*

heliography   1. the measurement of the duration and intensity of sunlight.
2. the system or process of signaling by reflecting the sun's rays in a mirror.
3. an early photographic process involving coat'd metal plates exposed to sunlight. —**heliographer,** *n.* —**heliographic, heliographical,** *adj.*

heliolatry   the worship of the sun. —**heliolator,** *n.*

heliology   *Archaic.* the science of the sun. —**heliologist,** *n.*

heliophobia   1. an abnormal fear of sunlight.
2. an avoidance of sunlight.

solarism   1. the explanation of myths by reference to the sun or the personification of the sun, as the hero as sun-figure.
2. an over-reliance on this method of interpretation. —**solarist,** *n.*

T

TEETH

bruxism   the habit of purposelessly grinding one's teeth, esp. during sleep. Also called **bruxomania.**

dedentition   the shedding of teeth.

dentition   the production or cutting of teeth; teething. Also called **odontogeny.**

odontalgia, odontalgy   a pain in a tooth; toothache. —**odontalgic,** *adj.*

odontology   1. the science that studies teeth and their surrounding tissues, esp. the prevention and cure of their diseases.
2. dentistry. —**odontologist,** *n.* —**odontological,** *adj.*

odontophobia   an abnormal fear of teeth, esp. of animal teeth.

orthodontics, orthodontia   the branch of dentistry that studies the prevention and correction of irregular teeth.—**orthodontist,** *n.* —**orthodontic,** *adj.*

periodontics, periodontia   the branch of dentistry that studies and treats disease of the bone, connecting tissue, and gum surrounding a tooth. —**periodontist,** *n.* —**periodontic,** *adj.*

THEOLOGY

Albertist a student or supporter of the theological ideas of Albertus Magnus, 13th cent. German Scholastic philosopher.

antinomianism the belief that Christians are freed from the moral law by the virtue of God's grace. —**antinomian,** *n., adj.*

Augustinianism 1. the doctrines and ideas of St. Augustine, 5th cent. archbishop of Hippo, and the religious rule developed by him.
2. the support of his doctrines.
3. adherence to his religious rule. —**Augustinian,** *n., adj.*

concursus any divine influence upon secondary causes, esp. the doctrine that before the fall man was kept from sin by God's direct intervention.

confessionalism an advocacy of the maintenance of a confession of faith as a prerequisite to membership in a religious group. —**confessionalian,** *n., adj.*

consubstantiation the doctrine that the substance of the body and blood of Christ coexist in and with the substance of the bread and wine of the Eucharist. Cf. **transubstantiation, receptionism.**

Occamism 1. the precepts and ideas of William of Occam, 14th cent. English Scholastic.
2. support of his precepts. —**Occamist, Occamite,** *n.* —**Occamistic,** *adj.*

Origenism 1. the doctrines and precepts of Origen of Alexandria, 3rd cent. Christian theologian and teacher.
2. adherence to his doctrines. —**Origenist,** *n.* —**Origenian, Origenistic,** *adj.*

ponerology a branch of theology that studies the doctrine of evil. Cf. **hamartiology.**

patrology 1. the branch of theology that studies the teachings of the early church fathers. Also called **patristics.**
2. a collection of the writings of the early church fathers. —**patrologist,** *n.* —**patrologic, patrological,** *adj.*

predestinarianism a belief in predestination. —**predestinarian,** *n., adj.*

Scholasticism the doctrines of the schoolmen; the system of theological and philosophical instruction of the Middle Ages, based chiefly upon the authority of the church fathers and Aristotle and his commentators. —**Scholastic,** *n., adj.*

predestination 1. the action of God in foreordaining from eternity whatever comes to pass.
2. the doctrine that God chooses those who are to come to salvation.

receptionism the doctrine that in the communion service the body and blood of Christ are received but the bread and wine remain unchanged. —**receptionist,** *n.* Cf. **consubstantiation, transubstantiation.**

stercoranism   the belief that the bread and wine consecrated in the Eucharist are subject to natural processes, as decay. —**stercorarian, stercoranist,** *adj.*

theologism   1. any theological speculation.
2. the assumption that other disciplines, as philosophy or science, are inferior to theology.

transubstantiation   the doctrine that the consecrated elements of the communion only appear as bread and wine, for they have been converted into the whole substance of the body and blood of Christ. —**transubstantiationalist,** *n.* Cf. **consubstantiation.**

virtualism   the doctrine attributed to Calvin and other reformers that the bread and wine of the communion remain unchanged but are the vehicle through which the spiritual body and blood of Christ are received by the communicant. Cf. **receptionism.**
See also CATHOLICISM, CHRISTIANITY, HERESY, PHILOSOPHY, *and* PROTESTANTISM.

THINKING

cogitation   1. the act of meditation or contemplation.
2. the faculty of thinking.
3. a thought; a design or plan. —**cogitator,** *n.* —**cogitative,** *adj.*

free association   *Psychoanalysis.* the unhampered and uncensored expression of ideas, impressions, etc., passing through the mind of the patient, used to permit access to the processes of the unconscious.

phrontistery   a place for study or thinking.

rumination   the act of pondering or meditating. —**ruminator,** *n.* —**ruminative,** *adj.*

speculation   1. the contemplation or consideration of some subject.
2. an instance of such activity.
3. a conclusion or opinion reached by such activity.
4. a conjecture or surmise; a guess. —**speculator,** *n.* —**speculative,** *adj.*

THUNDER

brontophobia   an abnormal fear of thunder and thunderstorms.

brontology   *Rare.* a treatise on thunder.

ceraunomancy   a form of divination involving the interpretation of an omen communicated by thunder.

keraunoscopia, keraunoscopy   a form of divination involving the observation of thunder.
See also LIGHTNING.

TIGHTROPE WALKING

funambulism the art or skill of tightrope walking. —**funambulist,** *n.*

schoenabatist a tightrope walker.

TIME

anachronism **1.** a person or a thing remaining or appearing after its own time period; archaism.
2. an error in chronology. —**anachronistic, anachronistical, anachronous,** *adj.*

chronology **1.** the science of arranging time in fixed periods for the purpose of dating events accurately and arranging them in order of occurrence.
2. a reference book organized according to the dates of past events. —**chronologer, chronologist,** *n.* —**chronological,** *adj.*

chronometry **1.** the art of measuring time accurately.
2. the measurement of time by periods or divisions. —**chronometric, chronometrical,** *adj.*

cunctation the practice or habit of delay or tardiness; procrastination. —**cunctator,** *n.* —**cunctatious, cunctatory,** *adj.*

dendrochronology the science of fixing dates in the past by the study of growth rings in trees. —**dendrochronologist,** *n.* —**dendrochronological,** *adj.*

diurnal of or pertaining to a day or each day; daily.

eon **1.** an indefinitely long period of time. Also called **aeon.**
2. *Geology.* any long stretch of geologic time, usu. longer than one named period, as Jurassic plus Triassic, but shorter than a geologic era.

geochronology the chronology of the earth as induced from geologic data. —**geochronologist,** *n.* —**geochronologic, geochronological,** *adj.*

horology the art or science of making timepieces or of measuring time. —**horologist,** *n.* —**horological,** *adj.*

millenium **1.** a period of a thousand years.
2. a thousandth anniversary.
3. *Eschatology.* the fulfillment of the beliefs underlying millenialism.

phenology the study of natural phenomena that occur periodically, as migration or blossoming, and their relation to climate and changes of season. —**phenologist,** *n.* —**phenological,** *adj.*

radiocarbon dating the determination of the age of fossil plants or objects by measuring the radioactivity of their radiocarbon content. Also called **carbon-14 dating.**

synchronism a coincidence in time; simultaneity. —**synchronistic, synchronistical,** *adj.*

TRADE

coemption   *Obsolete.* the purchase of all of a given commodity in order to control its price. —**coemptive,** *adj.*

duopoly   the market condition that exists when there are only two sellers. —**duopolist,** *n.* —**duopolistic,** *adj.*

duopsony   the market condition that exists when there are only two buyers. —**duopsonist,** *n.* —**duopsonistic,** *adj.*

monopoly   an exclusive control of a commodity or service in a particular market, or a control that makes possible the manipulation of prices. —**monopolist,** *n.* —**monopolistic,** *adj.*

monopsony   the market condition that exists when only one buyer will purchase the products of a number of sellers. —**monopsonist,** *n.* —**monopsonistic,** *adj.*

multiopoly   the condition of free enterprise, without restriction as to the number of sellers of a given product.

multiopsony   a market condition where no restriction on the number of buyers exists. —**multiopsonist,** *n.* —**multiopsonistic,** *adj.*

oligopoly   the market condition that exists when there are few sellers. —**oligopolistic,** *adj.*

TREASON

collaborationism   an act of cooperating with an invader of one's country. —**collaborationist,** *n.*

quisling   a traitor who accepts office with the enemy occupying his country. [allusion to V.A.L.J. Quisling, who accepted office under the Nazis in WW II]

TREES

dendrology   the branch of botany that studies trees. —**dendrologist,** *n.* —**dendrologic, dendrological,** *adj.*

silviculture   the cultivation of forest trees; forestry. Also called **sylviculture.** —**silviculturist,** *n.*

topiary   the art of trimming and training shrubs into ornamental, imitative, or fantastic shapes. —**topiarist,** *n.* —**topiarian,** *adj.*

TRUTH

alethiology   the branch of logic dealing with truth and error. —**alethiologist,** *n.* —**alethiological,** *adj.*

prevaricator   an evader of the truth; a liar.

truism   a self-evident, obvious truth. —**truistic, truistical,** *adj.*

TUNING

tonology the science of tones or of speech intonations, proceeding historically and comparatively. —**tonological,** *adj.*

tonometer an instrument for determining the pitch of a tone, as a tuning fork or graduated set of tuning forks. —**tonometric,** *adj.*

tonometry the art or science of measuring tones, esp. with a tonometer. —**tonometrist,** *n.* —**tonometric,** *adj.*

U

UNDERSTANDING

empathy the power of entering into another's personality and imaginatively experiencing his feelings. —**empathic,** *adj.*

noology the science of intuition and reason as phenomena of the mind. —**noological,** *adj.*

UTOPIA

Icarianism the precepts and opinions of Étienne Cabet and his followers, who settled communistic utopias in the U.S. during the 19th cent., as Nauvoo, Illinois (1849). —**Icarian,** *n., adj.*

utopianism 1. the views and habits of mind of a visionary or idealist, sometimes beyond realization.
2. impracticable schemes of political and social reform. —**utopian,** *n., adj.*

V

VALUES

axiology *Philosophy.* the study of values, as those of aesthetics, ethics, or religion. —**axiologist,** *n.* —**axiological,** *adj.*

derogation a lowering in value or estimation. —**derogatory,** *adj.*

floccinaucinihilipilification the categorizing of something as valueless trivia.

timology the theory or doctrine of values.

VEHICLES

amaxophobia an abnormal fear of being in or riding in vehicles.

autonumerology the study of unusual and distinctive licence plate numbers.

omnibology the study of motor buses.

VERSE

acrosticism   the art or skill of writing a poem in which the lines or stanzas begin with letters of the alphabet in regular order or one in which the first, middle, or final letters of the line spell a word or a phrase. —**acrostic,** *n., adj.*

amphigory   any nonsense verse that is apparently meaningful until scrutinized. Also called **amphigouri.** —**amphigoric,** *adj.*

bardism   **1.** the art or skill of one who composes and recites epic or heroic poetry, often to his own musical accompaniment.
2. membership in an ancient Celtic order of poets.

carmen figuratum   a poem so written or printed that its form suggests the subject matter, as the humorous "long and sad tail of the mouse" in *Alice in Wonderland.*

Imagism   a theory or practice of a group of English and American poets between 1909 and 1917, esp. emphasis upon the use of common speech, new rhythms, unrestricted subject matter, and clear and precise images. —**Imagist,** *n.* —**Imagistic,** *adj.*

leonist   a poet whose specialty is leonine rime.

lettrism   a technique of poetic composition originated by Isidore Isou, characterized by strange or meaningless arrangements of letters.

lyricism   the practice of writing verse in various song forms that embody the poet's thoughts and emotions rather than narrative. —**lyricist,** *n.* —**lyrical,** *adj.*

metricism   **1.** any of various theories and techniques of metrical composition.
2. the study of metrics. —**metricist,** *n.*

metrics   **1.** the science of meter. —**metricist,** *n.*
2. the art of composing metrical verse. —**metrician, metrist,** *n.*

metromania   an abnormal compulsion for writing verse.

monody   **1.** a Greek ode sung by a single voice in a tragedy.
2. a lament.
3. a poem in which one person laments another's death. —**monodist,** *n.*

panegyrist   a writer of panegyrics; eulogist.

Parnassianism   the theories and practice of a school of French poets in the 19th cent., esp. an emphasis upon art for art's sake, careful metrics, and the repression of emotive elements. —**Parnassian,** *n., adj.*

poetaster   an inferior poet; a writer who dabbles at verse.

poetics   **1.** *Lit. Crit.* the nature and laws of poetry.
2. the study of prosody.
3. a treatise on poetry.
4. (*cap.*) a treatise or collection of lecture notes on aesthetics composed by Aristotle.

poeticism the qualities of bad poetry: trite subject matter, banal or archaic and poetical language, easy rhymes, jingling rhythms, sentimentality, etc.; the standards of a poetaster.

prosody 1. the science or study of poetic meters and versification. **2.** a particular or distinctive system of metrics and versification, as that of Dylan Thomas. —**prosodist,** *n.* —**prosodic, prosodical,** *adj.*

rhapsodism the professional recitation of epic poems. —**rhapsodist,** *n.*

rhapsodomancy a form of divination involving verses.

rhopalism 1. the art or skill of writing verse in which each word in a line is longer by one syllable or in which each line of verse is longer by a syllable or a metrical foot. **2.** an instance of rhopalic form. —**rhopalist,** *n.* —**rhopalic,** *adj.*

stichomancy a form of divination involving lines of verse or passages from books.

Symbolism the principles of a literary movement originated during the latter part of the 19th cent. in France and highly influential in literature written in English, esp. an emphasis upon the associative character of verbal, often private, symbols and the use of synesthetic devices to suggest color and music. —**Symbolist,** *n., adj.*

VOLCANOES

volcanism the phenomena connected with volcanoes and volcanic activity. Also called **vulcanism.** —**volcanist,** *n.*

volcanology *Geology.* the scientific study of volcanoes and volcanic phenomena. Also called **vulcanology.** —**volcanologist,** *n.* —**volcanologic, volcanological,** *adj.*

W

WALKING

autoperipeteticus a learned coinage to describe a mechanism capable of independent movement, as a child's toy that "walks" down an inclined plane.

gyromancy a type of divination involving walking in a circle.

stasibasiphobia 1. an abnormal conviction that one cannot stand or walk. **2.** an abnormal fear of attempting to do either.

WAR

bellicism the advocacy of war, as opposed to *pacifism.* —**bellicist,** *n.*

copperheadism any expression of sympathy for the Confederate cause in the American Civil War. —**copperhead,** *n.*

doveism, dovism   the advocacy of peace or a conciliatory national attitude, esp. on the part of a public official.

hawkism   the advocacy of war or a belligerent national attitude, esp. on the part of a public official. —**hawk,** *n.* —**hawkish,** *adj.*

hypaspist   a shieldbearer.

irenicism   an advocacy of peace and conciliation. —**irenicist,** *n.*

logistics   the branch of military science concerned with the movement and supply of troops. —**logistician,** *n.*

pacifism   1. an opposition to war or violence of any kind.
2. the principle or policy of establishing and maintaining universal peace.
3. nonresistance to aggression. —**pacifist,** *n.* —**pacifistic,** *adj.*

martialism   1. an inclination to belligerency; bellicosity.
2. the qualities of a military existence. —**martialist,** *n.*

stratography   the art of directing an army. —**stratographer,** *n.*

WATER

bletonism   the skill or talent of water divining.

dowsing   a form of divination involving a rod or wand, esp. the art of finding underground supplies of water, ores, etc. Also called **rhabdomancy.**

fluviology   the science of watercourses, esp. rivers. —**fluviologist,** *n.*

hydrography   1. the study, description, and mapping of oceans, lakes, and rivers, esp. with reference to their use for navigational purposes.
2. those parts of the map, collectively, that represent surface waters. —**hydrographer,** *n.* —**hydrographic, hydrographical,** *adj.*

hydrology   the science that studies the occurrence, circulation, distribution, and properties of the waters of the earth and its atmosphere. —**hydrologist,** *n.* —**hydrologic, hydrological,** *adj.*

hydromancy   a form of divination involving observations of water or other liquids.

hydrophobia   an abnormal fear of water.

lecanomancy   a form of divination involving the examination of water in a basin.

lecanoscopy   a form of self-hypnotism involving staring at water in a basin.

limnology   the scientific study of bodies of fresh water, as lakes or rivers, with reference to their physical, geographical, and biological features. —**limnologist,** *n.* —**limnologic, limnological,** *adj.*

orohydrography   the branch of hydrography that studies the drainage phenomena of mountains. —**orohydrographic,** *adj.*

WAX

cerography   1. the art or process of writing or engraving on wax.
2. *Rare.* the art or process of making paintings with colors mixed with

beeswax and fixed with heat; encaustic painting. —**cerographist,** *n.* —**cerographic, cerographical,** *adj.*

ceromancy a form of divination involving dropping melted wax into water.

ceroplastics the art of modeling with wax. —**ceroplastic,** *adj.*

WEATHER

aerographics the study of atmospheric conditions. Also called **aerography.** —**aerographer,** *n.*

climatology the science that studies climate or climatic conditions. —**climatologist,** *n.* —**climatologic, climatological,** *adj.*

nephology the scientific study of clouds. —**nephologist,** *n.*

telemeteorography the recording of meteorological conditions at a distance, as in the use of sensing devices at various points that transmit their data to a central office. —**telemeteorgraphic,** *n.*
See also AIR *and* CLIMATE.

WIFE

uxoricide 1. the murder of a wife by a husband.
2. the husband who murders his wife. —**uxoricidal,** *adj.*

viduage the condition of widowhood. Also called **viduity.** —*Obsolete.*
vidual, *adj.*

WINE

oenology, enology the science of making wines. Also called *viniculture.* —**oenologist,** *n.*

oenomancy, oinomancy a form of divination involving observation of the colors and other features of wine.

oenophily, enophily the love of wine; connoisseurship concerning wines. —**oenophile,** *n.*

oenophobia, enophobia a dislike of or hatred for wine. —**oenophobe,** *n.*

vigneron a cultivator of grape vines; viticulturist.

viticulture 1. the science that studies grapes and their culture.
2. the cultivation of grapes and grapevines. —**viticulturist,** *n.* —**viticultural, viticulturist,** *adj.*

WOLF

lycanthrope 1. a person suffering from lycanthropy.
2. a werewolf or alien spirit in the form of a bloodthirsty wolf.
3. a person reputed to be able to change himself or another person into a wolf.

lycanthropy 1. *Psychiatry.* a kind of insanity in which the patient believes himself to be a beast, esp. a wolf.

2. the supposed or fabled assumption of the form of a wolf by a human being. —**lycanthropic,** *adj.*

WOMEN

femicide **1.** the murder of a woman.
2. the murderer of a woman. Also called **gynecide, gynaecide.** —**femicidal,** *adj.*

gynecolatry, gynaecolatry the worship of women. Also called **gyneolatry.** —**gynecolater,** *n.*

gynecology, gynaecology the branch of medical science that studies the diseases of women, esp. of the reproductive organs. —**gynecologist,** *n.* —**gynecologic, gynecological,** *adj.*

gynarchy a form of government by a woman or women. Also called **gynecocracy.** —**gynarchic,** *adj.*

gynephobia, gynophobia an abnormal fear of women. **gynephobe,** *n.*

philogyny a love of or liking for women. —**philogynist,** *n.* —**philogynous,** *adj.*

Soroptimist a member of a Soroptimist Club, an international organization of women executives and business women, devoted chiefly to welfare work.

WOOD

treen any small object made entirely of wood, as wooden spoons.

xylology a branch of dendrology that studies the structure of wood.

xylomancy a form of divination involving small pieces of wood.

xylotomy the art of cutting thin cross-sections of wood for microscopic examination. —**xylotomist,** *n.*

WORDS

acronym a word created from the initial letters of words in a phrase, as *ACTA,* for the *American Community Theatre Association.* Also called **abecedism.** —**acronymic, acronymous,** *adj.*

aphetism *Linguistics.* the loss of an initial unstressed vowel in a word, as *squire* for *esquire.* Also called **apharesis, aphesis.** —**aphetic,** *adj.*

archaism **1.** an archaic word or expression.
2. the deliberate use, for effect, of old-fashioned terminology in literature.

barbarism the use of terms or constructions felt by some to be undesirably foreign to the established customs of the language. — **barbarian,** *n., adj.*

catachresis **1.** a misuse or strained use of words.
2. the employment of a word under a false form through folk etymology: *gooseberry,* which is not attractive to geese and is not a berry, is the catachrestic form of a Dutch word. —**catachrestic,** *adj.* —**catachrestical,** *adj.*

cledonism *Rare.* the use of euphemisms in order to avoid the use of plain words and any misfortune associated with them.

derism an expression of scorn. —**deristic,** *adj.*

dysphemism **1.** a deliberate substitution of a disagreeable, offensive, or disparaging word for an otherwise inoffensive term, as *pig* for *policeman.* Cf. **euphemism.**
2. an instance of such substitution.

etymology **1.** the branch of linguistics that studies the origin and history of words.
2. an account of the historical changes of a word.
3. the derivation of a word. —**etymologist,** *n.* —**etymologic, etymological,** *adj.*

euphemism **1.** the deliberate or polite use of a pleasant or neutral word or expression to avoid the emotional implications of a plain term, as *passed over* for *died.* Cf. **dysphemism.**
2. an instance of such use. —**euphemist,** *n.* —**euphemistic, euphemistical, euphemious,** *adj.* See also **genteelism.**

genteelism **1.** the deliberate use of a word or phrase as a substitute for one thought to be less genteel, if not coarse, as *male cow* for *bull* or *limb* for *leg.*
2. an instance of such substitution.

glossography the writing or compilation of marginal or interlinear notes in a manuscript text. —**glossographer,** *n.* Cf. **tosaphoth.**

grammatolatry **1.** the worship of letters or words.
2. a devotion to the letter, as in law or Scripture; literalism.

heteronym a word with a different meaning and pronunciation from another, but with the same spelling, as *lead* "to conduct" and *lead* (the metal). —**heteronymous,** *adj.* Cf. **homonym, homophone.**

lexicography the writing or compiling of dictionaries. —**lexicographer,** *n.* —**lexicographic, lexicographical,** *adj.*

lexicology the study of the meanings of words and of idiomatic combinations. —**lexicologist,** *n.* —**lexicologic, lexicological,** *adj.*

logodaedaly *Rare.* a cunning with words; verbal legerdemain. Also called **logodaedalus.**

logomachy **1.** a dispute about or concerning words.
2. a contention marked by the careless or incorrect use of words; a meaningless battle of words. —**logomach, logomachist,** *n.* —**logomachic, logomachical,** *adj.*

logomancy a form of divination involving the observation of words and discourse.

malapropism **1.** the act or habit of misusing words ridiculously, esp. by the confusion of words similar in sound.

2. an instance of such misuse, as "comparisons are odorous". Also called **malapropoism.**

melioration *Linguistics.* a semantic change in a word to a higher, more respectable meaning, as in the change from *styward* to *steward.*

neologism **1.** a new word, usage, or phrase.
2. the coining or introduction of new words or new senses for established words. —**neologist,** *n.* —**neologistic, neologistical,** *adj.*

neophrasis *Rare.* neologism. —**neophrastic,** *adj.*

neoterism **1.** a neologism.
2. the use of neologisms.

orismology the science of defining technical terms. —**orismologic, orismological,** *adj.*

palindrome a word or phrase spelled the same way when read either forward or backward, as *Poor Dan is in a droop.* —**palindromist,** *n.* —**palindromic, palindromical,** *adj.*

paragoge the addition of a sound or group of sounds at the end of a word, as in the nonstandard *heighth* for *height.* —**paragogic, paragogical,** *adj.*

parisology the use of equivocal or ambiguous terms. —**parisological,** *adj.*

paronymous *Linguistics.* containing the same root or stem, as *perilous* and *parlous.* —**paronym,** *n.*

pejoratism *Linguistics.* a semantic change in a word to a lower, less respectable meaning, as in *hussy.* Also called **pejoration.** Cf. **melioration.**

philologue a lover of words.

pleonasm **1.** the use of more words than are necessary to convey the intended meaning; redundancy.
2. an instance of such redundancy, as *true fact.*
3. a redundant word or expression. —**pleonastic,** *adj.*

plurisignation a semantic quality in a word permitting to have two or more simultaneous interpretations; ambiguity.

portmanteau a blending of two words or their parts, as in *smog* (*smoke* + *fog*).

semantics *Linguistics.* **1.** a study of meaning.
2. the study of linguistic development by classifying and examining changes in meaning and form. —**semanticist, semantician,** *n.* —**semantic,** *adj.*

semeiology, semiology the science of signs, including words, and their meanings. —**semeiologist,** *n.* —**semeiologic, semeiological,** *adj.*

semasiology *Linguistics.* the science of semantics, esp. the study of semantic change. —**semasiologist,** *n.* —**semasiological,** *adj.*

semiotics *Logic, Philosophy.* a general theory of signs and symbolism, usually divided into pragmatics, semantics, and syntactics. Also called **semiotic, semeiotic.** —**semiotic,** *n., adj.*

sesquipedalianism the practice of using very long words. Also called **sesquipedalism, sesquipedality.** —**sesquipedal, sesquipedalian,** *adj.*

steganography *Archaic.* the use of a secret language or code; cryptography. —**steganographer,** *n.*

tautologism *Rare.* **1.** a needless repetition of an idea in other words without adding to emphasis or clarity; tautology.
2. an instance of such a repetition; a tautology.

tmesis *Rhetoric.* the interpolation of another word between two syllables of a compound word, as *what man soever.*

verbomania an excessive use of or attraction to words.
See also FIGURES OF SPEECH, LANGUAGE, RHETORIC.

WORK

dilutee a semiskilled or unskilled worker introduced into an industry to do what had been considered a skilled task.

ergasiophobia an abnormal fear of work.

ergograph an instrument that records the amount of work done when a muscle contracts. —**ergographic,** *adj.*

ergology the study of the effect of work on mind and body. —**ergologist,** *n.*

ergophile a person who loves to work.

ergophobia a hatred of work.

sinecurism a system under which it is possible to hold an office or position that brings profit while requiring little or no work and responsibility. Also called **sinecureship.** —**sinecurist,** *n.*

Taylorism the methods of scientific factory management first introduced in the early 19th cent. by the American engineer Frederick W. Taylor, esp. the differential piece-rate system.

WORMS

helminthology the branch of zoology that studies worms, esp. parasitic worms. —**helminthologist,** *n.* —**helminthologic, helminthological,** *adj.*

helminthophobia an abnormal fear of being infested with worms.

scoleciphobia an abnormal fear of worms.

WRITERS

pseudandry the use by a female writer of a male pseudonym. —**pseudandrous,** *adj.*

pseudogyny the use by a male writer of a female pseudonym. —**pseudogynous,** *adj.*

WRITING

acrology 1. the use of a symbol to represent phonetically the initial sound (syllable or letter) of the name of an object, as *A* is the first sound of Greek *alpha*.
2. the use of the name of the object as the name of the symbol representing its initial sound, as *A* in Greek is called *alpha* "ox". Also called **acrophony.** —**acrologic,** *adj.*

brachygraphy an abbreviated writing; shorthand. —**brachygraphic,** *adj.*

cacography 1. the possession of a bad handwriting. Cf. **calligraphy.**
2. the possession of poor spelling skills. Cf. **orthography.** —**cacographer,** *n.* —**cacographic, cacographical,** *adj.*

calligraphy 1. the art of beautiful penmanship.
2. handwriting in general.
3. the possession of good handwriting skills. Cf. **cacography.**
4. a script of a high aesthetic value produced by brush, esp. that of Chinese, Japanese, or Arabic origin. —**calligrapher, calligraphist,** *n.* —**calligraphic, calligraphical,** *adj.*

chirography 1. the penmanship of a person, esp. when used in an important document, as in an apostolic letter written and signed by the pope.
2. the art of beautiful writing; calligraphy. Also called **cheirography.** —**chirograph,** *n.* —**chirographer,** *n.* —**chirographic, chirographical,** *adj.*

chrysography 1. the art of writing in inks containing gold or silver in suspension.
2. the gold writing produced in this way. —**chrysographer,** *n.*

curiologics, curiology the representation of things or sounds by means of their pictures instead of by symbols or words, as in hieroglyphics or a rebus. —**curiologic, curiological,** *adj.*

graphemics *Linguistics.* the study of systems of writing and their relationship to the systems of the languages they represent. Also called **graphonomy.** —**graphemic,** *adj.*

graphology the study of handwriting, esp. as regarded as an expression of character. —**graphologist,** *n.* —graphologic, graphological, *adj.*

graphopathology *Psychology.* the study of handwriting as a symptom of mental or emotional disorder. —**graphopathologist,** *n.* —**graphopathological,** *adj.*

graptomancy a form of divination involving the examination of the client's handwriting.

haplography the accidental omission in writing or copying of one or more adjacent and similar letters, syllables, words, or lines, as *tagme* for *tagmeme.*

hieroglyphology   the study of hieroglyphic writing. —**hieroglyphologist,** *n.*

iconomaticism   a form of writing regarded as midway between picture writing, as hieroglyphics, and phonetic writing in which the names of the symbols are not the names of the objects they depict but phonetic elements only. —**iconomatic,** *adj.*

ideography   a form of writing in which a written symbol represents an object rather than a word or speech sound. —**ideographic, ideographical,** *adj.*

isography   *Rare.* the imitation of another person's handwriting. —**isographic, isographical,** *adj.*

logography   a method of reporting spoken language in longhand, using several reporters taking down a few words in succession. —**logographer,** *n.* —**logographic,** *adj.*

nomancy   a form of divination involving the examination of letters, possibly from a graphological stand point. Cf. **onomancy.**

ogham, ogam   **1.** an alphabetical script originally used for inscriptions in the Irish language from the 5th to the 10th cents.
2. any of the 20 characters of this script.
3. an inscription in this script. —**oghamist,** *n.*

pasigraphy   an artificial and international written language that uses signs and symbols instead of words. —**pasigraphic, pasigraphical,** *adj.*

phonography   **1.** any system of phonetic shorthand, as that of Pitman.
2. phonetic spelling, writing, or shorthand. —**phonographer, phonographist,** *n.* —**phonographic,** *adj.*

pictography   the use of pictorial symbols to communicate; picture writing with symbols that may be either ideographic or phonetic in function. —**pictograph,** *n.* —**pictographic,** *adj.*

rebus   **1.** a representation of a word, phrase, or sentence by pictures, symbols, etc., that suggest that word, phrase, or sentence, or its syllables: a *bridge and a pond make up one rebus for Bridgewater.*
2. a piece of writing using this system.

runology   the study of runes and runic writing. —**runologist,** *n.* —**runological,** *adj.*

sphenography   *Rare.* the art of writing and deciphering cuneiform characters. —**sphenographer, sphenographist,** *n.* —**sphenographic,** *adj.*

stenography   the art of writing in shorthand. —**stenographer, stenographist,** *n.* —**stenographic, stenographical,** *adj.*

stenotypy   a phonographic shorthand in which alphabetic letters, produced by hand or a special machine, are used to represent words and phrases. —**stenotypist,** *n.* —**stenotypic,** *adj.*

stignomancy   a form of divination involving the examination of writing on the bark of a tree.

syllabism 1. the use of characters in writing that represent syllables rather than individual sounds, as in the Cherokee syllabary.
2. a division of a word into syllables.

tachygraphy 1. the ancient Greek and Roman shorthand systems.
2. cursive writing.
3. the abbreviated Greek and Latin forms used in the medieval period.
—**tachygrapher, tachygraphist,** *n.* —**tachygraphic, tachygraphical,** *adj.*

XYZ

X-RAYS

fluoroscopy an examination by means of a screen coated with a fluorescent substance responsive to radiation from X-rays. —**fluoroscopic,** *adj.*

pyelography the science or technique of making X-ray photographs of the kidneys, renal pelves, and ureters, using injection of opaque solutions or radiopaque dyes. —**pyelographic,** *adj.*

radiography the production of photographic images on film using radiation from X-rays or other radioactive substances instead of light. Also called **shadowgraphy.** —**radiographer,** *n.* —**radiographic, radiographical,** *adj.*

radiology 1. the science that studies X-rays or radiation from radioactive substances, esp. for medical purposes.
2. the examination or photographing of parts of the body with such rays.
3. the interpretation of the resulting photographs. —**radiologist,** *n.* —**radiologic, radiological,** *adj.*

radiotherapy a method of treating diseases with X-rays or the radiation from other radioactive substances. —**radiotherapist,** *n.* —**radiotherapeutic,** *adj.*

tomography the X-ray photography of a selected plane of the body by a method that eliminates the outline of structures in other planes. —**tomographic,** *adj.*

xeroradiography a process of recording X-ray images by electrostatic means. —**xeroradiographic,** *adj.*

INDEX

A

abacist, NUMBERS
Abderian, LAUGHTER
abecedarian, ALPHABET
Abecedarian, BAPTISM
abecedary, ALPHABET
abecedism, WORDS
abiogenesis, LIFE
abiogenetic, LIFE
abiology, INANIMATE OBJECTS
ablepsia, BLINDNESS
ablepsy, BLINDNESS
ableptical, BLINDNESS
ablutomania, CLEANLINESS
abolitionism, SLAVES
abolitionist, SLAVES
aboriginal, PAST
aboriginality, PAST
abracadabra, MAGIC
abracadabrism, MAGIC
absentee, LAND
absenteeism, LAND
absinthial, ALCOHOL
absinthian, ALCOHOL
absinthism, ALCOHOL
absolutism, GOVERNMENT
absolutist, GOVERNMENT
absolutistic, GOVERNMENT
abstinence, ALCOHOL
abstinent, ALCOHOL
Abstract Expressionism, ART

Abstractism, ART
academic, LEARNING
academical, LEARNING
academicism, LEARNING
academism, LEARNING
academist, LEARNING
acalculia, NUMBERS
acapnotic, SMOKE
acarophobia, INSECTS, PHOBIAS
acatalepsy, KNOWLEDGE
acataleptic, KNOWLEDGE
accismus, LIES AND LYING
accubation, FOOD AND NUTRITION
Achephali, EASTERN ORTHODOXY
Achephalist, EASTERN ORTHODOXY
achromaticity, COLOR
achromatism, COLOR
acidophobia, PLANTS
acidophobic, PLANTS
acology, REMEDIES
acomia, BALDNESS
acomous, BALDNESS
acosmic, GOD AND GODS
acosmism, GOD AND GODS
acosmist, GOD AND GODS
acoustic, SOUNDS
acoustician, SOUNDS
acousticophobia, PHOBIAS
acoustics, SOUNDS
acritochromacy, COLOR
acrologic, WRITING
acrology, WRITING
acronym, WORDS

acronymic, WORDS
acronymous, WORDS
acrophile, MOUNTAINS
acrophobia, HEIGHTS
acrophony, WRITING
acrostic, VERSE
acrosticism, VERSE
actinic, HEAT
actinism, HEAT
actinographic, PHOTOGRAPHY
actinography, PHOTOGRAPHY
Action Painting, ART
active scopophilia, SEX
actualism, PHILOSOPHY
actualist, PHILOSOPHY
actualistic, PHILOSOPHY
acyanoblepsia, COLOR
acyrological, SPEECH
acyrology, SPEECH
Adamite, RELIGION
Adamitic, RELIGION
Adamitism, RELIGION
addenda, COLLECTIONS AND COLLECTING
adelphogamic, MARRIAGE
adelphogamy, MARRIAGE
ademonist, DEMONS
adevism, GOD AND GODS
adevist, GOD AND GODS
adiabolist, DEVIL
adiaphorism, PROTESTANTISM
adiaphorist, PROTESTANTISM
adiaphoristic, PROTESTANTISM
adnomination, PUN
adonism, BEAUTY
adoptianism, CHRIST
adoptionism, CHRIST
adoptionist, CHRIST
Adventism, PROTESTANTISM
Adventist, PROTESTANTISM
aedist, SPIRITS AND SPIRITUALISM
aelurophile, CATS
aelurophobia, CATS
aeolism, LANGUAGE STYLES
aeolistic, LANGUAGE STYLES
aeon, TIME
aerialist, AVIATION
aerobic, AIR
aerobics, AIR
aerodonetic, AVIATION
aerodonetics, AVIATION
aerodromics, AVIATION
aerodynamic, AIR

aerodynamical, AIR
aerodynamics, AIR
aerogeologist, GEOLOGY
aerogeology, GEOLOGY
aerographer, ATMOSPHERE
aerographic, ATMOSPHERE
aerographical, ATMOSPHERE
aerographics, ATMOSPHERE, WEATHER
aerography, ATMOSPHERE
aerography, WEATHER
aerolithology, ASTRONOMY, METEORITES
aerolitics, ASTRONOMY, METEORITES
aerologic, ATMOSPHERE
aerological, ATMOSPHERE
aerologist, ATMOSPHERE
aerology, ATMOSPHERE
aeromancy, AIR
aerometric, AIR
aerometry, AIR
aeronaut, AVIATION
aeronautic, AVIATION
aeronautical, AVIATION
aeronautics, AVIATION
aerophilately, COLLECTIONS AND COLLECTING
aerophobe, AIR
aerophobia, AIR
aerophysics, AVIATION
aerophyte, PLANTS
aerostatic, AVIATION
aerostatical, AVIATION
aerostatics, AVIATION
aesthetic, BEAUTY
aesthetical, BEAUTY
aesthetician, BEAUTY
aestheticism, ART, BEAUTY
aesthetics, BEAUTY
aetiology, DISEASE AND ILLNESS, NATURE
aficionado, BULLS
agathism, GOOD
agathist, GOOD
agathology, GOOD
Aggada, JUDAISM
Aggadah, JUDAISM
agmatology, BONES
agnoeology, KNOWLEDGE
Agnoete, HERESY
Agnoetism, HERESY
agnoiology, KNOWLEDGE
Agnoite, HERESY
agnomination, PUN
agnostic, GOD AND GODS
agnosticism, GOD AND GODS

agogic, MUSIC
agogics, MUSIC
agonist, ATHLETICS
agonistic, ATHLETICS
agonistical, ATHLETICS
agonistics, ATHLETICS
agoraphobia, SPACES
agrammatism, GRAMMAR
agrarian, POISON
agrarianism, POISON
agrarian reform, POISON
agriological, MAN
agriologist, MAN
agriology, MAN
agrobiologic, BIOLOGY
agrobiological, BIOLOGY
agrobiologist, BIOLOGY
agrobiology, BIOLOGY
agrological, SOILS
agrologist, SOILS
agrology, SOILS
agrostographer, GRASSES
agrostography, GRASSES
agrostologic, BOTANY
agrostological, BOTANY
agrostologist, BOTANY, GRASSES
agrostology, BOTANY, GRASSES
aichmophobia, SHARPNESS
ailurophile, CATS
ailurophobia, CATS
air plant, PLANTS
aischrolatreia, DIRT, OBSCENITY
aischrology, OBSCENITY
akosmism, GOD AND GODS
alacritous, ALERTNESS
alacrity, ALERTNESS
Albertist, THEOLOGY
Albigensianism, HERESY
albinal, DISEASE AND ILLNESS
albinic, DISEASE AND ILLNESS
albinism, DISEASE AND ILLNESS, SKIN
albinistic, DISEASE AND ILLNESS
albino, SKIN
albinoism, SKIN
albinotic, SKIN
albuminurophobia, PHOBIAS
alcoholic, ALCOHOL
alcoholism, ALCOHOL
alcoholphile, ALCOHOL
alcoholphilia, ALCOHOL
Alcoranist, ISLAM
alectoromachy, COCKS

alectoromancy, COCKS
alectryomachy, COCKS
alectryomancy, COCKS
alethiological, TRUTH
alethiologist, TRUTH
alethiology, TRUTH
alexipharmac, POISON
alexipharmic, POISON
algogenic, PAIN
algolagnia, PAIN, SEX
algolagnic, PAIN, SEX
algolagnist, PAIN, SEX
algological, BOTANY
algologist, BOTANY
algology, BOTANY
algophilia, PAIN
algophobia, PAIN
algorism, MATHEMATICS
algorismic, MATHEMATICS
algorist, MATHEMATICS
algraphic, PRINTING
algraphy, PRINTING
alienism, PSYCHOLOGY
alienist, PSYCHOLOGY
alimentology, FOOD AND NUTRITION
aliptic, REMEDIES
allomorph, LINGUISTICS
allomorphic, LINGUISTICS
allopath, REMEDIES
allopathic, REMEDIES
allopathist, REMEDIES
allopathy, REMEDIES
allophonic, LINGUISTICS
allotheism, GOD AND GODS
almanagist, ALMANACS
alogia, SPEECH
alogy, SPEECH
alopecia, BALDNESS, HAIR
alopecic, HAIR
alopecist, BALDNESS
altimetrical, HEIGHTS
altimetry, HEIGHTS
altruism, ATTITUDES
altruist, ATTITUDES
altruistic, ATTITUDES
aluminography, PRINTING
amateurism, ATTITUDES
amathophobia, PHOBIAS
amaxophobia, VEHICLES
ambidexterity, HANDS
ambidextrianism, HANDS
ambidextrous, HANDS

Americanism, CATHOLICISM, LANGUAGE
Ameslan, DEAFNESS
amicicide, KILLING
amnesia, MEMORY
amnesiac, MEMORY
amnesic, MEMORY
ampelographer, BOTANY
ampelography, BOTANY
amphibological, GRAMMAR
amphibology, GRAMMAR
amphibolous, GRAMMAR
amphiboly, GRAMMAR
amphierotic, SEX
amphierotism, SEX
amphigoric, VERSE
amphigory, VERSE
amphigouri, VERSE
Amyraldism, PROTESTANTISM
Anabaptism, BAPTISM
Anabaptist, BAPTISM
anabolic, ORGANISMS
anabolism, ORGANISMS
anachronism, TIME
anachronistic, TIME
anachronistical, TIME
anachronous, TIME
anacoluthia, GRAMMAR
anacoluthic, GRAMMAR
anacoluthon, GRAMMAR
anadiplosis, LANGUAGE STYLES
analogic, AGREEMENT
analogical, AGREEMENT
analogous, ARGUMENT
analogy, AGREEMENT, ARGUMENT
analphabetic, ALPHABET
analytical stasiology, POLITICS
anamnesis, MEMORY
anamnestic, MEMORY
anaphora, RHETORIC
anaphoral, RHETORIC
anaphrodisia, SEX
anaplasty, MEDICAL SPECIALTIES
anarchic, GOVERNMENT
anarchism, GOVERNMENT
anarchist, GOVERNMENT
anathema, CHRISTIANITY
anathematism, CHRISTIANITY
anatomy, ANATOMY
anchoret, MONKS
anchoretic, MONKS
anchorite, MONKS
anchoritic, MONKS

anchoritism, MONKS
andric, MALE
androcentric, MALE
androcracy, MALE
androcratic, MALE
androgenesis, MALE
androgenetic, MALE
androgyneity, BODIES
androgynism, BODIES
androgynous, BODIES
androlepsy, FOREIGNERS
androphagous, CANNIBALISM
androphagy, CANNIBALISM
androphilia, MALE
androphilic, MALE
androphobia, MALE
androphonomania, MURDER
anecdotalism, LITERATURE
anecdotalist, LITERATURE
anemographic, AIR
anemography, AIR
anemological, AIR
anemology, AIR
anemometric, AIR
anemometrical, AIR
anemometry, AIR
anemophile, AIR
anemophilia, AIR
anemophilous, AIR
anemophobe, AIR
anemophobia, AIR
aneroid, ATMOSPHERE
anesthesiologist, MEDICAL SPECIALTIES
anesthesiology, MEDICAL SPECIALTIES
aneurism, ARTERIES
aneurysm, ARTERIES
angelology, RELIGION
anginophobia, HEART, PHOBIAS
angiology, BLOOD
angiopathology, BLOOD
Anglicism, ENGLISH
Anglicist, ENGLISH
Anglist, ENGLAND
Anglomania, ENGLAND
Anglophile, ENGLAND
Anglophobia, ENGLAND
aniconic, GOD AND GODS
aniconism, GOD AND GODS
anima, PSYCHOLOGY
animalism, MAN
animalist, MAN
animalistic, MAN

animality, ANIMALS
animatism, INANIMATE OBJECTS
animatistic, INANIMATE OBJECTS
animism, GOD AND GODS
animist, GOD AND GODS
animistic, GOD AND GODS
animosity, ATTITUDES
animus, PSYCHOLOGY
ankylophobia, BODIES
annomination, PUN
anomia, LAW
anomic, LAW
anomie, LAW
anomy, LAW
anorexia, FOOD AND NUTRITION, HEALTH
anosmia, ODORS
anosmic, ODORS
anosphrasia, ODORS
antagonism, BEHAVIOR
antagonistic, BEHAVIOR
antediluvian, PAST
antediluvianism, PAST
anthoecology, ENVIRONMENT, FLOWERS
anthography, FLOWERS
anthomania, FLOWERS
anthophagous, FLOWERS
anthophagy, FLOWERS
anthophobia, FLOWERS
anthropographer, MAN
anthropographic, MAN
anthropography, MAN
anthropolatry, GOD AND GODS
anthropometric, ANATOMY
anthropometrical, ANATOMY
anthropometrist, ANATOMY
anthropometry, ANATOMY
anthropomorphic, ANATOMY, GOD AND GODS
anthropomorphical, ANATOMY, GOD AND GODS
anthropomorphism, ANATOMY, GOD AND GODS
anthropomorphist, GOD AND GODS
anthropomorphistic, GOD AND GODS
anthropomorphology, ANATOMY
anthropomorphous, ANATOMY
anthroponomical, MAN
anthroponomics, MAN
anthroponomist, MAN
anthroponomy, MAN
anthroponymist, NAMES
anthroponymy, NAMES
anthropopathic, ANIMALS, GOD AND GODS
anthropopathism, ANIMALS, GOD AND GODS
anthropopathite, GOD AND GODS

anthropopathy, ANIMALS, GOD AND GODS
anthropophagism, CANNIBALISM
anthropophagous, CANNIBALISM
anthropophagy, CANNIBALISM
anthropophilic, MAN
anthropophobia, MAN, SOCIETY
anthropophuism, GOD AND GODS
anthropophuistic, GOD AND GODS
anthropopsychic, NATURE
anthropopsychism, NATURE
anthroposcopy, ANATOMY, RACE
anthroposociological, RACE
anthroposociology, ENVIRONMENT
anthroposophical, MAN
anthroposophist, MAN
anthroposophy, MAN
anthropotheism, GOD AND GODS
anticlericalism, CATHOLICISM
anticlericalist, CATHOLICISM
antilapsarian, MAN
antinomia, LAW
antinomian, LAW, THEOLOGY
antinomianism, LAW, THEOLOGY
antinomic, LAW
antinomist, LAW
antinomy, LAW
antipaedobaptism, BAPTISM
antipedobaptism, BAPTISM
antipedobaptist, BAPTISM
antiphrasis, LITERATURE, RHETORIC
antiphrastic, LITERATURE, RHETORIC
antiphrastical, RHETORIC
antipodean, EQUATOR
antipodes, EQUATOR
antipope, POPE
antiquarian, ANTIQUITY, PAST
antiquarianism, ANTIQUITY, PAST
antiquary, PAST
Antiscians, EQUATOR
Antiscii, EQUATOR
antonomasia, NAMES
antonomastic, NAMES
anythingarian, POLITICS
anythingarianism, POLITICS
apagoge, ARGUMENT
apagogic, ARGUMENT
apartheid, GOVERNMENT
aphanite, GEOLOGY
aphanitism, GEOLOGY
apharesis, WORDS
aphasia, SPEECH
aphasiac, SPEECH

aphasic, SPEECH
aphephobia, PHOBIAS
aphesis, WORDS
aphetic, WORDS
aphetism, WORDS
aphnology, ECONOMICS, MONEY
aphorism, PROVERBS
aphorismic, PROVERBS
aphorismical, PROVERBS
aphorist, PROVERBS
aphoristic, PROVERBS
apiarian, BEES
apiarist, BEES
apiary, BEES
apiologist, BEES
apiology, BEES
apiophobia, BEES
apiphobia, BEES
apocalyptic, RELIGION
apocalypticism, RELIGION
apocalyptocal, RELIGION
Apollinarian, HERESY
Apollinarianism, HERESY
apologetical, DEFENSE
apologetics, DEFENSE
apologist, DEFENSE
apophasic, FIGURES OF SPEECH
apophasis, FIGURES OF SPEECH
aposiopesis, LANGUAGE STYLES, RHETORIC
aposiopetic, LANGUAGE STYLES, RHETORIC
apostrophe, FIGURES OF SPEECH
apostrophic, FIGURES OF SPEECH
apotelesm, ASTROLOGY
apotelesmatic, ASTROLOGY
apothegmatic, PROVERBS
apothegmatical, PROVERBS
apothegmatist, PROVERBS
apotropaic, MAGIC
apotropaism, MAGIC
aptotic, LANGUAGE
aquapontic, PLANTS
aquapontics, PLANTS
Arabism, POLITICS
arachnephobia, PHOBIAS
Aramaism, LANGUAGE
arbalest, JOBS
arbalist, JOBS
Arcadian, ATTITUDES
Arcadianism, ATTITUDES
archaeogeology, GEOLOGY
archaeolater, PAST
archaeolatrous, PAST

archaeolatry, PAST
archaeologic, ANTIQUITY
archaeological, ANTIQUITY
archaeologist, ANTIQUITY
archaeology, ANTIQUITY
archaic, PAST
archaicism, ANCESTORS, PAST
archaism, ANCESTORS, ART, PAST, WORDS
archaist, ANCESTORS, PAST
archaistic, ANCESTORS
archeogeology, GEOLOGY
archeology, ANTIQUITY
archology, GOVERNMENT, ORIGINS
arctophilist, COLLECTIONS AND COLLECTING
arcubalist, JOBS
areography, MARS
areologic, ASTRONOMY, MARS
areological, ASTRONOMY, MARS
areologist, ASTRONOMY, MARS
areology, ASTRONOMY, MARS
argyria, DISEASE AND ILLNESS
argyrism, DISEASE AND ILLNESS
argyrothecology, COLLECTIONS AND COLLECTING
Arianism, CHRIST
aristologist, DINING
aristology, DINING
Aristotelian, PHILOSOPHY
Aristotelianism, PHILOSOPHY
arithmancy, NUMBERS
arithmomancy, NUMBERS
arithmomania, NUMBERS
Arminian, PROTESTANTISM
Arminianism, PROTESTANTISM
Arnoldist, POLITICS
arsonist, FIRE
arthritic, DISEASE AND ILLNESS
arthritical, DISEASE AND ILLNESS
arthritism, DISEASE AND ILLNESS
arthropathology, DISEASE AND ILLNESS
aruspex, ANIMALS
Aryanism, RACE
Aryanist, RACE
ascetic, ATTITUDES
asceticism, ATTITUDES
asportation, LAW
asportator, LAW
asseveration, LAW
asseverative, LAW
Assideanism, JUDAISM
astatic, PHYSICS
astaticism, PHYSICS
asterism, ASTRONOMY

asterismal, ASTRONOMY
asteroids, PLANETS
asthenia, STRENGTH AND WEAKNESS
asthenic, ANATOMY, STRENGTH AND WEAKNESS
asthenophobia, PHOBIAS
astigmatic, EYES
astigmatism, EYES
astraphobia, LIGHTNING
astrapophobia, LIGHTNING
astrogation, ASTRONOMY
astrogator, ASTRONOMY
astrogeology, ASTRONOMY
astrognosy, ASTRONOMY
astrographic, ASTRONOMY
astrography, ASTRONOMY
astrolater, ASTRONOMY
astrolatry, ASTRONOMY
astrolithology, METEORITES
astrologer, ASTROLOGY
astrological, ASTROLOGY
astrologist, ASTROLOGY
astrology, ASTROLOGY
astromancer, ASTRONOMY
astromancy, ASTRONOMY
astromantic, ASTRONOMY
astrometric, ASTRONOMY
astrometrical, ASTRONOMY
astrometry, ASTRONOMY
astronautic, ASTRONOMY
astronautical, ASTRONOMY
astronautics, ASTRONOMY
astronavigation, ASTRONOMY
astronavigator, ASTRONOMY
astronomer, ASTRONOMY
astronomical, ASTRONOMY
astronomy, ASTRONOMY
astrophile, ASTRONOMY
astrophilic, ASTRONOMY
astrophobia, PHOBIAS
astrophysicist, ASTRONOMY
astrophysics, ASTRONOMY
ataraxia, HAPPINESS
ataraxic, HAPPINESS
atavism, ANCESTORS
atavist, ANCESTORS
atavistic, ANCESTORS
ataxiophobia, PHOBIAS
ataxophobia, PHOBIAS
Atenism, GOD AND GODS
Athanasian, CHRIST
Athanasianism, CHRIST
athedonia, HAPPINESS

athedonic, HAPPINESS
atheism, GOD AND GODS
atheist, GOD AND GODS
atheistic, GOD AND GODS
athletic, ANATOMY
atlas, MAPS
atomic theory, PHILOSOPHY
atomism, PHILOSOPHY
atomist, PHILOSOPHY
atomistic, PHILOSOPHY
atomistical, PHILOSOPHY
atonal, MUSIC
atonalism, MUSIC
atonalist, MUSIC
atonalistic, MUSIC
atonality, MUSIC
atrabilarian, BEHAVIOR
atrabilious, BEHAVIOR
atrichia, BALDNESS
atrichosis, BALDNESS
Atticism, HUMOR
Atticist, HUMOR
attitudinarian, ATTITUDES
attitudinarianism, ATTITUDES
audiclave, HEARING
audioanalgesia, HEARING
audiologist, EAR
audiology, EAR
audiometric, HEARING
audiometrician, HEARING
audiometrist, HEARING
audiometry, HEARING
audiophile, PHONOGRAPH RECORDS
audiophilia, PHONOGRAPH RECORDS
audiophilic, PHONOGRAPH RECORDS
auditognosis, HEARING
Augustinian, THEOLOGY
Augustinianism, THEOLOGY
aulic, LANGUAGE
aulicism, LANGUAGE
aurophobia, PHOBIAS
autarch, GOVERNMENT
autarchic, GOVERNMENT
autarchical, GOVERNMENT
autarchy, GOVERNMENT
autarkic, ECONOMICS
autarkical, ECONOMICS
autarkist, ECONOMICS
autarky, ECONOMICS
autecologic, ENVIRONMENT
autecological, ENVIRONMENT
autecology, BIOLOGY, ENVIRONMENT

authoritarian, ATTITUDES
authoritarianism, ATTITUDES
autism, DREAMS
autistic, DREAMS
autocracy, GOVERNMENT
autocrat, GOVERNMENT
autocratic, GOVERNMENT
autoerotic, SEX
autoeroticism, SEX
autoerotism, SEX
automatism, ACTION
automatist, ACTION
automysophobia, CLEANLINESS, DIRT
autonomism, COMMUNISM
autonomous, GOVERNMENT
autonomy, GOVERNMENT
autonumerology, VEHICLES
autoperipeteticus, WALKING
autophagia, FOOD AND NUTRITION
autophagous, FOOD AND NUTRITION
autophagy, FOOD AND NUTRITION
autophile, SELF
autophilia, SELF
autophilic, SELF
autophobia, SELF
autophoby, BEHAVIOR
autophoby, SELF
autopsy, CORPSE
autotelic, ART
autotelism, ART
autothaumaturgist, LIES AND LYING
autotheism, ATTITUDES, CHRIST
autotheist, CHRIST
autotheistic, CHRIST
auxanographic, BIOLOGY
auxanography, BIOLOGY
auxanology, GROWTH
auxographic, PLANTS
auxography, PLANTS
auxology, GROWTH
Averrhoism, PHILOSOPHY
Averroism, PHILOSOPHY
Averroist, PHILOSOPHY
Averroistic, PHILOSOPHY
aviary, BIRDS
avicide, BIRDS
aviculture, BIRDS
aviculturist, BIRDS
avinosis, AVIATION
avowtry, LAW
axiological, ETHICS, VALUES
axiologist, ETHICS, VALUES

axiology, ETHICS, VALUES
Ayurveda, HINDUISM
Ayurvedic, HINDUISM
Ayurvedism, HINDUISM
azoology, NATURE

B

Baalism, GOD AND GODS
Baalistic, GOD AND GODS
Baalite, GOD AND GODS
Babiism, ISLAM
Babism, ISLAM
Babist, ISLAM
Babouvism, POLITICS
Babouvist, POLITICS
bacchanalian, ALCOHOL
bacchanalianism, ALCOHOL
bacillophobia, PHOBIAS
Backuninism, COMMUNISM
bacteriologic, BACTERIA
bacteriological, BACTERIA
bacteriologist, BACTERIA
bacteriology, BACTERIA
bacteriophobia, PHOBIAS
baculometry, MEASUREMENT
Bahai, RELIGION
Bahaism, RELIGION
Bahaist, RELIGION
balladism, SONGS AND SINGING
balladist, SONGS AND SINGING
ballistic, MISSILES
ballistician, MISSILES
ballistics, MISSILES
ballistophobia, MISSILES
balneography, BATHING
balneologic, BATHING
balneological, BATHING
balneologist, BATHING
balneology, BATHING
baptisaphily, BAPTISM
baragnosis, GRAVITY
barbarian, WORDS
barbarism, WORDS
bardism, VERSE
barognosis, GRAVITY
barograph, ATMOSPHERE
barology, GRAVITY
barometry, ATMOSPHERE
barrator, LAW
barratrous, LAW, SHIPS

barratry, LAW, SHIPS
barretry, SHIPS
Bascology, LANGUAGE
basiphobia, PLANTS
basophobia, PLANTS
basophobic, PLANTS
bathmism, GROWTH
bathmophobia, PHOBIAS
bathometer, DEPTH
bathophobia, BATHING
bathyal, DEPTH
bathyalic, DEPTH
bathyclinograph, DEPTH, SEA
bathygram, SEA
bathygraph, SEA
bathygraphy, SEA
bathymeter, DEPTH
bathymetric, DEPTH
bathymetrical, DEPTH
bathymetry, DEPTH
bathyscape, DEPTH
bathyscaph, DEPTH
bathyscaphe, DEPTH
bathyseism, EARTHQUAKES
bathysphere, DEPTH
bathythermograph, DEPTH
batologist, BOTANY
batology, BOTANY
batophobia, BUILDINGS
batrachophobia, PHOBIAS
battery, LAW
battology, LANGUAGE STYLES
behaviorism, MIND, PSYCHOLOGY
behaviorist, MIND, PSYCHOLOGY
behavioristic, MIND, PSYCHOLOGY
Behmenism, MYSTICISM
belles lettre, LITERATURE
belles-lettrism, LITERATURE
belletrism, LITERATURE
belletrist, LITERATURE
belletristic, LITERATURE
bellicism, WAR
bellicist, WAR
belomancy, ARROWS
belonephobia, SHARPNESS
Benedictine, MONKS
Benedictinism, MONKS
Berengarian, HERESY
Berengarianism, HERESY
Bergsonian, PHILOSOPHY
Bergsonism, PHILOSOPHY
Berkeleian, PERCEPTION

Berkeleianism, PERCEPTION
Berkeleyan, PERCEPTION
Berkeleyanism, PERCEPTION
Berkeleyism, PERCEPTION
bestiality, BEHAVIOR
bestiarian, ANIMALS
bestiarist, ANIMALS
bestiary, ANIMALS
biarchy, GOVERNMENT
biblioclasm, BIBLE
biblioclast, BIBLE
bibliogenesis, BOOKS
bibliognost, BOOKS
bibliognostic, BOOKS
bibliogony, BOOKS
bibliographer, BOOKS
bibliographic, BOOKS
bibliographical, BOOKS
bibliography, BOOKS
biblioklept, BOOKS, STEALING
bibliokleptomania, BOOKS, STEALING
bibliokleptomaniac, STEALING
bibliologist, BOOKS
bibliology, BOOKS
bibliomancy, BIBLE
bibliomania, BOOKS
bibliomaniac, BOOKS
bibliomaniacal, BOOKS
bibliopegic, BOOKS
bibliopegist, BOOKS
bibliopegy, BOOKS
bibliophage, BOOKS
bibliophagous, BOOKS
bibliophagy, BOOKS
bibliophile, BOOKS
bibliophilic, BOOKS
bibliophilism, BOOKS
bibliophilist, BOOKS
bibliophily, BOOKS
bibliophobia, BOOKS
bibliopole, BOOKS
bibliopolic, BOOKS
bibliopolism, BOOKS
bibliopolist, BOOKS
bibliopoly, BOOKS
bibliotaph, BOOKS
bibliotaphic, BOOKS
bibliotaphy, BOOKS
bibliotherapeutic, BOOKS, REMEDIES
bibliotherapist, BOOKS, REMEDIES
bibliotherapy, BOOKS, REMEDIES
bicameral, GOVERNMENT

bicameralism, GOVERNMENT
bicameralist, GOVERNMENT
bigamist, MARRIAGE
bigamous, MARRIAGE
bigamy, MARRIAGE
bilateralism, ECONOMICS
bilateralistic, ECONOMICS
bilingual, LANGUAGE
bilingualism, LANGUAGE
bilinguality, LANGUAGE
bilinguist, LANGUAGE
Billingsgate, LANGUAGE STYLES
biloquism, SPEECH
biloquist, SPEECH
bimetallism, MONEY
bimetallist, MONEY
bimetallistic, MONEY
biochemical, LIFE
biochemist, LIFE
biochemistry, LIFE
bioclimatician, ATMOSPHERE
bioclimatological, ATMOSPHERE
bioclimatologist, ATMOSPHERE
bioclimatology, ATMOSPHERE
bioecologic, ANIMALS
bioecological, ANIMALS
bioecologist, ANIMALS, ENVIRONMENT
bioecology, ANIMALS, ENVIRONMENT
biofeedback, BRAIN
biogeography, BIOLOGY
biolinguist, SPEECH
biolinguistics, SPEECH
biometeorology, ATMOSPHERE
biophysiologist, BODIES
biophysiology, BODIES
bioscope, FILMS
biosophist, SELF
biosophy, SELF
biotechnology, ENVIRONMENT, MAN
biracial, RACE
biracialism, RACE
biracialist, RACE
bitheism, GOD AND GODS
bitheist, GOD AND GODS
bitheistic, GOD AND GODS
bletonism, WATER
Boehmenism, MYSTICISM
Boehmenist, MYSTICISM
Boehmenite, MYSTICISM
Boehmist, MYSTICISM
bohemian, BEHAVIOR
bohemianism, BEHAVIOR

Bollandist, SAINTS
Boloism, POLITICS
bolometric, RADIATION
bolometrist, RADIATION
bolometry, RADIATION
Bolshevik, COMMUNISM
Bolshevism, COMMUNISM
Bolshevist, COMMUNISM
boodleism, POLITICS
boodler, POLITICS
boodling, POLITICS
bossism, POLITICS
botanical, BOTANY
botanist, BOTANY
botany, BOTANY
botulism, FOOD AND NUTRITION, POISON
Bourbonian, POLITICS
Bourbonic, POLITICS
Bourbonism, POLITICS
Bourbonist, POLITICS
Bourigianism, MYSTICISM
bowdlerism, LITERATURE
bowdlerize, LITERATURE
brachygraphic, WRITING
brachygraphy, WRITING
brachylogy, BREVITY
Brahmanism, HINDUISM
Brahminism, HINDUISM
Braidism, SLEEP
brandophily, COLLECTIONS AND COLLECTING
brigand, STEALING
brigandage, STEALING
brigandish, STEALING
brigandism, STEALING
brinkmanship, POLITICS
brinksmanship, POLITICS
Briticism, LANGUAGE
bromatology, FOOD AND NUTRITION
bromidism, DISEASE AND ILLNESS
bromidrosiphobia, CLEANLINESS
brominism, DISEASE AND ILLNESS
bromism, DISEASE AND ILLNESS
brontology, THUNDER
brontophobia, THUNDER
Brownism, PROTESTANTISM
Brownist, PROTESTANTISM
Brownistic, PROTESTANTISM
Brutalism, ARCHITECTURE
bruxism, TEETH
bruxomania, TEETH
bryologist, BOTANY
bryology, BOTANY

Buchmanism, PROTESTANTISM
Buchmanite, PROTESTANTISM
bucolic, ATTITUDES
bucolical, ATTITUDES
bucolicism, ATTITUDES
Buddhism, BUDDHISM
Buddhist, BUDDHISM
Buddhistic, BUDDHISM
Buddhistical, BUDDHISM
buffoon, HUMOR
buffoonery, HUMOR
buffoonish, HUMOR
buffoonism, HUMOR
bulldogger, BULLS
bulldogging, BULLS
bumpologist, HEAD
bumpology, HEAD
Bund, FASCISM
Bundist, FASCISM
Bungaloid, ARCHITECTURE
bureaucracy, BUREAUCRACY
bureaucratic, BUREAUCRACY
burinist, ENGRAVING
Byzantinism, CHRISTIANITY

C

cabalism, JUDAISM
cabalist, JUDAISM
cabalistic, JUDAISM
cacesthesia, DISEASE AND ILLNESS
caciquism, GOVERNMENT
caciquismo, GOVERNMENT
cacodemonia, DEMONS
cacodemoniac, DEMONS
cacodemonic, DEMONS
cacodemonomania, DEMONS
cacoepy, PRONUNCIATION
cacoethes, DISEASE AND ILLNESS
cacoethic, DISEASE AND ILLNESS
cacogenic, RACE
cacogenics, RACE
cacographer, SPELLING
cacographic, SPELLING
cacographical, SPELLING
cacography, SPELLING, WRITING
cacology, PRONUNCIATION
caconymic, NAMES
cacophonic, SOUNDS
cacophonous, SOUNDS
cacophony, SOUNDS

cagophily, COLLECTIONS AND COLLECTING
Cahenslyism, CATHOLICISM
Cainism, HERESY, PHILOSOPHY
Cainite, HERESY
Cainitism, HERESY
cainophobia, CHANGE, NOVELTY
cainotophobia, CHANGE, NOVELTY
calciphilia, DISEASE AND ILLNESS
caliology, BIRDS
calisthenic, ATHLETICS
calisthenical, ATHLETICS
calisthenics, ATHLETICS
calligrapher, WRITING
calligraphic, WRITING
calligraphical, WRITING
calligraphist, WRITING
calligraphy, WRITING
Calvinism, PROTESTANTISM
Calvinist, PROTESTANTISM
Calvinistic, PROTESTANTISM
Calvinistical, PROTESTANTISM
calvities, BALDNESS
calvity, BALDNESS
calvous, BALDNESS
cambism, FINANCE, MONEY
cambist, FINANCE, MONEY
cambistry, FINANCE, MONEY
cameist, JOBS
campanarian, BELLS
campanario, BELLS
campanile, BELLS
campanist, BELLS
campanology, BELLS
cancerophobia, CANCER
cannabism, DRUGS
cantharidism, POISON
Caodaism, RELIGION
Caodaist, RELIGION
Caodism, RELIGION
capitalism, ECONOMICS
capitalist, ECONOMICS
capitalistic, ECONOMICS
capnomancy, SMOKE
carbon-14 dating, TIME
carcinogen, CANCER
carcinogenic, CANCER
carcinomatophobia, CANCER
carcinomophobia, CANCER
carcinophobia, CANCER
cardioangiology, HEART
cardiocentesis, HEART
cardiodynamics, HEART

cardiodynia, HEART
cardiogenesis, HEART
cardiograph, HEART
cardiographer, HEART
cardiographic, HEART
cardiography, HEART
cardiokinetic, HEART
cardiologic, HEART
cardiological, HEART
cardiologist, HEART
cardiology, HEART
cardiomalacia, HEART
cardiomegaly, HEART
cardiomyopathy, HEART
cardiopaludism, HEART
cardiopath, HEART
cardiopathy, HEART
cardiophobia, HEART
cardiopuncture, HEART
cardioversion, HEART
carmen figuratum, VERSE
carnal, SEX
carnalism, SEX
carnality, SEX
carpological, BOTANY
carpologist, BOTANY
carpology, BOTANY
cartel, ECONOMICS
cartelism, ECONOMICS
Cartesian, PHILOSOPHY
Cartesianism, PHILOSOPHY
cartographer, MAPS
cartographic, MAPS
cartography, MAPS
cartophily, COLLECTIONS AND COLLECTING
casuist, BEHAVIOR
casuistic, BEHAVIOR
casuistry, BEHAVIOR
catabaptist, BAPTISM
catabolic, ORGANISMS
catabolism, ORGANISMS
catachresis, WORDS
catachrestic, WORDS
catachrestical, WORDS
cataclasm, DECADENCE
cataclasmic, DECADENCE
catacoustics, ECHOES
catalepsis, DISEASE AND ILLNESS
catalepsy, DISEASE AND ILLNESS
cataleptic, DISEASE AND ILLNESS
cataphonics, ECHOES
catastrophism, GEOLOGY

catastrophist, GEOLOGY
catechesis, QUESTIONING
catechetic, QUESTIONING
catechetical, QUESTIONING
catechetics, QUESTIONING
catechism, CHRISTIANITY
catechist, CHRISTIANITY, QUESTIONING
catechumen, CATHOLICISM
catechumenal, CATHOLICISM
catechumenate, CATHOLICISM
catechumenical, CATHOLICISM
catechumenism, CATHOLICISM
Cathar, HERESY
Cathari, HERESY
Catharism, HERESY
Catharist, HERESY
Catharistic, HERESY
cathisophobia, PHOBIAS
Catholic, CHRISTIANITY
Catholicism, CHRISTIANITY
catopromancy, FUTURE
catoptromancy, FUTURE
catoptrophobia, PHOBIAS
causticism, LANGUAGE STYLES
causticity, LANGUAGE STYLES
causticness, LANGUAGE STYLES
cavear, LAW
caveatee, LAW
caveator, LAW
cecidiology, PLANTS
cecidology, PLANTS
cecity, BLINDNESS
ceilometer, CLOUDS
celestial, ASTRONOMY
celidographer, PLANETS
celidography, PLANETS, SUN
celo-navigation, ASTRONOMY
Celticism, LANGUAGE
Celtophobia, PHOBIAS
cenobite, MONKS
cenobitic, MONKS
cenobitism, MONKS
cenophobia, SPACES
cento, LITERATURE
centonical, LITERATURE
centonism, LITERATURE
centonization, LITERATURE
centralism, GOVERNMENT
centralist, GOVERNMENT
centralistic, GOVERNMENT
cephalalgia, PAIN
cephalgia , PAIN

cephalodynia, PAIN
cephalomancy, HEAD
cephalometer, HEAD
cephalometric, HEAD
cephalometry, HEAD
ceramicist, POTTERY
ceramics, POTTERY
ceramist, POTTERY
ceramography, POTTERY
ceraunography, LIGHTNING
ceraunomancy, THUNDER
ceraunophobia, LIGHTNING
ceraunoscopia, LIGHTNING
cerebrology, BRAIN
ceremonialism, ATTITUDES
ceremonialist, ATTITUDES
cerographic, WAX
cerographical, WAX
cerographist, WAX
cerography, WAX
ceromancy, WAX
ceroplastic, WAX
ceroplastics, WAX
chalcography, DRAWING
chalcologue, BRASSES
chalcomancy, BRASSES
chalcotript, BRASSES
Chaldaic, LANGUAGE
Chaldaism, LANGUAGE
change ringing, BELLS
characterologic, PERSONALITY
characterological, PERSONALITY
characterologist, PERSONALITY
characterology, PERSONALITY
charisticary, EASTERN ORTHODOXY
Chartism, POLITICS
Chartist, POLITICS
chartography, MAPS
chartology, MAPS
Chasidism, JUDAISM
chauvinism, NATIONALISM
chauvinist, NATIONALISM
chauvinistic, NATIONALISM
cheirognomy, HANDS
cheirograph, POPE
cheirography, WRITING
cheirology, HANDS
cheiromancy, FUTURE, HANDS
cheironomy, GESTURE
chekist, JOBS
chemocracy, SOCIETY
chemocrat, SOCIETY

chemotherapeutic, REMEDIES
chemotherapist, REMEDIES
chemotherapy, REMEDIES
cherophobia, HAPPINESS
chiarooscuro, DRAWING
chiaroscurist, DRAWING
chiaroscuro, DRAWING
chiasmus, LANGUAGE STYLES
chiastic, LANGUAGE STYLES
chiliasm, CHRIST
chiliast, CHRIST
chiliastic, CHRIST
chionablepsia, BLINDNESS
chiragra, HANDS
chirapsia, HANDS
chirocosmetic, HANDS
chirocosmetics, HANDS
chirognomist, HANDS
chirognomy, HANDS
chirograph, POPE, WRITING
chirographer, WRITING
chirographic, WRITING
chirographical, WRITING
chirography, WRITING
chirology, HANDS
chiromancy, FUTURE, HANDS
chironomic, GESTURE
chironomy, GESTURE
chiroplasty, HANDS
chiropodial, FEET
chiropodist, FEET
chiropody, FEET
chiropractic, REMEDIES
chiropractor, REMEDIES
chirothesia, HANDS
chirotony, HANDS
cholerophobia, PHOBIAS
chondrology, BODIES
choralism, MUSIC
choralistic, MUSIC
choregraphy, DANCING
choreographer, DANCING
choreographic, DANCING
choreography, DANCING
chorizontist, CRITICISM
chorographer, MAPS
chorographic, MAPS
chorography, MAPS
chorologic, BIOLOGY
chorological, BIOLOGY
chorology, BIOLOGY
choromania, DISEASE AND ILLNESS

chrematheism, GOD AND GODS
chrematist, ATTITUDES
chrematistic, ATTITUDES, MONEY
chrematistics, MONEY
chrematophobia, PHOBIAS
chrestomathic, COLLECTIONS AND COLLECTING, KNOWLEDGE
chrestomathics, KNOWLEDGE
chrestomathy, COLLECTIONS AND COLLECTING
chrism, CATHOLICISM
chrismation, EASTERN ORTHODOXY
Christadelphian, PROTESTANTISM
Christadelphianism, PROTESTANTISM
Christological, CHRIST
Christology, CHRIST
Christophany, CHRIST
chromaticism, MUSIC
chromatics, COLOR
chromatophobia, BACTERIA
chromatophobic, BACTERIA
chromesthesia, PERCEPTION
chromophobia, COLOR
chronologer, TIME
chronological, TIME
chronologist, TIME
chronology, TIME
chronomancy, FUTURE
chronometric, TIME
chronometrical, TIME
chronometry, TIME
chronophobia, PHOBIAS
chrysographer, WRITING
chrysography, WRITING
cibophobia, FOOD AND NUTRITION
cigrinophily, COLLECTIONS AND COLLECTING
cinchonology, DRUGS
cinematic, PHOTOGRAPHY
cinematics, FILMS, PHOTOGRAPHY
cinematographer, FILMS
cinematographic, FILMS
cinematographist, FILMS
cinematography, FILMS
circularism, ARGUMENT
circularity, ARGUMENT
cirplanology, PROTESTANTISM
Cistercian, MONKS
Cistercianism, MONKS
citharist, MUSIC
civism, NATIONALISM
classicalism, LITERATURE
classicalize, LITERATURE
classicism, ARCHITECTURE, ART

classicist, ART
classicistic, ART
claustrophile, -PHILIA
claustrophilia, -PHILIA
claustrophilic, -PHILIA
claustrophobia, SPACES
cledonism, WORDS
cleisiophobia, SPACES
cleptomania, STEALING
cleptophobia, STEALING
clericalism, CATHOLICISM
clericalist, CATHOLICISM
climatologic, WEATHER
climatological, WEATHER
climatologist, WEATHER
climatology, WEATHER
cloacal, LITERATURE
codicology, MANUSCRIPTS
coemption, TRADE
coemptive, TRADE
coenobitism, MONKS
cogitation, THINKING
cogitative, THINKING
cogitator, THINKING
coitophobia, SEX
Colbertism, ECONOMICS
coleopterist, ENTOMOLOGY, INSECTS
coleopterological, INSECTS
coleopterology, ENTOMOLOGY
collaborationism, TREASON
collaborationist, TREASON
collectivism, POLITICS
collectivist, POLITICS
collectivistic, POLITICS
colloquial, LANGUAGE
colloquialism, LANGUAGE
colonialism, GOVERNMENT
colonialist, GOVERNMENT
colonialistic, GOVERNMENT
color hearing, PERCEPTION
colportage, BIBLE
colporteur, BIBLE
cometophobia, PHOBIAS
commensal, FOOD AND NUTRITION
commensalism, FOOD AND NUTRITION
commensality, FOOD AND NUTRITION
commercialism, ECONOMICS
commercialist, ECONOMICS
commercialistic, ECONOMICS
commonsense realism, PHILOSOPHY
communalism, POLITICS
communalist, POLITICS

communalistic, POLITICS
communism, COMMUNISM
communist, COMMUNISM
communistic, COMMUNISM
compaternity, PARENTS
compendium, COLLECTIONS AND COLLECTING
compilation, COLLECTIONS AND COLLECTING
compurgation, LAW
compurgator, LAW
compurgatory, LAW
conceptualism, IDEAS
conceptualist, IDEAS
conceptualistic, IDEAS
concettism, LANGUAGE STYLES
conchologist, COLLECTIONS AND COLLECTING
conchologize, COLLECTIONS AND COLLECTING
conchology, COLLECTIONS AND COLLECTING
concursus, THEOLOGY
conditional baptism, BAPTISM
condominate, GOVERNMENT
condominium, GOVERNMENT
confessionalian, THEOLOGY
confessionalism, THEOLOGY
Congregationalism, PROTESTANTISM
Congregationalist, PROTESTANTISM
congruence, AGREEMENT
congruent, AGREEMENT
congruity, AGREEMENT
coniology, AIR
consciencism, ATTITUDES
conservational, NATURE
conservationist, NATURE
conservatism, POLITICS
conservative, POLITICS
consociational, PROTESTANTISM
consociationism, PROTESTANTISM
constitutional monarchy, GOVERNMENT
constitutionalism, POLITICS
constitutionalist, POLITICS
consubstantiation, THEOLOGY
contemplation, MEDITATION
contemplative, MEDITATION
continentalism, POLITICS
continentalist, POLITICS
continuity, FILMS
contortionist, ATHLETICS
contortionistic, ATHLETICS
contrapuntalist, MUSIC
contrapuntist, MUSIC
contumacious, LAW
contumacy, LAW
conurbation, CITIES

conventionalism, ATTITUDES
conventionalist, ATTITUDES
Copernicanism, ASTRONOMY
Copernican system, the, ASTRONOMY
copoclephile, COLLECTIONS AND COLLECTING
copoclephily, COLLECTIONS AND COLLECTING
copperhead, WAR
copperheadism, WAR
coprology, OBSCENITY
coprophilia, OBSCENITY, SEX
coprophobia, PHOBIAS
coronagraphic, SUN
coronagraphy, SUN
corrigenda, COLLECTIONS AND COLLECTING
corrigendum, COLLECTIONS AND COLLECTING
corybantiasm, MENTAL STATES
corybantism, MENTAL STATES
cosmetological, BEAUTY
cosmetologist, BEAUTY
cosmetology, BEAUTY
cosmism, COSMOLOGY
cosmist, COSMOLOGY
cosmocracy, GOVERNMENT
cosmogonic, COSMOLOGY
cosmogonist, COSMOLOGY
cosmogony, COSMOLOGY
cosmographer, COSMOLOGY
cosmographic, COSMOLOGY
cosmographical, COSMOLOGY
cosmography, COSMOLOGY
cosmologic, COSMOLOGY
cosmological, COSMOLOGY
cosmologist, COSMOLOGY
cosmology, COSMOLOGY
cosmopolitan, ATTITUDES
cosmopolitanism, ATTITUDES, COMMUNISM
cosmotheism, COSMOLOGY
cosmotheist, COSMOLOGY
cosmozoism, COSMOLOGY
Couéism, PSYCHOLOGY
counteridea, IDEAS
courier, GUIDE
craniological, HEAD
craniologist, HEAD
craniology, HEAD
craniometric, HEAD
craniometrical, HEAD
craniometrist, HEAD
craniometry, HEAD
cranioscopical, HEAD
cranioscopist, HEAD
cranioscopy, HEAD

creationism, COSMOLOGY, SOUL
creationist, COSMOLOGY, SOUL
creationistic, SOUL
credenda, COLLECTIONS AND COLLECTING
cremnophobia, HEIGHTS
creophagism, FLESH
creophagous, FLESH
creophagy, FLESH
crescograph, PLANTS
crescographic, PLANTS
cretinism, IDIOCY
cretinoid, IDIOCY
cretinous, IDIOCY
criminal, LAW
criminalism, LAW
criminality, LAW
criminologic, CRIME
criminological, CRIME
criminologist, CRIME
criminology, CRIME
critic, LITERARY STUDY
criticism, LITERARY STUDY
crotism, HEART
crustalogy, GEOLOGY
crymotherapy, REMEDIES
cryogenic, COLD
cryogenics, COLD
cryology, COLD
cryophile, COLD
cryophilia, COLD
cryophilic, COLD
cryotherapy, REMEDIES
cryptaesthesia, PSYCHOLOGY
cryptanalysis, CODE
cryptanalyst, CODE
cryptanalytic, CODE
cryptesthesia, PSYCHOLOGY
cryptesthetic, PSYCHOLOGY
cryptoclimate, CLIMATE
cryptogram, CODE
cryptogrammic, CODE
cryptograph, CODE
cryptographal, LANGUAGE
cryptographer, CODE, LANGUAGE
cryptographic, CODE, LANGUAGE
cryptographical, LANGUAGE
cryptographist, CODE, LANGUAGE
cryptography, CODE, LANGUAGE
cryptologist, LANGUAGE
cryptology, CODE, LANGUAGE
cryptomnesia, MEMORY
cryptomnesic, MEMORY

crystallographer, PHYSICS
crystallographic, PHYSICS
crystallographical, PHYSICS
crystallography, PHYSICS
crystallophobia, PHOBIAS
ctetology, BIOLOGY
cubebism, DRUGS
Cubism, ART
Cubist, ART
Cubistic, ART
culpability, LAW
culpable, LAW
culteranismo, LANGUAGE STYLES
cultismo, LANGUAGE STYLES
cultural anthropology, ANTHROPOLOGY
culturology, ANTHROPOLOGY
cumaphytic, PLANTS
cumaphytism, PLANTS
cumyxaphily, COLLECTIONS AND COLLECTING
cunctation, TIME
cunctatious, TIME
cunctator, TIME
cunctatory, TIME
Curialism, CATHOLICISM
curiologic, WRITING
curiological, WRITING
curiologics, WRITING
curiology, WRITING
curiosa, COLLECTIONS AND COLLECTING
cybernetic, AUTOMATION
cyberneticist, AUTOMATION
cybernetics, AUTOMATION, BRAIN
cyclic, HISTORY
cyclicism, HISTORY
cyclicity, HISTORY
cyclothyme, MOODS
cyclothymia, MOODS
cyclothymic, MOODS
cyesiology, PREGNANCY
cyesis, PREGNANCY
cymography, MEASUREMENT
cynanthropy, DOGS
cynegetic, HUNTING
cynegetics, HUNTING
cynic, ATTITUDES
Cynic, PHILOSOPHY
cynical, ATTITUDES
Cynical, PHILOSOPHY
cynicism, ATTITUDES
Cynicism, PHILOSOPHY
cynism, ATTITUDES
cynologist, DOGS

cynology, DOGS
cynophobia, DOGS, PHOBIAS
cypridophobia, DISEASE AND ILLNESS, SEX
Cyrillian, HERESY
Cyrillianism, HERESY
cytogenetic, LIFE
cytogenetical, LIFE
cytogenetics, LIFE
cytogeneticist, LIFE
cytologic, CELLS
cytological, CELLS
cytologist, BIOLOGY, CELLS
cytology, BIOLOGY, CELLS
cytopathologic, LIFE
cytopathological, LIFE
cytopathology, LIFE
czarism, POLITICS
czarist, POLITICS

D

dactyliology, DEAFNESS
dactyliomancy, FINGERS
dactylitis, FINGERS
dactylogram, FINGERS
dactylographer, FINGERS
dactylographic, FINGERS
dactylography, FINGERS
dactylology, DEAFNESS
dactylonomy, FINGERS
dactyloscopic, FINGERS
dactyloscopist, FINGERS
dactyloscopy, FINGERS
Dadaism, ART
Dadaist, ART
Daltonism, COLOR
Dantesque, DANTE
Dantophily, DANTE
Darbyism, PROTESTANTISM
Darbyite, PROTESTANTISM
Darwinian, EVOLUTION
Darwinism, EVOLUTION
decadarchy, GOVERNMENT
decarchy, GOVERNMENT
decretalist, CATHOLICISM
decretist, CATHOLICISM
dedentition, TEETH
defeatism, ATTITUDES
defeatist, ATTITUDES
defoliant, LEAVES
defoliate, LEAVES

defoliation, LEAVES
deicidal, GOD AND GODS
deicide, GOD AND GODS
deipnophobia, PHOBIAS
deipnosophist, DINING
deism, GOD AND GODS
deist, GOD AND GODS
deistic, GOD AND GODS
deja vu, MEMORY
dekarchy, GOVERNMENT
delitescence, DISEASE AND ILLNESS
delitescent, DISEASE AND ILLNESS
deltiology, COLLECTIONS AND COLLECTING
demagogism, POLITICS
demagoguery, POLITICS
demagoguism, POLITICS
demagogy, POLITICS
demiurge, GOD AND GODS
demiurgic, GOD AND GODS
demiurgism, GOD AND GODS
democracy, GOVERNMENT
democrat, GOVERNMENT
democratic, GOVERNMENT
demographer, MAN
demographic, MAN
demography, MAN
demological, MAN
demology, MAN
demoniac, DEMONS
demoniacism, DEMONS
demonian, DEMONS, INSANITY
demonianism, DEMONS, INSANITY
demonolatry, DEMONS
demonologic, DEMONS
demonological, DEMONS
demonologist, DEMONS
demonology, DEMONS
demonomancy, DEMONS
demonomania, INSANITY
demonopathy, INSANITY
demonophobia, DEMONS, PHOBIAS
demophil, CROWDS
demophile, CROWDS
demophilia, CROWDS
demophobia, CROWDS, MAN
demotic, LANGUAGE
demotist, LANGUAGE
dendrochronological, TIME
dendrochronologist, TIME
dendrochronology, TIME
dendrologic, TREES
dendrological, TREES

dendrologist, TREES
dendrology, TREES
dendrophilia, PLANTS
dendrophilous, PLANTS
denigration, BLACKENING
denigrator, BLACKENING
denominationalism, PROTESTANTISM
denominationalist, PROTESTANTISM
dentition, TEETH
deontological, ETHICS
deontologist, ETHICS
deontology, ETHICS
deoppilation, IMPROVEMENT
depauperate, POVERTY
depauperation, POVERTY
depauperization, POVERTY
dereism, MENTAL STATES
dereistic, MENTAL STATES
derism, WORDS
deristic, WORDS
derivation, ORIGINS
derivative, ORIGINS
dermatoglyphic, SKIN
dermatoglyphics, SKIN
dermatographia, SKIN
dermatographic, SKIN
dermatographism, SKIN
dermatography, SKIN
dermatological, SKIN
dermatologist, SKIN
dermatology, SKIN
dermatopathophobia, SKIN
dermatophobia, SKIN
dermatosiophobia, SKIN
dermographia, SKIN
dermographism, SKIN
derogation, VALUES
derogatory, VALUES
descendental, PHILOSOPHY
descendentalism, PHILOSOPHY
descendentalist, PHILOSOPHY
descendentalistic, PHILOSOPHY
descriptive linguistics, LINGUISTICS
despot, GOVERNMENT
despotic, GOVERNMENT
despotism, GOVERNMENT
deteriorism, DECADENCE
determinism, PHILOSOPHY
determinist, PHILOSOPHY
deterministic, PHILOSOPHY
deuterogamy, MARRIAGE
deviationalism, COMMUNISM

deviationism, COMMUNISM
deviationist, COMMUNISM
devotionalism, RELIGION
devotionalist, RELIGION
diabetophobia, PHOBIAS
diabolepsy, INSANITY
diabolism, DEVIL
diabolist, DEVIL
diabolology, DEVIL
diachronic, LINGUISTICS
diachronism, LINGUISTICS
diachrony, LINGUISTICS
diacoustics, SOUNDS
dialectician, LINGUISTICS
dialecticism, LANGUAGE
dialectologist, LINGUISTICS
dialectology, LINGUISTICS
dianoetic, MIND
dianoia, MIND
diarch, GOVERNMENT
diarchy, GOVERNMENT
diastrophe, EARTH
diastrophic, EARTH
diastrophism, EARTH
diathermia, REMEDIES
diathermic, REMEDIES
diathermy, REMEDIES
diatonicism, MUSIC
diatonism, MUSIC
dictatorial, GOVERNMENT
dictatorship, GOVERNMENT
didachist, CHRISTIANITY
didact, ATTITUDES, LEARNING
didactic, ATTITUDES, LEARNING
didacticism, ATTITUDES, LEARNING
didactics, LEARNING
didascalic, ATTITUDES
digamism, MARRIAGE
digamist, MARRIAGE
digamous, MARRIAGE
digamy, MARRIAGE
dilettante, BEHAVIOR
dilettantism, BEHAVIOR
dilutee, WORK
dinophobia, PHOBIAS
diplomatics, MANUSCRIPTS
diplomatic text, MANUSCRIPTS
diplopiaphobia, PHOBIAS
dipsomania, ALCOHOL
dipsomaniac, ALCOHOL
dipsomaniacal, ALCOHOL
dipsophobe, ALCOHOL

dipsophobia, ALCOHOL
Diptera, INSECTS
dipterology, INSECTS
disc jockey, PHONOGRAPH RECORDS
discographer, PHONOGRAPH RECORDS
discographical, PHONOGRAPH RECORDS
discography, PHONOGRAPH RECORDS
discophile, PHONOGRAPH RECORDS
discophily, COLLECTIONS AND COLLECTING,
    PHONOGRAPH RECORDS
disk jockey, PHONOGRAPH RECORDS
diskographer, PHONOGRAPH RECORDS
diskography, PHONOGRAPH RECORDS
diskophile, PHONOGRAPH RECORDS
diskophily, PHONOGRAPH RECORDS
dispauperization, POVERTY
dispauperize, POVERTY
dittology, BIBLE
diurnal, TIME
Docetic, CHRIST
Docetism, CHRIST
doctrinaire, ARGUMENT
doctrinairism, ARGUMENT
doctrinarianism, ARGUMENT
dodecaphonic, MUSIC
dodecaphonism, MUSIC
dodecaphonist, MUSIC
dodecaphony, MUSIC
dodecatonality, MUSIC
dogmatic, ARGUMENT
dogmatism, ARGUMENT
dogmatist, ARGUMENT
dolor, PAIN
dolorous, PAIN
dolour, PAIN
domatophobia, HOUSES
Donatism, HERESY
Donatist, HERESY
Donatistic, HERESY
Doppelgänger, GHOSTS
doraphobe, ANIMALS
doraphobia, ANIMALS
doubleganger, GHOSTS
doulocracy, GOVERNMENT
doveism, WAR
dovism, WAR
Down's syndrome, IDIOCY
dowsing, WATER
doxographer, COLLECTIONS AND COLLECTING,
    PHILOSOPHY
doxographic, COLLECTIONS AND COLLECTING
doxographical, PHILOSOPHY

doxography, COLLECTIONS AND COLLECTING,
    PHILOSOPHY
doxological, MUSIC
doxology, MUSIC
Draconian, LAW
Draconianism, LAW
dragoman, JOBS
dramaticism, BEHAVIOR
dromophobia, PHOBIAS
Druid, RELIGION
Druidic, RELIGION
Druidical, RELIGION
Druidism, RELIGION
dualism, PHILOSOPHY, RELIGION
dualist, PHILOSOPHY, RELIGION
dualistic, PHILOSOPHY, RELIGION
dulocracy, GOVERNMENT
duopolist, TRADE
duopolistic, TRADE
duopoly, TRADE
duopsonist, TRADE
duopsonistic, TRADE
duopsony, TRADE
dwarfism, SIZE
dyarchy, GOVERNMENT
dynamism, PHILOSOPHY
dynamist, PHILOSOPHY
dynamistic, PHILOSOPHY
dynast, GOVERNMENT
dynasticism, GOVERNMENT
dynasty, GOVERNMENT
Dyophysite, CHRIST
Dyophysitic, CHRIST
Dyophysitism, CHRIST
Dyothelete, CHRIST
Dyotheletism, CHRIST
Dyothelite, CHRIST
Dyothelitism, CHRIST
Dyothetism, CHRIST
dyscrasia, HEALTH
dyscrasic, HEALTH
dyscratic, HEALTH
dysgenics, RACE
dyslalia, SPEECH
dyslexia, READING
dyslexic, READING
dyslogia, SPEECH
dyslogistic, PRAISE
dyslogy, SPEECH
dysmorphophobia, PHOBIAS
dyspepsia, DISEASE AND ILLNESS, HEALTH
dyspepsy, HEALTH

dyspeptic, DISEASE AND ILLNESS, HEALTH
dyspeptical, DISEASE AND ILLNESS
dysphemia, SPEECH
dysphemism, WORDS
dysteleological, PHILOSOPHY
dysteleologist, PHILOSOPHY
dysteleology, PHILOSOPHY
dysthymia, MOODS
dysthymic, MOODS

E

Early Federal Style, ARCHITECTURE
Early Republican, ARCHITECTURE
Eastern Orthodox, CHRISTIANITY
Eastern Orthodoxy, CHRISTIANITY
Ebionism, HERESY, PHILOSOPHY
Ebionite, HERESY
Ebionitic, HERESY
Ebionitism, HERESY
ebriety, ALCOHOL
ecclesiarch, CATHOLICISM, CHURCH
ecclesiarchy, CATHOLICISM
ecclesioclasticism, CHURCH
ecclesiolatry, CHURCH
ecclesiologic, CHURCH
ecclesiological, CHURCH
ecclesiologist, CHURCH
ecclesiology, CHURCH
ecclesiophobia, CHURCH
eccrinology, ANATOMY
echoic, LINGUISTICS
echoism, LINGUISTICS
echolalia, SPEECH
echolalic, SPEECH
eclampsia, DISEASE AND ILLNESS
eclamptism, DISEASE AND ILLNESS
eclectic, PHILOSOPHY
eclecticism, ARCHITECTURE, ART, PHILOSOPHY
eclecticist, ART
ecologic, ENVIRONMENT
ecological, BIOLOGY, ENVIRONMENT
ecologist, BIOLOGY, ENVIRONMENT
ecology, BIOLOGY, ENVIRONMENT
ecophobia, HOUSES
ectomorphic, ANATOMY
ectomorphy, ANATOMY
ecumenicalism, PROTESTANTISM
ecumenicism, PROTESTANTISM
Ecumenicist, CHURCH
Ecumenism, CHURCH

ecumenism, PROTESTANTISM
edaphic, SOILS
edaphology, SOILS
educationalist, LEARNING
educationist, LEARNING
effigiate, IMAGES
effigiation, IMAGES
effoliation, LEAVES
egalitarian, POLITICS
egalitarianism, POLITICS
egoism, ATTITUDES
egoist, ATTITUDES
egoistic, ATTITUDES
egomania, SELF
egomaniac, SELF
egotheism, SELF
egotism, ATTITUDES
egotist, ATTITUDES
egotistical, ATTITUDES
Egyptian Revivalism, ARCHITECTURE
eidolism, GHOSTS
eidology, PSYCHOLOGY
eidolon, GHOSTS
Eight-Fold Path, The, BUDDHISM
eisoptrophobia, PHOBIAS
elastic, PHYSICAL CHARACTERISTICS
elasticity, PHYSICAL CHARACTERISTICS
Eleatic, PHILOSOPHY
Eleaticism, PHILOSOPHY
election, CHRISTIANITY
electrograph, PHOTOGRAPHY
electrographic, PHOTOGRAPHY
electrography, PHOTOGRAPHY
electrologist, HAIR
electrology, HAIR
electrotyper, PRINTING
electrotypic, PRINTING
electrotypist, PRINTING
electrotypy, PRINTING
eleutheromania, FREEDOM
Elohist, BIBLE
elurophobia, CATS
emanational, PHILOSOPHY
emanationism, PHILOSOPHY
emanationist, PHILOSOPHY
emanatism, PHILOSOPHY
embolic, CALENDAR
embolism, ARTERIES, CALENDAR
embolismic, CALENDAR
embolismical, CALENDAR
emesis, DISEASE AND ILLNESS
emetic, DISEASE AND ILLNESS

emetophobia, PHOBIAS
emotionalism, ATTITUDES
emotionalist, ATTITUDES
emotionalistic, ATTITUDES
empathic, UNDERSTANDING
empathy, UNDERSTANDING
empirical, PHILOSOPHY
empiricism, KNOWLEDGE, PHILOSOPHY
empiricist, KNOWLEDGE, PHILOSOPHY
empirism, KNOWLEDGE
empyromancy, SMOKE
encomiast, PRAISE
encomiastic, PRAISE
encyclopedism, KNOWLEDGE
encyclopedist, KNOWLEDGE
endarchy, GOVERNMENT
endogamic, MARRIAGE
endogamous, MARRIAGE
endogamy, MARRIAGE
endomorphic, ANATOMY
endomorphy, ANATOMY
energeticist, PHYSICS
energeticistic, PHYSICS
energetics, PHYSICS
enigmatographer, PUZZLES
enigmatography, PUZZLES
enigmatology, PUZZLES
enology, WINE
enophily, WINE
enophobia, WINE
entelechial, PHILOSOPHY
entelechy, PHILOSOPHY
entomologic, ENTOMOLOGY
entomological, ENTOMOLOGY, INSECTS
entomologist, ENTOMOLOGY, INSECTS
entomology, ENTOMOLOGY, INSECTS
entomophobia, PHOBIAS
enzymologist, FERMENTATION
enzymology, FERMENTATION
eonism, SEX
eosophobia, PHOBIAS
epagogic, ARGUMENT
epagogue, ARGUMENT
ephemeris, ALMANACS
epicure, PLEASURE
epicurean, FOOD AND NUTRITION
Epicurean, PHILOSOPHY
epicurean, PLEASURE
epicureanism, FOOD AND NUTRITION, PLEASURE
Epicureanism, PHILOSOPHY
Epicurism, PHILOSOPHY
epicurism, PLEASURE

epidemiologic, MEDICAL SPECIALTIES
epidemiological, MEDICAL SPECIALTIES
epidemiologist, MEDICAL SPECIALTIES
epidemiology, MEDICAL SPECIALTIES
epigrammatic, LANGUAGE STYLES
epigrammatism, LANGUAGE STYLES
epigrammatist, LANGUAGE STYLES
epigrapher, ANTIQUITY
epigraphic, ANTIQUITY
epigraphical, ANTIQUITY
epigraphist, ANTIQUITY
epigraphy, ANTIQUITY
epiphenomenal, PHILOSOPHY
epiphenomenalism, PHILOSOPHY
epiphenomenalist, PHILOSOPHY
epiphora, LANGUAGE STYLES
epiphyte, PLANTS
epiphytic, PLANTS
epiphytical, PLANTS
epiphytology, PLANTS
Episcopal, PROTESTANTISM
Episcopalian, PROTESTANTISM
Episcopalianism, PROTESTANTISM
episcopalism, PROTESTANTISM
epistemic, KNOWLEDGE
epistemological, KNOWLEDGE
epistemologist, KNOWLEDGE
epistemology, KNOWLEDGE
epistemophilia, KNOWLEDGE
epistemophiliac, KNOWLEDGE
epistolographic, LITERARY STUDY
epistolography, LITERARY STUDY
epistrophe, LANGUAGE STYLES
epizootiologic, ANIMALS
epizootiological, ANIMALS
epizootiology, ANIMALS
epizootology, ANIMALS
eponymic, NAMES
eponymism, NAMES
eponymous, NAMES
eponymy, NAMES
epopt, MYSTICISM
epoptae, MYSTICISM
epoptic, MYSTICISM
equivoke, PUN
equivoque, PUN
eremiophobia, SELF
eremite, DESERTS
eremitic, DESERTS
eremology, DESERTS
eremophobia, SELF
erethism, DISEASE AND ILLNESS

erethistic, DISEASE AND ILLNESS
erethitic, DISEASE AND ILLNESS
ergasiophobia, WORK
ergatocracy, GOVERNMENT
ergograph, WORK
ergographic, WORK
ergoism, BEHAVIOR
ergologist, WORK
ergology, WORK
ergonomic, ENVIRONMENT, MAN
ergonomics, ENVIRONMENT, MAN
ergophile, WORK
ergophobia, WORK
ergotism, ARGUMENT, POISON
ergotize, ARGUMENT
eroticism, SEX
erotism, SEX
erotophobia, SEX
errinophily, COLLECTIONS AND COLLECTING
erythrism, DISEASE AND ILLNESS
erythrismal, DISEASE AND ILLNESS
erythristic, DISEASE AND ILLNESS
erythrophobia, COLOR
eschatological, ENDS
eschatologist, ENDS
eschatology, ENDS
esoterica, COLLECTIONS AND COLLECTING,
    NOVELTY
esotericism, NOVELTY
esoterism, NOVELTY
esoterist, NOVELTY
essentialism, PHILOSOPHY
essentialist, PHILOSOPHY
essentialistic, PHILOSOPHY
esthetician, BEAUTY
estheticism, BEAUTY
esthetics, BEAUTY
ethicism, ATTITUDES
ethnobotanic, BOTANY
ethnobotanical, BOTANY
ethnobotanist, BOTANY
ethnobotany, BOTANY
ethnocentric, ANTHROPOLOGY
ethnocentrism, ANTHROPOLOGY
ethnocracy, RACE
ethnocratic, RACE
ethnogenic, ANTHROPOLOGY
ethnogenist, ANTHROPOLOGY
ethnogeny, ANTHROPOLOGY
ethnogeographer, RACE
ethnogeographic, RACE
ethnogeography, RACE

ethnographer, ANTHROPOLOGY, MAN
ethnographic, ANTHROPOLOGY, MAN
ethnographical, ANTHROPOLOGY, MAN
ethnography, ANTHROPOLOGY, MAN
ethnologic, ANTHROPOLOGY
ethnological, ANTHROPOLOGY
ethnologist, ANTHROPOLOGY
ethnology, ANTHROPOLOGY
ethnomania, NATIONALISM
ethnomaniac, NATIONALISM
ethnopsychological, RACE
ethnopsychology, RACE
ethologic, MAN
ethological, ANIMALS, MAN
ethologist, ANIMALS
ethology, ANIMALS, MAN
etiologic, DISEASE AND ILLNESS, NATURE
etiological, DISEASE AND ILLNESS, NATURE
etiologist, DISEASE AND ILLNESS
etiology, DISEASE AND ILLNESS, NATURE
Etruscologist, HISTORY
Etruscology, HISTORY
etymologic, WORDS
etymological, WORDS
etymologist, WORDS
etymology, WORDS
Euchologion, EASTERN ORTHODOXY
Euchology, EASTERN ORTHODOXY
euchology, EASTERN ORTHODOXY
Euclidean, MATHEMATICS
Euclidian, MATHEMATICS
eucrasia, HEALTH
eucrasic, HEALTH
eucratic, HEALTH
Eucratism, CHRISTIANITY
Eucratite, CHRISTIANITY
eudaemonics, ETHICS, HAPPINESS
eudaemonism, ETHICS
eudaemonist, ETHICS
eudemonia, HAPPINESS
eudemonic, HAPPINESS
eudemonical, HAPPINESS
eudemonics, HAPPINESS
eudemonism, ETHICS
eugenic, IMPROVEMENT, RACE
eugenicist, IMPROVEMENT
eugenics, IMPROVEMENT
eugenism, RACE
euhemerism, GOD AND GODS
euhemerist, GOD AND GODS
euhemeristic, GOD AND GODS
eulogist, PRAISE

eulogistic, PRAISE
eulogistical, PRAISE
eupepsia, HEALTH
eupepsy, HEALTH
eupeptic, HEALTH
euphemious, WORDS
euphemism, WORDS
euphemist, WORDS
euphemistic, WORDS
euphemistical, WORDS
euphonic, SOUNDS
euphonical, SOUNDS
euphonious, SOUNDS
euphony, SOUNDS
euphoria, HAPPINESS
euphoric, HAPPINESS
euphory, HAPPINESS
Euphuism, LANGUAGE STYLES
euphuistic, LANGUAGE STYLES
eurotophobia, PHOBIAS
eurysomatic, ANATOMY
euthanasia, KILLING
euthanasic, KILLING
Eutychian, CHRIST
Eutychianism, CHRIST
evangelical, CHRISTIANITY
evangelicalism, CHRISTIANITY
evangelism, CHRISTIANITY
evangelistic, CHRISTIANITY
examination, CORPSE
exarch, EASTERN ORTHODOXY
exarchal, EASTERN ORTHODOXY
exegete, BIBLE
exegetics, BIBLE
exhibitionism, BEHAVIOR
exhibitionist, BEHAVIOR
exhibitionistic, BEHAVIOR
existentialism, PHILOSOPHY
existentialist, PHILOSOPHY
exobiology, PLANETS
exogamic, MARRIAGE
exogamous, MARRIAGE
exogamy, MARRIAGE
exorcism, DEMONS
exorcismal, DEMONS
exorcisory, DEMONS
exorcist, DEMONS
exorcistic, DEMONS
exorcistical, DEMONS
expansionism, POLITICS
expansionistic, POLITICS
Expressionism, ART

Expressionist, ART
Expressionistic, ART
extrascripturalism, CATHOLICISM
extraversion, SELF
extraversive, SELF
extravert, SELF
extravertive, SELF
extroversion, SELF

F

Fabian, ECONOMICS
Fabianism, ECONOMICS
fabism, DISEASE AND ILLNESS
facetiae, HUMOR
facetious, HUMOR
faddish, FADS
faddishness, FADS
faddism, FADS
faddist, FADS
Falangism, FASCISM, POLITICS
Falangist, FASCISM, POLITICS
fanatic, ATTITUDES, RELIGION
fanatical, ATTITUDES
fanaticism, ATTITUDES, RELIGION
farrier, HORSES
fascism, FASCISM, GOVERNMENT
fascist, FASCISM, GOVERNMENT
fascistic, FASCISM, GOVERNMENT
fatalism, ATTITUDES, PHILOSOPHY
fatalist, ATTITUDES, PHILOSOPHY
fatalistic, ATTITUDES, PHILOSOPHY
faunology, ANIMALS
Fauve, ART
Fauvism, ART
Fauvist, ART
favism, DISEASE AND ILLNESS
febriphobia, PHOBIAS
Federalism, ARCHITECTURE
federalism, GOVERNMENT
federalist, GOVERNMENT
federalistic, GOVERNMENT
felinophile, CATS
felinophobia, CATS
femicidal, WOMEN
femicide, WOMEN
feminism, ATTITUDES
feminist, ATTITUDES
feministic, ATTITUDES
Fenian, POLITICS
Fenianism, POLITICS

fermentologist, ALCOHOL
fermentology, ALCOHOL
ferroequinologist, RAILROADS
ferroequinology, RAILROADS
fetichism, SEX
fetishism, SEX
fetishistic, SEX
feudal, GOVERNMENT
feudalism, GOVERNMENT
feudalistic, GOVERNMENT
feuilletonism, MEDIA
feuilletonist, MEDIA
fideism, FAITH
fideist, FAITH
fideistic, FAITH
fiducial, LAW
fiduciary, LAW
fiefdom, LAND
filicidal, CHILD
filicide, CHILD
filionymic, NAMES
finical, ATTITUDES
finicalism, ATTITUDES
finicality, ATTITUDES
finicalness, ATTITUDES
finicism, ATTITUDES
Flacian, PROTESTANTISM
Flacianism, PROTESTANTISM
flagellant, CHRISTIANITY
flagellantism, CHRISTIANITY
Fletcherism, FOOD AND NUTRITION
Fletcherite, FOOD AND NUTRITION
Fletcherize, FOOD AND NUTRITION
floccinaucinihilipilification, VALUES
floricultural, FLOWERS
floriculture, FLOWERS
floriculturist, FLOWERS
floriferous, FLOWERS
florilegium, COLLECTIONS AND COLLECTING
floristry, PLANTS
fluoroscopic, X-RAYS
fluoroscopy, X-RAYS
fluviologist, WATER
fluviology, WATER
fogeyism, ATTITUDES
fogyish, ATTITUDES
fogyism, ATTITUDES
forensic, ARGUMENT
forensics, ARGUMENT
formalism, CRITICISM
formalist, CRITICISM
formalistic, CRITICISM

formicarium, ANTS
formicary, ANTS
formulism, ATTITUDES
formulist, ATTITUDES
formulistic, ATTITUDES
fortuist, CHANCE
fortuitism, CHANCE
fortuitous, CHANCE
fortuitousness, CHANCE
fortuity, CHANCE
Fourierism, COMMUNALISM
Fourierist, COMMUNALISM
Fourierite, COMMUNALISM
Francophile, FRANCE
Francophobia, FRANCE
fratricidal, MURDER
fratricide, MURDER
free association, THINKING
Froebelian, LEARNING
Froebelist, LEARNING
fromology, CHEESE
fruitarian, FOOD AND NUTRITION
fruitarianism, FOOD AND NUTRITION
fuguism, MUSIC
fuguist, MUSIC
funambulism, TIGHTROPE WALKING
funambulist, TIGHTROPE WALKING
functionalism, ARCHITECTURE
fundamentalism, BIBLE, CATHOLICISM,
   PROTESTANTISM
fundamentalist, BIBLE, PROTESTANTISM
futilitarian, ATTITUDES
futilitarianism, ATTITUDES
Futurism, ART
futurism, PAST
Futurist, ART
futurist, PAST
Futuristic, ART
futuristic, PAST

G

galenic, MEDICAL SPECIALTIES
Galenism, MEDICAL SPECIALTIES
galeophilia, CATS
galeophobia, PHOBIAS
Gallican, CATHOLICISM
Gallicanism, CATHOLICISM
Gallicism, LANGUAGE
Gallomania, FRANCE
Gallophil, FRANCE

Gallophile, FRANCE
Gallophobia, FRANCE
gambist, MUSIC
gamomania, MARRIAGE
gamophobia, MARRIAGE, PHOBIAS
Gandhian, POLITICS
Gandhiism, POLITICS
Gandhiist, POLITICS
Gandhism, POLITICS
Gandhist, POLITICS
gastriloquism, SPEECH
gastronome, FOOD AND NUTRITION
gastronomic, FOOD AND NUTRITION
gastronomist, FOOD AND NUTRITION
gastronomy, FOOD AND NUTRITION
gatophobia, CATS
gazumping, HOUSES
gelastic, BEHAVIOR
geloscopy, LAUGHTER
gelotoscopy, LAUGHTER
Ge-lup-Ka, BUDDHISM
gemmological, GEMS
gemmologist, GEMS
gemmology, GEMS
gemology, GEMS
genealogic, HISTORY
genealogist, HISTORY
genealogy, HISTORY
genecologic, ENVIRONMENT
genecological, ENVIRONMENT
genecologist, ENVIRONMENT
genecology, ENVIRONMENT
geneological, HISTORY
genethlialogic, ASTROLOGY
genethlialogical, ASTROLOGY
genethlialogy, ASTROLOGY
genetic, BIOLOGY, HEREDITY
geneticist, BIOLOGY, HEREDITY
genetics, BIOLOGY, HEREDITY
genocidal, RACE
genocide, RACE
genophobia, SEX
genteelism, LITERATURE, WORDS
geocentric, COSMOLOGY
geocentricism, COSMOLOGY
geocentrism, COSMOLOGY
geochronologic, EARTH, TIME
geochronological, EARTH, TIME
geochronologist, EARTH, TIME
geochronology, EARTH, TIME
geodesist, MATHEMATICS
geodesy, MATHEMATICS

geodetic, MATHEMATICS
geodetical, MATHEMATICS
geodetics, MATHEMATICS
geognosist, GEOLOGY
geognost, GEOLOGY
geognostic, GEOLOGY
geognosy, GEOLOGY
geogonic, EARTH
geogony, EARTH
geographer, GEOGRAPHY
geographic, GEOGRAPHY
geographical, GEOGRAPHY
geography, GEOGRAPHY
geologic, EARTH
geological, EARTH
geologist, EARTH
geology, EARTH
geomalic, EARTH
geomalism, EARTH
geomancer, EARTH
geomancy, EARTH
geomorphologic, EARTH, FORM
geomorphological, EARTH, FORM
geomorphologist, EARTH, FORM
geomorphology, EARTH, FORM
geophagia, EARTH
geophagism, EARTH
geophagist, EARTH
geophagous, EARTH
geophagy, EARTH
geophysical, PHYSICS
geophysicist, PHYSICS
geophysics, PHYSICS
Georgianism, ARCHITECTURE
geotectology, GEOLOGY
geotectonic, GEOLOGY
geotectonics, GEOLOGY
geothermometry, HEAT
geotropic, GRAVITY
geotropism, GRAVITY
gephyrophobia, PHOBIAS
gerascophobia, OLD AGE
geratologic, DECADENCE, OLD AGE
geratological, OLD AGE
geratologous, DECADENCE, OLD AGE
geratology, DECADENCE, OLD AGE
gereology, DECADENCE
geriatric, OLD AGE
geriatrician, OLD AGE
geriatrics, OLD AGE
geriatrist, OLD AGE
geriatry, OLD AGE

Germanophobia, PHOBIAS
gerocomy, OLD AGE
gerodontics, OLD AGE
gerodontist, OLD AGE
geromorphism, OLD AGE
gerontological, OLD AGE
gerontologist, OLD AGE
gerontology, OLD AGE
gerontophile, SEX
gerontophilia, SEX
gerontophilic, SEX
geumophobia, PHOBIAS
Ghibellinism, POLITICS
gigantism, SIZE
gigmanism, ATTITUDES
glaciological, GEOLOGY
glaciologist, GEOLOGY
glaciology, GEOLOGY
glossographer, WORDS
glossography, WORDS
glossolalia, SPEECH
glossolalist, SPEECH
glossology, LINGUISTICS
glossophobia, SPEECH
glottochronological, LINGUISTICS
glottochronologist, LINGUISTICS
glottochronology, LINGUISTICS
glottogonic, LANGUAGE, ORIGINS
glottogonist, LANGUAGE
glottogony, ORIGINS
glottology, LINGUISTICS
glycophilia, DISEASE AND ILLNESS
glyphographer, PRINTING
glyphographic, PRINTING
glyphography, PRINTING
glyptic, GEMS
glyptographer, GEMS
glyptographic, GEMS
glyptography, GEMS
glyptology, ENGRAVING, GEMS
gnathonic, BEHAVIOR
gnathonism, BEHAVIOR
gnomonology, PROVERBS
gnoseological, KNOWLEDGE
gnoseology, KNOWLEDGE
gnosiological, KNOWLEDGE
gnosiology, KNOWLEDGE
Gnostic, HERESY, PHILOSOPHY
Gnosticism, HERESY, PHILOSOPHY
Gobinism, RACE
gombeen, MONEY
gombeenism, MONEY

gombeen-man, MONEY
Gongoresque, LANGUAGE STYLES
Gongorism, LANGUAGE STYLES
Gongoristic, LANGUAGE STYLES
gormandism, BEHAVIOR
Gothic, ARCHITECTURE
gothic, LITERATURE
Gothicism, ARCHITECTURE, ART
gothicism, LITERATURE
Gothicist, ART
gothicist, LITERATURE
Gothic Revivalism, ARCHITECTURE
gourmand, BEHAVIOR
gourmandism, BEHAVIOR
gourmetism, ATTITUDES
gradualism, PHILOSOPHY, POLITICS
gradualist, PHILOSOPHY, POLITICS
gradualistic, PHILOSOPHY, POLITICS
gramary, MAGIC
gramarye, MAGIC
grammarianism, GRAMMAR
grammaticism, GRAMMAR
grammatism, GRAMMAR
grammatist, GRAMMAR
grammatolatry, WORDS
gramophile, PHONOGRAPH RECORDS
grangerism, BOOKS
grangerize, BOOKS
graphemic, WRITING
graphemics, WRITING
graphologist, WRITING
graphology, WRITING
graphonomy, WRITING
graphopathological, WRITING
graphopathologist, WRITING
graphopathology, WRITING
graphophobia, PHOBIAS
graptomancy, WRITING
graver, ENGRAVING
gravid, PREGNANCY
gravidity, PREGNANCY
gravidness, PREGNANCY
Greek Revivalism, ARCHITECTURE
Gregorian, MUSIC
Gregorianist, MUSIC
gringophobia, PHOBIAS
Grundyism, ATTITUDES
Grundyist, ATTITUDES
Grundyite, ATTITUDES
Guelfic, POLITICS
Guelfism, POLITICS
Guelphic, POLITICS

Guelphism, POLITICS
Guesdism, POLITICS
Guesdist, POLITICS
gymnopaedia, NAKEDNESS
gymnopedia, NAKEDNESS
gymnopedic, NAKEDNESS
gymnophobia, NAKEDNESS
gymnosophical, NAKEDNESS
gymnosophist, NAKEDNESS
gymnosophy, NAKEDNESS
gynaecide, WOMEN
gynaecolatry, WOMEN
gynaecology, WOMEN
gynarchic, WOMEN
gynarchy, WOMEN
gynecide, WOMEN
gynecocracy, WOMEN
gynecolater, WOMEN
gynecolatry, WOMEN
gynecologic, WOMEN
gynecological, WOMEN
gynecologist, WOMEN
gynecology, WOMEN
gynecomastia, BODIES
gynecomastism, BODIES
gynecomasty, BODIES
gyneolatry, WOMEN
gynephobe, WOMEN
gynephobia, WOMEN
gynophobia, WOMEN
gyromancy, WALKING

H

haemaphobia, BLOOD
haematology, BLOOD
haemophilia, BLOOD, DISEASE AND ILLNESS
Haggada, JUDAISM
Haggadah, JUDAISM
haggadic, JUDAISM
haggadical, JUDAISM
Haggadist, JUDAISM
hagiarchy, GOVERNMENT
hagiocracy, GOVERNMENT
hagiographer, SAINTS
hagiographic, SAINTS
hagiographical, SAINTS
hagiography, SAINTS
hagiolater, SAINTS
hagiolatrous, SAINTS
hagiolatry, SAINTS

hagiologic, SAINTS
hagiological, SAINTS
hagiologist, SAINTS
hagiology, SAINTS
hagiophobia, PHOBIAS
Halachah, JUDAISM
Halachist, JUDAISM
Halaka, JUDAISM
Halakah, JUDAISM
Halakic, JUDAISM
Halakist, JUDAISM
halophyte, PLANTS
halophytic, PLANTS
halophytism, PLANTS
hamartia, STRENGTH AND WEAKNESS
hamartiology, SIN
hamartophobia, PHOBIAS
haphephobia, PHOBIAS
haplography, WRITING
haplologic, SPEECH
haplology, SPEECH
haptephobia, PHOBIAS
Harmonite, COMMUNALISM
haruspex, ANIMALS
haruspical, ANIMALS
haruspicy, ANIMALS
Hasidic, JUDAISM
Hasidim, JUDAISM
Hasidism, JUDAISM
hawk, WAR
hawkish, WAR
hawkism, WAR
hazard, GAMBLING
heathenism, RELIGION
heathenistic, RELIGION
hebdomadary, MONKS
Hebraic, LANGUAGE
Hebraica, COLLECTIONS AND COLLECTING
Hebraism, JUDAISM, LANGUAGE
Hebraist, JUDAISM, LANGUAGE
Hebraistic, JUDAISM, LANGUAGE
Hebraistical, JUDAISM
hecatonarchy, GOVERNMENT
Heckerism, CATHOLICISM
hectographic, COPYING
hectography, COPYING
hedonism, PLEASURE
hedonist, PLEASURE
hedonistic, PLEASURE
hedonophobia, PHOBIAS
Hegelian, PHILOSOPHY
Hegelian dialectic, PHILOSOPHY

Hegelianism, PHILOSOPHY
Hegelian triad, PHILOSOPHY
hektography, COPYING
helcology, MEDICAL SPECIALTIES
heliocentric, COSMOLOGY
heliocentricism, COSMOLOGY
heliocentricity, COSMOLOGY
heliocentrism, COSMOLOGY
heliographer, SUN
heliographic, SUN
heliographical, SUN
heliography, SUN
heliolator, SUN
heliolatry, SUN
heliologist, SUN
heliology, SUN
heliophile, PLANTS
heliophilia, PLANTS
heliophilic, PLANTS
heliophilous, PLANTS
heliophobia, PHOBIAS, SUN
heliotrope, PLANTS
heliotropic, PLANTS
heliotropism, PLANTS
Hellenism, GREECE AND GREEKS
Hellenist, GREECE AND GREEKS
helminthologic, WORMS
helminthological, WORMS
helminthologist, WORMS
helminthology, WORMS
helminthophobia, WORMS
helotage, SLAVES
helotism, SLAVES
helotry, SLAVES
hemadynamometry, BLOOD
hemaphobia, BLOOD
hematidrosis, BLOOD
hematologic, BLOOD
hematological, BLOOD
hematologist, BLOOD
hematology, BLOOD
hematopathology, BLOOD
hematophobia, BLOOD
hemautograph, BLOOD
hemautographic, BLOOD
hemautography, BLOOD
hemerobaptism, BAPTISM
hemerobaptist, BAPTISM
hemicrania, PAIN
hemipterology, INSECTS
hemopathology, BLOOD
hemophilia, BLOOD, DISEASE AND ILLNESS

hemophiliac, BLOOD, DISEASE AND ILLNESS
hemophobia, BLOOD
hemorrhaphilia, BLOOD
henotheism, GOD AND GODS
henotheist, GOD AND GODS
heortological, CALENDAR
heortology, CALENDAR
herbalism, COLLECTIONS AND COLLECTING
herbarism, BOTANY
heredofamilial, HEREDITY
heresiarch, HERESY
heresimach, HERESY
heresiography, HERESY
heresiologist, HERESY
heresiology, HERESY
heresy, HERESY
heretic, HERESY
heretical, HERESY
heretication, HERESY
hereticator, HERESY
heretocidal, HERESY
heretocide, HERESY
hermaphrodite, BODIES
hermaphroditic, BODIES
hermaphroditism, BODIES
hermeneutics, BIBLE
hermeneutist, BIBLE
hermitic, ATTITUDES
hermitical, ATTITUDES
hermitism, ATTITUDES
hermitry, ATTITUDES
hermitship, ATTITUDES
herpetologic, REPTILES
herpetological, REPTILES
herpetologist, REPTILES
herpetology, REPTILES
herpetophobia, REPTILES
Hesychasm, EASTERN ORTHODOXY
hesychast, EASTERN ORTHODOXY
hesychastic, EASTERN ORTHODOXY
hetaerism, SEX
hetaerist, SEX
hetaeristic, SEX
hetairism, SEX
hetericism, SPELLING
hetericist, SPELLING
heterographic, SPELLING
heterographical, SPELLING
heterography, SPELLING
heterologous, MEDICAL SPECIALTIES
heterology, MEDICAL SPECIALTIES
heteronym, WORDS

heteronymous, FREEDOM, WORDS
heteronymy, FREEDOM
heteroousian, CHRIST
heteroousianism, CHRIST
heterophemism, LANGUAGE STYLES
heterophemy, LANGUAGE STYLES
heterousianism, CHRIST
heuristic, ARGUMENT
Hibernian, LANGUAGE
Hibernianism, LANGUAGE
Hibernicism, LANGUAGE
hieratic, RELIGION
hieraticism, RELIGION
hierocracy, CATHOLICISM
hieroglyphologist, WRITING
hieroglyphology, WRITING
hierologic, THE SACRED
hierological, THE SACRED
hierologist, THE SACRED
hierology, THE SACRED
hieromancy, THE SACRED
hierophobia, THE SACRED
Higher Criticism, BIBLE
Hildebrandic, CATHOLICISM
Hildebrandine, CATHOLICISM
Hildebrandism, CATHOLICISM
Hinayana, BUDDHISM
Hinayanism, BUDDHISM
hippology, HORSES
hippomobile, HORSES
hippopathology, HORSES
hippophile, HORSES
hippophobia, HORSES
hirsute, HAIR
hirsutism, HAIR
histiology, ORGANISMS
histologic, ORGANISMS
histological, ANATOMY, ORGANISMS
histologist, ANATOMY, ORGANISMS
histology, ANATOMY, ORGANISMS
historical linguistics, LINGUISTICS
historicism, HISTORY
historicist, HISTORY
historiographer, HISTORY
historiographic, HISTORY
historiographical, HISTORY
historiography, HISTORY
historiology, HISTORY
historism, HISTORY
histriconism, BEHAVIOR
histrionic, BEHAVIOR
histrionicism, BEHAVIOR

histrionics, BEHAVIOR
Hitlerism, FASCISM
Hitlerite, FASCISM
hodometer, DISTANCE
holism, PHILOSOPHY
holist, PHILOSOPHY
holistic, PHILOSOPHY
holobaptism, BAPTISM
holobaptist, BAPTISM
holophrase, LANGUAGE
holophrasis, LANGUAGE
holophrasm, LANGUAGE
holophrastic, LANGUAGE
homeopath, REMEDIES
homeopathic, REMEDIES
homeopathist, REMEDIES
homeopathy, REMEDIES
homeotherapeutic, REMEDIES
homeotherapy, REMEDIES
homicidal, MURDER
homicide, MURDER
homilophobia, PHOBIAS
homoeanism, CHRIST
homoeopathy, REMEDIES
homoerotic, HOMOSEXUALITY
homoeroticism, HOMOSEXUALITY
homoerotism, HOMOSEXUALITY
homograph, SOUNDS
homoiousian, CHRIST
homoiousianism, CHRIST
homologoumena, COLLECTIONS AND COLLECTING
homologumena, COLLECTIONS AND COLLECTING
homonym, SOUNDS
homonymic, SOUNDS
homonymous, SOUNDS
homoousian, CHRIST
homoousianism, CHRIST
homophone, SOUNDS
homophonic, SOUNDS
homophonous, SOUNDS
horological, TIME
horologist, TIME
horology, TIME
hostelaphily, COLLECTIONS AND COLLECTING
Hsüan Chiao, RELIGION
Huguenot, PROTESTANTISM
Huguenotic, PROTESTANTISM
Huguenotism, PROTESTANTISM
humanism, MAN
humanist, MAN
humanistic, MAN
humanitarian, ANIMALS, PHILOSOPHY

humanitarianism, PHILOSOPHY
humoral, BEHAVIOR
humoralism, BEHAVIOR
humouralism, BEHAVIOR
Hussism, PROTESTANTISM
Hussite, PROTESTANTISM
Hussitism, PROTESTANTISM
Hutterian Brethren, COMMUNALISM
Hutterites, COMMUNALISM
hyalophobia, PHOBIAS
hybridism, ANTHROPOLOGY
hybridity, ANTHROPOLOGY
hydriotaphia, BURYING
hydrographer, WATER
hydrographic, WATER
hydrographical, WATER
hydrography, WATER
hydrologic, WATER
hydrological, WATER
hydrologist, WATER
hydrology, WATER
hydromancy, WATER
hydrophily, PLANTS
hydrophobia, PHOBIAS, RABIES, WATER
hydrophobophobia, PHOBIAS
hydrophyte, PLANTS
hydrophytic, PLANTS
hydrophytism, PLANTS
hydrotherapeutic, BATHING
hydrotherapeutical, BATHING
hydrotherapeutics, BATHING
hydrotherapist, BATHING
hydrotherapy, BATHING
hyetographic, RAIN
hyetographical, RAIN
hyetography, RAIN
hyetological, RAIN
hyetologist, RAIN
hyetology, RAIN
hygiastics, HEALTH
hygienic, HEALTH
hygienics, HEALTH
hygienist, HEALTH
hygieology, HEALTH
hygiology, HEALTH
hygrophobia, DAMPNESS, PHOBIAS
hylephobia, PHOBIAS
hylic, MAN
hylicism, MAN
hylicist, MAN
hylism, MAN
hylomorphic, PHILOSOPHY

hylomorphism, PHILOSOPHY
hylomorphist, PHILOSOPHY
hylotheism, GOD AND GODS
hylotheist, GOD AND GODS
hylozoism, MATTER
hylozoist, MATTER
hylozoistic, MATTER
hymenopterology, INSECTS
hymnodist, MUSIC
hymnody, MUSIC
hypallactic, FIGURES OF SPEECH
hypallage, FIGURES OF SPEECH
hypaspist, WAR
hypengyophobia, PHOBIAS
hyperaesthesia, DISEASE AND ILLNESS
hyperbole, FIGURES OF SPEECH
hyperbolic, FIGURES OF SPEECH
hypercritic, BEHAVIOR
hypercritical, BEHAVIOR
hypercriticism, BEHAVIOR
hyperdulia, MARY
hyperesthesia, DISEASE AND ILLNESS
hyperesthetic, DISEASE AND ILLNESS
hypermetropia, EYES
hypermetropic, EYES
hypnologic, SLEEP
hypnological, SLEEP
hypnologist, SLEEP
hypnology, SLEEP
hypnopaedia, SLEEP
hypnopedia, SLEEP
hypnophobia, SLEEP
hypnotism, PSYCHOLOGY
hypnotist, PSYCHOLOGY
hypnotistic, PSYCHOLOGY
hypochondriac, HEALTH
hypochondriacal, HEALTH
hypochondriacism, HEALTH
hypochondriasis, HEALTH
hypocorism, NAMES
hypocoristic, NAMES
hypomania, MENTAL STATES
hypopotencia, STRENGTH AND WEAKNESS
hypopotency, STRENGTH AND WEAKNESS
hypsiphobia, HEIGHTS
hypsographic, GEOGRAPHY, HEIGHTS
hypsographical, GEOGRAPHY, HEIGHTS
hypsography, GEOGRAPHY, HEIGHTS
hypsophobia, HEIGHTS
hysteron proteron, FIGURES OF SPEECH

I

iatralipsis, REMEDIES
iatraliptics, REMEDIES
iatrochemist, ALCHEMY
iatrochemistry, ALCHEMY
iatrology, MEDICAL SPECIALTIES
iatrophobia, PHOBIAS
Icarian, UTOPIA
Icarianism, UTOPIA
ichnographic, DRAWING
ichnographical, DRAWING
ichnography, DRAWING
ichnological, FOSSILS
ichnology, FOSSILS
ichthyism, FISH
ichthyismus, FISH
ichthyolatry, FISH
ichthyological, FISH
ichthyologist, FISH
ichthyology, FISH
ichthyomancy, FISH
ichthyophagist, FISH
ichthyophagous, FISH
ichthyophagy, FISH
ichthyophobia, FISH, PHOBIAS
iconoclasm, IMAGES
iconoclast, EASTERN ORTHODOXY, IMAGES
iconoclastic, EASTERN ORTHODOXY, IMAGES
iconoclasticism, EASTERN ORTHODOXY
iconography, ART
iconolater, IMAGES
iconolatry, IMAGES
iconological, ART, IMAGES
iconologist, ART, IMAGES
iconology, ART, IMAGES
iconomatic, WRITING
iconomaticism, WRITING
idealism, PHILOSOPHY
idealist, PHILOSOPHY
idealistic, PHILOSOPHY
ideographic, WRITING
ideographical, WRITING
ideography, WRITING
ideologic, POLITICS
ideological, POLITICS
ideologist, POLITICS
ideology, POLITICS
idiolect, LANGUAGE
idiotic, IDIOCY
idiotism, IDIOCY

Idoism, LANGUAGE
Idoist, LANGUAGE
Idoistic, LANGUAGE
idolatry, IMAGES
idoloclast, EASTERN ORTHODOXY
ikebana FLOWERS
illeism, LANGUAGE STYLES
illeist, LANGUAGE STYLES
Illuminati, KNOWLEDGE
Illuminism, KNOWLEDGE
Illuminist, KNOWLEDGE
illuminist, KNOWLEDGE
illusionism, PHILOSOPHY
illusionist, MAGIC, PHILOSOPHY
illusionistic, PHILOSOPHY
Imagism, VERSE
Imagist, VERSE
Imagistic, VERSE
immersionism, BAPTISM
immunologic, MEDICAL SPECIALTIES
immunological, MEDICAL SPECIALTIES
immunologist, MEDICAL SPECIALTIES
immunology, MEDICAL SPECIALTIES
impotence, STRENGTH AND WEAKNESS
impotency, STRENGTH AND WEAKNESS
impotent, STRENGTH AND WEAKNESS
impotentness, STRENGTH AND WEAKNESS
Impressionism, ART
Impressionist, ART
Impressionistic, ART
impuberty, BEHAVIOR
impubic, BEHAVIOR
incendiarism, FIRE
incendiary, FIRE
inchoate, ORIGINS
inchoation, ORIGINS
inchoative, ORIGINS
incipiency, ORIGINS
incipient, ORIGINS
incubus, DEMONS
incunabula, BOOKS
incunabular, BOOKS
incunabulist, BOOKS
incunabulum, BOOKS
individualism, ATTITUDES
individualist, ATTITUDES
individualistic, ATTITUDES
industrialism, ECONOMICS
industrialist, ECONOMICS
inebriety, ALCOHOL
infallibilism, CATHOLICISM
infralapsarian, CHRISTIANITY

infralapsarianism, CHRISTIANITY
insobriety, ALCOHOL
inspirationist, RELIGION
institutionalism, POLITICS
institutionalist, POLITICS
instrumentalism, PHILOSOPHY
instrumentalist, PHILOSOPHY
intellectualism, KNOWLEDGE
intellectualistic, KNOWLEDGE
Internationalism, ARCHITECTURE
International Style, ARCHITECTURE
interracial, RACE
interracialism, RACE
introversion, SELF
introversive, SELF
introvert, SELF
introvertive, SELF
intuitionalism, KNOWLEDGE
intuitionalist, KNOWLEDGE
intuitionism, KNOWLEDGE
intuitionist, KNOWLEDGE
invalidism, DISEASE AND ILLNESS
invultuation, EVIL
Ionicism, GREECE AND GREEKS
Ionism, GREECE AND GREEKS
iophobia, POISON
ipseity, SELF
ipsism, SELF
irascibility, BEHAVIOR
irascible, BEHAVIOR
irascibleness, BEHAVIOR
irenicism, WAR
irenicist, WAR
irrationalism, PHILOSOPHY
irrationalist, PHILOSOPHY
irrationalistic, PHILOSOPHY
irredentism, POLITICS
irredentist, POLITICS
isagogic, BIBLE
isagogics, BIBLE
isiac, GOD AND GODS
Islamism, ISLAM
Islamist, ISLAM
Islamitic, ISLAM
isographic, WRITING
isographical, WRITING
isography, WRITING
isolationism, POLITICS
isolationist, POLITICS
isometric projection, DRAWING
isopterophobia, PHOBIAS

J

Jain, RELIGION
Jainism, RELIGION
Jainist, RELIGION
Jansenism, HERESY
Jansenist, HERESY
jarovization, PLANTS
jingo, NATIONALISM
jingoism, NATIONALISM
jingoist, NATIONALISM
jingoistic, NATIONALISM
jocose, HUMOR
jocosity, HUMOR
journalism, MEDIA
journalist, MEDIA
journalistic, MEDIA
Judaeophobia, PHOBIAS
Judaica, COLLECTIONS AND COLLECTING
Judophobia, PHOBIAS
Judophobism, PHOBIAS
jujuism, MAGIC
jujuist, MAGIC
Julianism, CHRIST
Julianist, CHRIST
Junker, NATIONALISM
Junkerism, NATIONALISM
jusquaboutism, POLITICS
jusquaboutisme, POLITICS
jusquaboutist, POLITICS
justicialism, GOVERNMENT
Justinian code, LAW
Justinianist, LAW
juvenilia, LITERATURE
juvenilism, BEHAVIOR
juvenility, BEHAVIOR

K

Kaaba, ISLAM
Kaabism, ISLAM
kakistocracy, GOVERNMENT
kakorrhaphiophobia, PHOBIAS
Kantian, PHILOSOPHY
Kantianism, PHILOSOPHY
Kantist, PHILOSOPHY
karyologic, CELLS
karyological, CELLS
karyology, BIOLOGY, CELLS
katabolism, ORGANISMS

kenophobia, SPACES
kenosis, CHRIST
kenotic, CHRIST
kenoticism, CHRIST
kenoticist, CHRIST
keramics, POTTERY
keraunograph, LIGHTNING
keraunographic, LIGHTNING
keraunography, LIGHTNING
keraunophobia, LIGHTNING
keraunoscopia, LIGHTNING, THUNDER
keraunoscopy, LIGHTNING, THUNDER
kerugma, CHRISTIANITY
kerygma, CHRISTIANITY
kerygmatic, CHRISTIANITY
Keynesian, ECONOMICS
Keynesianism, ECONOMICS
kibbutz, COMMUNALISM
kibbutzim, COMMUNALISM
kinemics, GESTURE
kinesic, GESTURE
kinesics, GESTURE
kinesiologic, BODIES
kinesiological, BODIES
kinesiology, BODIES
kinestherapy, BODIES
kinesthesia, PERCEPTION
kinesthetic, PERCEPTION
kinetics, MOVEMENT
Kiplingesque, LITERATURE
Kiplingism, LITERATURE
kitharist, MUSIC
Klanism, ATTITUDES
kleptomania, STEALING
kleptomaniac, STEALING
kleptophobia, STEALING
knacker, BUILDINGS, HORSES
Kneippism, BATHING
koniology, AIR
kopophobia, FATIGUE
Koreshan, PROTESTANTISM
Koreshanity, PROTESTANTISM
Krishnaism, HINDUISM
kritarchy, GOVERNMENT
ktenology, DEATH
Ku Kluxery, ATTITUDES
Ku Kluxism, ATTITUDES
kvutzah, COMMUNALISM
kymograph, MEASUREMENT
kymographic, MEASUREMENT
kymography, MEASUREMENT
kynophobia, PHOBIAS

L

labdacism, PRONUNCIATION
labeorphile, BEER
labeorphily, BEER
laclabphily, CHEESE
laconic, BREVITY, LANGUAGE STYLES
laconical, BREVITY
laconicism, BREVITY, LANGUAGE STYLES
laconism, BREVITY, LANGUAGE STYLES
ladron, STEALING
ladrone, STEALING
ladronism, STEALING
laicism, CATHOLICISM
laity, CATHOLICISM
laliophobia, PHOBIAS
lallation, PRONUNCIATION
lalopathic, SPEECH
lalopathology, SPEECH
lalopathy, SPEECH
lalophobia, PHOBIAS, SPEECH
Lamaism, BUDDHISM
Lamaist, BUDDHISM
Lamaistic, BUDDHISM
Lamarckian, EVOLUTION
Lamarckism, EVOLUTION
lambdacism, PRONUNCIATION
laparotomaphilia, -PHILIA
lapidarian, GEMS
lapidarist, GEMS
lapidary, GEMS
lapidist, GEMS
Latinism, LANGUAGE
Latinize, LANGUAGE
latrocination, LAW
latrocinium, LAW
Laudian, PROTESTANTISM
Laudianism, PROTESTANTISM
lecanomancy, WATER
lecanoscopy, WATER
leccator, SEX
legalism, LAW, RELIGION
legalist, RELIGION
legalistic, LAW, RELIGION
legenda, COLLECTIONS AND COLLECTING
legendary, COLLECTIONS AND COLLECTING
legitimism, GOVERNMENT
legitimist, GOVERNMENT
Leibnitzian, PHILOSOPHY
Leibnitzianism, PHILOSOPHY
Leibnizian, PHILOSOPHY

Leibnizianism, PHILOSOPHY
Leninism, COMMUNISM
Leninist, COMMUNISM
Leninite, COMMUNISM
leonist, VERSE
Lepidoptera, BUTTERFLIES
lepidopteral, BUTTERFLIES
lepidopterist, BUTTERFLIES
lepidopterology, BUTTERFLIES
lepidopterous, BUTTERFLIES
lepraphobia, PHOBIAS
leprologist, SKIN
leprology, SKIN
leptosomatic, ANATOMY
leptosomic, ANATOMY
lesbian, HOMOSEXUALITY
lesbianism, HOMOSEXUALITY
lettrism, VERSE
leucippotomy, HORSES
levophobia, PHOBIAS
lexicographer, LANGUAGE, WORDS
lexicographic, LANGUAGE, WORDS
lexicographical, LANGUAGE, WORDS
lexicography, LANGUAGE, WORDS
lexicologic, WORDS
lexicological, WORDS
lexicologist, WORDS
lexicology, WORDS
lexiphanic, LANGUAGE STYLES
lexiphanicism, LANGUAGE STYLES
liberalism, POLITICS, PROTESTANTISM
liberalist, POLITICS, PROTESTANTISM
liberalistic, POLITICS, PROTESTANTISM
libertarian, FREEDOM
libertarianism, FREEDOM, PHILOSOPHY
liberticidal, FREEDOM
liberticide, FREEDOM
libertine, BEHAVIOR
libertinism, BEHAVIOR
lichenologic, PLANTS
lichenological, PLANTS
lichenologist, PLANTS
lichenology, PLANTS
limnologic, WATER
limnological, WATER
limnologist, GEOLOGY, WATER
limnology, GEOLOGY, WATER
linguist, LANGUAGE
linguistician, LANGUAGE
Linnaean, BOTANY
Linnean, BOTANY
Linneanism, BOTANY

lionism, BEHAVIOR, DISEASE AND ILLNESS
lionize, BEHAVIOR
lipsanographer, ANTIQUITY
lipsanography, ANTIQUITY
literalism, ALPHABET, BIBLE
literalist, ALPHABET
lithiasis, DISEASE AND ILLNESS
lithographer, PRINTING
lithographic, PRINTING
lithography, PRINTING
lithoidolater, ROCKS
lithoidolatrous, ROCKS
lithoidolatry, ROCKS
lithoidology, ROCKS
lithologic, GEOLOGY
lithological, GEOLOGY
lithology, GEOLOGY
lithomancy, ROCKS
lithophane, LIGHT
lithophanic, LIGHT
lithophany, LIGHT
litigiomania, LAW
litigious, BEHAVIOR, LAW
litigiousness, BEHAVIOR, LAW
litotes, FIGURES OF SPEECH
localism, LANGUAGE
localist, LANGUAGE
localistic, LANGUAGE
Locofoco, POLITICS
Locofocoism, POLITICS
logical positivism, PHILOSOPHY
logistician, WAR
logistics, WAR
logodaedalus, WORDS
logodaedaly, WORDS
logographer, WRITING
logographic, WRITING
logography, WRITING
logogriph, PUZZLES
logogriphic, PUZZLES
logologist, PUZZLES
logology, PUZZLES
logomach, WORDS
logomachic, WORDS
logomachical, WORDS
logomachist, WORDS
logomachy, WORDS
logomancy, WORDS
logopaedia, SPEECH
logopaedics, SPEECH
logopedia, SPEECH
logopedic, SPEECH

logopedics, SPEECH
logorrhea, LANGUAGE STYLES
logorrheic, LANGUAGE STYLES
Lollard, PROTESTANTISM
Lollardism, PROTESTANTISM
Lollardry, PROTESTANTISM
Lollardy, PROTESTANTISM
longuanimity, PAIN
longuanimous, PAIN
Lower Criticism, BIBLE
Loyalism, POLITICS
Loyalist, POLITICS
lucid, LANGUAGE STYLES
lucidity, LANGUAGE STYLES
lucidness, LANGUAGE STYLES
lucubrate, LIGHT
lucubration, LIGHT
lucubrator, LIGHT
Luddism, LABOR
Luddite, LABOR
Ludditism, LABOR
luetic, DISEASE AND ILLNESS
luetism, DISEASE AND ILLNESS
luminarism, ART
luminarist, ART
luminism, ART
luminist, ART
lunambulism, SLEEP
lunambulist, SLEEP
lunambulistic, SLEEP
Lutheran, PROTESTANTISM
Lutheranism, PROTESTANTISM
lycanthrope, WOLF
lycanthropic, WOLF
lycanthropy, WOLF
lyrical, VERSE
lyricism, VERSE
lyricist, VERSE
Lysenkoism, BIOLOGY
lyssophobia, INSANITY, RABIES

M

macarism, HAPPINESS
macarize, HAPPINESS
macaroni, BEHAVIOR
macaronic, LANGUAGE STYLES
macaronism, BEHAVIOR
maccaroni, BEHAVIOR
Machiavellian, POLITICS
Machiavellianism, POLITICS

Machiavellism, POLITICS
macrobiosis, LIFE
macrobiotics, LIFE
macrobiotist, LIFE
macrocephalic, HEAD
macrocephaly, HEAD
macrology, LANGUAGE STYLES
maculate, DIRT
maculation, DIRT
Magianism, ASTROLOGY
magirics, FOOD AND NUTRITION
magirist, FOOD AND NUTRITION
Mahayana, BUDDHISM
Mahayanism, BUDDHISM
maieusiophobia, BIRTH
maieutic, KNOWLEDGE
maieutics, KNOWLEDGE
maihem, LAW
Malanism, POLITICS
malapropism, WORDS
malapropoism, WORDS
malism, ATTITUDES, EVIL
malleability, PHYSICAL CHARACTERISTICS
malleable, PHYSICAL CHARACTERISTICS
Malthusian, ECONOMICS
Malthusianism, ECONOMICS
Mammonism, GOD AND GODS
mammonism, MONEY
Mammonist, GOD AND GODS
Mammonite, GOD AND GODS
manaism, RELIGION
manaistic, RELIGION
mancinism, HANDS
mangonism, PLANTS
mania, FADS, MENTAL STATES
maniac, MENTAL STATES
maniacal, MENTAL STATES
maniaphobia, INSANITY
Manichaeism, HERESY
Manichean, HERESY
Manicheanism, HERESY, PHILOSOPHY
Manicheism, HERESY
Manicheistic, HERESY
mannerism, ACTION, ART
Mannerism, ART
mannerist, ACTION, ART
Mannerist, ART
manneristic, ACTION, ART
manualism, DEAFNESS
manualist, DEAFNESS
Marcionism, CHRISTIANITY
Marcionite, CHRISTIANITY

mareography, SEA
Marianism, CATHOLICISM
marigraphic, SEA
marigraphy, SEA
Mariolater, CATHOLICISM, MARY
Mariolatrous, CATHOLICISM, MARY
Mariolatry, CATHOLICISM, MARY
Mariologist, MARY
Mariology, MARY
Maronism, CATHOLICISM
Maronite, CATHOLICISM
marranism, CATHOLICISM
marrano, CATHOLICISM
marranoism, CATHOLICISM
martialism, WAR
martialist, WAR
martinet, BEHAVIOR
martinetish, BEHAVIOR
martinetism, BEHAVIOR
martyrologic, CATHOLICISM
martyrological, CATHOLICISM
martyrologist, CATHOLICISM
martyrology, CATHOLICISM
Marxian, COMMUNISM
Marxism, COMMUNISM
Marxist, COMMUNISM
Maryolatry, CATHOLICISM
Maryology, CATHOLICISM
masculinism, ATTITUDES
masochism, PAIN
masochist, PAIN
masochistic, PAIN
materialism, MATTER, PHILOSOPHY
materialist, MATTER, PHILOSOPHY
materialistic, MATTER, PHILOSOPHY
matriarch, GOVERNMENT
matriarchal, GOVERNMENT
matriarchy, GOVERNMENT
matricentric, FATHER, MOTHER
matricidal, MOTHER, PARENTS
matricide, MOTHER, PARENTS
matronymic, NAMES
maudlin, BEHAVIOR
maudlinism, BEHAVIOR
maximist, PROVERBS
mayhem, CRIME, LAW
Mazdaism, GOD AND GODS, RELIGION
McCarthyism, POLITICS
meadophile, BEER
meadophily, BEER
mechanism, LIFE, PHILOSOPHY
mechanist, LIFE, PHILOSOPHY

mechanistic, LIFE, PHILOSOPHY
mechanomorphic, GOD AND GODS
mechanomorphism, GOD AND GODS
meconism, DRUGS
meconophagism, DRUGS
medievalism, PAST
medievalist, HISTORY, PAST
medievalistic, PAST
mediumism, SPIRITS AND SPIRITUALISM
mediumistic, SPIRITS AND SPIRITUALISM
megalomania, GRANDEUR, INSANITY
megalomaniac, GRANDEUR, INSANITY
Megarianism, ARGUMENT
meiosis, FIGURES OF SPEECH
meiotic, FIGURES OF SPEECH
melanism, BLACKENING
melioration, WORDS
meliorism, IMPROVEMENT, PHILOSOPHY
meliorist, IMPROVEMENT, PHILOSOPHY
melioristic, IMPROVEMENT, PHILOSOPHY
melismatics, SONGS AND SINGING
melissophobia, BEES
melittologist, BEES
melittology, BEES
melodramatic, LITERATURE, MUSIC
melodramaticism, LITERATURE, MUSIC
melodramatist, LITERATURE, MUSIC
melograph, MUSIC
melomane, MUSIC
melomania, MUSIC
melomaniac, MUSIC
memorabilia, COLLECTIONS AND COLLECTING
memoranda, COLLECTIONS AND COLLECTING
Mendelian, HEREDITY
Mendelism, HEREDITY
meningitophobia, PHOBIAS
Menologion, CALENDAR
menology, CALENDAR
Menshevik, COMMUNISM
Menshevism, COMMUNISM
mentalism, KNOWLEDGE, PHILOSOPHY
mentalist, KNOWLEDGE, PHILOSOPHY
mentalistic, KNOWLEDGE, PHILOSOPHY
menticide, BRAIN
mercantilism, ECONOMICS
mercantilist, ECONOMICS
mercantilistic, ECONOMICS
merinthophobia, PHOBIAS
Mesmerism, HYPNOSIS
mesmerist, HYPNOSIS
mesmerization, HYPNOSIS
mesmerizer, HYPNOSIS

mesomorphic, ANATOMY
mesomorphy, ANATOMY
mesophyte, PLANTS
mesophytic, PLANTS
mesophytism, PLANTS
Messianic, JUDAISM
Messianism, JUDAISM
metabolism, CHANGE
metabolize, CHANGE
metaboly, BODIES
metagraphic, ALPHABET
metagraphy, ALPHABET
metallophobia, PHOBIAS
metaphrase, LANGUAGE STYLES
metaphrasis, LANGUAGE STYLES
metaphrast, LANGUAGE STYLES
metaphrastic, LANGUAGE STYLES
metaphrastical, LANGUAGE STYLES
metapsychological, PSYCHOLOGY
metapsychology, PSYCHOLOGY
metempsychic, SOUL
metempsychosic, SOUL
metempsychosical, SOUL
metempsychosis, SOUL
meteorism, DISEASE AND ILLNESS
meteorist, METEORITES
meteoritics, METEORITES
meteorology, CLIMATE
meteorophobia, PHOBIAS
Methodism, PROTESTANTISM
Methodist, PROTESTANTISM
metonymic, FIGURES OF SPEECH
metonymy, FIGURES OF SPEECH
metrician, VERSE
metricism, VERSE
metricist, VERSE
metrics, VERSE
metrist, VERSE
metrological, MEASUREMENT
metrologist, MEASUREMENT
metrology, MEASUREMENT
metromania, VERSE
metronymic, NAMES
miasmology, AIR
microbiologist, BACTERIA
microbiology, BACTERIA
microbiophobia, BACTERIA
microphobia, BACTERIA
microphobic, BACTERIA
microscopical anatomy, ANATOMY
militaria, COLLECTIONS AND COLLECTING
militarism, POLITICS

militarist, POLITICS
militaristic, POLITICS
millenarian, CHRIST
millenarianism, CHRIST
millenarist, CHRIST
millenialism, CHRIST
millenialist, CHRIST
millenium, TIME
Millerism, ENDS
Millerite, ENDS
mimesis, LITERATURE
mimetic, LITERATURE
mimicism, BEHAVIOR
mineralogist, GEOLOGY
mineralogy, GEOLOGY
miniaturist, ART
minor planets, PLANETS
misandria, ATTITUDES, MALE
misandry, ATTITUDES, MALE
misanthrope, ATTITUDES, MAN
misanthropic, ATTITUDES, MAN
misanthropism, MAN
misanthropist, ATTITUDES
misanthropy, ATTITUDES, MAN
miscegenation, RACE
miserotia, SEX
misocainea, IDEAS
misocapnic, SMOKE
misocapnist, SMOKE
misogamic, MARRIAGE
misogamist, MARRIAGE
misogamy, MARRIAGE
misogynism, ATTITUDES
misogyny, ATTITUDES
misologist, ARGUMENT, KNOWLEDGE
misology, ARGUMENT, KNOWLEDGE
misoneism, CHANGE, NOVELTY
misopaedia, CHILD
misopaterism, FATHER
misopaterist, FATHER
misopedia, CHILD
misopedist, CHILD
misophobia, DIRT
misosophist, ATTITUDES
misosophy, ATTITUDES
misotheism, GOD AND GODS
Mithraic, GOD AND GODS
Mithraism, GOD AND GODS
Mithraist, GOD AND GODS
mithridatism, POISON
mithridatize, POISON
mnemonic, MEMORY

mnemonics, MEMORY
mnemotechnics, MEMORY
mnestic, MEMORY
modalism, HERESY
modalist, HERESY
modalistic, HERESY
Modalistic Monarchianism, HERESY
moderantism, POLITICS
moderantist, POLITICS
modist, JOBS
modiste, JOBS
Molinism, CATHOLICISM
Molinist, CATHOLICISM
molysomophobia, DISEASE AND ILLNESS
momism, MOTHER
monachal, MONKS
monachism, MONKS
monachist, MONKS
monadism, PHILOSOPHY
monadistic, PHILOSOPHY
monadology, PHILOSOPHY
monandrous, MARRIAGE
monandry, MARRIAGE
monarchical, GOVERNMENT
monarchy, GOVERNMENT
monastic, CHRISTIANITY, MONKS
monastical, CHRISTIANITY
monasticism, CHRISTIANITY, MONKS
monergism, HERESY
monergist, HERESY
monergistic, HERESY
mongolic, IDIOCY
mongolism, IDIOCY
monism, HISTORY, LEARNING, MATTER,
    PHILOSOPHY
monist, HISTORY, MATTER, PHILOSOPHY
monistic, HISTORY, MATTER, PHILOSOPHY
monistical, MATTER, PHILOSOPHY
monochromist, ART
monocracy, GOVERNMENT
monodist, VERSE
monody, VERSE
monogamous, MARRIAGE
monogamy, MARRIAGE
monoglot, LANGUAGE
monolatry, GOD AND GODS
monologic, SELF
monological, SELF
monologist, SELF
monology, SELF
monomania, MENTAL STATES
monomaniac, MENTAL STATES

monomanical, MENTAL STATES
monometallism, MONEY
monometallist, MONEY
monopathophobia, PHOBIAS
monophobia, SELF
Monophysite, CHRIST
Monophysitic, CHRIST
Monophysitical, CHRIST
Monophysitism, CHRIST
monopolist, TRADE
monopolistic, TRADE
monopoly, TRADE
monopsonist, TRADE
monopsonistic, TRADE
monopsony, TRADE
monotheism, GOD AND GODS
monotheist, GOD AND GODS
Monothelete, CHRIST
Monotheletic, CHRIST
Monotheletism, CHRIST
Monothelism, CHRIST
Monothelite, CHRIST
Monothelitic, CHRIST
Monothelitism, CHRIST
moralism, ETHICS
moralist, ETHICS
moralistic, ETHICS
morganatic, MARRIAGE
Mormon, PROTESTANTISM
Mormondom, PROTESTANTISM
Mormonism, PROTESTANTISM
morpheme, LINGUISTICS
morphemicist, LINGUISTICS
morphemics, LINGUISTICS
morphinmania, DRUGS
morphiomania, DRUGS
morphologic, ANIMALS, PLANTS
morphological, ANIMALS, LANGUAGE, PLANTS
morphologist, ANIMALS, LANGUAGE, PLANTS
morphology, ANIMALS, FORM, LANGUAGE, PLANTS
morphophoneme, LINGUISTICS
morphophonemic, LINGUISTICS
morphophonemicist, LINGUISTICS
morphphonemics, LINGUISTICS
motorphobia, PHOBIAS
mugwump, POLITICS
mugwumpery, POLITICS
mugwumpian, POLITICS
mugwumpish, POLITICS
mugwumpism, POLITICS
multilateralism, ECONOMICS
multiopoly, TRADE

multiopsonist, TRADE
multiopsonistic, TRADE
multiopsony, TRADE
muscology, PLANTS
museologist, COLLECTIONS AND COLLECTING
museology, COLLECTIONS AND COLLECTING
musicological, MUSIC
musicologist, MUSIC
musicology, MUSIC
musicophobia, PHOBIAS
musophobia, DIRT
mutism, SPEECH
mycetism, POISON
mycetismus, POISON
mycologic, BOTANY
mycological, BOTANY
mycologist, BOTANY
mycology, BOTANY, PLANTS
mycteric, NOSE
myographic, ANATOMY
myography, ANATOMY
myologic, ANATOMY
myology, ANATOMY
myopia, EYES
myopic, EYES
myrmecologist, ANTS
myrmecology, ANTS
myrmecophobia, ANTS
myrmecophobic, ANTS
myrmicophile, ANTS
myrmicophilism, ANTS
myrmicophilous, ANTS
myrmicophily, ANTS
mysophilia, DIRT, -PHILIA
mysophobia, DIRT
mystagogic, MYSTICISM
mystagogical, MYSTICISM
mystagogics, MYSTICISM
mystagogue, MYSTICISM
mystagogy, MYSTICISM
mysticism, RELIGION
mythicist, MYTHS
mythoclast, MYTHS
mythoclastic, MYTHS
mythogenesis, MYTHS
mythogenetic, MYTHS
mythogeny, MYTHS
mythographer, MYTHS
mythographist, MYTHS
mythography, MYTHS
mythologem, MYTHS
mythologer, MYTHS

mythological, MYTHS
mythologist, MYTHS
mythology, MYTHS
mythomania, LIES AND LYING
mythophobia, LIES AND LYING
mythopoeic, MYTHS
mythopoeist, MYTHS
mythopoesis, MYTHS
mythos, MYTHS
mythus, MYTHS
myxomatosis, DISEASE AND ILLNESS

N

naive realism, PHILOSOPHY
nanism, SIZE
naology, BUILDINGS
narcism, BEHAVIOR
narcissism, BEHAVIOR
narcissist, BEHAVIOR
narcissistic, BEHAVIOR
narcist, BEHAVIOR
narcistic, BEHAVIOR
narcoanalysis, SLEEP
narcohypnia, SLEEP
narcolepsy, DISEASE AND ILLNESS, SLEEP
narcoleptic, DISEASE AND ILLNESS, SLEEP
narcoma, DRUGS
narcomania, DRUGS
narcosis, DRUGS
narcotherapist, SLEEP
narcotherapy, SLEEP
narcoticism, DRUGS
narcotism, DRUGS
nasalism, PRONUNCIATION
nasality, PRONUNCIATION
nasillate, NOSE
nasological, NOSE
nasologist, NOSE
nasology, NOSE
nasoscope, NOSE
nasoscopic, NOSE
nationalism, NATIONALISM
nationalist, NATIONALISM
nationalistic, NATIONALISM
naturalism, ART
naturalist, ART
naturalistic, ART, MAN
natural realism, PHILOSOPHY
naturism, NAKEDNESS
naturist, NAKEDNESS

naturistic, NAKEDNESS
naturopath, REMEDIES
naturopathic, REMEDIES
naturopathism, REMEDIES
naturopathy, REMEDIES
navigation, ASTRONOMY
Nazi, FASCISM, POLITICS
Naziism, POLITICS
Nazism, FASCISM, POLITICS
necessarianism, PHILOSOPHY
necessitarianism, PHILOSOPHY
necessitarian, PHILOSOPHY
necrolatry, DEATH
necrologist, DEATH
necrologue, DEATH
necrology, DEATH
necromancer, DEATH
necromancy, DEATH
necromant, DEATH
necromantic, DEATH
necrophagous, CORPSE
necrophagy, CORPSE
necrophile, SEX
necrophilia, CORPSE, SEX
necrophilic, SEX
necrophilism, CORPSE
necrophily, CORPSE
necrophobia, CORPSE
necropsy, CORPSE
necrosadism, SEX
necrosadist, SEX
necrotomic, CORPSE
necrotomist, CORPSE
necrotomy, CORPSE
negrophobia, PHOBIAS
Neo-Classic, ART
Neo-Classical, ART
Neo-Classicism, ART
Neo-Classicist, ART
neocracy, GOVERNMENT
Neo-Expressionism, ARCHITECTURE
Neo-Impressionism, ART
neolalia, MENTAL STATES
neolater, NOVELTY
neolatry, NOVELTY
neologism, WORDS
neologist, WORDS
neologistic, WORDS
neologistical, WORDS
neonatologist, MEDICAL SPECIALTIES
neonatology, MEDICAL SPECIALTIES

neontological, BEING
neontologist, BEING
neontology, BEING
neophilism, NOVELTY
neophobia, CHANGE, NOVELTY
neophrasis, WORDS
neophrastic, WORDS
neophyte, CONVERT
neophytic, CONVERT
neophytism, CONVERT
Neoplatonic, PHILOSOPHY
Neoplatonism, PHILOSOPHY
NeoPlatonism, PHILOSOPHY
Neoplatonist, PHILOSOPHY
neossology, BIRDS
neoteric, IDEAS
neoterism, WORDS
nephalism, ALCOHOL
nephalist, ALCOHOL
nephalistic, ALCOHOL
nephologist, CLOUDS, WEATHER
nephology, CLOUDS, WEATHER
nephrologist, BODIES
nephrology, BODIES
nepotic, FAVORITISM
nepotism, FAVORITISM
nepotist, FAVORITISM
neptunism, GEOLOGY
neptunist, GEOLOGY
Nestorian, CHRIST
Nestorianism, CHRIST
neuralgia, NERVES
neuralgic, NERVES
neurasthenia, NERVES
neurasthenic, NERVES
neuritic, NERVES
neuritis, NERVES
neuroanatomical, NERVES
neuroanatomy, NERVES
neurological, NERVES
neurologist, NERVES
neurology, NERVES
neuromechanism, MEDICAL SPECIALTIES
neuromimesis, NERVES
neuromimetic, NERVES
neuropathologic, MEDICAL SPECIALTIES, NERVES
neuropathological, MEDICAL SPECIALTIES,
  NERVES
neuropathologist, MEDICAL SPECIALTIES, NERVES
neuropathology, MEDICAL SPECIALTIES, NERVES
neuropsychiatric, NERVES

neuropsychiatrist, NERVES
neuropsychiatry, NERVES
neuropterology, INSECTS
neuroticism, PSYCHOLOGY
neurotomist, NERVES
neurotomy, NERVES
neutralism, POLITICS
neutralist, POLITICS
New Critic, CRITICISM
New Criticism, CRITICISM
New Formalism, ARCHITECTURE
New Realism, ART
nidologist, BIRDS
nidology, BIRDS
Nietzschean, PHILOSOPHY
Nietzscheanism, PHILOSOPHY
nihilism, ATTITUDES
Nihilism, GOVERNMENT
nihilist, ATTITUDES, GOVERNMENT
nihilistic, ATTITUDES, GOVERNMENT
noctambulant, SLEEP
noctambulation, SLEEP
noctambule, SLEEP
noctambulism, SLEEP
noctambulist, SLEEP
noctambulistic, SLEEP
noctambulous, SLEEP
noctiphobia, PHOBIAS
noetic, ARGUMENT, MIND
noetics, ARGUMENT
nomadic, BEHAVIOR
nomadism, BEHAVIOR
nomancy, NAMES, WRITING
nomism, LAW
nomographer, LAW
nomographic, LAW
nomography, LAW
nomological, LAW, MIND
nomologist, LAW, MIND
nomology, LAW, MIND
nonconformism, ATTITUDES, PROTESTANTISM
nonconformist, ATTITUDES, PROTESTANTISM
nonconformity, ATTITUDES
nonjuror, PROTESTANTISM
nonjurorism, PROTESTANTISM
nonpartisan, POLITICS
nonpartisanism, POLITICS
nonpartisanship, POLITICS
noological, UNDERSTANDING
noology, UNDERSTANDING
nosism, SELF
nosologic, DISEASE AND ILLNESS

nosological, DISEASE AND ILLNESS
nosologist, DISEASE AND ILLNESS
nosology, DISEASE AND ILLNESS
nosonomy, DISEASE AND ILLNESS
nosophilia, DISEASE AND ILLNESS
nosophobia, DISEASE AND ILLNESS
nostalgia, HOMESICKNESS
nostalgic, HOMESICKNESS
nostalgy, HOMESICKNESS
nostology, OLD AGE
nostomania, HOMESICKNESS
nostopathy, PLACES
notaphily, COLLECTIONS AND COLLECTING
nothingarian, POLITICS
nothingarianism, POLITICS
noumenal, PHILOSOPHY
noumenalism, GOD AND GODS, PHILOSOPHY
noumenalist, GOD AND GODS, PHILOSOPHY
noumenon, PHILOSOPHY
Novationism, CATHOLICISM
Novationist, CATHOLICISM
nucleation, RAIN
nucleator, RAIN
nudiphobia, PHOBIAS
nudism, BEHAVIOR, NAKEDNESS
nudist, BEHAVIOR, NAKEDNESS
nudophobia, PHOBIAS
nullibism, SOUL
nullibist, SOUL
nullifidian, RELIGION
numerological, NUMBERS
numerologist, NUMBERS
numerology, NUMBERS
numismatics, COLLECTIONS AND COLLECTING
numismatist, COLLECTIONS AND COLLECTING
numismatology, COLLECTIONS AND COLLECTING
nyctalopia, BLINDNESS
nyctalopic, BLINDNESS
nyctophilia, -PHILIA
nyctophobia, DARKNESS
nympholepsy, DEMONS
nympholeptic, DEMONS
nymphomania, SEX

O

obeahism, MAGIC
obi , MAGIC
obism, MAGIC
objectivism, PHILOSOPHY
objectivist, PHILOSOPHY

objectivity, ATTITUDES
obscurant, ARGUMENT
obscurantic, ARGUMENT
obscuranticism, ARGUMENT
obscurantism, ARGUMENT
obscurantist, ARGUMENT
obstetric, BIRTH
obstetrical, BIRTH
obstetrician, BIRTH
obstetrics, BIRTH
obstructionism, ARGUMENT
obstructionist, ARGUMENT
obstructionistic, ARGUMENT
Occamism, THEOLOGY
Occamist, THEOLOGY
Occamistic, THEOLOGY
Occamite, THEOLOGY
occultism, RELIGION
occultist, RELIGION
oceanographer, SEA
oceanographic, SEA
oceanographical, SEA
oceanography, SEA
oceanology, SEA
ochlocracy, MOB
ochlocrat, MOB
ochlocratic, MOB
ochlocratical, MOB
ochlophobia, CROWDS, MOB
ochlophobic, MOB
ochlophobist, MOB
oculist, EYES
odalisk, SLAVES
odalisque, SLAVES
odograph, DISTANCE
odometer, DISTANCE
odontalgia, PAIN, TEETH
odontalgic, PAIN, TEETH
odontalgy, TEETH
odontogeny, TEETH
odontological, TEETH
odontologist, TEETH
odontology, TEETH
odontophobia, PHOBIAS, TEETH
odylic, HYPNOSIS
odylism, HYPNOSIS
odynophobia, PAIN
oecist, JOBS
oecology, BIOLOGY
oecophobia, HOUSES
Oecumenism, CHURCH
oekist, JOBS

oenologist, WINE
oenology, WINE
oenomancy, WINE
oenophile, WINE
oenophily, WINE
oenophobe, WINE
oenophobia, WINE
officialism, BUREAUCRACY
ogam, WRITING
ogham, WRITING
oghamist, WRITING
oikophobia, HOUSES
oinomancy, WINE
oleographic, PRINTING
oleography, PRINTING
olfactologist, ODORS
olfactology, ODORS
olfactophobia, PHOBIAS
oligarch, GOVERNMENT
oligarchic, GOVERNMENT
oligarchy, GOVERNMENT
oligopolistic, TRADE
oligopoly, TRADE
ombrological, RAIN
ombrology, RAIN
ombrophilic, PLANTS
ombrophilous, PLANTS
ombrophily, PLANTS
ombrophobia, PHOBIAS, RAIN
ommatophobia, EYES
omnibology, VEHICLES
omnipotence, STRENGTH AND WEAKNESS
omnipotent, STRENGTH AND WEAKNESS
omophagia, FLESH
omophagic, FLESH
omphalism, MEDITATION
omphalopsychism, MYSTICISM
omphalopsychite, MYSTICISM
omphaloskepsis, MEDITATION, MYSTICISM
onanism, SEX
onanist, SEX
onanistic, SEX
oncologic, MEDICAL SPECIALTIES
oncologist, MEDICAL SPECIALTIES
oncology, MEDICAL SPECIALTIES
Oneida Perfectionists, COMMUNALISM
oneirocritic, DREAMS
oneirocritical, DREAMS
oneirocriticism, DREAMS
oneirodynia, DREAMS
oneirology, DREAMS
oneiromancer, DREAMS

oneiromancy, DREAMS
oneiroscopy, DREAMS
oniomania, MENTAL STATES
oniomaniac, MENTAL STATES
onomancy, NAMES
onomastic, NAMES
onomasticon, NAMES
onomastics, NAMES
onomatology, NAMES
onomatomania, NAMES
onomatophobia, NAMES, PHOBIAS
onomatopoeia, SOUNDS
onomatopoeial, SOUNDS
onomatopoeic, SOUNDS
onomatopoetic, SOUNDS
onomatopoietic, SOUNDS
ontologic, BEING
ontological, BEING
ontologism, BEING, RELIGION
ontologist, BEING, RELIGION
ontologistic, BEING, RELIGION
ontology, BEING
oologic, BIRDS
oological, BIRDS
oologist, BIRDS
oology, BIRDS
ophicleidist, MUSIC
ophidiophobia, REPTILES, SNAKES
ophiolator, SNAKES
ophiolatry, SNAKES
ophiologic, SNAKES
ophiological, SNAKES
ophiologist, SNAKES
ophiology, SNAKES
ophiomancy, SNAKES
ophiophobia, SNAKES
Ophism, RELIGION
Ophite, RELIGION
Ophitic, RELIGION
Ophitism, RELIGION
ophthalmologic, EYES
ophthalmological, EYES
ophthalmologist, EYES
ophthalmology, EYES
opiomania, DRUGS
opportunism, ATTITUDES
opportunist, ATTITUDES
opportunistic, ATTITUDES
optician, EYES
optimism, PHILOSOPHY
optimist, PHILOSOPHY
optimistic, PHILOSOPHY

optology, EYES
optometrical, EYES
optometrist, EYES
optometry, EYES
oracularity, FUTURE
oralism, DEAFNESS
oralist, DEAFNESS
orchesis, DANCING
orchesography, DANCING
orchestics, DANCING
orchidologist, PLANTS
orchidology, PLANTS
oreography, MOUNTAINS
oreology, MOUNTAINS
organicism, MEDICAL SPECIALTIES, PHILOSOPHY
organicist, MEDICAL SPECIALTIES, PHILOSOPHY
organicistic, MEDICAL SPECIALTIES, PHILOSOPHY
organologic, ANIMALS, PLANTS
organological, ANIMALS, PLANTS
organologist, ANIMALS, PLANTS
organology, ANIMALS, PLANTS
Orientalist, HISTORY
origami, ART
origamist, ART
Origenian, THEOLOGY
Origenism, PHILOSOPHY, THEOLOGY
Origenist, PHILOSOPHY, THEOLOGY
Origenistic, PHILOSOPHY, THEOLOGY
orismologic, WORDS
orismological, WORDS
orismology, WORDS
ornamentalism, ART
ornithologic, BIRDS
ornithological, BIRDS
ornithologist, BIRDS
ornithology, BIRDS
ornithomancy, BIRDS
ornithopter, AVIATION
ornithoscopy, BIRDS
orogenesis, MOUNTAINS
orogenic, MOUNTAINS
orogeny, MOUNTAINS
orographic, GEOGRAPHY, MOUNTAINS
orographical, GEOGRAPHY, MOUNTAINS
orography, GEOGRAPHY, MOUNTAINS
orohydrographic, WATER
orohydrography, WATER
orological, MOUNTAINS
orologist, MOUNTAINS
orology, MOUNTAINS
orometric, MOUNTAINS
orometry, MOUNTAINS

orophilous, MOUNTAINS
Orphic, RELIGION
Orphicism, RELIGION
Orphism, ART, RELIGION
Orphist, ART
orthodontia, TEETH
orthodontic, TEETH
orthodontics, TEETH
orthodontis, TEETH
orthoepic, PRONUNCIATION
orthoepical, PRONUNCIATION
orthoepist, PRONUNCIATION
orthoepistic, PRONUNCIATION
orthoepy, PRONUNCIATION
orthographer, SPELLING
orthographic, SPELLING
orthographic projection, DRAWING
orthography, SPELLING
orthopedic, MEDICAL SPECIALTIES
orthopedics, MEDICAL SPECIALTIES
orthopedist, MEDICAL SPECIALTIES
orthopsychiatric, MENTAL STATES
orthopsychiatrical, MENTAL STATES
orthopsychiatrist, MENTAL STATES
orthopsychiatry, MENTAL STATES
orthopterology, INSECTS
orthoptic, EYES
orthoptics, EYES
orthoptist, EYES
oryctognosy, GEOLOGY
oryctology, GEOLOGY
oscillographic, PHYSICS
oscillography, PHYSICS
osmatic, ODORS
osmatism, ODORS
osmic, ODORS
osmology, ODORS
osmonologist, ODORS
osmonosology, ODORS
osmophobia, ODORS, PHOBIAS
osphresiology, ODORS
osphresiophilia, ODORS
osphresiophobia, ODORS
osteologer, BONES
osteologic, BONES, MEDICAL SPECIALTIES
osteological, BONES, MEDICAL SPECIALTIES
osteologist, BONES, MEDICAL SPECIALTIES
osteology, BONES, MEDICAL SPECIALTIES
osteomancy, BONES
osteopath, BONES, REMEDIES
osteopathic, BONES, REMEDIES
osteopathist, BONES

osteopathology, BONES
osteopathy, BONES, REMEDIES
ostiary, CATHOLICISM
ostracism, BANISHMENT
otalgia, EAR, PAIN
otalgic, PAIN
otiatric, EAR
otiatrics, EAR
otiatry, EAR
oticodinia, EAR
oticodinosis, EAR
otitic, EAR
otitis, EAR
otocleisis, HEARING
otologic, EAR
otological, EAR
otologist, EAR
otology, EAR
otomyasthenia, HEARING
otomyasthenic, HEARING
otophone, HEARING
otoscopic, EAR
otoscopy, EAR
otosis, HEARING
Owenism, COMMUNALISM, ECONOMICS
Owenite, COMMUNALISM, ECONOMICS

P

pacifism, WAR
pacifist, WAR
pacifistic, WAR
paedobaptism, BAPTISM
paedogogics, LEARNING
paedonymic, NAMES
paedophobia, DOLLS
paganism, RELIGION
paganist, RELIGION
paganistic, RELIGION
Pajonism, PROTESTANTISM
palaeobiology, FOSSILS
palaeobotany, FOSSILS
palaeontology, FOSSILS
palaeopedology, SOILS
palaetiological, PAST
palaetiology, PAST
Palamitism, EASTERN ORTHODOXY
paleobiologic, FOSSILS
paleobiological, FOSSILS
paleobiologist, FOSSILS
paleobiology, FOSSILS

paleobotanic, FOSSILS
paleobotanical, FOSSILS
paleobotanist, FOSSILS
paleobotany, FOSSILS
paleoecologic, ENVIRONMENT
paleoecological, ENVIRONMENT
paleoecology, ENVIRONMENT
paleoethnography, MAN
paleogeographer, GEOGRAPHY
paleogeographic, GEOGRAPHY
paleogeographical, GEOGRAPHY
paleogeography, GEOGRAPHY
paleographer, ANTIQUITY, LITERARY STUDY
paleographic, ANTIQUITY, LITERARY STUDY
paleography, ANTIQUITY, LITERARY STUDY
paleological, PAST
paleologist, PAST
paleology, PAST
paleontologic, FOSSILS
paleontological, FOSSILS
paleontologist, BEING, FOSSILS
paleontology, BEING, FOSSILS
paleopathology, PAST
paleopedology, GEOLOGY, SOILS
paletiology, PAST
palillogy, RHETORIC
palilogy, RHETORIC
palimpsest, MANUSCRIPTS
palimpsestic, MANUSCRIPTS
palindrome, WORDS
palindromic, WORDS
palindromical, WORDS
palindromist, WORDS
palingenesian, BAPTISM
palingenesis, BAPTISM
palingenesist, BAPTISM
palingenesy, BAPTISM
Palladianism, ARCHITECTURE
pallid, COLOR
pallidity, COLOR
pallograph, SHIPS
pallographic, SHIPS
palmist, HANDS
palmistry, HANDS
palynological, PAST
palynology, PAST
panarchy, GOVERNMENT
pancosmic, COSMOLOGY
pancosmism, COSMOLOGY
pandect, LAW
pandectist, LAW
pandemonism, DEMONS

panderage, SEX
panderism, SEX
pandiatonic, MUSIC
pandiatonicism, MUSIC
panegyrist, PRAISE, VERSE
panentheism, GOD AND GODS
panentheist, GOD AND GODS
Panhellenic, GREECE AND GREEKS
Panhellenism,GREECE AND GREEKS
Panhellenist, GREECE AND GREEKS
panlogical, PHILOSOPHY
panlogism, PHILOSOPHY
panlogist, PHILOSOPHY
panlogistic, PHILOSOPHY
panlogistical, PHILOSOPHY
panmnesia, MEMORY
panophobe, FEAR
panophobia, FEAR
panophobic, FEAR
panphobia, FEAR
panpsychism, PHILOSOPHY, SOUL
panpsychist, PHILOSOPHY, SOUL
panpsychistic, PHILOSOPHY, SOUL
Pansatanism, COSMOLOGY
PanSatanism, DEVIL
pansexualism, PSYCHOLOGY
pansexualist, PSYCHOLOGY
pansexuality, PSYCHOLOGY
pansophic, KNOWLEDGE
pansophism, KNOWLEDGE
pansophist, KNOWLEDGE
pansophistical, KNOWLEDGE
pansophy, KNOWLEDGE
Pantagruelian, HUMOR
Pantagruelism, HUMOR
pantaphobia, FEAR
pantaraxia, ALERTNESS
pantheism, GOD AND GODS
pantheist, GOD AND GODS
pantisocracy, GOVERNMENT
pantisocratic, GOVERNMENT
pantisocratical, GOVERNMENT
pantisocratist, GOVERNMENT
pantograph, COPYING
pantographic, COPYING
pantologic, KNOWLEDGE
pantological, KNOWLEDGE
pantologist, KNOWLEDGE
pantology, KNOWLEDGE
pantophobia, FEAR
papalism, CATHOLICISM
papalist, CATHOLICISM

papaphobia, PHOBIAS
papism, CATHOLICISM
papist, CATHOLICISM
papistic, CATHOLICISM
papistical, CATHOLICISM
papistry, CATHOLICISM
papyrological, PAST
papyrologist, PAST
papyrology, PAST
Paraclete, CHRISTIANITY
paragoge, PRONUNCIATION, WORDS
paragogic, PRONUNCIATION, WORDS
paragogical, PRONUNCIATION, WORDS
paralipophobia, PHOBIAS
paralipsis, FIGURES OF SPEECH
paralogia, ARGUMENT, MENTAL STATES, SPEECH
paralogical, MENTAL STATES
paralogism, ARGUMENT
paralogist, ARGUMENT
paralogistic, ARGUMENT
paralogy, ARGUMENT, MENTAL STATES
paramnesia, MEMORY
paranoia, GRANDEUR
paranoiac, GRANDEUR
paranoid, GRANDEUR, INSANITY
paranoidism, INSANITY
paraphilia, SEX
paraphilic, SEX
paraphobia, PHOBIAS
parapsychological, PSYCHOLOGY
parapsychology, PSYCHOLOGY
parasitologist, BIOLOGY
parasitology, BIOLOGY
parasitophobia, PHOBIAS
paratactic, GRAMMAR
parataxis, GRAMMAR
paremiography, PROVERBS
parentalism, PARENTS
parentation, PARENTS
parenticide, PARENTS
parisological, WORDS
parisology, WORDS
parmacopedic, DRUGS
Parnassian, VERSE
Parnassianism, VERSE
parochialism, ATTITUDES
parochialist, ATTITUDES
parodist, LITERATURE
parodistic, LITERATURE
parody, LITERATURE
paroemia, PROVERBS
paroemiac, PROVERBS

paroemiographer, PROVERBS
paroemiography, PROVERBS
paroemiologist, PROVERBS
paroemiology, PROVERBS
paromologia, RHETORIC
paronomasia, FIGURES OF SPEECH, PUN
paronomastic, PUN
paronym, WORDS
paronymous, WORDS
parosmia, ODORS
parosphresia, ODORS
parosphresis, ODORS
parrhesia, LANGUAGE STYLES, SPEECH
parricidal, KILLING, PARENTS
parricide, KILLING, PARENTS
parricidism, KILLING
Parseeism, GOD AND GODS
Parsi, GOD AND GODS
Parsiism, GOD AND GODS
parthenogenesis, LIFE
parthenogenetic, LIFE
parthenophobia, PHOBIAS
partialism, SEX
partisan, FAVORITISM, POLITICS
partisanism, FAVORITISM, POLITICS
partisanship, POLITICS
parturiency, BIRTH
parturient, BIRTH
pasigraphic, LANGUAGE, WRITING
pasigraphical, WRITING
pasigraphy, LANGUAGE, WRITING
pasimology, GESTURE
passive scopophilia, SEX
Patarene, HERESY
Pataria, HERESY
Patarine, HERESY
Patarinism, HERESY
pathologic, DISEASE AND ILLNESS
pathological, DISEASE AND ILLNESS
pathologist, DISEASE AND ILLNESS
pathology, DISEASE AND ILLNESS
pathophilia, DISEASE AND ILLNESS
pathophobia, DISEASE AND ILLNESS
patriarch, GOVERNMENT
patriarchic, FATHER
patriarchical, FATHER
patriarchism, GOVERNMENT
patriarchist, FATHER, GOVERNMENT
patriarchy, FATHER, GOVERNMENT
patricentric, FATHER
patricidal, PARENTS
patricide, PARENTS

patriot, NATIONALISM
patriotic, NATIONALISM
patriotism, NATIONALISM
Patripassian, CHRIST
Patripassianism, CHRIST
Patripassianist, CHRIST
patristics, THEOLOGY
patrologic, THEOLOGY
patrological, THEOLOGY
patrologist, THEOLOGY
patrology, THEOLOGY
patronymic, NAMES
Paulian, CHRIST
Paulianism, CHRIST
Paulianist, CHRIST
pauperage, POVERTY
pauperism, POVERTY
paysagist, JOBS
peccatiphobia, SIN
peccatophobia, SIN
pedagog, LEARNING
pedagogic, LEARNING
pedagogical, LEARNING
pedagogics, CHILD, LEARNING
pedagogism, LEARNING
pedagogist, LEARNING
pedagogue, CHILD, LEARNING
pedagogy, CHILD, LEARNING
pedant, LEARNING
pedantic, LEARNING
pedanticism, LEARNING
pedantry, LEARNING
pederast, CHILD
pederasty, CHILD
pedestrian, LANGUAGE STYLES
pedestrianism, LANGUAGE STYLES
pediatrician, CHILD
pediatrics, CHILD
pediculophobia, INSECTS
pediculosis, INSECTS
pediculous, INSECTS
pedobaptism, BAPTISM
pedobaptist, BAPTISM
pedodontia, CHILD
pedodontics, CHILD
pedodontist, CHILD
pedologic, SOILS
pedological, CHILD, PLANTS, SOILS
pedologist, CHILD, PLANTS, SOILS
pedology, CHILD, PLANTS, SOILS
pedometer, DISTANCE
pedophilia, CHILD

pedophiliac, CHILD
pedophilic, CHILD
pedophobia, CHILD, DOLLS
pedophobiac, CHILD
pejoration, WORDS
pejoratism, WORDS
peladophobia, BALDNESS
Pelagian, HERESY
Pelagianism, HERESY
pellagraphobia, PHOBIAS
pellucid, LANGUAGE STYLES
pellucidity, LANGUAGE STYLES
pellucidness, LANGUAGE STYLES
Pelmanism, MIND
peniaphobia, PHOBIAS
penisterophily, BIRDS
penologist, CRIME
penology, CRIME
Pentecostal, PROTESTANTISM
Pentecostalism, PROTESTANTISM
peonage, ECONOMICS
peonism, ECONOMICS
perastadic, AVIATION
perastadics, AVIATION
perfectionism, ATTITUDES
perfectionist, ATTITUDES
perfectionistic, ATTITUDES
periodontia, TEETH
periodontic, TEETH
periodontics, TEETH
periodontist, TEETH
Peripatetic, PHILOSOPHY
Peripateticism, PHILOSOPHY
periphrasis, GRAMMAR, LANGUAGE STYLES
periphrastic, GRAMMAR, LANGUAGE STYLES
perissology, LANGUAGE STYLES
persona, PSYCHOLOGY
personification, FIGURES OF SPEECH
personificative, FIGURES OF SPEECH
pessimism, ATTITUDES, PHILOSOPHY
pessimist, ATTITUDES, PHILOSOPHY
pessimistic, ATTITUDES, PHILOSOPHY
pessomancy, ROCKS
petalism, BANISHMENT
Petrinism, CATHOLICISM
Petrinist, CATHOLICISM
petroglyph, ROCKS
petroglyphic, ROCKS
petroglyphy, ROCKS
petrographer, GEOLOGY
petrographic, GEOLOGY
petrographical, GEOLOGY

petrography, GEOLOGY
petrologic, GEOLOGY
petrological, GEOLOGY
petrologist, GEOLOGY
petrology, GEOLOGY
pettifogger, LAW
pettifoggery, LAW
phaenology, ORGANISMS
phagophobia, FOOD AND NUTRITION, PHOBIAS
phalacrosis, BALDNESS
phalansterianism, COMMUNALISM
phallicism, GOD AND GODS
phallicist, GOD AND GODS
phallist, GOD AND GODS
Pharisaic, JUDAISM
pharisaic, JUDAISM
Pharisaism, JUDAISM
Pharisee, JUDAISM
pharisee, JUDAISM
Phariseeism, JUDAISM
pharmacist, DRUGS
pharmacognosia, DRUGS
pharmacognosis, DRUGS
pharmacognosist, DRUGS
pharmacognostic, DRUGS
pharmacognosy, DRUGS
pharmacologia, DRUGS
pharmacologic, DRUGS
pharmacological, DRUGS
pharmacologist, DRUGS
pharmacology, DRUGS
pharmacopedia, DRUGS
pharmacopedics, DRUGS
pharmacophobia, DRUGS
pharmacy, DRUGS
phengophobia, LIGHT
phenologic, CLIMATE, ORGANISMS
phenological, CLIMATE, ORGANISMS, TIME
phenologist, CLIMATE, ORGANISMS, TIME
phenology, CLIMATE, ORGANISMS, TIME
phenomenalism, PHILOSOPHY
phenomenalist, PHILOSOPHY
phenomenalistic, PHILOSOPHY
phenomenologic, PHILOSOPHY
phenomenology, PHILOSOPHY
phenomonological, PHILOSOPHY
phenomonologist, PHILOSOPHY
philanthropic, ATTITUDES
philanthropical, MAN
philanthropism, MAN
philanthropist, ATTITUDES, MAN
philanthropy, ATTITUDES

philarchaic, PAST
philarchaist, PAST
philatelist, COLLECTIONS AND COLLECTING
philately, COLLECTIONS AND COLLECTING
Philhellenic, GREECE AND GREEKS
Philhellenism, GREECE AND GREEKS
Philippism, PROTESTANTISM
Philippist, PROTESTANTISM
Philippistic, PROTESTANTISM
philistine, ATTITUDES
philistinism, ATTITUDES
Phillenist, GREECE AND GREEKS
phillumeny, COLLECTIONS AND COLLECTING
philobiblist, BOOKS
philobotanist, PLANTS
philocalist, BEAUTY
philocubist, GAMBLING
philogynist, WOMEN
philogynous, WOMEN
philogyny, WOMEN
philologer, LANGUAGE
philologic, LANGUAGE
philological, LANGUAGE
philologist, LANGUAGE
philologue, WORDS
philology, LANGUAGE
philomath, MATHEMATICS
philomathean, MATHEMATICS
philomathic, MATHEMATICS
philomathical, MATHEMATICS
philomathy, MATHEMATICS
philometry, COLLECTIONS AND COLLECTING
philoneism, NOVELTY
Philonian, JUDAISM
Philonic, JUDAISM
Philonism, JUDAISM
Philonist, KNOWLEDGE
philonoist, KNOWLEDGE
philopolemic, ARGUMENT
philopolemist, ARGUMENT
philosophical existentialism, PHILOSOPHY
philosophical humanism, MAN
philosophobia, PHOBIAS
phlebotomic, BLOOD
phlebotomical, BLOOD
phlebotomist, BLOOD
phlebotomize, BLOOD
phlebotomy, BLOOD
phobophobia, FEAR
phonautographic, DEAFNESS
phonautography, DEAFNESS
phoneme, LINGUISTICS

phonemic, LINGUISTICS
phonemicist, LINGUISTICS
phonemics, LINGUISTICS
phonetic, LANGUAGE
phonetical, LANGUAGE
phonetician, LANGUAGE
phonetics, LANGUAGE
phonocamptics, ECHOES
phonocardiography, MEDICAL SPECIALTIES
phonographer, SPELLING, WRITING
phonographic, SPELLING, WRITING
phonographical, SPELLING
phonographist, SPELLING, WRITING
phonography, SPELLING, WRITING
phonological, LANGUAGE, SPEECH
phonologist, LANGUAGE, SPEECH
phonology, LANGUAGE, SPEECH
phonophile, COLLECTIONS AND COLLECTING
phonophily, COLLECTIONS AND COLLECTING,
  PHONOGRAPH RECORDS
phonophobia, PHOBIAS
phorologist, DISEASE AND ILLNESS
phorology, DISEASE AND ILLNESS
photangiophobia, PHOBIAS
Photinianism, HERESY
photism, PERCEPTION
photodysphoria, LIGHT
photometric, LIGHT
photometrician, LIGHT
photometrist, LIGHT
photometry, LIGHT
photonastic, PLANTS
photonasty, PLANTS
photopathy, LIGHT
photoperiod, BIOLOGY
photoperiodic, BIOLOGY, PLANTS
photoperiodical, PLANTS
photoperiodicity, BIOLOGY, PLANTS
photoperiodism, BIOLOGY, PLANTS
photophile, PLANTS
photophilia, PLANTS
photophilic, PLANTS
photophilous, PLANTS
photophily, LIGHT, PLANTS
photophobia, LIGHT
phrenologic, HEAD
phrenological, HEAD
phrenologist, HEAD
phrenology, HEAD
phrontistery, THINKING
phthiriophobia, INSECTS, PHOBIAS
phthisiology, DISEASE AND ILLNESS

phthisiophobia, PHOBIAS
phycology, BOTANY
phylogenetic, EVOLUTION
phylogenist, EVOLUTION
phylogeny, EVOLUTION
physical anthropology, ANTHROPOLOGY
physicist, PHYSICS
physics, PHYSICS
physiocrat, POLITICS
physiocratic, POLITICS
physiocratism, POLITICS
physiogenic, DISEASE AND ILLNESS
physiognomic, FACE
physiognomical, FACE
physiognomics, FACE
physiognomy, FACE
physiolater, NATURE
physiolatrous, NATURE
physiolatry, NATURE
physiologic, BODIES
physiological, BODIES, LIFE
physiologist, BODIES, LIFE
physiology, BODIES, LIFE
physiosophy, NATURE
physiotherapist, REMEDIES
physiotherapy, REMEDIES
physitheism, GOD AND GODS, NATURE
physiurgic, NATURE
phytographer, BOTANY
phytographic, BOTANY
phytographical, BOTANY
phytographist, BOTANY
phytography, BOTANY
phytoillumination, PLANTS
phytology, BOTANY
phytoserology, PLANTS
phytosociologic, BOTANY
phytosociological, BOTANY
phytosociologist, BOTANY
phytosociology, BOTANY
pictograph, WRITING
pictographic, WRITING
pictography, WRITING
Pietism, PROTESTANTISM
Pietist, PROTESTANTISM
Pietistic, PROTESTANTISM
Pietistical, PROTESTANTISM
pilose, HAIR
pilosism, HAIR
pilosity, HAIR
pilpulist, ARGUMENT
pilpulistic, ARGUMENT

piscatology, FISH
piscator, FISH
pistic, FAITH
pistology, FAITH
plagiarism, STEALING
plagiarist, STEALING
plagiaristic, STEALING
planetoid, PLANETS
planetoidal, PLANETS
planganologist, DOLLS
planktology, FISH
planktonology, FISH
plastic, PHYSICAL CHARACTERISTICS
plasticity, PHYSICAL CHARACTERISTICS
platitudinarian, LANGUAGE STYLES
platitudinarianism, LANGUAGE STYLES
Platonism, PHILOSOPHY
Platonist, PHILOSOPHY
Platonistic, PHILOSOPHY
plein-air, ART
Plein-airism, ART
plenism, PHYSICS
plenist, PHYSICS
pleomorphic, PLANTS
pleomorphism, PLANTS
pleomorphous, PLANTS
pleomorphy, PLANTS
pleonasm, LANGUAGE STYLES, WORDS
pleonastic, LANGUAGE STYLES, WORDS
plumbism, POISON
pluralism, PHILOSOPHY, POLITICS
pluralist, PHILOSOPHY, POLITICS
pluralistic, PHILOSOPHY, POLITICS
plurisignation, WORDS
plutocracy, GOVERNMENT
plutocrat, GOVERNMENT
plutolatry, MONEY
plutology, ECONOMICS, MONEY
plutomania, MONEY
plutonism, GEOLOGY, POISON
plutonist, GEOLOGY
pluviographic, RAIN
pluviographical, RAIN
pluviography, RAIN
pluviometric, RAIN
pluviometrical, RAIN
pluviometry, RAIN
pneumatics, AIR
pneumatism, MAN
pneumatologic, CHRISTIANITY, RELIGION
pneumatological, CHRISTIANITY
pneumatological, RELIGION

pneumatologist, CHRISTIANITY, RELIGION, SPIRITS AND SPIRITUALISM
pneumatology, CHRISTIANITY, RELIGION, SPIRITS AND SPIRITUALISM
pneumodynamics, AIR
pneumological, AIR
pneumology, AIR
pnigophobia, PHOBIAS
pococurante, BEHAVIOR
pococurantism, BEHAVIOR
pococurantist, BEHAVIOR
podiatric, FEET
podiatrist, FEET
podiatry, FEET
podology, FEET
poecilonymy, NAMES
poetaster, VERSE
poeticism, VERSE
poetics, VERSE
pogoniasis, BEARDS
pogonologist, BEARDS
pogonology, BEARDS
pogonophile, BEARDS
pogonotomy, BEARDS
pogonotrophy, BEARDS
Pointillism, ART
Pointillist, ART
Pointillistic, ART
polemical, ARGUMENT
polemicist, ARGUMENT
polemist, ARGUMENT
politicophobia, PHOBIAS
Polonist, LANGUAGE
poltergeist, SPIRITS AND SPIRITUALISM
poltroon, COWARDICE
poltroonery, COWARDICE
polyandrous, MARRIAGE
polyandry, MARRIAGE
polychrest, REMEDIES
polychrestic, REMEDIES
polydaemonism, DEMONS
polydemonism, DEMONS
polydemonistic, DEMONS
polygamous, MARRIAGE
polygamy, MARRIAGE
polyglot, LANGUAGE
polyglottism, LANGUAGE
polygynious, MARRIAGE
polygynous, MARRIAGE
polygyny, MARRIAGE
polyhistor, KNOWLEDGE
polyhistoric, KNOWLEDGE

polymath, KNOWLEDGE
polymathy, KNOWLEDGE
polymorphism, ENTOMOLOGY
polymorphous, ENTOMOLOGY
polyonymous, NAMES
polyonymy, NAMES
polyphagia, FOOD AND NUTRITION
polyphagian, FOOD AND NUTRITION
polyphagic, FOOD AND NUTRITION
polyphagous, FOOD AND NUTRITION
polyphagy, FOOD AND NUTRITION
polyphobia, FEAR
polypragmacy, BEHAVIOR
polypragmatic, BEHAVIOR
polypragmatism, BEHAVIOR
polypragmatist, BEHAVIOR
polypragmaty, BEHAVIOR
polypsychic, SOUL
polypsychical, SOUL
polypsychism, SOUL
polytheism, GOD AND GODS
polytheist, GOD AND GODS
polytonal, MUSIC
polytonalism, MUSIC
polytonalist, MUSIC
polytonality, MUSIC
pomologist, BOTANY
pomology, BOTANY
ponerology, EVIL, THEOLOGY
ponophobia, FATIGUE
Pop Art, ART
popeism, CATHOLICISM
popery, CATHOLICISM
Poplarism, POVERTY
Poplarist, POVERTY
popular sovereignty, POLITICS
populism, POLITICS
populist, POLITICS
populistic, POLITICS
poriomania, DISEASE AND ILLNESS
porism, MATHEMATICS
porismatic, MATHEMATICS
pornerastic, BEHAVIOR
portiforium, CATHOLICISM
portmanteau, WORDS
positivism, PHILOSOPHY
positivist, PHILOSOPHY
positivistic, PHILOSOPHY
posologic, MEDICAL SPECIALTIES
posological, MEDICAL SPECIALTIES
posology, MEDICAL SPECIALTIES
Post-Impressionism, ART

Post-Impressionist, ART
post-mortem, CORPSE
potamological, RIVERS
potamologist, RIVERS
potamology, RIVERS
potamophobia, RIVERS
potanadromous, FISH
powwow, MAGIC
powwowism, MAGIC
pragmaticist, PHILOSOPHY
pragmatism, PHILOSOPHY
pragmatist, PHILOSOPHY
pragmatistic, PHILOSOPHY
pragmatistism, PHILOSOPHY
praxeological, BEHAVIOR
praxeology, BEHAVIOR
praxiology, BEHAVIOR
precisionism, ATTITUDES
precisionist, ATTITUDES
precisionistic, ATTITUDES
predestinarian, THEOLOGY
predestinarianism, THEOLOGY
predestination, THEOLOGY
pregnancy, PREGNANCY
pre-Raphaelite, ART
pre-Raphaelitism, ART
Presbyterian, PROTESTANTISM
Presbyterianism, PROTESTANTISM
prestidigitation, HANDS, MAGIC
prestidigitator, HANDS, MAGIC
prestidigitatorial, HANDS, MAGIC
prestidigitatory, HANDS, MAGIC
prestigiation, HANDS
preterism, CHRISTIANITY
preterist, CHRISTIANITY
prevaricator, TRUTH
priapism, SEX
priapismic, SEX
primitivism, ART
primitivist, ART
primitivistic, ART
primordialism, EVOLUTION
Priscillianism, HERESY
Priscillianist, HERESY
probabilism, PHILOSOPHY
probabilist, PHILOSOPHY
probabilistic, PHILOSOPHY
proctologic, MEDICAL SPECIALTIES
proctological, MEDICAL SPECIALTIES
proctologist, MEDICAL SPECIALTIES
proctology, MEDICAL SPECIALTIES
proctophobia, PHOBIAS

professional, ATTITUDES
professionalism, ATTITUDES
prognostication, FUTURE
prognosticative, FUTURE
prognosticator, FUTURE
progressism, POLITICS
progressivism, POLITICS
progressivist, POLITICS
Prohibition, ALCOHOL
prohibitionism, ALCOHOL
prohibitionist, ALCOHOL
proletarian, POLITICS
proletarianism, POLITICS
prolicidal, CHILD
prolicide, CHILD
propaedeutic, LEARNING
propaedeutical, LEARNING
propaedeutics, LEARNING
propagandism, MEDIA
propagandist, MEDIA
propagandistic, MEDIA
proselyte, CONVERT
proselyter, CONVERT
proselytism, CONVERT
proselytist, CONVERT
proselytistic, CONVERT
prosodic, VERSE
prosodical, VERSE
prosodist, VERSE
prosody, VERSE
prosopographer, FACE
prosopography, FACE
protectionism, ECONOMICS
protectionist, ECONOMICS
proteinphobia, PHOBIAS
protervity, BEHAVIOR
Protestant, CHRISTIANITY
Protestantism, CHRISTIANITY
provenance, ORIGINS
proverbialism, LANGUAGE STYLES
proverbialist, LANGUAGE STYLES
provincialism, LANGUAGE
proxenetism, SEX
psalmodial, MUSIC
psalmodic, MUSIC
psalmodical, MUSIC
psalmodist, MUSIC
psalmody, MUSIC
psephological, POLITICS
psephologist, POLITICS
psephology, POLITICS, ROCKS
pseudandrous, WRITERS

pseudandry, WRITERS
pseudepigrapha, BIBLE
pseudepigraphic, BIBLE
pseudepigraphical, BIBLE
pseudepigraphous, BIBLE
pseudogynous, WRITERS
pseudogyny, WRITERS
pseudomania, LIES AND LYING
psilanthropic, CHRIST
psilanthropism, CHRIST
psilanthropist, CHRIST
psilology, LANGUAGE STYLES
psittacism, SPEECH
psittacosis, BIRDS
psittacotic, BIRDS
psychagogic, SOUL
psychagogics, BEHAVIOR
psychagogue, BEHAVIOR, SOUL
psychagogy, BEHAVIOR, SOUL
psychiatric, MEDICAL SPECIALTIES
psychiatrist, MEDICAL SPECIALTIES
psychiatry, MEDICAL SPECIALTIES
psychism, MAN
psychoanalysis, MENTAL STATES
psychoanalyst, MENTAL STATES
psychoanalytic, MENTAL STATES
psychobiologic, BIOLOGY, MIND
psychobiological, BIOLOGY, MIND
psychobiologist, BIOLOGY, MIND
psychobiology, BIOLOGY, MIND
psychodiagnostic, MENTAL STATES
psychodiagnostics, MENTAL STATES
psychodynamic, MENTAL STATES
psychodynamics, MENTAL STATES
psychogenic, DISEASE AND ILLNESS
psychogenicity, DISEASE AND ILLNESS
psychographic, SPIRITS AND SPIRITUALISM
psychography, SPIRITS AND SPIRITUALISM
psycholepsy, MENTAL STATES
psycholeptic, MENTAL STATES
psycholinguist, LINGUISTICS
psycholinguistic, LINGUISTICS
psycholinguistics, LINGUISTICS
psychologic, MIND
psychological, MIND
psychologist, MIND
psychology, MIND
psychometric, MENTAL STATES
psychometrics, MENTAL STATES
psychometrist, MENTAL STATES
psychometry, MENTAL STATES
psychopannychian, CHRISTIANITY

psychopannychism, CHRISTIANITY
psychopannychist, CHRISTIANITY
psychopannychistic, CHRISTIANITY
psychopath, MIND
psychopathic, DISEASE AND ILLNESS, MIND
psychopathist, MENTAL STATES
psychopathologic, MEDICAL SPECIALTIES,
    MENTAL STATES
psychopathological, MEDICAL SPECIALTIES,
    MENTAL STATES
psychopathologist, MEDICAL SPECIALTIES,
    MENTAL STATES
psychopathology, MEDICAL SPECIALTIES, MENTAL
    STATES
psychopathy, DISEASE AND ILLNESS, MIND
psychopharmacologic, MENTAL STATES
psychopharmacological, MENTAL STATES
psychopharmacology, MENTAL STATES
psychophobia, MIND
psychophysic, MIND
psychophysical, MIND
psychophysicist, MIND
psychophysics, MIND
psychorrhagic, SOUL
psychorrhagy, SOUL
psychosomatic, MEDICAL SPECIALTIES
psychosomaticist, MEDICAL SPECIALTIES
psychosomatics, MEDICAL SPECIALTIES
psychostatic, MENTAL STATES
psychostatical, MENTAL STATES
psychostatics, MENTAL STATES
psychosurgeon, BRAIN
psychosurgery, BRAIN
psychotheism, GOD AND GODS
psychotherapeutic, MENTAL STATES
psychotherapist, MENTAL STATES, REMEDIES
psychotherapy, MENTAL STATES, REMEDIES
psychrometric, DAMPNESS
psychrometrical, DAMPNESS
psychrometry, DAMPNESS
psychrophobia, COLD, PHOBIAS
pteridologist, BOTANY
pteridology, BOTANY
pterylography, BIRDS
pterylology, BIRDS
ptochocracy, GOVERNMENT, POVERTY
ptochology, POVERTY
Ptolemaic system, the, ASTRONOMY
Ptolemaism, ASTRONOMY
Ptolemaist, ASTRONOMY
ptyalism, POISON
publicist, LAW, MEDIA

pugilism, BOXING
pugilist, BOXING
pugilistic, BOXING
Puritan, PROTESTANTISM
Puritanism, PROTESTANTISM
purposivism, PHILOSOPHY
purposivist, PHILOSOPHY
pusillanimity, COWARDICE
pusillanimous, COWARDICE
putschism, FASCISM
putschist, FASCISM
pyelographic, X-RAYS
pyelography, X-RAYS
pyknic, ANATOMY
pyragravure, ART
pyretology, DISEASE AND ILLNESS
pyrexiophobia, PHOBIAS
pyrochromatography, FOSSILS
pyrogenic, FIRE
pyrogenous, FIRE
pyrograph, FIRE
pyrographer, ART, FIRE
pyrographic, ART, FIRE
pyrography, ART, FIRE
pyrolatry, FIRE
pyromancy, FIRE
pyromania, FIRE
pyrophobia, FIRE, PHOBIAS
pyrotechnic, FIREWORKS
pyrotechnical, FIREWORKS
pyrotechnician, FIREWORKS
pyrotechnics, FIREWORKS
pyrotechnist, FIREWORKS
pyrotechny, FIREWORKS
Pyrrhonian, PHILOSOPHY
Pyrrhonic, PHILOSOPHY
Pyrrhonism, PHILOSOPHY
Pyrrhonist, PHILOSOPHY
Pythagorean, MATHEMATICS
Pythagoreanism, MATHEMATICS
Pythagorism, MATHEMATICS
Pythagorist, MATHEMATICS
pythoness, FUTURE

Q

Quaker, PROTESTANTISM
Quakerdom, PROTESTANTISM
Quakerism, PROTESTANTISM
quietism, HERESY
quietist, HERESY

quisling, TREASON
quixotic, BEHAVIOR
quixotical, BEHAVIOR
Quixotism, BEHAVIOR

R

rabbinic, JUDAISM
rabbinical, JUDAISM
rabbinism, JUDAISM
rabulism, BEHAVIOR
rabulistic, BEHAVIOR
rabulous, BEHAVIOR
racialism, RACE
racialist, RACE
racialistic, RACE
racism, ATTITUDES
racist, ATTITUDES
radar, AVIATION
radicalism, POLITICS
radiesthesia, RADIATION
radiesthetic, RADIATION
radioastronomy, ASTRONOMY
radiocarbon dating, TIME
radiogenetics, HEREDITY
radiogenic, HEREDITY
radiographer, X-RAYS
radiographic, X-RAYS
radiographical, X-RAYS
radiography, X-RAYS
radiologic, X-RAYS
radiological, X-RAYS
radiologist, X-RAYS
radiology, X-RAYS
radiotherapeutic, X-RAYS
radiotherapist, X-RAYS
radiotherapy, X-RAYS
Ramaism, HINDUISM
Ramaite, HINDUISM
Rappite, COMMUNALISM
rationalism, PHILOSOPHY
rationalist, PHILOSOPHY
rationalistic, PHILOSOPHY
reactological, PSYCHOLOGY
reactologist, PSYCHOLOGY
reactology, PSYCHOLOGY
Realism, ART
realism, PHILOSOPHY
Realist, ART
realist, PHILOSOPHY
rebus, WRITING

receptionism, THEOLOGY
receptionist, THEOLOGY
recidivism, CRIME
recidivist, CRIME
recidivistic, CRIME
recidivous, CRIME
red-tapeism, BUREAUCRACY
red-tapism, BUREAUCRACY
reflexological, PSYCHOLOGY
reflexologist, PSYCHOLOGY
reflexology, PSYCHOLOGY
regalism, GOVERNMENT
regicidal, KILLING
regicide, KILLING
regicidism, KILLING
regionalism, LITERATURE
regionalist, LITERATURE
regionalistic, LITERATURE
relationism, PHILOSOPHY
relationist, PHILOSOPHY
relativism, PHILOSOPHY
relativist, PHILOSOPHY
relativistic, PHILOSOPHY
religious, MONKS
Renaissance Revivalism, ARCHITECTURE
representationalism, ART
reprography, COPYING, PHOTOGRAPHY
republicanism, GOVERNMENT
resistentialism, INANIMATE OBJECTS
restitutionism, PROTESTANTISM
restorationism, PROTESTANTISM
restorationist, PROTESTANTISM
resurrectionism, CORPSE
resurrection man, CORPSE
retinoscopist, EYES
retinoscopy, EYES
revisionism, COMMUNISM
revisionist, COMMUNISM
revivalism, PROTESTANTISM
revivalist, PROTESTANTISM
revivalistic, PROTESTANTISM
Rexist, FASCISM
rhabdomancy, WATER
rhabdophobia, PHOBIAS
rhapsodism, VERSE
rhapsodist, VERSE
rhapsodomancy, VERSE
rheologic, MATTER
rheological, MATTER
rheologist, MATTER
rheology, MATTER
rheumatic, DISEASE AND ILLNESS

rheumatism, DISEASE AND ILLNESS
rheumatologist, DISEASE AND ILLNESS
rheumatology, DISEASE AND ILLNESS
rhinologic, NOSE
rhinological, NOSE
rhinologist, NOSE
rhinology, NOSE
rhopalic, VERSE
rhopalism, VERSE
rhopalist, VERSE
rhotacism, PRONUNCIATION
rhotacistic, PRONUNCIATION
rhotaticize, PRONUNCIATION
rhyparographer, OBSCENITY
rhyparographic, OBSCENITY
rhyparography, OBSCENITY
rhypophobia, PHOBIAS
rigid, PHYSICAL CHARACTERISTICS
rigidity, PHYSICAL CHARACTERISTICS
rigorism, PHILOSOPHY
risibility, LAUGHTER
ritualism, ATTITUDES
ritualist, ATTITUDES
ritualistic, ATTITUDES
robotism, AUTOMATION
robotistic, AUTOMATION
Romanticism, ART
Romanticist, ART
Ronsardism, LANGUAGE STYLES
Rosicrucian, RELIGION
Rosicrucianism, RELIGION
Rosminian, PHILOSOPHY
Rosminianism, PHILOSOPHY
royalism, POLITICS
royalist, POLITICS
royalistic, POLITICS
rubrician, ATTITUDES
rubricism, ATTITUDES
rumination, MEDITATION, THINKING
ruminative, MEDITATION, THINKING
ruminator, MEDITATION, THINKING
runological, WRITING
runologist, WRITING
runology, WRITING
ruralism, ATTITUDES
ruralist, ATTITUDES
Russellites, PROTESTANTISM
Russophobia, PHOBIAS

S

Sabaism, ASTRONOMY
sabbatarian, CHRISTIANITY
Sabbatarian, JUDAISM
sabbatarianism, CHRISTIANITY
Sabbatarianism, JUDAISM
Sabellian, HERESY
Sabellianism, HERESY
sacerdotal, CATHOLICISM
sacerdotalism, CATHOLICISM
sacramentalism, CHRISTIANITY
sacramentalist, CHRISTIANITY
sacrist, CHURCH
Sadducean, JUDAISM
Sadducee, JUDAISM
Sadduceeism, JUDAISM
Sadducism, JUDAISM
sadism, PAIN
sadist, PAIN
sadistic, PAIN
sadomasochism, PAIN
sadomasochist, PAIN
sadomasochistic, PAIN
sagittary, ARROWS
sagittate, ARROWS
Saivism, HINDUISM
Saktism, HINDUISM
salivation, POISON
salmonellosis, POISON
salvational, PROTESTANTISM
salvationism, PROTESTANTISM
salvationist, PROTESTANTISM
sanscullotic, POLITICS
sanscullotish, POLITICS
sanscullotism, POLITICS
sanscullotist, POLITICS
Sanusi, ISLAM
Sanusism, ISLAM
Sanusiya, ISLAM
saponaceous, PERSONALITY
saponacity, PERSONALITY
saprophyte, PLANTS
saprophytic, PLANTS
saprophytism, PLANTS
sarcology, MEDICAL SPECIALTIES
sardonicism, LANGUAGE STYLES
Satanism, DEVIL
Satanist, DEVIL
Satanophobia, PHOBIAS
sati, HINDUISM

saturnism, POISON
satyr, SEX
satyriasis, SEX
satyric, SEX
satyrism, SEX
satyromania, SEX
scabiophobia, PHOBIAS
scatologic, OBSCENITY
scatological, OBSCENITY
scatology, FOSSILS, OBSCENITY
scenarist, FILMS
scenographer, DRAWING
scenographic, DRAWING
scenographical, DRAWING
scenography, DRAWING
scepticism, ATTITUDES
Scepticism, PHILOSOPHY
schoenabatist, TIGHTROPE WALKING
Scholastic, THEOLOGY
Scholasticism, THEOLOGY
scholiast, LITERARY STUDY
scholiastic, LITERARY STUDY
scientific, MAN
scientism, ATTITUDES
scientistic, ATTITUDES
Scientologist, RELIGION
Scientology, RELIGION
scintilla, SIZE
sciolism, KNOWLEDGE
sciolist, KNOWLEDGE
sciolistic, KNOWLEDGE
sciolous, KNOWLEDGE
sciosophist, KNOWLEDGE
sciosophy, KNOWLEDGE
scoleciphobia, WORMS
scopophilia, SEX
scopophiliac, SEX
scopophilic, SEX
scopophobia, PHOBIAS
scoptophilia, SEX
scoptophobia, PHOBIAS
Scoticism, LANGUAGE
Scotism, PHILOSOPHY
scotist, PHILOSOPHY
Scotistic, PHILOSOPHY
scotistical, PHILOSOPHY
scotophobia, DARKNESS
Scotticism, LANGUAGE
Scottishism, LANGUAGE
scriptorium, MANUSCRIPTS
Scripturalism, BIBLE, CATHOLICISM
Second Adventist, PROTESTANTISM

sectarian, PROTESTANTISM
sectarianism, PROTESTANTISM
secularism, RELIGION
secularist, RELIGION
secularistic, RELIGION
segregationist, RACE
seism, EARTHQUAKES
seismic, EARTHQUAKES
seismicity, EARTHQUAKES
seismism, EARTHQUAKES
seismogram, EARTHQUAKES
seismograph, EARTHQUAKES
seismographer, EARTHQUAKES
seismographic, EARTHQUAKES
seismographical, EARTHQUAKES
seismography, EARTHQUAKES
seismologic, EARTHQUAKES
seismological, EARTHQUAKES
seismologist, EARTHQUAKES
seismology, EARTHQUAKES
seismometer, EARTHQUAKES
seismometric, EARTHQUAKES
seismometry, EARTHQUAKES
selenographer, ASTRONOMY, MOON
selenographic, ASTRONOMY, MOON
selenographical, ASTRONOMY, MOON
selenographist, ASTRONOMY, MOON
selenography, ASTRONOMY, MOON
selenolatry, MOON
selenological, MOON
selenologist, MOON
selenology, MOON
selenomancy, MOON
semantic, LANGUAGE, WORDS
semantician, WORDS
semanticist, LANGUAGE, WORDS
semantics, LANGUAGE, WORDS
semasiological, WORDS
semasiologist, WORDS
semasiology, WORDS
sematology, LANGUAGE
semeiologic, LANGUAGE, WORDS
semeiological, LANGUAGE, WORDS
semeiologist, LANGUAGE, WORDS
semeiology, DISEASE AND ILLNESS, LANGUAGE,
    WORDS
semeiotic, WORDS
semiology, LANGUAGE, WORDS
semiotic, WORDS
semiotics, WORDS
Semi-Pelagianism, HERESY
Semiticism, LANGUAGE

semology, LANGUAGE
senectitude, OLD AGE
senicidal, OLD AGE
senicide, OLD AGE
sensationalism, LITERATURE, PHILOSOPHY
sensationalist, LITERATURE, PHILOSOPHY
sensationalistic, LITERATURE, PHILOSOPHY
sensualism, PHILOSOPHY
sentimentalism, LITERATURE
sentimentalist, LITERATURE
Senusi, ISLAM
Senusism, ISLAM
Senusiya, ISLAM
separatism, POLITICS
separatist, POLITICS
Sepher Torah, JUDAISM
sequacious, BEHAVIOR
sequaciousness, BEHAVIOR
sequacity, BEHAVIOR
seraphism, BEHAVIOR
serendipitous, CHANCE
serendipity, CHANCE
serfism, GOVERNMENT
serigrapher, ART
serigraphy, ART
servomechanical, AUTOMATION
servomechanism, AUTOMATION
sesquipedal, WORDS
sesquipedalian, WORDS
sesquipedalianism, WORDS
sesquipedalism, WORDS
sesquipedality, WORDS
Sethian, GOD AND GODS
Sethite, GOD AND GODS
sexdigitism, HANDS
sexological, SEX
sexologist, SEX
sexology, SEX
sexual anesthesia, SEX
shadowgraphy, X-RAYS
Shaker, PROTESTANTISM
Shakerism, PROTESTANTISM
Shakta, HINDUISM
Shakti, HINDUISM
Shaktism, HINDUISM
shamanism, RELIGION
shamanist, RELIGION
shamanistic, RELIGION
Shandyism, BEHAVIOR
Shiism, ISLAM
Shiite, ISLAM
Shinto, RELIGION

Shintoism, RELIGION
Shintoistic, RELIGION
Shivaism, HINDUISM
sialism, DISEASE AND ILLNESS
sialismus, DISEASE AND ILLNESS
siderodromophobia, RAILROADS
sideromancy, ASTRONOMY
siderophobia, PHOBIAS
sigillographer, SEALS
sigillographic, SEALS
sigillography, SEALS
sigmatism, SPEECH
sillographer, LITERATURE
sillography, LITERATURE
silviculture, TREES
silviculturist, TREES
similarity, AGREEMENT
simoniac, RELIGION
simoniacal, RELIGION
simonism, CATHOLICISM, RELIGION
simonist, RELIGION
simplism, ARGUMENT
simplistic, ARGUMENT
Sinarquism, POLITICS
Sinarquist, POLITICS
sindology, DEATH
sinecureship, WORK
sinecurism, WORK
sinecurist, WORK
Sinicism, CHINA
Sinological, CHINA
Sinologist, CHINA
Sinology, CHINA
Sinonism, LIES AND LYING
sitiophobia, FOOD AND NUTRITION
sitophobia, FOOD AND NUTRITION
Sivaism, HINDUISM
Sivaite, HINDUISM
skeptic, ATTITUDES
Skeptic, PHILOSOPHY
skeptical, ATTITUDES
skepticism, ATTITUDES
Skepticism, PHILOSOPHY
skiagram, DRAWING
skiagrapher, DRAWING
skiagraphy, DRAWING
skiascopy, EYES
slangism, LANGUAGE
Slavicism, LANGUAGE
snob, ATTITUDES
snobbish, ATTITUDES
snobbism, ATTITUDES

snobby, ATTITUDES
social anthropology, ANTHROPOLOGY
socialism, POLITICS
socialist, POLITICS
socialistic, POLITICS
Socinian, HERESY
Socinianism, HERESY
sociogram, MAN, SOCIETY
sociographic, MAN
sociography, MAN
sociologic, SOCIETY
sociological, MAN, SOCIETY
sociologist, MAN, SOCIETY
sociology, MAN, SOCIETY
sociometric, MAN, SOCIETY
sociometrist, MAN, SOCIETY
sociometry, MAN, SOCIETY
solarism, SUN
solarist, SUN
solecism, GRAMMAR, SPEECH
solecist, GRAMMAR, SPEECH
solecistic, GRAMMAR, SPEECH
solecistical, GRAMMAR, SPEECH
solidarism, SOCIETY
solidarist, SOCIETY
solidaristic, SOCIETY
solipsism, PHILOSOPHY
solipsist, PHILOSOPHY
solipsistic, PHILOSOPHY
somatism, MEDICAL SPECIALTIES
somatist, MEDICAL SPECIALTIES
somatogenic, DISEASE AND ILLNESS
somatologic, BODIES
somatological, BODIES
somatology, ANTHROPOLOGY, BODIES, MATTER
somnambulant, SLEEP
somnambulism, SLEEP
somnambulist, SLEEP
somnambulistic, SLEEP
somniloquism, SLEEP
somniloquist, SLEEP
somniloquous, SLEEP
somnolence, SLEEP
somnolency, SLEEP
somnolent, SLEEP
Sophianism, EASTERN ORTHODOXY
Sophianist, EASTERN ORTHODOXY
Sophiology, EASTERN ORTHODOXY
sophiology, IDEAS
sophism, ARGUMENT
sophister, ARGUMENT
sophistic, ARGUMENT

sorcerer, MAGIC
sorcerous, MAGIC
sorcery, MAGIC
Soroptimist, WOMEN
sororicidal, MURDER
sororicide, MURDER
sortition, GAMBLING
soteriologic, CHRIST
soteriological, CHRIST
soteriology, CHRIST
spagyrist, ALCHEMY
Spartacist, POLITICS
spartan, ATTITUDES
spartanism, ATTITUDES
spasmodic, BEHAVIOR
spasmodical, BEHAVIOR
spasmodism, BEHAVIOR
spasmodist, BEHAVIOR
spasmophile, DISEASE AND ILLNESS
spasmophilia, DISEASE AND ILLNESS
speaking in tongues, SPEECH
specialism, KNOWLEDGE
specialist, KNOWLEDGE
specialistic, KNOWLEDGE
spectrological, GHOSTS
spectrology, GHOSTS
spectrophobia, PHOBIAS
speculation, THINKING
speculative, THINKING
speculator, THINKING
spelaeology, CAVES
speleological, CAVES
speleologist, CAVES
speleology, CAVES
spelunk, CAVES
spelunker, CAVES
sphacelation, DECADENCE
sphenographer, WRITING
sphenographic, WRITING
sphenographist, WRITING
sphenography, WRITING
sphragistic, SEALS
sphragistics, SEALS
sphygmology, ARTERIES
spiritualism, SPIRITS AND SPIRITUALISM
spiritualist, SPIRITS AND SPIRITUALISM
spiritualistic, SPIRITS AND SPIRITUALISM
spirometer, BODIES
spirometry, BODIES
splanchnology, BODIES
spontaneous generation, LIFE
spookology, GHOSTS

Spoonerism, LANGUAGE STYLES
spoonerize, LANGUAGE STYLES
Stakhanovism, COMMUNISM
Stakhanovite, COMMUNISM
Stalinism, COMMUNISM
Stalinist, COMMUNISM
Stalinistic, COMMUNISM
stasibasiphobia, WALKING
stateism, GOVERNMENT
statism, GOVERNMENT
statist, GOVERNMENT
steganographer, WORDS
steganography, WORDS
stenographer, WRITING
stenographic, WRITING
stenographical, WRITING
stenographist, WRITING
stenography, WRITING
stenotypic, WRITING
stenotypist, WRITING
stenotypy, WRITING
stercoranism, THEOLOGY
stercoranist, THEOLOGY
stercorarian, THEOLOGY
stereographer, DRAWING
stereographic, DRAWING
stereographical, DRAWING
stereography, DRAWING
stethographic, MEDICAL SPECIALTIES
stethography, MEDICAL SPECIALTIES
stichomancy, VERSE
stichometric, LANGUAGE STYLES
stichometrical, LANGUAGE STYLES
stichometry, LANGUAGE STYLES
stigmata, CATHOLICISM
stigmatic, CATHOLICISM
stigmatism, CATHOLICISM
stignomancy, WRITING
stoic, PAIN, PLEASURE
Stoic, PHILOSOPHY
stoical, PAIN, PLEASURE
stoicism, PAIN, PLEASURE
Stoicism, PHILOSOPHY
stomatologic, MEDICAL SPECIALTIES
stomatological, MEDICAL SPECIALTIES
stomatologist, MEDICAL SPECIALTIES
stomatology, MEDICAL SPECIALTIES
storiologist, LITERARY STUDY
storiology, LITERARY STUDY
stratigrapher, GEOLOGY
stratigraphic, GEOLOGY
stratigraphical, GEOLOGY

stratigraphy, GEOLOGY
stratocracy, GOVERNMENT
stratographer, WAR
stratography, WAR
strephosymbolia, READING
strephosymbolic, READING
structuralism, ARCHITECTURE, LINGUISTICS
structuralist, LINGUISTICS
structural linguistics, LINGUISTICS
Stundism, PROTESTANTISM
Stundist, PROTESTANTISM
subjectivism, ATTITUDES, PHILOSOPHY
subjectivist, PHILOSOPHY
subjectivistic, PHILOSOPHY
subjectivity, ATTITUDES
subordinationism, CHRISTIANITY
subordinationist, CHRISTIANITY
suburbanism, ATTITUDES
succubae, DEMONS
succubi, DEMONS
succubus, DEMONS
suffragism, POLITICS
suffragist, POLITICS
Sufi, ISLAM
Sufiism, ISLAM
Sufism, ISLAM
Sumerologist, LANGUAGE
Sumerology, LANGUAGE
Sunnism, ISLAM
Sunnite, ISLAM
Superrealism, ART
supersonic, AVIATION
supralapsarian, CHRISTIANITY
supralapsarianism, CHRISTIANITY
Surrealism, ART
Surrealist, ART
Surrealistic, ART
suttee, HINDUISM
sutteeism, HINDUISM
Swedenborgian, PROTESTANTISM
Swedenborgianism, PROTESTANTISM
Swedenborgism, PROTESTANTISM
sybarite, BEHAVIOR
sybaritic, BEHAVIOR
sybaritism, BEHAVIOR
sybotism, ANIMALS
sycophant, BEHAVIOR
sycophantic, BEHAVIOR
sycophantism, BEHAVIOR
syllabism, WRITING
syllepsis, FIGURES OF SPEECH, GRAMMAR
sylleptic, FIGURES OF SPEECH

syllogism, ARGUMENT
syllogistic, ARGUMENT
sylviculture, TREES
symbiosis, BIOLOGY
symbiotic, BIOLOGY
symbolaeographer, LAW
symbolaeography, LAW
Symbolism, VERSE
Symbolist, VERSE
symetallic, MONEY
symmetalism, MONEY
symptomatologic, DISEASE AND ILLNESS
symptomatological, DISEASE AND ILLNESS
symptomatology, DISEASE AND ILLNESS
synaeresis, SPEECH
synaesthesia, PERCEPTION
synaesthetic, PERCEPTION
synaxarist, EASTERN ORTHODOXY
synchronic linguistics, LINGUISTICS
synchronism, ART, TIME
synchronist, ART
synchronistic, ART, TIME
synchronistical, TIME
syncretic, PHILOSOPHY, PROTESTANTISM
syncretical, PHILOSOPHY, PROTESTANTISM
syncretism, PHILOSOPHY, PROTESTANTISM
syncretistic, PHILOSOPHY, PROTESTANTISM
syncretistical, PHILOSOPHY, PROTESTANTISM
syndicalism, COMMUNISM, POLITICS
syndicalist, COMMUNISM, POLITICS
syndicalistic, COMMUNISM, POLITICS
synecdoche, FIGURES OF SPEECH
synecdochic, FIGURES OF SPEECH
synecdochical, FIGURES OF SPEECH
synecologic, ENVIRONMENT
synecological, ENVIRONMENT
synecology, BIOLOGY, ENVIRONMENT
synectics, BRAIN
syneresis, SPEECH
synergism, DRUGS, HERESY
synergist, HERESY
synergistic, DRUGS, HERESY
synergy, DRUGS
synesthesia, PERCEPTION
synesthetic, PERCEPTION
synodal, CATHOLICISM
synodical, CATHOLICISM
synodist, CATHOLICISM
synoptic, BIBLE
synoptist, BIBLE
syphiliphobia, PHOBIAS
syphilophobia, PHOBIAS

systematician, CLASSIFICATION
systematics, CLASSIFICATION
systematist, CLASSIFICATION
systematy, CLASSIFICATION

T

tabophobia, PHOBIAS
Tachism, ART
Tachisme, ART
Tachist, ART
Tachiste, ART
tachygrapher, WRITING
tachygraphic, WRITING
tachygraphical, WRITING
tachygraphist, WRITING
tachygraphy, WRITING
talisman, MAGIC
talismanic, MAGIC
talismanist, ISLAM
Talmudic, JUDAISM
Talmudism, JUDAISM
Talmudist, JUDAISM
tanist, GOVERNMENT
tanistry, GOVERNMENT
Tantrayana, BUDDHISM
Tantrayanic, BUDDHISM
Tantric, HINDUISM
Tantrism, HINDUISM
Tantrist, HINDUISM
Taoism, RELIGION
taphephobia, BURYING
taphiphobia, BURYING
taphophilia, BURYING, DEATH
taphophobia, BURYING
tapinophobia, PHOBIAS
tarantism, DISEASE AND ILLNESS
Targumic, BIBLE
Targumist, BIBLE
Targumistic, BIBLE
tauricide, BULLS
taurobolium, BULLS
tauroboly, BULLS
taurokathapsia, BULLS
tauromachian, BULLS
tauromachic, BULLS
tauromachy, BULLS
tauromaquia, BULLS
Taurus, BULLS
tautologism, WORDS
taxidermist, ANIMALS

taxidermy, ANIMALS
taxology, CLASSIFICATION
taxonomic, CLASSIFICATION
taxonomical, CLASSIFICATION
taxonomist, CLASSIFICATION
taxonomy, CLASSIFICATION
Taylorism, WORK
Technocracy, GOVERNMENT
Technocrat, GOVERNMENT
Technocratic, GOVERNMENT
tecnology, CHILD
teetotaler, ALCOHOL
teetotalism, ALCOHOL
tegestologist, BEER
tegestology, BEER
telegony, HEREDITY
telekinesis, GRAVITY
telekinetic, GRAVITY
telemeteorgraphic, WEATHER
telemeteorography, WEATHER
teleologic, PHILOSOPHY
teleological, ENDS, PHILOSOPHY
teleologism, COSMOLOGY, ENDS
teleologist, COSMOLOGY, ENDS, PHILOSOPHY
teleology, COSMOLOGY, ENDS, PHILOSOPHY
teleophobia, PHOBIAS
telepathic, PSYCHOLOGY
telepathist, PSYCHOLOGY
telepathy, PSYCHOLOGY
telephonophobia, PHOBIAS
telephotographic, PHOTOGRAPHY
telephotography, PHOTOGRAPHY
teleportation, GRAVITY
telic, ENDS
tellurian, EARTH
tellurist, EARTH
telmatology, GEOGRAPHY
tepid, HEAT
tepidity, HEAT
teratism, MONSTERS
teratoid, MONSTERS
teratological, GROWTH, LITERATURE, MONSTERS
teratologist, BIOLOGY, GROWTH, LITERATURE,
    MONSTERS
teratology, BIOLOGY, GROWTH, LITERATURE,
    MONSTERS
teratophobia, MONSTERS
teratosis, MONSTERS
territorialism, POLITICS
territorialist, POLITICS
territorial system, POLITICS
terrorism, POLITICS

terrorist, POLITICS
terroristic, POLITICS
tetrarch, GOVERNMENT
tetrarchate, GOVERNMENT
tetrarchic, GOVERNMENT
tetrarchical, GOVERNMENT
tetrarchy, GOVERNMENT
Teutonophobia, PHOBIAS
Teutophobia, PHOBIAS
Thalassa, SEA
thalassocracy, SEA
thalassocrat, SEA
thalassographer, SEA
thalassographic, SEA
thalassographical, SEA
thalassography, SEA
thalassophobia, SEA
thanatism, DEATH
thanatoid, DEATH
thanatological, DEATH
thanatology, DEATH
thanatophobia, CORPSE
thaumatology, MIRACLES
thaumaturge, MIRACLES
thaumaturgic, MIRACLES
thaumaturgical, MIRACLES
thaumaturgist, MIRACLES
thaumaturgus, MIRACLES
thaumaturgy, MIRACLES
theanthropic, CHRIST
theanthropism, CHRIST, GOD AND GODS
theanthropist, CHRIST, GOD AND GODS
theanthropology, CHRIST
theanthroposophy, GOD AND GODS
thearchic, GOVERNMENT
thearchy, GOVERNMENT
theatricalism, BEHAVIOR
theatrophobia, PHOBIAS
thebaism, POISON
theism, GOD AND GODS
theocentric, GOD AND GODS
theocentricity, GOD AND GODS
theocentrism, GOD AND GODS
theocracy, GOVERNMENT
theocrasia, GOD AND GODS
theocrasy, GOD AND GODS
theocrat, GOVERNMENT
theocratic, GOVERNMENT
theogonist, GOD AND GODS
theogony, GOD AND GODS
theolepsy, GOD AND GODS
theoleptic, GOD AND GODS

theological, GOD AND GODS
theologism, THEOLOGY
theologist, GOD AND GODS
theology, GOD AND GODS
theomachist, GOD AND GODS
theomachy, GOD AND GODS
theomancy, GOD AND GODS
theomania, GOD AND GODS, RELIGION
theomorphic, RELIGION
theomorphism, RELIGION
Theopaschite, HERESY
Theopaschitism, HERESY
theophanic, RELIGION
theophanous, RELIGION
theophany, RELIGION
theophilanthropic, RELIGION
theophilanthropism, RELIGION
theophilanthropist, RELIGION
theophobia, GOD AND GODS
theorematic, MATHEMATICS
theorematist, MATHEMATICS
theosophical, MYSTICISM
theosophism, MYSTICISM
theosophist, MYSTICISM
theosophy, MYSTICISM
therianthropism, ANIMALS
theriolatry, ANIMALS
theriomancy, ANIMALS
theriomorphic, ANIMALS
theriomorphism, ANIMALS
theriomorphous, ANIMALS
thermatology, HEAT
thermochemical, HEAT
thermochemist, HEAT
thermochemistry, HEAT
thermodynamic, HEAT
thermodynamical, HEAT
thermodynamicist, HEAT
thermodynamics, HEAT
thermogenesis, HEAT
thermogenic, HEAT
thermogenous, HEAT
thermographer, HEAT, PRINTING
thermographic, HEAT, PRINTING
thermography, HEAT, PRINTING
thermology, HEAT
thermoluminescence, HEAT
thermoluminescent, HEAT
thermolysis, HEAT
thermolytic, HEAT
thermometric, HEAT
thermometry, HEAT

thermonastic, PLANTS
thermonasty, PLANTS
thermoperiod, BIOLOGY
thermoperiodic, BIOLOGY, PLANTS
thermoperiodical, PLANTS
thermoperiodicity, PLANTS
thermoperiodism, BIOLOGY, PLANTS
thermophobia, HEAT
thermoscope, HEAT
thermoscopic, HEAT
thermotactic, HEAT
thermotaxic, HEAT
thermotaxis, HEAT
thermotherapy, HEAT
thermotics, HEAT
thermotropic, PLANTS
thermotropical, PLANTS
thermotropism, PLANTS
theurgic, GOD AND GODS, MAGIC
theurgical, GOD AND GODS, MAGIC
theurgist, GOD AND GODS, MAGIC
theurgy, GOD AND GODS, MAGIC
Thomism, PHILOSOPHY
Thomist, PHILOSOPHY
Thomistic, PHILOSOPHY
thremmatology, ANIMALS
threnodic, MUSIC
threnodist, MUSIC
threnody, MUSIC
thrombophilia, DISEASE AND ILLNESS
thug, HINDUISM
thuggee, HINDUISM
thuggeeism, HINDUISM
thuggery, HINDUISM
thyroidism, DISEASE AND ILLNESS
tidology, GRAVITY
timbrology, COLLECTIONS AND COLLECTING
time lapse photography, PHOTOGRAPHY
timocracy, GOVERNMENT
timocratic, GOVERNMENT
timocratical, GOVERNMENT
timology, VALUES
Timonism, BEHAVIOR
tintinabular, BELLS
tintinabulation, BELLS
Titoism, COMMUNISM
Titoist, COMMUNISM
tmesis, WORDS
toady, BEHAVIOR
toadyish, BEHAVIOR
toadyism, BEHAVIOR
tocology, BIRTH

tocophobia, BIRTH
tokology, BIRTH
tokophobia, BIRTH
tomographic, X-RAYS
tomography, X-RAYS
tomophobia, DISEASE AND ILLNESS, PHOBIAS
tonitrophobia, PHOBIAS
tonitruphobia, PHOBIAS
tonological, TUNING
tonology, TUNING
tonometer, TUNING
tonometric, TUNING
tonometrist, TUNING
tonometry, TUNING
topiarian, TREES
topiarist, TREES
topiary, TREES
topographer, MAPS
topographic, MAPS
topography, MAPS
topologic, GEOGRAPHY, MATHEMATICS
topological, GEOGRAPHY, MATHEMATICS
topologist, GEOGRAPHY, MATHEMATICS
topology, GEOGRAPHY, MATHEMATICS
toponym, NAMES
toponymic, NAMES
toponymical, NAMES
toponymy, NAMES
topophobe, PLACES
topophobia, PLACES
Torah, JUDAISM
torminal, PAIN
Tory, POLITICS
Toryish, POLITICS
Toryism, POLITICS
tosaphist, JUDAISM
tosaphoth, JUDAISM
total abstinence, ALCOHOL
totalitarian, GOVERNMENT
totalitarianism, GOVERNMENT
totalizator, GAMBLING
totemic, SOCIETY
totemism, SOCIETY
toxaemia, BLOOD
toxemia, BLOOD
toxemic, BLOOD
toxicologic, MEDICAL SPECIALTIES, POISON
toxicological, MEDICAL SPECIALTIES, POISON
toxicologist, MEDICAL SPECIALTIES, POISON
toxicology, MEDICAL SPECIALTIES, POISON
toxicomania, DRUGS
toxicophobia, POISON

toxiphobe, POISON
toxiphobia, POISON
toxiphobiac, POISON
toxophilite, ARCHERY
toxophily, ARCHERY
Tractarian, PROTESTANTISM
Tractarianism, PROTESTANTISM
traditionalism, ATTITUDES, CATHOLICISM
traditionalist, ATTITUDES, CATHOLICISM
traditionalistic, CATHOLICISM
traditionism, ATTITUDES
traducianism, SOUL
traducianist, SOUL
traducianistic, SOUL
tragic flaw, STRENGTH AND WEAKNESS
trampoline, ATHLETICS
trampoliner, ATHLETICS
trampolinist, ATHLETICS
transatlanticism, LANGUAGE
transcendentalism, PHILOSOPHY
transcendentalist, PHILOSOPHY
transcendentalistic, PHILOSOPHY
transformationalist, LINGUISTICS
transliteration, ALPHABET
transmigrationism, SOUL
transmutationist, ALCHEMY
transubstantiation, THEOLOGY
transubstantiationalist, THEOLOGY
transvestism, SEX
transvestitism, SEX
traulism, PRONUNCIATION
traumatologist, MEDICAL SPECIALTIES
traumatology, MEDICAL SPECIALTIES
traumatophilia, DISEASE AND ILLNESS
traumatophobia, PHOBIAS
treen, WOOD
tremophobia, PHOBIAS
triarchy, GOVERNMENT
tribade, HOMOSEXUALITY
tribadic, HOMOSEXUALITY
tribadism, HOMOSEXUALITY
tribady, HOMOSEXUALITY
tribalism, GOVERNMENT
tribology, PHYSICS
trichinophobia, PHOBIAS
trichoanesthesia, HAIR
trichobezoar, HAIR
trichologia, HAIR
trichologist, HAIR
trichology, HAIR
trichopathophobia, PHOBIAS
trichophobia, PHOBIAS

trichosis, HAIR
trichotillomania, HAIR
trichotomic, MAN
trichotomous, MAN
trichotomy, MAN
tricopathic, HAIR
tricopathy, HAIR
tricophagy, HAIR
tridecaphobia, PHOBIAS
trierarchy, DEFENSE
trinitarian, CHRIST
trinitarianism, CHRIST
triskaidekaphobia, PHOBIAS
tritheism, CHRISTIANITY, GOD AND GODS
tritheist, CHRISTIANITY, GOD AND GODS
tritheistic, CHRISTIANITY
tritheistical, CHRISTIANITY
troglodyte, ATTITUDES
troglodytic, ATTITUDES
troglodytism, ATTITUDES
tromometer, EARTHQUAKES
trophology, FOOD AND NUTRITION
tropism, MOVEMENT
tropistic, MOVEMENT
tropologic, FIGURES OF SPEECH
tropological, BIBLE, FIGURES OF SPEECH
tropology, BIBLE, FIGURES OF SPEECH
Trotskyism, COMMUNISM
Trotskyite, COMMUNISM
truism, TRUTH
truistic, TRUTH
truistical, TRUTH
tsarism, POLITICS
tsiology, FOOD AND NUTRITION
tuberculophobia, PHOBIAS
tuchungism, GOVERNMENT
tuism, LANGUAGE STYLES
tulipomania, PLANTS
tulipomaniac, PLANTS
tutiorism, PHILOSOPHY
tutiorist, PHILOSOPHY
tychism, EVOLUTION
typhlology, BLINDNESS
typhlophile, BLINDNESS
typhlosis, BLINDNESS
typhlotic, BLINDNESS
typmanites, DISEASE AND ILLNESS
tyrannicidal, KILLING
tyrannicide, KILLING
tyrannophobia, PHOBIAS
tyrology, LEARNING
tyromancy, CHEESE

tyrosemiophily, CHEESE
tzarism, POLITICS

U

Ubiquitarian, PROTESTANTISM
Ubiquitism, PROTESTANTISM
udometric, RAIN
udometry, RAIN
ultraism, ATTITUDES, POLITICS
ultraist, ATTITUDES, POLITICS
ultraistic, ATTITUDES, POLITICS
ultramontane, CATHOLICISM
ultramontanism, CATHOLICISM
ultramontanist, CATHOLICISM
ultramontanistic, CATHOLICISM
Uniat, CATHOLICISM
Uniate, CATHOLICISM
Uniatism, CATHOLICISM
unicameral, GOVERNMENT
unicameralism, GOVERNMENT
unicameralist, GOVERNMENT
unicism, PERSONALITY
unicist, PERSONALITY
unicity, PERSONALITY
uniformitarian, EVOLUTION, GEOLOGY
uniformitarianism, EVOLUTION, GEOLOGY
unitarian, CHRIST
Unitarian, PROTESTANTISM
unitarianism, CHRIST
Unitarianism, PROTESTANTISM
Universalism, PROTESTANTISM
Universalist, PROTESTANTISM
Universalistic, PROTESTANTISM
universology, COSMOLOGY
uranianism, ASTRONOMY, HOMOSEXUALITY
uranism, HOMOSEXUALITY
uranist, HOMOSEXUALITY
uranographer, ASTRONOMY
uranographic, ASTRONOMY
uranographical, ASTRONOMY
uranographist, ASTRONOMY
uranography, ASTRONOMY
uranology, ASTRONOMY
Uranophobia, PHOBIAS
urbanism, ATTITUDES
urbanistic, ATTITUDES
urbiculture, CITIES
uredinology, PLANTS
urning, HOMOSEXUALITY
urningism, HOMOSEXUALITY

urnism, HOMOSEXUALITY
urophobia, PHOBIAS
uteromania, SEX
utilitarian, ETHICS
utilitarianism, ETHICS
utopian, UTOPIA
utopianism, UTOPIA
utopian socialism, POLITICS
Utraquism, PROTESTANTISM
Utraquist, PROTESTANTISM
uxoricidal, WIFE
uxoricide, WIFE

V

vaccinophobia, PHOBIAS
vacuism, PHYSICS
vacuist, PHYSICS
vagabond, BEHAVIOR
vagabondage, BEHAVIOR
vagabondism, BEHAVIOR
Vaishnava, HINDUISM
Vaishnavism, HINDUISM
Vaishnavite, HINDUISM
Valentinian, HERESY
Valentinianism, HERESY, PHILOSOPHY
valet-de-place, GUIDE
valetudinarian, DISEASE AND ILLNESS, HEALTH
valetudinarianism, DISEASE AND ILLNESS, HEALTH
vassalism, GOVERNMENT
Vaticanism, CATHOLICISM
Vaticanist, CATHOLICISM
vaticidal, FUTURE
vaticide, FUTURE
vaticination, FUTURE
vaticinator, FUTURE
vectograph, PHOTOGRAPHY
vectographic, PHOTOGRAPHY
vectography, PHOTOGRAPHY
vecturist, COLLECTIONS AND COLLECTING
Vedaic, HINDUISM
Vedaism, HINDUISM
Vedantic, HINDUISM
Vedantism, HINDUISM
Vedic, HINDUISM
Vedism, HINDUISM
vegetarian, FOOD AND NUTRITION
vegetarianism, FOOD AND NUTRITION
venatic, HUNTING
venatical, HUNTING
venation, HUNTING

venational, HUNTING
venenation, POISON
venereophobia, DISEASE AND ILLNESS
venerer, HUNTING
venery, HUNTING
venesection, BLOOD
ventriloquism, SPEECH
ventriloquist, SPEECH
ventriloquistic, SPEECH
ventriloquy, SPEECH
verbalism, LANGUAGE STYLES
verbomania, WORDS
Verism, ART
verism, MUSIC
Verist, ART
Verismo MUSIC
verist, MUSIC
Veristic, ART
veristic, MUSIC
vermiphobia, PHOBIAS
vernacular, LANGUAGE
vernacularism, LANGUAGE
vernalization, PLANTS
vernalize, PLANTS
vexillary, FLAGS
vexillium, FLAGS
vexillological, FLAGS
vexillologist, FLAGS
vexillology, FLAGS
videologist, MEDIA
viduage, WIFE
vidual, WIFE
viduity, WIFE
vigneron, WINE
virological, MEDICAL SPECIALTIES
virologist, MEDICAL SPECIALTIES
virology, MEDICAL SPECIALTIES
virtualism, THEOLOGY
visible speech, DEAFNESS
vitalism, LIFE, PHILOSOPHY
vitalist, LIFE, PHILOSOPHY
vitalistic, LIFE, PHILOSOPHY
viticultural, WINE
viticulture, WINE
viticulturist, WINE
vitrailist, JOBS
vitreosity, PHYSICAL CHARACTERISTICS
vitreous, PHYSICAL CHARACTERISTICS
viviparism, BIRTH
viviparity, BIRTH
viviparous, BIRTH
vocalism, LINGUISTICS

volcanism, VOLCANOES
volcanist, VOLCANOES
volcanologic, VOLCANOES
volcanological, VOLCANOES
volcanologist, VOLCANOES
volcanology, VOLCANOES
Volsteadism, ALCOHOL
voluntarism, PHILOSOPHY
voluntarist, PHILOSOPHY
voluntaristic, PHILOSOPHY
voodooism, MAGIC
voodooist, MAGIC
Vorticism, ART
Vorticist, ART
voudouism, MAGIC
voyeur, BEHAVIOR, SEX
voyeurism, BEHAVIOR, SEX
voyeuristic, BEHAVIOR, SEX
vulcanism, VOLCANOES
vulcanology, VOLCANOES
vulpicide, ANIMALS

W

Wesleyan, PROTESTANTISM
Wesleyanism, PROTESTANTISM
Wesleyism, PROTESTANTISM
Whitefieldism, PROTESTANTISM
Whitley Council, LABOR
Whitleyism, LABOR
witticism, LANGUAGE STYLES
wizard, MAGIC
wizardry, MAGIC
Wycliffism, PROTESTANTISM

XYZ

xenophobia, FOREIGNERS
xerographic, COPYING
xerography, COPYING
xerophilia, PLANTS
xerophilous, PLANTS
xerophily, PLANTS
xerophobia, PHOBIAS
xerophyte, PLANTS
xerophytic, PLANTS
xerophytism, PLANTS
xeroradiographic, X-RAYS
xeroradiography, X-RAYS
xylographer, ENGRAVING, PRINTING

xylographic, ENGRAVING, PRINTING
xylographical, ENGRAVING, PRINTING
xylography, ENGRAVING, PRINTING
xylology, WOOD
xylomancy, WOOD
xylotomist, WOOD
xylotomy, WOOD
Yahooism, BEHAVIOR
Yahwist, BIBLE
Yankeeism, LANGUAGE
Yiddishism, LANGUAGE
Yoga, HINDUISM
Yogi, HINDUISM
Yogin, HINDUISM
Yogism, HINDUISM
Zarathustrism, RELIGION
zealotism, BEHAVIOR
Zealotism, JUDAISM
zealotry, BEHAVIOR
Zemiism, GOD AND GODS
Zendaic, MAGIC
Zendic, MAGIC
Zendicism, MAGIC
Zendik, MAGIC
Zenic, BUDDHISM
Zenism, BUDDHISM
zeugma, FIGURES OF SPEECH
zeugmatic, FIGURES OF SPEECH
Zionism, JUDAISM
Zionist, JUDAISM
Zionistic, JUDAISM
Zionite, JUDAISM
zoanthropic, ANIMALS
Zoanthropy, ANIMALS
Zoili, CRITICISM
Zoilism, CRITICISM
Zoilus, CRITICISM
zoism, LIFE
zoist, LIFE
zoistic, LIFE
Zolaism, LITERATURE
zoobiology, ANIMALS
zoolater, ANIMALS
zoolatry, ANIMALS
zoological, ANIMALS
zoologist, ANIMALS
zoology, ANIMALS
zoomancy, ANIMALS
zoomorphic, ANIMALS
zoomorphism, ANIMALS, GOD AND GODS
zoonosis, DISEASE AND ILLNESS
zoonotic, DISEASE AND ILLNESS

zoophile, ANIMALS
zoophilia, ANIMALS, SEX
zoophilic, SEX
zoophilist, SEX
zoophilous, SEX
zoophobe, ANIMALS
zoophobia, ANIMALS
zoopsychology, ANIMALS
zoosadism, PAIN
zoosadist, PAIN
zoosadistic, PAIN
zootechnical, ANIMALS
zootechnician, ANIMALS
zootechnics, ANIMALS
zootechny, ANIMALS
zootheism, ANIMALS
zootheist, ANIMALS
Zoroastrian, RELIGION
Zoroastrianism, RELIGION
Zoroastrism, RELIGION
zymetology, FERMENTATION
zymology, FERMENTATION
zymometer, FERMENTATION
zymotic, FERMENTATION
zymurgy, FERMENTATION